Corpora and Language Change in Late Modern English

Linguistic Insights

Studies in Language and Communication

Edited by Maurizio Gotti,
Emeritus Professor,
University of Bergamo (Italy).

Volume 308

Javier Calle-Martín / Jesús Romero-Barranco (eds.)

Corpora and Language Change in Late Modern English

PETER LANG
Lausanne - Berlin - Bruxelles - Chennai - New York - Oxford

Bibliographic information published by die Deutsche Nationalbibliothek
Die Deutsche Nationalbibliothek lists this publication in the Deutsche Nationalbibliografie; detailed bibliographic data is available on the Internet at ‹http://dnb.d-nb.de›.

Library of Congress Cataloging- in- Publication Data
A CIP catalog record for this book has been applied for at the Library of Congress.

This book has been funded by the research project "Compilation, Tagging and Exploitation of the Málaga Corpus of Early English Scientific Prose: The Late Modern English Period (1700-1900)"(Referenced P18-RT-2782), granted by the Autonomous Government of Andalusia (Consejería de Universidad, Investigación e Innovación); and by the Department of English, French and German Philology (University of Málaga). Both fundings are hereby gratefully acknowledged.

ISSN 1424-8689
E-ISBN 978-3-0343-4826-3 (E-PDF)
DOI 10.3726/b21562
ISBN 978-3-0343-4642-9 (Print)
E-ISBN 978-3-0343-4827-0 (E-PUB)

Published by Peter Lang Group AG, Lausanne, Switzerland

info@peterlang.com
http://www.peterlang.com/

Table of Contents

Section 2. Empirical Studies

Javier Calle-Martín

From Corpora to Data: Sources for the Study of Late Modern English[1]

1. Introduction

Scholars traditionally refer to the language used between 1500 and 1900 as Modern English and draw a fine distinction between Early Modern English (1500–1700) (henceforth EModE) and Late Modern English (1700–1900) (henceforth LModE). It is widely known that the most radical changes in English grammar had occurred in the Early Modern period, such as the incipient standardization of spelling, the Great Vowel Shift, the collapse of the inflectional system or the fixing of SVO order, among others, along with the huge amount of foreign words incorporated into the lexicon. Even though LModE has been deemed as a period of stability in the system (Romaine 1998: 7), a cursory look at some linguistic factors reveals that much was going on then. The rise of technological innovations and the expansion of the British empire all over the world, both under the shelter of the Industrial Revolution, led to a process of geographical and social mobility with tangible implications in the development of the language, inasmuch as the new social networks acted, in Milroy's terms, as a "norm enforcement mechanism" (1987) subsequently hoping from one centre of population to the other (Milroy and Milroy 1985: 378; see also Tieken-Boon van Ostade

1 The present research has been funded by the Spanish Ministry of Science and Innovation (grant number PID2021-126496NB-I00) and by the Andalusian Regional Government (grant numbers PY18-2782 and UMA18-FEDERJA-129). These grants are hereby gratefully acknowledged.

2009: 10). Letter-writing, as a typical stance of ego-writing, lent itself well for the endorsement of personal variation and the ideal mode of transmission of some of these social innovations (Tieken-Boon van Ostade 2009: 39–41; Mugglestone 2006: 279–81).

The eighteenth and the nineteenth centuries thus witnessed the birth of modern sociolinguistics, which brought into play the social concept of language itself and, more importantly, the need of standardization to comply with the social requirements of the time, which primarily focused on differentiating new money from the old (Beal 2004: 94). These standards of correctness were in need of codification and it was in the LModE period when the precepts of the spelling reformers, grammarians and lexicographers became of paramount importance (Tieken-Boon van Ostade 2019: 8). These circumstances did not only favour the codification of British English. Within this trend of prescriptivism, the LModE period witnessed the creation of a distinctly American variety, pioneered by Noah Webster as the central actor in the creation of the American orthography (Upward and Davidson 2011: 302), whose norms soon permeated among the early immigrants in search for linguistic correctness (Tottie 2002: 9).

A linguistic period such as LModE, characterized by the search for standardization and codification, while still giving room to personal and social variation, stands out as a challenge for linguists, who ought to put some order out of the apparent chaos pertaining to the origin and driving force of particular linguistic features. It may become really hazardous to determine whether a given feature is just the result of the intrinsic development of the language, whether it responds to external motivations like the prescriptive bias of grammarians and lexicographers or whether it answers to any social, textual or idiosyncratic variation. It is at this point where corpora have come to play an outstanding role in language analysis and today we may congratulate on the release of medium-size and large corpora which, to a certain extent, come to satisfy many of the linguists' needs.

The last decades have witnessed the proliferation of many diachronic corpora of LModE. Rather than aspiring to exhaustiveness, the following list is just limited to mentioning the corpora deemed as remarkable for their dimension, tagging and reputation in the discipline. Widely used are the *Hansard Corpus* (1803–2005) or the *Eighteenth-Century Collections Online* (ECCO) (1700–1799) for the analysis of British English; and the *Corpus of Historical American English* (COHA) (1820–2019) or the *Evans Early American Imprints* corpus (Evans) (1639–1800) for the newly-formed American variety in the period. The release of the *Old Bailey Corpus* also stands out as an added asset, housing c.134 million words from speech-related texts used in London's Central Criminal Court between 1674 and 1913. In addition to these, other specialized corpora have proliferated which do not only illustrate usage over time, but also allow for the study of variation across particular genres, registers or text types, such as the latest version of *A Representative Corpus of Historical English Registers* (*ARCHER*) for the period 1600–1999; the *Corpus of Historical English Law Reports* covering 1535–1999; and Hendrik de Smet's *Corpus of Late Modern English Texts* (*CLMET*) (1710–1920) with novels written by English and American authors. Among all these, Terttu Nevalainen's *The Corpus of Early English Correspondence Extension* (*CEECE*) deserves special attention, containing more than two million words of letter-writing for the period 1680–1800, with a long-standing tradition and reputation for sociolinguistic research in the LModE period.

The present volume focuses on the leading role of corpora for the study of LModE, be it from a qualitative or a quantitative stance. For the purpose, the book has been divided into two parts. The first presents some of the currently available corpora for the study of the English language in the LModE period, where six different proposals are hereby presented: *The Corpus of Irish English Correspondence*; *The Coruña Corpus of English Scientific Writing*; *The Málaga Corpus of Late Modern English Scientific Prose*; *The Corpus of Late Modern English Medical Writing*; *The Salamanca Corpus: Digital Archive of English Dialect Texts*; and *The Mary Hamilton Papers*. The second section, in turn, houses a selection of corpus-based empirical studies combining the use of current corpora with up-to-date methods of linguistic analysis at different linguistic levels, from spelling to morpho-syntactic and lexical issues of eighteenth and nineteenth-century English.

2. The Primary Sources: Corpora

This first part begins with Amador-Moreno's *The Corpus of Irish English Correspondence* (CORIECOR), a corpus especially conceived to provide insight into Irish English from a diachronic perspective. The corpus contains personal letters written by Irish emigrants and their recipients between the late seventeenth (1731) and the early twentieth centuries (1940), the period when Ireland became an English-speaking country (Amador-Moreno 2022: 49–56). In addition to the diachronic scope of the corpus, the compilers have been careful to select material from informants all over Ireland, a valuable asset to investigate the origin and development of linguistic features from the perspective of stylistic, regional and social variation, gender studies also included.[2]

The corpus is freely available at the project's webpage (https://corviz.h.uib.no/index.php), where users may find a general description of the project and access the letters themselves along with their bibliographic details, such as the year, the sender and recipient, their relationship, origin, occupation, gender and religion. More important, in our view, is the advanced search tool, which allows to search for a particular word or string of words in the whole corpus – or a part of it – specifying, if necessary, a restricted set of conditions. CORIECOR has now become a primary source for linguistic research into Irish English not only synchronically and diachronically, but also from the perspective of variationist sociolinguistics. Despite being originally conceived in the year 2008 and materialized throughout the 2010s, the number of publications stemming from the corpus stands as a solid indication of the maturity and suitability of the product for research.[3]

2 The letters, initially classified by individual informants, were later grouped into networks of family, friends, colleagues and business associates, among others, in order to facilitate research on social network approaches (Milroy 1987). This notion of "communities of practice" is also endorsed by Tyrkkö (2013: 155; also Conde-Silvestre 2019; 2020), who argues that these nertwoks "have formed communicative communities capable of shaping linguistic practice".

3 See the project's webpage for the complete list of publications derived from the corpus, including books, book chapters, journal articles and PhD theses.

CORIECOR is followed by Crespo and Moskowich's *The Coruña Corpus of English Scientific Writing* (*CC*), an electronic corpus especially compiled for the study of eighteenth and nineteenth century scientific writing in English. In its current form, the corpus displays more than two million words, with approximately one million words for the eighteenth and the nineteenth centuries, respectively. The great advantage of the corpus is the inclusion of sample material from different disciplines in the attempt to account for the particular writing traditions and restrictions of each discipline. Accordingly, the corpus is divided into different subcorpora based on the UNESCO's classification (1988), the list including *CETA*, *Corpus of English Texts on Astronomy* (2012); *CEPhiT, Corpus of English Philosophy Texts* (2016); *CHET*, *Corpus of* History English Texts (2019); CELiST, the *Corpus of English Life Sciences Texts* (2020); and *CEChe T*, the *Corpus of English Chemistry Text* (2022).[4]

The compilers of the corpus have been careful in the selection of the material. When it comes to authors, both well-known and less famous figures have been included across the disciplines. As far as texts are concerned, edited and printed scientific prose is the prerogative, favouring first editions whenever possible. The corpus samples have also been selected in accordance with other extralinguistic factors, such as (i) genre, relying on the text categories that existed in eighteenth- and ninenteenth-century scientific texts (Görlach 2004); (ii) gender, giving room to women writing in spite of the evident minority of female authors at the time; (iii) geography, with details about the writers' place of education for the analysis of variation within scientific discourse; and (iv) the age of authors in the attempt to investigate features from the perspective of the writers' age groups. The project's webpage hosts all the information about the corpus, the different subcorpora and the particularities of the tagged version of the product (https://www.udc.es/grupos/muste/corunacorpus/index.html). The corpus is also available in open access in the project's webpage and on CQPweb at Lancaster University. The *CC* has had a long-standing trajectory since its inception

4 CETeL, the *Corpus of English Texts on Languages* is now in preparation for publication.

in 2004 and has now become an essential source for the investigation of any linguistic feature in the period.

The volume follows with Calle-Martín's description of *The Málaga Corpus of Late Modern English Scientic Prose* (*CoLaMESP*), the third component of *The Málaga Corpus of Early English Scientific Prose*. This corpus houses a collection of medical writing in the vernacular from the eighteenth and nineteenth centuries, the current version with 1.1 million words for the eighteenth century and another 1.2 million for the nineteenth. The corpus displays representative material from the three branches of medical writing in English, that is, theoretical treatises, surgical treatises and recipe collections. The product has been conceived as a primary source for linguistic research both over time and across text types. On the one hand, the corpus is organized into eight sub-periods of 25 years so that any linguistic feature may be surveyed from a diachronic standpoint. Textual variation, on the other hand, may be surveyed in light of the different rationale of medical writing, especially when it comes to theoretical/surgical treatises and recipe colections, the former as the most academic register written by surgeons and practitioners of the highest class and the latter as the language used by laypeople written by non-practitioners and barber surgeons.

The corpus is published and made available in the project's webpage (https://latemodernmss.uma.es), offered in three different formats: the plain text version, the modernized version and the tagged version. The normalized version of the corpus is taken as the source data for the tagging of the corpus through an automatic process performed by CLAWS, a rule-based tagger that provides every running word with its corresponding POS-tag in view of its context. This tagged version consists of more than 160 different tags which, if properly combined, present a great potential for research on the levels of spelling and morphosyntax. The CQPweb version is also available for online use (https://latemodern mss.uma.es/cqpweb/).

The Corpus of Late Modern English Medical Writing (LMEMT) is the third and final component of *The Corpus of Early English Medical Writing*, compiled by Prof. Taavitsainen's VARIENG research team at the University of Helsinki (Finland). Released in the year 2019, this part contains eighteenth-century printed material covering a wide range of text types of medical writing, from learned treatises and journal articles to health guides and popular books on medicine. Periodicals are also given room as a new type of writing in vogue throughout the eighteenth century.[5] The corpus is offered in two formats, the annotated version using TEI-compliant XML and the unannotated plain-text version, both of them sold with the accompanying book *Late Modern English Medical Texts* (Taavitsainen and Hiltunen 2019).

This release of the corpus incorporates over two million words out of 628 sample texts, with a limitation of 10,000-word extracts in the case of longer texts. Notwithstanding the size of the product, the extracts have been carefully selected to represent the full range of printed medical texts in the eighteenth century. The resulting corpus incorporates heterogeneous material inasmuch as "the authors and the audiences of the texts extend from lay people to educated elites" (Suhr, Taavitsainen and Hiltunen 2024: this volume). It therefore stands out as an ideal source for insight into common grammatical and discursive features as well as text structure in view of the length of some extracts. If used in combination with the other components of *The Corpus of Early English Medical Writing*, the Helsinki product turns into an excellent primary source for diachronic research in English. As a matter of fact, Prof. Taavitsainen's outstanding project has been the source of a plethora of research studies for the past two decades, with surely an endless list to come.

García-Bermejo Giner and Ruano-García's *The Salamanca Corpus* (*SC*) is a digital archive of diachronic dialect material covering the period 1500–1950 and providing valuable information about dialect variation and change in EModE and LModE. Released in 2011, the current version of the corpus presents more than 14 million words stemming from novels, short stories, poetry collections and plays. Divided into three chronological periods (1500–1699, 1700–1799 and 1800–1950), the 571 digitized works contain references of the different dialect varieties, of which Lancashire, Yorkshire, Devonshire and Cornwall are those with highest number of references. As the authors explicitly state, the *SC* "represents our most important source of information about

5 LMEMT incorporates material from the following seven categories: general treatises and textbooks; specialized treatises; medical recipe collections; regimens; surgical and anatomical texts; public health; and periodicals.

regional English variation in centuries from which we have very little contemporary information" (García-Bermejo Giner and Ruano-García 2024: this volume), thus becoming the ideal supplement to Joseph Wright's *English Dialect Dictionary* (1898–1905).

The *SC* is also available for consultation in the project's webpage (http://www.thesalamancacorpus.com), where users are offered the catalogues of the relevant texts for each variety and news about the texts incorporated into the archive, along with other information about research on the corpus. Of particular interest is the tool that enables the researcher to look for a particular word or string of words. As published in its webpage, the *SC* has been the source of information for a number of studies since the year 1991, a fact which corroborates the potential of the Salamanca project not only for the study of diachronic linguistics itself, but also for other areas such as dialectal variation and standardization in the Early and Late Modern periods of English (see, among others, Ruano-García 2020: 185–205).

The Mary Hamilton Papers is Denison, Yáñez-Bouza and Tino Oudesluijs's proposal for the study of English in the period c.1740–c.1850. This compilation incorporates ego-documents related to Mary Hamilton (1756–1816), the bulk of which are her private letter collection along with "manuscript diaries", "manuscript volumes" along with the additional documents related to Hamilton herself, all of which amounting to c.875,500 words. This unique material provides the opportunity "to exploit an almost untouched archive and answer questions about literary practice, letter-writing and everyday language use in Georgian England", apart from "shedding light on the socio-economic, cultural and political landscape or the region and period in which they were created" (Denison, Yáñez-Bouza and Oudesluijs 2024: this volume). The corpus is divided into seven different periods in accordance with the important milestones of Mary Hamilton's life, thus affording the opportunity to also investigate any particular feature also over time.

Following the rationale of other similar corpora, the corpus material is manually transcribed and made available, both in diplomatic and normalized versions, in the digitial edition hosted in Manchester Digital Collections. One of the great advantages of the project is the possibility of accessing the high-resolution images of the material, surely of interest not only to historical linguists but also to those from other side areas such as Manuscript Studies or Ecdotics. The normalized transcriptions make up the basis of the linguistic corpus, which is subsequently tagged for part of speech by the CLAWS tagger and for semantic analysis by the USAS tagger. Even though the transcribed version is accessible through the Manchester Digital Collections (hwww.digitalcollections.manchester.ac.uk/collections/maryhamilton/1), the tagged version is also indexed on CQPweb at Lancaster University. In a nutshell, *The Mary Hamilton Papers* will soon become, if not already, a compulsory source for the study of LModE language, history and culture in view of the uniqueness of the material, its handwritten condition and the potential of its part-of-speech and semantic annotations.

3. The Secondary Sources: Empirical Studies

Blanco-Suárez opens this second part proposing the analysis of the intensifying adverbs *ridiculously* and *madly* from their origins in the thirteenth and sixteenth centuries, respectively, down to the LModE period, exploring the diachronic evolution of the adverbs along with the mechanisms and processes involved in their development. The study proposes a collocational analysis surveying variables such as (i) the type of words modified by these *-ly* adverbs; (ii) the semantic types (whether literal meanings, ambiguous interpretations or pure intensifying readings are concerned); and (iii) their function as manner adjuncts, premodifiers, intensifiers or disjuncts. The author relies on the evidence of the *Oxford English Dictionary*, the *Early English Books Online Corpus 1.0* (EEBOCorp 1.0) and the online collections *Eighteenth Century Fiction* (ECF) and *Nineteenth Century Fiction* (NCF), thus covering a timespan or more than six hundred years from their earliest records. These intensifiers seem to have acquired the new function out of their original uses as manner adverbs conveying stance or evaluation. Importantly enough, the new intensifying functions of *ridiculously* and *madly* have since then coexisted with other functions, literal meanings included, which has resulted in typical instances of homonymy and polysemy in English.

Blanco-García's contribution, in turn, assesses the origin, development and decline of ephemeral causal adverbial subordinators in the Early and Late Modern periods, paying particular attention to *for as much as*, *for because*, *for why*, *in as much as*, *in so much as*, *sin* and *sithen*. The selection of the seven subordinators has been carried out in view of the fact that (i) they are only attested in EModE; (ii) they are attested in both EModE and Middle English; and (iii) they are attested in EModE and Present-day English but archaic, obsolete or without a causal meaning today. For the purpose, the author makes use of the *Penn-Helsinki Parsed Corpus of Middle English*, the *Penn-Helsinki Parsed Corpus of Early Modern English* and the *Penn-Helsinki Parsed Corpus of Modern British English*. The study concludes that these connectives are very low-frequency items which had their momentum in the EModE period, with an intrinsic tendency to appear in combination with pleonastic *that*, when placed in final position, and in written texts and formal registers.

The next paper examines the use and distribution of demonstrative *them* in American English in the period 1820–2019, a variety in which the neutral form *them* is sporadically found as a substitute of the plural forms *these* and *those*. Criado-Peña uses *COHA* as the source data to compile all the instances of the sequence *them* + noun from the twenty most-frequent constructions in the corpus. The study is, in itself, a corpus-based variationist analysis of the construction both over time and across text types, also assessing the participation of some linguistic factors in the choice of the demonstrative. This contribution points to the diffusion of demonstrative *them* as a nineteenth-century phenomenon mostly instigated by grammars, school textbooks and television programmes, reaching its peak one century later. As a dialectal form, *them* finds more room in speech-like text types such as fiction books and television/movies while it becomes restricted in the more formal domains. The author also comes to provide evidence on the participation of linguistic factors such as the animate entity of the noun or when it acts as the object of the utterance.

Fernández-Domínguez contributes to the field of word formation with his paper on the development of the suffix *-ment* in the 1820–2010 time frame for the creation of deverbal nominalizations in the category ACTION. The author relies on the evidence of *COHA* for his analysis, focusing on *hapax legomena* as the appropriate benchmark for the measurement of corpus-based productivity. The identification of the lexical base of the derivatives of *-ment* are taken as the input to detect derivatives of other word-formation processes, whose frequencies are subsequently measured in *COHA* for comparison. Even though *-ment* has been a highly-productive suffix between the seventeenth and the nineteenth centuries both with Romance and Germanic bases, the study shows that its lexical productivity is found to decrease one century later to the extent that it may be regarded as unproductive in Present-day English, plausibly as a result of the rivalry with other nominalizers in the same morphological domain, such as *-al* and *-ing*.

The next paper tackles another case of linguistic competition in the history of English. Lorente-Sánchez looks into the morphological rivalry of *-ed* and -(*e*)*n* in both British and American English for the expression of the past participle in a set of six irregular verbs. The study is based on the evidence from *Early English Books Online* corpus (*EEBO*), *ECCO* and *CLMET* for the analysis of the British English practices, while the Evans collection and *COHA* are the input for the analysis of the phenomenon in American English. The results confirm the tendency for to use *-ed* throughout the seventeenth and the eighteenth centuries across the two varieties, -(*e*)*n* diffusing more significantly one century later in British English and in the twentieth century in American English. The study also points to the existence of functional differences between the forms over time, the strong forms of the verb predominating in the expression of the past aspect and the passive voice.

Pacheco-Franco addresses the issue of the orthographic standardization of American English in her analysis of *colour*-type words. For that purpose, she puts forward a corpus-based study that draws its data from *Evans* (1640–1800) and from *COHA* (1820–2019), as well as from a precept corpus consisting of lexicographic works produced in the United States. In spite of the attention paid to Webster as the enactor of orthographic reform in American English, the author concludes that *colour*-type words were re-spelled into *-or* prior to his endeavours. Rather than participating in the selection or diffusion of the form, the lexicographer took part on its codification, successfully imbuing the *-or* spelling with the sentiments of Americanness that were flourishing after Independence.

In line with the previous contribution, Pacheco-Franco and Calle-Martín's paper delves into the use and frequency of contractions with the verb *be*, the verb *have*, the shortened forms of the negative particle *not* and the modal auxiliary verbs *will* and *would*. The study is based on the data provided by *ARCHER* for the historical period 1600–1999, when the phenomenon is observed to have its most widespread distribution in the history of English. In itself, the study has been conceived not only diachronically, but also as a variationist analysis surveying their status across both genre and gender. The paper concludes that the LModE period was crucial in the diffusion of contractions among the speakers of English, with a higher incidence in speech-like and the more informal text types, often authored by female speakers. The issue seems to boil down to the overall democratization of the language throughout the nineteenth and twentieth centuries, with the spread of colloquial linguistic traits onto a wider domain.

Next, Rodríguez-Álvarez and von der Fecht-Fernández address the issue of lexical borrowing with their analysis of the Amerindian words that entered the English language from the sixteenth century onwards, focusing on how they were later disseminated over the seventeenth century and recorded into the dictionaries of the eighteenth. For the purpose, the primary source for the study is Richard Hakluyt's *The Principall Navigations* (1589), one of the top sources used in the compilation of the *OED*. The use of travel literature, and Hakluyt's work in particular, stands out as the ideal input for this lexicographic study as his intention was none other but "to compile all the records on the travels and discoveries of his countrymen over the course of history" (Markham 1896: 7–8; Rodríguez-Alvarez and von der Fecht-Fernández 2024: this volume). The study identifies a number of Amerindian words in Hakluyt's work, which are later checked against the set of secondary sources, that is, digitized corpora (*EEBO*, *ECCO* and Google Books) and lexical and lexicographical databases (*AMERLEX*). The study safely concludes that, even though sixteenth- and seventeenth-century bilingual and monolingual dictionaries echoed many of the words of widespread use in the period, it was the eighteenth-century bilingual and monolingual dictionaries which made substantial room for the Amerindian words. This change of attitude is explained by the greater need for the publication of this kind of texts to satisfy the commercial interests of eighteenth-century England in this new land.

The book closes with Yáñez-Bouza and Tino Oudesluijs's paper on the different forms of address in the Late Georgian period. The paper pursues the analysis of both direct address and self-reference in private correspondence from the LModE period to discern how "this reflects diachronic variation and change at both the societal and interactive level of communication" (Nevala 2004: 4). For the purpose, the study is based on the collection of letters in the project *Unlocking the Mary Hamilton Papers* (Denison, Yáñez-Bouza and Oudesluijs 2024: this volume), which has been especially tagged to identify the linguistic strategies relating to addressee-oriented and author-oriented forms of address. The authors analyse the use of direct address to recipients and self-reference expressions according to the following variables: (i) the structure of the letter; (ii) the particular trends with individual correspondents; and (iii) the gender of the correspondents.

References

Amador-Moreno, Carolina P., 'Contact, Variation and Change: Mapping the History of Irish English through CORIECOR', *Nexus* 2 (2022), 49–56.

Beal, Joan C., *English in Modern Times* (New York: Arnold, 2004).

Conde-Silvestre, Juan Camilo, 'Spelling Focusing and Proto-Standardisation in a Fifteenth-Century English Community of Practice', *Studia Neophilologica* 91/1 (2019), 1–30.

——, 'Communities of Practice, Protostandardisation and Spelling Focusing in the Stonor Letters', in Laura Wright, ed., *The Multilingual Origins of Standard English* (Berlin: Mouton de Gruyter, 2020), 443–66.

Denison, David, Nuria Yáñez-Bouza and Tino Oudesluijs, 'Editing *The Mary Hamilton Papers* (c. 1740–c. 1850)', in Javier Calle-Martín and Jesús Romero-Barranco, eds., *Corpora and Language Change in Late Modern English* (Bern: Peter Lang, 2024).

García-Bermejo Giner, María F. and Javier Ruano-García, 'Investigating Variation and Change in Late Modern English Dialects: *The Salamanca Corpus*', in Javier Calle-Martín and Jesús Romero-Barranco, eds., *Corpora and Language Change in Late Modern English* (Bern: Peter Lang, 2024).

Görlach, Manfred, *Text Types and the History of English* (New York: Walter de Gruyter, 2004).

Markham, Clements R., *Richard Hakluyt: His Life and Work. With a Short Account of the Aims and Achievements of the Hakluyt Society* (London: Bedford Press, 1896).

Milroy, Lesley, *Language and Social Networks* (Oxford: Blackwell, 1987).

Milroy, James and Lesley Milroy, 'Linguistic Change, Social Network and Speaker Innovation', *Journal of Linguistics* 21 (1985), 339–84.

Mugglestone, Lynda, 'English in the Nineteenth Century', in Lynda Mugglestone, ed., *The Oxford History of English* (Oxford: Oxford University Press, 2006), 274–304.

Nevala, Minna, *Address in Early English Correspondence: Its Forms and Socio-Pragmatic Functions* (Helsinki: Société Néophilologique, 2004).

Rodríguez-Álvarez, Alicia and Sara von der Fecht-Fernández, 'Amerindian Loanwords in Richard Hakluyt's *The Principall Navigations* (1589) and Their Inclusion in Early and Late Modern English Dictionaries: Applications and Limitations of Digital Corpora, Databases and Tools in Lexicoigraphical Research', in Javier Calle-Martín and Jesús Romero-Barranco, eds., *Corpora and Language Change in Late Modern English* (Bern: Peter Lang, 2024).

Romaine, Suzanne, 'Introduction', in Suzanne Romaine, ed., *The Cambridge History of the English Language. Volume IV: 1776–1997* (Cambridge: Cambridge University Press, 1998), 1–56.

Ruano-García, Javier, 'Shaping the Other in the Standardization of English: The Case of the "Northern" Dialect', *International Journal of English Studies* 20/2 (2020), 185–205.

Suhr, Carla, Irma Taavitsainen and Turo Hiltunen, '*The Corpus of Late Modern English Medical Writing*: Scientific and Social Change in the Eighteenth Century', in Javier Calle-Martín and Jesús Romero-Barranco, eds., *Corpora and Language Change in Late Modern English* (Bern: Peter Lang, 2024).

Taavitsainen, Irma and Turo Hiltunen, eds., *Late Modern English Medical Texts. Writing Medicine in the Eighteenth Century* (Amsterdam: John Benjamins, 2019).

Tieken-Boon van Ostade, Ingrid, *An Introduction to Late Modern English* (Edinburgh: Edinburgh University Press, 2009).

——, 'Usage guides and the Age of Prescriptivism', in Claudia Claridge and Birte Bös, eds., *Norms and Conventions in the History of English* (Amsterdam: John Benjamins, 2019), 7–28.

Tottie, Gunnel, *An Introduction to American English* (Oxford: Blackwell, 2002).

Tyrkkö, Jukka, 'Printing Houses as Communities of Practice: Orthography in Early Modern Medical Books', in Joanna Kopaczyk and Andreas H. Jucker, eds., *Communities of Practice in the History of English* (Amsterdam: John Benjamins, 2013), 151–76.

UNESCO, *United Nations Educational, Scientific and Cultural Organisation. Proposed International, Standard Nomenclature for Fields of Science and Technology* (Paris, 1988).

Upward, Christopher and George Davidson, *The History of English Spelling* (Chichester: Wiley-Blackwell, 2011).

Wright, Joseph, ed., *English Dialect Dictionary*, 6 Vols. (Oxford: Henry Frowde, 1898–1905).

Section 1. Corpora

Carolina P. Amador-Moreno

Language Change in Ireland: Compiling and Using a Diachronic Corpus to Study the Evolution of an Early New English[1]

1. Introduction

This chapter presents the *Corpus of Irish English Correspondence* (CORIECOR), which contains mostly personal letters written by Irish emigrants and their families, friends and associates between the late seventeenth and the early twentieth century. The overarching aim of the creation of CORIECOR was to further our knowledge of how Irish English (IrE) has evolved. To this end, a number of interrelated projects conducted since 2008 (see Amador-Moreno 2022) have allowed us to compile and classify the data while engaging in different specific studies that have focused on the manner in which certain structures (grammatical, pragmatic and lexical) are used diachronically. The overall project has resulted in a number of publications, the majority of which are listed in the Resources section of https://corviz.h.uib.no.[2]

An ancillary objective of the CORIECOR project was to consider the (historical) sociolinguistic issues underpinning the relationships

1 Research project funded by the Ministerio de Ciencia e Innovación. Agencia Estatal de Investigación, Spain. Funder DOI: 10.13039/501100011033. Award Number: PID2019-106609GB-I00.

2 CORIECOR data has also been used for a monograph by Corrigan (2020), a PhD thesis at the University of Manchester (van Hattum 2012), and the research on emigrant letters conducted by Hickey (2019) and by Elsweiler and Ronan (2023). Present collaboration between the author, Karen P. Corrigan, Javier Ruano-García and Laura Rupp will also lead to new research output.

between language, migration and identity. To these ends, a recent approach to the data has combined corpus-analytic tools and visualization techniques. A key outcome of the most recent research on CORIECOR has been to create a publicly accessible, sustainable electronic correspondence corpus, which is now part of a research project titled "CORIECOR Visualized (CORVIZ)". At the time of writing (March 2023), CORVIZ (https://corviz.h.uib.no) provides direct access to some of the CORIECOR material, which can be used for further research by the wider academic community, for training Early Career Researchers (ECRs) and as an engagement tool for broadening knowledge amongst the general public.

CORVIZ was conceived as a complement and continuation of our previous work on Irish emigrant letters. As discussed in Amador-Moreno (2022), CORIECOR has been put together in three stages. The initial stage consisted in the compilation of the corpus and the devise of some pilot projects that gave rise to a number of publications by members of the research team, the majority of which focused on language contact, variation and change, and involved the mining of data at a larger scale. The impetus of the initial CORIECOR project, which has demonstrated proof of concept, then needed to be capitalized upon by further developing the knowledge and insights gained with respect to both digital corpus creation and curation as well as deepening our understanding of the evolution of IrE.

Thus, building on, and further developing the knowledge and expertise gained from the initial stages, CORVIZ has allowed us to carry out a series of micro-analyses that will permit a closer look at the language of correspondence. By combining methodological approaches and theoretical perspectives within the area of linguistics, we aim to determine how language use contributed to the construction of the emigrant experience in different realms.

2. Background to CORIECOR

Until recently, accounts of the evolution of IrE as found in the major surveys (e.g., Barry 1982; Kallen 1994, 2013; Filppula 1999; Hickey

2005, 2007; Corrigan 2010; Amador-Moreno 2010) were not based on empirical diachronic linguistic research. This is primarily on account of the paucity of large-scale historical IrE corpora. As a result, the exact evolution of only a few features of IrE has thus far been studied in detail. Earlier research was occasioned either to take a longer-term view or to examine literary data which is likely to be unrepresentative of the spoken word in numerous respects (see McCafferty and Amador-Moreno 2023). Several historical studies attempted to evaluate whether present-day usage derives from Irish or earlier English antecedents (e.g. Bliss 1979; Harris 1984; Filppula 1999; Corrigan 2000, 2003; Hickey 2005, 2007; Filppula et al. 2008). Other existing historical work had an even narrower focus and included case studies of historical documents and folklore material which examined aspects of the use of specific features in particular locations and/or periods (e.g., Montgomery 1997; Corrigan 1992, 2010; Kirk 2000; McCafferty 2003, 2005). Consequently, although we knew something of certain features and their use by some (literary) authors in key periods of the development of IrE as a dialect, it unfortunately remained the case that linguists needed to systematically exploit written evidence for earlier IrE in a way that would allow it to be studied longitudinally and in relation to both input varieties of British English and other overseas varieties that it may have contributed to.

This state of affairs was the impetus for McCafferty and Amador-Moreno's idea of creating a *Corpus of Irish English Correspondence* (CORIECOR) with the aim of accomplishing a more thorough diachronic study of IrE than had been previously possible.

2.1. CORIECOR Online

The majority of the letters in CORIECOR were initially classified by individual informants (letter writers in this case), which aids historical sociolinguistic study, enabling us to extract and encode data that could for the first time in this field of study take account of aspects of the backgrounds of individual writers (geographical origin, gender, social status, ethnicity/religion, social mobility, and so on) and other factors that might influence language use (e.g. relationship to addressee, purpose of writing, etc.). Individuals were also grouped into networks of family, friends, colleagues, business associates and the like, to facilitate research based on social network approaches that have proved fruitful in the study of the present-day language (Milroy 1987) and earlier English (Fitzmaurice 2007). However, after the first stages of the corpus were completed, it became obvious that the nascent electronic corpus required additional work so that it could become a state-of-the-art corpus that is sustainable and which complies with the most up-to-date guidelines for the creation and encoding of digital material. The initial work needed to be capitalized upon by further developing the knowledge and insights gained with respect to both digital corpus creation and curation as well as deepening our understanding of the evolution of IrE. As regards the latter, new goals were identified with the aim to undertake original research in three key overlapping sub-fields of linguistics:

2.1.1. Variation, Perceptions and Change

This part of our new research plan considers the role of metalinguistic discourse in language change by focusing on how language change may happen below the level of consciousness: when processes of overt social conditioning such as stigmatization take place, they can be very powerful determinants of change. Some of the features contained in the letters are features that users were strongly aware of; these can be studied in order to explore how individual forms were stigmatized with negative epithets referring either to education, errors, or social evaluation. Taking Agha's notion of *enregisterment*, which refers to the "process through which a linguistic repertoire becomes differentiable within a language as a socially recognized register of forms" (2003: 231–32), we aim to examine these features in the context of qualitative metalinguistic discourse, so as to gain more refined insights into the ideologies behind the use of such linguistic forms. In this regard, by studying prescriptivist attitudes towards some of these linguistic features, we will explore how certain linguistic traits take on sociocultural meaning in the context of IrE, which will allow us to determine whether these indexical meanings have shifted over time (Amador-Moreno and Ruano-García 2024). Indeed, it may be possible to trace the decline of non-standard usage over time by comparing the earliest letters in CORIECOR with those of later periods (or indeed less highly educated writers – often female – with those whose biographies suggest a closer engagement with schooling). Such an approach engages with the recent turn to the third wave of (historical) sociolinguistics, where intra-speaker variation or meaningful individual choices to project and construct social personae has taken centre stage (e.g., Conde-Silvestre 2016; Hernández-Campoy and García-Vidal 2018).

This area of the CORVIZ project will also concentrate on the investigation of specific features of IrE, the origins of which are hotly contested in the scholarly literature and are irresolvable without access to a large digital database like CORIECOR. These will include embedded inverted questions, zero relatives, zero copula, the use of present/past tenses (including past be), and *for-to* infinitives. The majority of these features are included in the list provided by Görlach (2001: 25), which contains a number of forms affected by the eighteenth-century drive to prescribe grammatical forms, where the aim, as he puts it, "was not only to make Standard English as homogeneous as possible, at least in its written form [...], but also to select from the existing variation the forms that best fitted logical requirements and to suppress those that conflicted with it." Some of the developments listed by Görlach are obviously a consequence of this language planning process that affected how other varieties of English were perceived not only by other English speakers but also by the users of that particular variety. In addition to tracing the development of these specific features, CORVIZ tools will facilitate the use of the metadata in order to interpret the features in context.

2.1.2. Pragmatics and Emotion Discourse in Letter Writing

While there has been an explosion of enthusiasm and research efforts in studying emotion using corpora, we still know very little about the relationship between linguistic patterns and emotion. Recently, Bednarek (2008) has investigated the language of emotion across corpora. Her focus is on four registers: conversation, fiction, news reportage and academic discourse. However, patterns of affect in letters remain to be studied from this perspective. Such study could have important implications for our understanding of pragmatics and register since it may well be the case that affect in personal letters plays a significantly greater role than it does in other domains. The structuring function of emotive terms is also noted by Precht (2003), who has investigated the construals of affective portrayal and creation – emotional responses such as empathy or identification or evaluative reactions, associated with cultural norms.

Our aim as part of this section of the current project is to analyse pragmatic features in context, in order to obtain a better picture of language use in letter writing. As Dossena (2016), for example, points out, in the study of authorial voices and textual personae present in letters, it is clear that a very important role is played (in more or less explicit ways) by attitude (i.e., emotional or affectual responses), engagement (i.e., acknowledging, ignoring or rejecting different viewpoints), and graduation (i.e., strengthening or downtoning statements or their semantic focus). In particular, expressions of attitude comprise three sub-systems: affect (relating to emotion), judgement (relating to the implicit or explicit evaluation of behaviour with respect to social norms), and appreciation (relating to the evaluation of objects). All these traits occur in CORIECOR as a genre and ongoing work on the topic (Ávila-Ledesma forthcoming) leads us to believe that this is an area that is well worth investigating in the context of IrE specifically, but with respect to personal letters as a text type more broadly too. When all these phenomena are taken into consideration from a historical sociolinguistic perspective, it may be useful to rely on appraisal theory (Martin and White 2005), which provides a comprehensive and accurate framework for the study of texts in which the interaction of semantics and pragmatics is particularly important. Also, when mapping affect in letters, (im)politeness issues will equally be worthy of analysis, as the research currently conducted by Sotoca-Fernández is showing (see Sotoca-Fernández and Ávila-Ledesma, 2024).

2.1.3. Sociolinguistic Issues Related to Style, Recipient and Authorship

Historical socio-linguistic analyses grounded on the third-wave approach to the study of variation are feasible, but they depend, as Conde-Silvestre (2007) points out, on the possibility of having access to a coherent corpus of documents from the past that reveals a network of individuals engaged in a joint enterprise; speakers linked in this way often shared linguistic behaviours that constitute the source of some social meanings pertaining to the identity of the community itself.

Thus, the third area of the CORVIZ project will focus on social network theory as it applies to corpus data.

Thus far, CORIECOR has been mined from a large-scale perspective and the CORVIZ project will allow us to undertake micro-analyses that take a closer look at the language of correspondence as an example of intimate discourse (Clancy 2016). In that sense, CORVIZ will allow us to analyse language production distinctions or choices due to the addressees' differences in terms of audience design (Bell 1984), which proposes that style is essentially the speakers' response to their audience, or other stylistic resources that may be significant (see Hernández-Campoy 2016; Martínez-Insua and Pérez-Guerra 2018). As in other forms of written and spoken communication, the use of language in the letters may vary depending on the addressee. By the same token, authorship also determines language choice based on ideology, cultural background, and speaker's experience, so a more systematic analysis of language use in the letters based on geographical origin, gender, social status and ethnicity/religion will facilitate the observation of this variety of English more comprehensively.

2.2. Main Objectives of CORVIZ

In order to attain its main objectives, CORVIZ aims to answer a number of research questions connected with the areas listed above. While we still plan to analyse how certain features of IrE have developed over time, we also aim to explore how these features compare to other varieties of English in the Inner, Outer and Expanding circles. When looking at the origin of these features, we will measure Celticity besides other (sociopragmatic) factors at play that may explain the use of dialectal features.

By taking into account sociolinguistic factors that influence attitudes towards dialect maintenance or dialect leveling, we look at how group and individual identities have been shaped and influenced by language in the context of emigration.

All emigration, whether voluntary or forced, is tied to life stories and to narratives of journeys, departures, arrivals and processes of settling down, so one of our goals is to investigate how language choice influenced the way Irish emigration was narrated by its protagonists.

We will also explore the ways in which a large corpus can provide new insights into how Irish emigrants and their families/friends talked about their own and others' emotions: does authorship determine language choice based on ideology, cultural background, and speaker's experience? How does the area of Pragmatics interact with variation, for example, when studying affect, engagement or graduation in a particular variety of English?

The question about how statistical evidence and corpus-linguistic methods can be combined with qualitative text analyses, in order to systematically examine the use of IrE across time is directly related to the issue of visualization: how can data be connected in such a way that it allows for the visualization of linguistic features proper to IrE in combination with other factors such as gender, social/educational/ethnic background, occupation and region, and other (socio)pragmatic elements proper to the language of private communication?

In answering some of these questions, CORVIZ aims to reach a number of goals. Thus, arising from the intersection of the three interrelated areas mentioned above, one of the most immediate needs was to connect the CORIECOR data in such a way that it would allow for the visualization of key concepts related to emigration, linguistic features proper to IrE, and (socio)pragmatic elements proper to the language of private communication. With that purpose in mind, the piloting of CORVIZ involved the creation of visualization tools based on specific linguistic features, as well as topics, networks of the letter authors, gender, and origin of the letter, which will provide pathways through the data. This will be described in the section that follows.

3. Moving Forward in Historical Sociolinguistic Analyses of Irish English

In recent years, new methods of socio-historical analyses have been closely connected with the developments in digital humanities/computational linguistics (see Beal et al. 2007; López-Couso 2016). As Säily et al. (2017: 1) point out, "in some respects, a move has taken place from more philological and qualitative approaches to more expert quantitative approaches and /or combinations between them." The Salamanca Corpus project, for example, led by some of the collaborators in the CORVIZ project, was a pioneering work on English dialects in Spain, and Amador-Moreno, Corrigan and McCafferty have discussed issues related to the creation and curation of diachronic databases in various publications (see Amador-Moreno et al. 2016).

As argued in an influential essay by Nevalainen (2015), variationist sociolinguistics, or the study of language variation and change in relation to external factors, is only possible for documented periods of the language in question, and it requires access to primary textual materials by identifiable individuals and groups such as ego-documents (private letters and diaries). However, a *layered simultaneity* between the various micro- and macro-levels of contextual meaning is necessary (Säily et al. 2017: 3), particularly when investigating different varieties of English (Seoane and Suárez-Gómez 2016), where visualization and statistical techniques can help reveal variability (see for example the EWAVE Atlas, http://ewave-atlas.org), time periods and specific social groups (Vartiainen et al. 2013).

Recent decades have witnessed an increasing interest in non-standard features of English attested in varieties spoken around the globe from a broader perspective. Associated with this broader perspective on the study of English is a more inclusive language history that questions the notion of the standard language itself. Such inclusive approach also takes account of variation and change within and between BrE and AmE (e.g. Mair 2006; Leech et al. 2009), and pays more attention to non-mainstream, non-standard varieties (e.g. Crystal 2004; Hogg and Denison 2006; Mugglestone 2006). Recent edited volumes focusing on worldwide studies (e.g. see for example bibliography in Bergs and Brinton 2017) vouch for the progress in raising awareness in relation to variation and change within the English-speaking world. However, while variation now is more visible than it was in the past, there are still few in-depth historical studies of many of the local, regional and national varieties encountered in the field, and fewer even that combine corpus and visualization techniques of the type that we are conducting in CORVIZ (Moreton and Culy 2019; O'Leary and Moreton 2017).

Also, as pointed out by Nevalainen (2015: 252), macro-level processes associated with broader contexts (e.g. ideologies) need to be combined with more micro-analyses of linguistic features in the context of the social and discursive practices in which they were produced. The availability of comparable corpora nowadays allows researchers to combine macro- and micro-levels by making use of private and public writing (newspapers) to investigate, for example, language change from the perspective of standardization in the wake of nationalism and the concomitant language ideologies (Corrigan 2003).

4. Some Initial Results through CORVIZ

4.1. Creating Visualizations

As pointed out above, the CORVIZ project is grounded in methodologies associated with both quantitative variationist sociolinguistics (multivariate analyses, among others) and corpus linguistics (e.g. generating concordances). The emphasis is on how certain structures have developed, how they have been perceived over time by their users and by those with whom they were in contact, and on how style, register, recipient and authorship may or may not determine the choice of words related to emotions, culture, and identity. The analysis of all these factors allows both for a holistic view of variation and change and a more specific diagnosis that takes into account context.

In order to achieve such diagnosis, the website that we have developed is based on the principles of the Visualization of Language and Linguistic Data. Visualization techniques offer the potential for creating new methods that reveal structure and detail in data. Culy (2014) discusses innovative suites of tools for performing linguistic analyses of correspondence generally, and O'Leary and Moreton (2017) highlight how "historical migrant correspondence offers a relatively unexploited source of Big Data ripe for analysis." Pushing the boundaries of how electronic corpora can be accessed, shared and visualized, one of the goals of CORVIZ is to make our work accessible to other researchers by using innovative digital service development techniques that will allow us to present our work in an interactive web platform. This interactive platform allows users to explore the letters by entering different parameters. The combination of different parameters (e.g. relation between sender and reader, place of origin of the letter, writer/reader sex, ethnic/educational background of writer/reader, etc.) allows users to analyse the language of the letters, taking into account sociolinguistic factors that may have been at play, as will be demonstrated below.

Following the method(s) employed by O'Leary (see O'Leary and Moreton 2017), CORIECOR is now part of a web-based solution that uses a server-side program (written in PHP) to query data and present it to the user in a web browser. A PHP script handles the dynamic requirements of the site. When the database is queried, the results are formatted into JSON (JavaScript Object Notation), a lightweight data-interchange format that is particularly well suited to JavaScript programming. Thus, once all parameters have been selected by the user/researcher, the chosen variables are submitted to the web server and from there to the PHP program. This automatically generates the appropriate database calls (the SQL statements incorporating the parameters) and submit them to the database. The database returns the results dataset. The PHP program then formats this dataset into a format appropriate for visualization and generates the HTML code of the results page for display.

Texts in CORIECOR are already classified and some of the metadata have been coded and classified in spreadsheets. The first task was to create a database (within MySQL) and use these spreadsheets to populate it. This required data modelling, preparation and import as described next.

4.2. Interpreting and Using Visualizations

As stated by Murray (2013: 71) "data visualization is a process of mapping data to visuals." This subsection describes how such mapping has taken place in CORVIZ.

A relational database is comprised of tables (analogous to individual spreadsheets) formed of fields (cells) that interrelate with each other through a series of relationships based on specific fields. Thus, a

LETTERS table was initially created with unique identifiers for each letter, a field for sender, a field for date, origin, etc. The sender field was populated with a unique identifier that relates to another record in a PEOPLE table with specific data on that person. Another biographical table details attributes associated with all individuals, for instance, gender, socio-economic status, etc. This facilitates dynamic graphs like the ones shown in https://corviz.h.uib.no/. A table dedicated to places (storing geo-spatial coordinates required for mapping) is also ready, providing visualizations like the one shown in https://corviz.h.uib.no/index.php?convar_function=21, and another dedicated to relationships (thus allowing us to identify family members, friends, etc.) produces visualizations using the different combinations available from https://corviz.h.uib.no/index.php?convar_function=24.

Data has been normalized to ensure consistency. Once the spreadsheets were prepared they were saved as Comma Separated Value files (CSV) and imported into each table. The text of letters is now stored in the database and used to populate the website.

The visualizations that have been created so far are based on JavaScript libraries such as Leaflet (for mapping), Dimple (for graphs), etc. JavaScript is another web-oriented programming language often used that is executed locally within the user's web browser rather than on the server. Generally, these libraries work well with data formatted in JavaScript Object Notation or JSON. As mentioned above, the PHP formats the data appropriately. The requisite JavaScript has been written by the PHP into the page code.

The work was based on former projects on Visual Correspondence (www.correspondence.ie), where O'Leary (see O'Leary and Moreton 2017) follows the above methodology exactly and uses technologies that are open-source, but have been adapted and developed for the purposes of this specific project. Other similar initiatives more centered on language change include the project *Image to Text: the Mary Hamilton Papers*[3] (Denison, Yañez-Bouza and Oudesluijs 2024: this volume); and Stanford's *Mapping the Republic of Letters*[4], indexing a variety

3 *Image to Text: Mary Hamilton Papers*. Available from: http://www.projects.alc.manchester.ac.uk/image-to-text/. Accessed 18.05.2023.

4 *Mapping the Republic of Letters* 2013. Available from: http: //republicofletters.stanford.edu/. Accessed 18.07.2018.

of sources of sixteenth, seventeenth and eighteenth century letters for its site.

Another example of how these types of visualization work can be seen in the analysis of the Lough Letters (Moreton 2016), where O'Leary and Moreton test similar visualization options to those that we envisage. The map in https://corviz.h.uib.no/index.php?convar_function=21 shows the connections between the letter writers contained in CORIECOR, while https://corviz.h.uib.no/index.php?convar_function=24 is shown as an example of multiple dynamic graphs that show social networks. In combination, these types of data visualization form a context within which the analysis of IrE across time can gain definition.

5. Summary and Conclusion

The aim of this chapter was to introduce the *Corpus of Irish English Correspondence* (CORIECOR) as a source for the investigation of language change in Ireland. The chapter has discussed some issues related to the compilation and use of the corpus by focusing more extensively on its access online through a recently created website still under development, which is part of the CORVIZ (CORIECOR Visualized) project. Other aspects of the emergence of the corpus in the context of World Englishes, and the place that IrE has in this context are also discussed.

Various interrelated theoretical frameworks have recently become the focus of interest in the CORIECOR research agenda. These are integrated into the three research areas that the CORVIZ project aims to focus on: firstly, variation, perceptions and change issues are currently being analysed, taking into account the notion of enregisterment and qualitative metalinguistic discourse; secondly, other sociolinguistic issues related to style, recipient and authorship are also under way; and thirdly, questions connected with Pragmatics, and more specifically with emotion discourse and (im)politeness aspects of letter writing are also being investigated.

The piloting of CORVIZ involved the creation of visualization tools based on specific linguistic features, as well as topics, networks of the letter authors, gender, and origin of the letter, which could facilitate pathways through the data.

The field of linguistic visualization is rapidly developing. CORVIZ integrates some visualizations, as shown in this chapter, and the data is ready so that other visualizations can be developed depending on the research questions devised.

The combination of corpus tools and visualization aids nowadays allows researchers to combine macro- and micro-level analyses. Our aim is to make use of private writing to investigate the evolution of an early New English that has often been overlooked in the context of the history of English in favour of English and Scottish varieties from other parts of the British Isles. This omission is unfortunate, as we have argued, because IrE is often claimed to have influenced important developments in other Englishes in the Late Modern English period (1700–1900).

The use of data visualization for the detection of language variation and change is part of the current trend in historical linguistics. One of the goals of CORVIZ is to generate new breakthroughs that push research forward by investigating multifaceted data that explain the interface between linguistic parameters existing within a variety of English that is worth investigating further.

References

Agha, Asif, 'The Social Life of Cultural Value', *Language & Communication* 23 (2003), 231–273.

Amador-Moreno, Carolina P., *An Introduction to Irish English* (London: Equinox, 2010).

——, 'Contact, Variation and Change: Mapping the History of Irish English through CORIECOR', *Nexus* 2 (2022), <https://aedean.org/wp-content/uploads/nexus-2022-02-completo.pdf>, accessed 08 July 2023.

Amador-Moreno, Carolina P. and Javier Ruano-García, '*Linguistic Perceptions of Irish English in Nineteenth-century Emigrant*

Letters: A Micro-perspective Analysis of John Kerr's Letters' (Special Issue on Third Wave English Historical Sociolinguistics), *International Journal of English Linguistics* (2024).

Amador-Moreno, Carolina P., Karen P. Corrigan, Kevin McCafferty and Emma Moreton, 'Migration Databases as Impact Tools in the Education and Heritage Sectors', in Karen P. Corrigan and Adam J. Mearns, eds., *Creating and Digitizing Language Corpora – Volume 3: Databases for Public Engagement* (Houndmills, Basingstoke: Palgrave Macmillan, 2016), 25–67.

Ávila-Ledesma, Nancy E., *A Corpus Pragmatic Analysis of Irish Emigrants' Letters* (Basingstoke, New York: Palgrave Macmillan, forthcoming).

Barry, Michael. V., 'The English Language in Ireland', in Richard. W. Bailey and Manfred Görlach, eds., *English as a World Language* (Ann Arbor: University of Michigan Press, 1982), 84–133.

Beal, Joan C., Karen P. Corrigan and Hermann L. Moisl, eds., *Creating and Digitizing Language Corpora, Volume 2: Diachronic Databases* (Basingstoke, New York: Palgrave Macmillan, 2007).

Bednarek, Monika, *Emotion Talk across Corpora* (Basingstoke, New York: Palgrave Macmillan, 2008).

Bell, Allan, 'Language Style as Audience Design', *Language in Society* 13 (1984), 145–204.

Bergs, Alexander and Laurel J. Brinton, eds, *Varieties of English,* Vol. 5 (Berlin: Mouton de Gruyter, 2017).

Bliss, Alan J., *Spoken English in Ireland 1600–1740* (Dublin: Dolmen, 1979).Clancy, Brian, *Investigating Intimate Discourse. Exploring the Spoken Interaction of Families, Couples and Friends* (Abingdon: Routledge, 2016).

Conde-Silvestre, Juan Camilo, *Sociolingüistica histórica* (Madrid: Gredos, 2007).

——, 'A Third-Wave Historical Sociolinguistic Approach to Late Middle English Correspondence: Evidence from the Stonor Letters', in Cinzia Russi, ed., *Current Trends in Historical Sociolinguistics* (Warsaw and Berlin: De Gruyter Open, 2016), 46–66.

Corrigan, Karen P., '*Glens* Dialect from Moira O'Neill to Michael J. Murphy', *Ulster Folklife* 38 (1992), 98–108.

——, 'What Bees to Be Maun Be: Aspects of Deontic and Epistemic Modality in a Northern Dialect of Irish English', *English World-Wide: A Journal of Varieties of English* 21/1 (2000), 25–62.

——, '*For-to* Infinitives and Beyond: Interdisciplinary Approaches to Non-Finite Complementation in a Rural Celtic English', in Hildegard L. C. Tristram, ed., *The Celtic Englishes III* (Heidelberg: Universitatsverlag Winter Heidelberg, 2003), 318–338.

——, *Irish English. Vol. 1, Northern Ireland* (Edinburgh: Edinburgh University Press, 2010).

——, *Linguistic Communities and Migratory Processes: Newcomers Acquiring Sociolinguistic Variation in Northern Ireland*. (Berlin: de Gruyter Mouton, 2020).

Crystal, David, *The Stories of English* (London: Penguin, 2004).

Culy, Chris, 'Getting inside the Letter: Using Visualisation Tools to Explore the Language of Emigrant Correspondence', invited presentation at the Workshop on visualizing letter collections, Omagh. 14–15 March 2014. http://linguistics.chrisculy.net/lx/presentations/CulyPresentation_Omagh.pdf, accessed 08 July 2023.

Denison, David, Nuria Yáñez-Bouza and Tino Oudesluijs, 'Editing *The Mary Hamilton Papers* (c.1740–c.1850)', in Javier Calle-Martín and Jesús Romero-Barranco, eds., *Corpora and Language Change in Late Modern English* (Bern: Peter Lang, 2024).

Dossena, Marina. 'Advice to Prospectors (and Others). Knowledge Dissemination, Power and Persuasion in Late Modern English Emigrants' Guides and Correspondence', in Russi, C., ed., *Current Trends in Historical Sociolinguistics* (Berlin: De Gruyter Open, 2016), 67–80.

Elsweiler, Christine and Patricia Ronan. "'From I am, with sincere regard, your most obedient servant to Yours sincerely": The Simplification of Leavetaking Formulae in 18th-Century Scottish and Irish English Letters', *ICAME Journal* 47/1 (2023), 1–17.

Filppula, Markku, *The Grammar of Irish English. Language in Hibernian Style* (London: Routledge, 1999).

Filppula, Markku, Juhani Klemola and Heli Paulasto, *English and Celtic in Contact* (London: Routledge, 2008).

Fitzmaurice, Susan, 'Questions of Standardization and Repre-Sentativeness in the Development of Social Networks-Based

Corpora: the Story of the Network of Eighteenth-Century English Texts', in Joan C. Beal, Karen P. Corrigan and Hermann L. Moisl, eds., *Creating and Digitizing Language Corpora, Volume 2: Diachronic Databases* (London: Palgrave Macmillan, 2007), 49–81.

Görlach, Manfred, *Eighteenth-Century English* (Heidelberg: Winter, 2001).

Harris, John, 'English in the North of Ireland', in Peter Trudgill, ed., *Language in the British Isles* (Cambridge: Cambridge University Press, 1984), 115–134.

Hernández-Campoy, Juan Manuel, 'Authorship and Gender in English Historical Sociolinguistic Research: Samples from the *Paston Letters*', in Cinzia Russi, ed., *Current Trends in Historical Sociolinguistics* (Warsaw and Berlin: Open De Gruyter, 2016), 108–142.

Hernández-Campoy, Juan Manuel and Tamara García-Vidal, 'Style-Shifting and Accommodative Competence in Late Middle English Written Correspondence: Putting Audience Design to the Test of Time', *Folia Linguistica* 39/2 (2018), 383–420.

Hickey, Raymond, *Dublin English. Evolution and Change* (Amsterdam: John Benjamins, 2005).

——, *Irish English. History and Present-Day Forms* (Cambridge: Cambridge University Press, 2007).

——, *Keeping in Touch: Familiar Letters across the English-Speaking World* (Amsterdam: John Benjamins, 2019).

Hogg, Richard and David Denison, eds, *A History of the English Language* (Cambridge: Cambridge University Press, 2006).

Kallen, Jeffrey L., 'English in Ireland', in Robert Burchfield, ed., *The Cambridge History of the English Language,* Vol. 5. (Cambridge: CUP, 1994), 148–196.

——, *Irish English, Vol. 2: The Republic of Ireland* (Edinburgh: Edinburgh University Press, 2013).

Kirk, John M., 'Two Ullans Texts', in John M. Kirk and Donall P. Ó Baoill, eds., *Language and Politics. Northern Ireland, the Republic of Ireland, and Scotland* (Belfast: Cló Ollscoil na Banríona, 2000), 33–44.

Leech, Geoffrey, Marianne Hundt, Christian Mair and Nicholas Smith, *Change in Contemporary English. A Grammatical Study.* (Cambridge: Cambridge University Press, 2009).

López-Couso, María José, 'Corpora and Online Resources in English Historical Linguistics', in Merja Kytö and Päivi Pahta, eds., *The Cambridge Handbook of English Historical Linguistics* (Cambridge: Cambridge University Press, 2016), 127–145.

Mair, Christian, *Twentieth-Century English. History, Variation and Standardization* (Cambridge: Cambridge University Press, 2006).

Martin, James R. and Peter R.R. White, *The Language of Evaluation, Appraisal in English* (London: Palgrave Macmillan, 2005).

Martínez-Insua, Ana Elina and Javier Pérez-Guerra, 'Text Types, Audience and Thematic Organisation in the Recent History of English', in Dominique Legallois, Thierry Charnois and Meri Lerjavaara, eds., *The Grammar of Genres and Styles. From Discrete to Non-discrete Units* (Berlin: Mouton de Gruyter, 2018), 14–38.

McCafferty, Kevin, '"I'll bee after telling dee de raison" ... Be after V-ing as a Future Gram in Irish English, 1601–1750', in Hildegard L. C. Tristram, ed., *The Celtic Englishes III* (Heidelberg: Universitatsverlag Winter Heidelberg, 2003), 298–317.

——, 'William Carleton between Irish and English: Using Literary Dialect to Study Language Contact and Change', *Language and Literature* 14/4 (2005), 339–362.

McCafferty, Kevin and Carolina P. Amador-Moreno, 'Emigrant Letters from Ireland', in Raymond Hickey, ed., *The Oxford Handbook of Irish English.* (Oxford: Oxford University Press, 2023).

Milroy, Lesley, *Language and Social Networks* (Oxford: Blackwell, 1987).

Montgomery, Michael, 'Making Transatlantic Connections between Varieties of English: the Case of Plural Verbal *-s*', *Journal of English Linguistics* 25 (1997), 122–141.

Moreton, Emma, '"I never could forget my darling mother": The Language of Recollection in a Corpus of Female Irish Emigrant Correspondence', *The History of the Family* 21/3 (2016), 315–336.

Moreton, Emma and Chris Culy, 'Homesickness, Recollections and Reunions: Using the Interesting Items Visualisation Tool (IIVT) to Explore Topics and Emotions in a Corpus of Female Irish Migrant Correspondence', in Raymond Hickey, ed.,

Keeping in Touch-Familiar Letters across the Anglophone World (Amsterdam: John Benjamins, 2019), 87–118.

Mugglestone, Lynda, ed., *The Oxford History of English.* (Oxford University Press, 2006).

Murray, Scott, *Interactive Data Visualization for the Web* (Beijing and Boston: O'Reilly Media, 2013).

Nevalainen, Terttu, 'What are Historical Sociolinguistics?', *Journal of Historical Sociolinguistics* 1/2 (2015), 243–269.

O'Leary, Niall and Emma Moreton, 'The Migrant Letter Digitised: Visualising Metadata', *Journal of Cultural Analytics* (2017) <https://culturalanalytics.org/article/11071-the-migrant-letter-digitised-visualising-metadata>, accessed 28 March 2023.

Precht, Kristen, 'Stance Moods in Spoken English: Evidentiality and Affect in British and American Conversation', *Text* 23 (2003), 239–57.

Säily, Tanja, Arja Nurmi, Minna Palander-Collin and Anita Auer, eds., *Exploring Future Paths for Historical Sociolinguistics* (Amsterdam: John Benjamins, 2017).

Seoane, Elena and Cristina Suárez-Gómez, eds, *World Englishes: New Theoretical and Methodological Considerations* (Amsterdam and Philadelphia: John Benjamins, 2016).

Sotoca-Fernández, David and Nancy E. Ávila-Ledesma. ' "I hope that a correspondence may still be kept up between us": Exploring Conversational Dynamics through the Lens of (Im)politeness Studies in CORIECOR', in Carolina P. Amador-Moreno, Dagmar Haumann and Arne Peters, eds., *Digitally-Assisted Historical English Linguistics* (Abingdon: Routledge, 2024).

van Hattum, Marije, *Irish English Modal Verbs from the 14th to the 20th Centuries*. Unpublished PhD thesis, University of Manchester.

Vartiainen, Turo, Tanja Säily and Mikko Hakala, 'Variation in Pronoun Frequencies in Early English Letters: Gender-Based or Relationship-Based?', in Jukka Tyrkkö, Olga Timofeeva and Maria Salenius, eds., *Ex Philologia Lux: Essays in Honour of Leena Kahlas-Tarkka* (Helsinki: Société Néophilologique, 2013), 233–255. https://core.ac.uk/reader/33735186, accessed 08 July 2023.

Begoña Crespo and Isabel Moskowich

The Coruña Corpus of English Scientific Writing: The Gift That Keeps on Giving[1]

1. Introduction

The Coruña Corpus of English Scientific Writing (henceforth *CC*) is a purpose-built electronic corpus conceived as a resource for the study of eighteenth and nineteenth-century scientific writing in English. The project began in 2003 as a means of exploring the historical background of English as the language of science, and is founded on solid grounds: socio-external considerations, theoretical principles of Corpus Linguistics, and technical robustness, all of which serve to confirm its value as a resource for research.

From the seventeenth century onwards, and with the increasing literacy of the times, different types of readerships emerged in response to a variety of discursive patterns (Crespo and Moskowich 2020). One of the main consequences of the shift from scholastic paradigms in the Middle Ages to modern science during the seventeenth century was a dramatic change in the way knowledge and technical advances were conveyed (Beal 2004). The *CC* tries to reflect this and includes samples of printed texts from a variety of domains in which the language and discourse of science was used by practitioners as a means of negotiating knowledge. These text extracts are of potential interest not only to linguists but also historians of science. The *CC* provides researchers with

1 The research here reported on has been funded by the Spanish Ministerio de Ciencia e Innovación (MICINN), grant number PID2022-136500NB-I00. This grant is hereby gratefully acknowledged.

significant new tools for a better understanding of science, language and society during the period it covers. Likewise, it allows for the study of material from a diachronic perspective, and due to the inclusion of different genres it is also useful for other approaches, such as comparative studies or other synchronic analyses within diachrony.

Since every field of scientific endeavour has its own writing traditions and restrictions, each subcorpus contains samples of texts from different scientific disciplines, given that the notion of rigid "disciplines" in the sciences had not fully emerged in this period (Crespo and Moskowich 2020). Such an overlapping of areas of work constitutes a fundamental difficulty in the selection of representative samples of scientific language, in that we are not dealing here with present-day science but rather something looser and more fluid in nature. Instead of developing our own taxonomy of disciplines for compilation, we turned to UNESCO's (1988) existing classification, founded on rationalist premises.

Thus, the first subcorpus compiled was *CETA*, *Corpus of English Texts on Astronomy* (2012), and the second was *CEPhiT, Corpus of English Philosophy Texts* (2016). The third, the *Corpus of History English Texts* (*CHET*) was released in 2019. Shortly afterwards, in 2020, the fourth corpus, the *Corpus of English Life Sciences Texts* (CELiST) was published, followed by the *Corpus of English Chemistry Text (CEChe T*) in 2022. The *Corpus of English Texts on Languages* (*CETeL*) is currently being prepared for publication. The characteristics of these open-access subcorpora will be presented in the following pages.

2. Criteria for Selection and Compilation

The principles applied to the compilation of the *CC* embrace criteria such as time-span delimitation, the possible range of registers involved, and discipline selection. Other relevant factors pertaining to issues of corpus linguistics methodology, balance, representativeness and sampling, have also been considered.

2.1. Time-Span Delimitation

It is widely acknowledged that changes in scientific thought lead to changes in the corresponding discourse (Crespo and Moskowich 2020: 665–84). The time limits used for our selection are based on non-linguistic considerations, but nevertheless have consequences for the study of language change. These non-linguistic considerations are closely related to the birth of the scientific revolution and the creation of the Royal Society of London. Together with Bacon and Boyle's 1661 recommendations about clarity and simplicity of expression in scientific works, these factors are the hallmark of the collection of texts from the very earliest samples in the *CC*.

A similar rationale was adopted to establish the end-point of our timespan, around 1900. This date coincides with the discovery of the electron by Thompson (1896), plus the crisis in mechanical physics and the proposal of quantum mechanics by Planck, both in the same year; less than a decade later Einstein's Special Theory of Relativity was published (1905). These new ideas once again provoked a change in the discursive patterns of science, shifting it towards greater simplicity, clarity and the use of specific jargon. Indeed, a call for changes in scientific communication on these lines was made by Thomas Huxley in the final years of the nineteenth century, echoing similar calls by Bacon and Boyle more than two centuries before.

One of the first decisions for the design of the corpus was whether to compile whole texts or samples. Based on the experiences reported for other projects (the Lampeter Corpus, the ARCHER), we opted for the selection of samples. Following a number of pilot studies we found that smaller samples, as proposed by Biber (1993), were not adequate for the study of variation in our texts, since the scientific register used therein was still not standardised. We therefore decided to compile two 10,000-words text files per decade, leading to a dataset of approximately 200,000 words per century and per discipline. Table 1 sets out the word-count for the subcorpora compiled so far:

Table 1: Style Word counts on the *CC* subcorpora

Century	***CETA***	***CEPhiT***	***CHET***	***CELisT***	***CECheT***	**Words/ century**
18th c. words	208,079	200,022	202,342	200,220	201,528	1,012,191
19th c. words	201,830	201,107	202,815	200,085	200,975	1,006,812
Words/ sub-corpus	409,909	401,129	405,157	403,965	402,503	2,019,003

Sample size is related to the principles of representativeness and balance, the two most significant aspects of a corpus (McEnery and Wilson 1996). A close study of the different disciplines involved, and how they develop over time, helped us in selecting which authors to include, both well-known writers and less famous ones. We restricted our selection to edited and printed texts in prose, and, whenever possible, first editions originally written in English were used. Where a first edition was not available, we resorted to any other edition of the work published within a thirty-year period, since this is generally taken as the timespan in which periods of language change can usefully be separated (Kytö, Rudanko and Smitterberg 2000: 85–97).

Texts shorter than 10,000 words were included in toto. For longer works, samples were selected from different parts of the work so as to obtain an accurate representation of the stylistic and pragmatic devices used by that writer and in that period (Biber, Conrad and Reppen 1998; Meyer 2002; Hardie and McEnery 2011). However, these text samples exclude any prefatory material as it does not constitute scientific prose per se. Since the *CC* is a diachronic corpus, the text extracts it contains naturally testify to the evolution of science from the eighteenth to the nineteenth centuries, that is, the period during which a move from Scholasticism to Empiricism took place (Puente-Castelo 2017: 111–29). The role of scientists at this time is also seen to shift from the amateur to the professional spheres, which may itself have had a transformative effect on their writing styles. In other words, there are many external factors that may cause linguistic differences in the samples from the two centuries represented.

The UNESCO classification of the six Fields of Science and Technology (1988) served as the basis for the disciplines to select. Using this taxonomy as a starting point, we then broadened the perspective to include certain texts which today would not be considered to fit any scientific discipline, given that late Modern English science did not have the degree of specialisation found in present-day science, and hence a degree of discipline-related fuzziness was to be expected. The disciplines finally represented in the various subcorpora of the *CC* are shown in Figure 1, with those already published in darker blue:

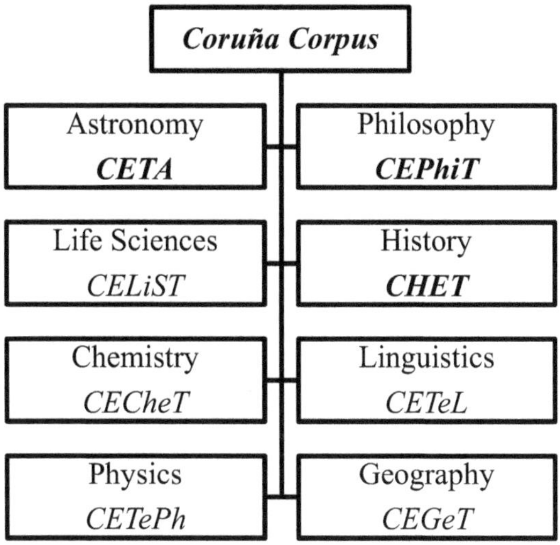

Figure 1: Disciplines and subcorpora in the *CC*.

One of the factors that contributes to the balance of the corpus as a whole is that the discipline-defined subcorpora fall into loose but natural pairings. Thus, we have the same number of words in the so-called 'hard' and 'soft' sciences. Balance is achieved by means of a focus on extra-linguistic factors, in that these are also crucial for the study of language from many perspectives. The intimate relation between languages and their users convinced us of the need to accompany each text sample with a metadata file, this divided in two sections: 'about the author' provides information on the author and a number of variables that can be used for searches in the Coruña Corpus Tool (CCT): sex and age of the author when the work was published, geographical provenance, etc. (Crespo and Moskowich 2020). The second part of the metadata file contains information about the text sampled, including year of publication, genre, the source of the sample, and cross-references to other texts in the *CC*. From the beginning of the project in the early 2000s both the text samples and the corresponding metadata files have been encoded in TEI-compliant XML.

Whereas balance is important in corpus compilation, so too is representativeness. On occasions, the *CC* is representative to the detriment of balance, in the sense that we believe that the corpus should serve as a reflection of a larger reality. Once again, socio-external rather than linguistic factors have played their part here.

3. Extralinguistic Factors in the Corpus

3.1. Genre

All the samples in the corpus can be identified with a particular genre, which we used to call text-type taking Görlach's (2004) textual typology as a starting point. He states that definitions of types of text are "indispensable before, for instance, corpus linguistics can claim to make reliable statements based on a representative text selection" (Görlach 2004). Therefore, we reviewed the text categories that existed in eighteenth and nineteenth-century scientific texts, and found that all the categories proposed by Görlach were already in use during the late Modern period, which clearly makes his classification particularly useful in a diachronic corpus like ours. His definitions are based on those found in the OED, and we have also followed these latter definitions when deciding to which genre each text fragment should be assigned. For these decisions we have used a systematic method: after consulting Görlach's classification we also considered the titles of the works themselves, sometimes self-explanatory. We also read any existing prefatory material to locate the author's opinions about their work or the kind of readership they sought to address, since this is also indicative of the genre to which a sample can be assigned. In addition, the interaction between writer and reader can help to classify texts (Moessner 2001: 131–8). However, one of the most important things here is to read the sample itself, especially in eighteenth-century books, since they often contain a variety of works in different formats, and given that only a particular fragment will be included in the *CC* (other than in the case of short texts), it is important that the genre classification reflects only the fragment sampled. This reading process is of especial value in helping to solve the philologist's dilemma (Rissanen 1996: 229–42) and ensures accuracy in our classification (Moskowich and Crespo 2016: 308–20).

Figure 2 below shows the distribution of genres across the whole *CC*. Treatise is the most popular genre among late Moden scientific authors. This tendency is also observed for Textbook and Essay, in that they occupy the second and third positions in all disciplines. It is worth noting that the fourth position is taken by Lecture, a genre that originates in the oral register, something which no doubt reflects the ways in which knowledge came to be transmitted in the late Modern period.

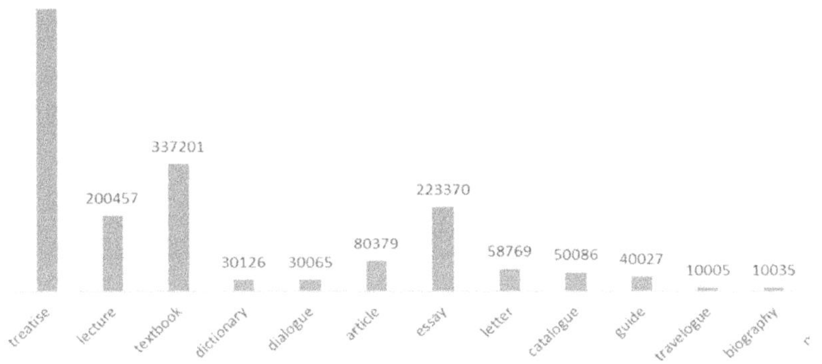

Figure 2: Genres in *CC*.

The different genres in the corpus can be seen to reflect a social reality in which knowledge is found in universities and other institutions (lecture, treatise and textbook/handbook) as well as outside these institutions, following the process of the vernacularisation of science in the fourteenth century and its subsequent popularisation across a wider audience. Long scientific works were very popular in the eighteenth century, whereas journal articles blossomed over the next hundred years (Allen, Qin and Lancaster 1994: 279–310). Other formats, such as letters and dialogues, were less frequent, and this depended on discipline. The range of genres present in the *CC* seems to be determined by the field of knowledge. Thus, the corpus on astronomy, CETA, contains: Treatise, Lecture, Textbook, Dialogue, Others (Dictionary), Article, Essay and Letter. Specifically, Textbook (156,057 words) is the most abundant genre, followed by Treatise (128,857), Article (34,014), Lecture (30,054) and Essay (22,259). There are just two samples from Letters (18,717), and one from the Dictionary (10,044) and Dialogue (9,907) genres.

The Philosophy texts (CEPhiT) fall into fewer genres than those in Astronomy, History, Life Sciences or Chemistry. They represent six types: Treatise (219,762), Essay (100,326), Lecture (50,133), Textbook (10,065), Dialogue (10,077) and Article (10,053). This variety may be explained by the newly emerging situation of nineteenth-century Philosophy as an independent discipline that was now available to a wider readership.

CELiST (Life Sciences) contains eight different genres: Treatise (180,176), Guide (60,068), Textbook (50,074), Letter (30,052), Catalogue (30,045), Essay (20,020) and Lecture (20,099) and Article (9,771). Here we find discipline-specific genres such as Guide and Catalogue.

The corpus of History (CHET) also contains eight genres. Treatise (282,907 words) is the most frequent, followed by Essay (30,323) and Lecture (30,091). There are two samples of Textbook (20,203) and one of Article (10,730), Dictionary (10,017), Travelogue (10,005) and Biography (10,035). The last two are again discipline-specific.

Finally, the texts on Chemistry (CECheT) are grouped in nine categories, the most abundant being Treatise (125,129 words), Textbook (100,802), Lecture (70,080), Essay (50,442), Article (15,811), Dialogue (10,081), Dictionary (10,065), Letter (10,000) and Manual (10, 063).

We have sought to represent all epistemological levels, from very technical ones to those accessible to a wide readership. For this reason, we have identified a number of cross-disciplinary genres (Treatise, Textbook, Essay, Article, Letter, Dialogue, Lecture) as well as discipline-specific ones (Manual, Travelogue, Guide, Catalogue, Biography).

3.2. Sex

The sex of the authors is included in the metadata files since we consider it to be an extralinguistic element with a potentially significant linguistic effect. As a reflection of the realities of late Modern English science writing, female authors represent an evident minority. Only 12 per cent of the total words in the five subcorpora were written by women (242,892 words vs 1,775,552 words by men). Female activity was often invisible in the Late Modern period, and more so in science, a typically masculine sphere of endeavour. Hence, it is difficult to trace the careers of female scientists; they often worked for their husbands or brothers, or used a masculine pseudonym so that their work would be taken seriously (Herrero-López 2007: 73–96). They were also excluded from official forums and organisations of knowledge such as the Royal Society and the universities, and this is seen in the degree of their representation in the *CC*.

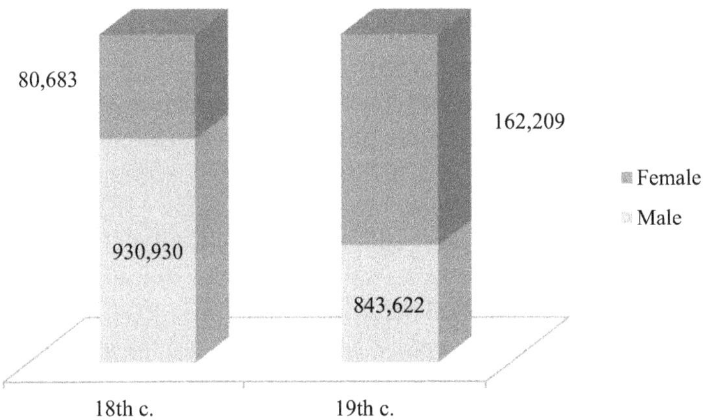

Figure 3: Distribution of sex of authors by century.

The situation for women changes somewhat in the nineteenth century, at a time of increased literacy and the social expansion of science, and this is reflected in the growing number of words by women in the *CC* in that century. Female scientists now found more opportunities to write and publish their own work. Yet this new situation can also be explained in terms of the social context of such women and the education they had received. They were often members of families in which the father occupied a prestigious position and had certain intellectual interests. From the mid-seventeenth century onwards, there were also efforts in Europe to find a female audience for science (Crespo

2016: 53–78), although publishing remained uncommon for women. For this reason, there are only two samples by women (Margaret Bryan for the eighteenth century and Agnes Mary Clerke for the nineteenth) in CETA, in that it was still the case that few women signed their own writing.

Female-authored works on philosophy were very infrequent, and we included none in the nineteenth-century section of CEPhiT. The three samples by female authors included (30,192 words) are all from the previous century: Mary Astell (1700), Catharine Macaulay (1783) and Mary Wollstonecraft (1792).

The corpus on Life Sciences (CELiST) contains extracts from eight female writers: Elizabeth Blackwell (1737), Priscilla Wakefield (1816), Almira Phelps Lincoln (1832), Pratt (1840), Agassiz (1859), Lankester (1879) and Emily Gregory (1895).

Meanwhile, there are only two texts by women in the eighteenth-century part of CHET, Catherine Justice (1700) and Sarah Scott (1783), but a greater number for the nineteenth-century section: Mercy Otis Warren (1805), Mary Callcott (1828), Lucy Aikin (1833), Elizabeth Sewell (1857), Martha Freer (1860) and Alice Cooke (1893). History seems to have been a more welcoming domain for women than the hard sciences, and this is reflected here.

Also, we found that overall, female authors use the same genres as their male counterparts. In fact, Treatise (81,378) and Textbook (40,333) are the two most frequent categories for both sexes, followed by Letters (20,043) and Guides (20,041). The remaining genres are represented by just one sample each in terms of female authorship. We found, then, that women followed the tendencies imposed by men and used both the genres typical of a discipline and those that gave them more visibility as authors (Lecture, Article).

Finally, the three women writing in the field of Chemistry resort to different genres: Fullhame, the only female writer in the eighteenth-century part of the CECheT subcorpus, uses the Essay genre (sample of 10,090 word). At the very beginning of the nineteenth century, Jane Marcet publishes a Dialogue (10,081 words), and almost at the turn of that century Ellen Richards chooses to author a Textbook, of which we have a sample of 10,042 words.

3.3. The Geographical Variable

One of the tenets underpinning the *CC* is that both knowledge and its dissemination depend on the socio-historical situations of writers and their readers, in that these constitute the context that determines their particular view of reality. In this sense, language plays a central role in the interpretation and transmission of facts and ideas. Context also determines the linguistic habits of writers, and for this reason we also consider the places where these habits were acquired. To this end, our metadata files include information regarding the place of education of each author, rather than the place where they were born, since education has a determinant influence on their writing style. The *CC* thus allows for the analysis of variation within scientific discourse. The need to provide information about an author's education itself implies that we have compiled texts from authors whose basic biographical information is known.

All the samples in the *CC* pertain to native English-speaking authors originally writing in English. Texts translated from other languages (mainly Latin) were avoided. Both European and American authors have been included, as shown in Figure 4:

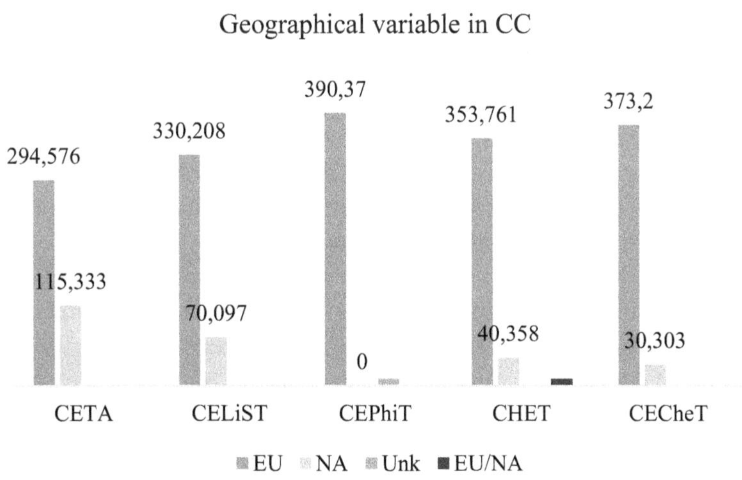

Figure 4: The geographical variable in *CC*.

Not all disciplines contain the same proportion of samples from any specific origin. Thus, in CETA, 50 per cent of the authors acquired their linguistic habits somewhere in England and 28 per cent in North America. These are the two predominating territories here, although Ireland (14 per cent of authors) and Scotland (8 per cent) are also represented. Scientific knowledge was developing in Europe at the time under the influence of Empiricism, while North America was recovering from a convulsive eighteenth century.

Social and political shifts are reflected in the compilation of the philosophy texts in CEPhiT. More broadly, the absence of American authors in the nineteenth-century section of the *CC* overall can be explained by the Civil War and its effects on scientific production there. Also, the fact that England was the dominant colonising power at the time helps to explain why most writers are English, whereas the emergence of the Scottish Enlightenment explains the high number of samples by authors educated in Scotland (Abbagnano 1982).

The presence of American authors is limited to 13 per cent in the corpus of Life Sciences, and Scottish authors are not as abundant as they were in Philosophy (18 per cent). Three factors can be said to determine the fact that 58 per cent of the samples here were written by authors educated in England: the influence of Linneus' taxonomies, Darwin's description of new species, and the colonisation process, leading to the documentation of new territories and peoples.

The same tendency in which European authors predominate can be seen in the History subcorpus, in contrast to the difficulties experienced at the time in the ex-colony, America, which as a new country was probably more concerned with immediate, practical applications of knowledge than with historical accounts.

As for Chemistry, the same tendency can be seen. More than half the samples belong to English authors, with a further fourteen distributed among Scotland (8), Ireland (5) and Wales (1). Only three of the total of 41 samples were written in America, and there are another two for which we only know that their authors had been educated in Europe.

The final sociolinguistic variable to be discussed is the age of authors when they published their works.

3.4. Age of Authors

Although the metadata files accompanying the samples of the five sub-corpora provide the exact age of authors at the moment that their work was published, this information is presented here in six ten-year age groups, from authors aged between 25 and 35 to those older than 75.

The youngest authors seem to be found in the Chemistry texts. There are two writers under 25 and a further nine belonging to our first age-group (25–35). The second group (36–45 years old) contains the highest number of authors (54). Since this range might be seen as roughly corresponding to the first stage of an established scientific life, the abundance of authors found here could be well expected. This is followed by the 43 authors whose works were published when they were between 46 and 55 years old. Not many authors belong to the rest of the ten-year periods, which might be explained on the grounds of another socio-external factor, namely, life expectancy, especially so for the 75+ group.

In what follows, technical aspects of the compilation process are briefly described.

4. Digitalisation and Some Peculiarities

In the early 2000s, the *CC* was designed as a collection of TEI-XML files containing both text samples and metadata, these subsequently being processed to create an index, in such a way that the accompanying *CC* Tool searches indexes rather than individual texts. XML tags are used to render faithful replicas of texts and allow the compilers, when creating the indexes, to exclude from the searchable material any language that does not belong to the author, thus yielding more reliable search results. However, all the linguistic material excluded from searches is shown to the final user in red so that no contextual information is lost.

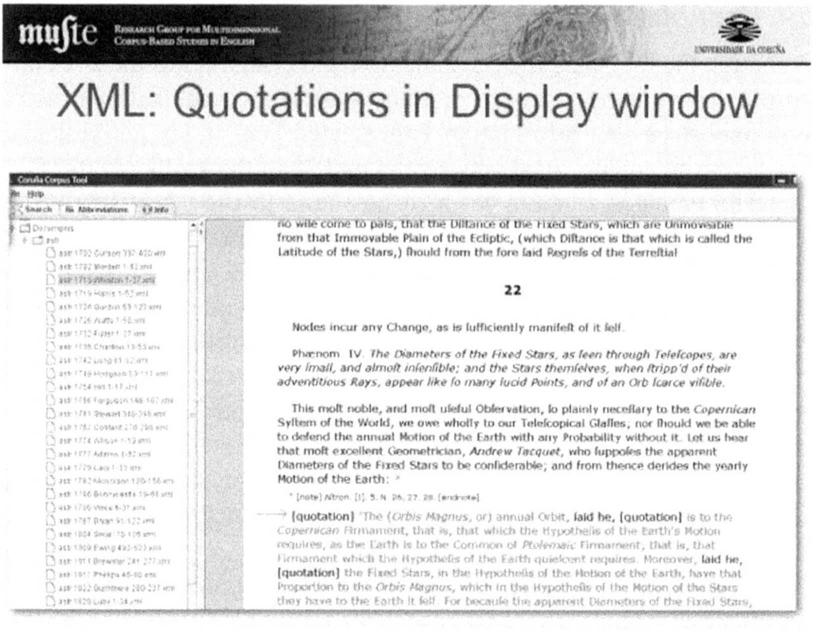

Figure 5: XML representation of elided text in red.

Unicode has been used extensively to present fragments as close to their original form as possible through the reproduction of special symbols and characters. Thus, the first fragment in Figure 6 below contains various signs of the zodiac, whereas the second fragment includes

The *Zodiack* is a Zone having eight degrees on either ſide of the Eclyptick, in which ſpace the Planets make their Revolutions, divided into 12 Signs, having 30 Degrees to each ſign, as *Aries* ♈, *Taurus* ♉, *Gemini* ♊, *Cancer* ♋, *Leo* ♌, *Virgo* ♍, which are called Northern Signs. *Libra* ♎, *Scorpio* ♏, *Sagittarius* ♐, *Capricornus* ♑, *Aquarius* ♒, and *Piſces* ♓, called the Southern Signs.

By the word *Sphære* we underſtand that common Inſtrument of a round Figure conſiſting of ſeveral Circles, invented to explain and repreſent the Heavenly Motions and the Fabrick of the whole World, which like a little Ball is in the Center of the Sphære having an Axis thro it, the extremities whereof are called Poles, about which the whole Body of the Heavens is ſuppoſed to turn round in the ſpace of 24 Hours. But for more Explanation,

Figure 6: Representation of special characters and symbols.

graphemes no longer in use. The software has been designed to recognise these archaic spellings when a search is made.

Another peculiarity of the *CC* is the use of certain editorial marks created by the compilers. These marks are the result of manual typing and a process of disambiguation. In this way, elements that are homograph with linguistic items, but do not in fact carry the same meaning, are set within square brackets; for example, the form [I] when it is not the personal pronoun but a Roman number, among others. A full account of the editorial policy adopted can be found in the manual accompanying the CCT (Camiña and Lareo 2016: 45–60).

Both the *CC* and the CCT provide researchers in language and the history of science with a rigorous collection of texts and bespoke retrieval tools that have already led to insights into this particular field of English for Special Purposes, that is, the language of science. With these freely available resources offered by the *CC*, it is hoped that many more findings regarding the emergence and development of English scientific discourse will come to light in future research.

References

Abbagnano, Nicolás, *Historia de la Filosofía,* Vol. 2 (Barcelona: Hora, 1982).

Allen, Bryce, Juan Qin and F.W. Lancaster, 'Persuasive Communities: A Longitudinal Analysis of References in the Philosophical Transactions of the Royal Society, 1665–1990', *Social Studies of Science* 24/2 (1994), 279–310.

Beal, Joan, *English in Modern Times: 1700–1945* (London: Arnold, 2004).

Biber, Douglas, 'Representativeness in Corpus Design', *Literary and Linguistic Computing* 8/4 (1993), 243–57.

Biber, Douglas. Susan Conrad and Randi Reppen, *Corpus Linguistics: Investigating Language Structure and Use* (Cambridge: Cambridge University Press, 1998).

Boyle, Robert. *A PROEMIAL ESSAY, WHEREIN, With some Considerations Touching EXPERIMENTAL ESSAYS in General, Is*

Interwoven such an Introduction to All Those Written by the Author, as Is Necessary to Be Perus'd for the Better Understanding of Them (London, 1661).

Camiña, Gonzalo and Inés Lareo. 'Editorial Policy in the Corpus of English Philosophy Texts: Criteria, Conventions, Encoding and Other Marks', in Isabel Moskowich, Gonzalo Camiña, Inés Lareo and Begoña Crespo, eds., *'The Conditioned and the Unconditioned': Late Modern English Texts on Philosophy* (Amsterdam: John Benjamins, 2016), 45–60.

Crespo, Begoña, 'On Writing Science in the Age of Reason', *Revista Canaria de Estudios Ingleses* 72 (2016), 53–78.

Crespo, Begoña and Isabel Moskowich, 'Astronomy, Philosophy, Life Sciences and History Texts: Setting the Scene for the Study of Modern Scientific Writing', *English Studies* 101/6 (2020), 665–84.

Görlach, Manfred, *Text Types and the History of English* (New York: Walter de Gruyter, 2004).

Hardie, Andrew and Tony McEnery, *Corpus Linguistics: Method, Theory and Practice* (Cambridge: Cambrdge University Press, 2011).

Herrero López, Concepción, 'Las mujeres en la investigación científica', *Criterio* 8 (2007), 73–96.

Kyto, Merja, Juhani Rudanko and Erik Smitterberg, 'Building a Bridge between the Present and the Past: A Corpus of 19th Century English', *ICAME Journal* 24 (2000), 85–97.

McEnery, Tony and Andrew Wilson, *Corpus Linguistics, An Introduction* (Edinburgh: Edinburgh University Press, 1996).

Meyer, Charles F., *English Corpus Linguistics: An Introduction* (Cambridge: Cambridge University Press, 2002).

Moessner, Lilo, 'Genre, Text Type, Style, Register: A Terminological Maze?', *International Journal of English Studies* 5/2 (2001), 131–8.

Moskowich, Isabel and Begoña Crespo, 'Classifying Communicative Formats in CHET, CECHeT and Others', in Antonio Moreno Ortiz and Chantal Pérez-Hernández, eds., *CILC2016. 8th International Conference on Corpus Linguistics,* Vol. 1 (EasyChair: EPiC Series in Language and Linguistics, 2016), 308–20.

Moskowich, Isabel, Inés Lareo, Gonzalo Camiña Rioboó and Begoña Crespo, comps., *Corpus of English Texts on Astronomy* (Amsterdam: John Benjamins, 2012) (Also open access at <https://ruc.udc.es/dspace/handle/2183/21848>).

Moskowich, Isabel, Gonzalo Camiña Rioboó, Inés Lareo and Begoña Crespo, comps., *A Corpus of English Texts on Philosophy* (CEPhiT) (Amsterdam: John Benjamins, 2016) (Also open access at <https://ruc.udc.es/dspace/handle/2183/21847>).

Moskowich, Isabel, Inés Lareo, Paula Lojo Sandino and Estefanía Sánchez-Barreiro, comps., *Corpus of History English Texts* (A Coruña: University of A Coruña., 2019) <http://hdl.handle.net/2183/21849>.

Oxford English Dictionary online. <http://www.oed.com>.

Puente-Castelo, Luis, '"If I mistake not". Conditionals as Stance Markers in Late Modern English Scientific Discourse', in Francisco Alonso-Almeida, ed., *Stancetaking in Late Modern English Scientific Writing: Evidence from the Coruña Corpus: Essays in Honour of Santiago González y Fernández-Corugedo* (Cambridge: Cambridge Scholars Publishing, 2017), 111–29.

Rissanen, Matti, 'Genres, Texts and Corpora in the Study of Medieval English', in Jürgen Klein and Dirk Vanderbeke, eds., *Anglistentag 1995 Greifswald: Proceedings* (Tübingen: Max Niemeyer Verlag, 1996), 229–42.

UNESCO, *United Nations Educational, Scientific and Cultural Organisation. Proposed International, Standard Nomenclature for Fields of Science and Technology* (Paris, 1988).

Javier Calle-Martín

Medical English Writing in the Period 1700–1900: *The Málaga Corpus of Late Modern English Scientific Prose*[1]

1. Antecedents

The Málaga Corpus of Early English Scientific Prose is a collection of English vernacular medical writing, consisting of three diachronically divided components, i.e. *The Málaga Corpus of Late Middle English Scientific Prose* (1350–1500); *The Málaga Corpus of Early Modern English Scientific Prose* (1500–1700); and *The Málaga Corpus of Late Modern English Scientific Prose* (1700–1900) – the latter shortened as CoLaMESP for brevity. The three components have been purposely designed so as to contain evidence from the three text types of medical writing in English, from "theoretical treatises transmitting specialized top-level knowledge through learned surgical and anatomical texts to simple recipes for practical use and miscellaneous collections" (Pahta and Taavitsainen 2004: 7). While theoretical treatises are considered the most academic register, remedies portray the language used by lay people, thus becoming an appropriate source for the investigation of textual variation in the period. In itself, the corpus stems from actual linguistic evidence of the period, both handwritten and printed, standing out as the ideal input for diachronic linguistic research at the levels of

1 The present research has been funded by the Spanish Ministry of Science and Innovation (grant number PID2021-126496NB-I00) and by the Andalusian Regional Government (grant numbers PY18–2782 and UMA18-FEDERJA-129). These grants are hereby gratefully acknowledged.

spelling, morphosyntax and lexis, among others. The early components of the corpus rely on manuscript material, which is taken as an added asset allowing introspection from other side areas such as Codicology, Palaeography or Ecdotics, among others.

In the first place, *The Málaga Corpus of Late Middle English Scientific Prose* is a collection of medical treatises written in the period 1350–1550 containing approximately one million words (Miranda-García and Calle-Martín 2012: 51–65). Compiled in the period 2007–2015, the corpus was based on complete hitherto unedited manuscripts housed in the special collections departments of two British Libraries: Glasgow University Library and The Wellcome Library. The project was initially conceived to offer the electronic edition of these manuscript texts providing faithful representation of the scribal practice in the period in such a way that lineation, punctuation and corrections were reproduced as in the original, while abbreviations were rendered in italics. The transcribed material was the source for the compilation of the raw and the annotated version of the corpus, the latter containing the lemma, word class and accidence of all the running words in the text (Calle-Martín and Miranda-García 2011: 3–20). The annotated version was unfortunately offered as an Excel spreadsheet, therefore complicating the actual process of data retrieval from the corpus. This inconvenience perhaps explains the limited repercussion of this component of the corpus among scholars interested in this kind of material.

The Málaga Corpus of Early Modern English Scientific Prose, in turn, is the second component of *The Málaga Corpus of Early English Scientific Prose* (Calle-Martín and Esteban-Segura 2020: 31–42). The corpus covers the period 1500–1700 and, as its predecessor, it contains hitherto unedited medical material from the three main branches of medical writing. This component houses approximately 1.5 million tokens portraying the language of the three text types of medical writing. Even though this component of the corpus follows the same rationale when it comes to the selection of hitherto unedited full manuscripts and the semi-diplomatic transcription of the material, the corpus format drastically differs from our late Middle English proposal. The corpus is offered in three versions corresponding to the three different stages of its compilation: the raw files (.txt), holding the transcribed version of the text as found in the original sources; the normalized files (.norm), with the modernized version of the material in present-day English; and the pos-tagged files (.pos), automatically carried out by means of Constituent Likelihood Automatic Word-tagging System (henceforth CLAWS), which assigns a morphosyntactic tag to each word in the corpus, punctuation marks included. The new format of the corpus has decidedly contributed to its on-going dissemination among scholars interested in the language of the period, becoming the primary source for multi-faceted studies in the last decade (Thaisen 2020: 11–30; Tyrkkö 2020: 67–93).

2. The Málaga Corpus of Late Modern English Scientific Prose

2.1. The Corpus

CoLaMESP (1700–1900) is the third component of *The Málaga Corpus of Early English Scientific Prose*, which has been recently published and made available in the project's webpage.[2] In its current form, the corpus amounts to 2.3 million words, of which 1.1 million belong to the eighteenth century and the other 1.2 million to the nineteenth century.[3] Following the rationale of the early modern English component, the product has also been organized into the three types of medical writing, with a balanced number of items in each category. Table 1 reproduces the total number of running words in the corpus classified in terms of their text type and sub-period:

2 https://latemodernmss.uma.es.

3 Unlike the earlier components of the Málaga corpus, the late modern component is based on printed documents rather than handwritten material, thus allowing for studies concerning the influence of the printing press on the development of the English language.

Table 1: Word count

	1700–1724	**1725–1749**	**1750–1774**	**1775–1799**	**1800–1824**	**1825–1849**	**1850–1874**	**1875–1899**
Theor.	90,425	210,957	123,165	92,442	38,123	57,896	289,320	157,177
Surg.	165,456	179,762	0	24,893	150,303	163,551	151,090	89,364
Recip.	231,432	94,479	206,054	31,020	29,193	18,910	31,245	52,705
TOTAL	157,177	485,198	329,219	148,355	217,619	240,357	471,655	299,246

As shown, the corpus has been conceived to represent medical writing in Late Modern English both over time and across text types. As far as the former is concerned, the different sub-periods were initially planned to exceed 300,000 words, considered to be a representative input to facilitate a diachronic survey. Even though there are sub-periods which substantially fulfil this criterion, the upcoming release of the corpus will sort out this same issue for the sub-periods 1700–1724, 1775–1799 and 1800–1824, which in the current version do not still satisfy this requirement as of today. When it comes to textual variation, on the other hand, the initial impetus is to provide researchers with a balanced corpus to explore text-type variation. Table 1 shows some differences across the three categories insofar as theoretical and surgical treatises amount to approximately one million tokens (1,059,505 and 924,419 words, respectively), while recipe collections lag considerably behind with approximately 700,000 tokens. Although a higher number of tokens of recipe material is a desideratum and the future version of the corpus aims to give more room to this kind of medical writing, especially for the nineteenth century, the truth is that recipe collections did not then have a wide circulation in England at the time, at least in their published form. The advent of the new concept of medicine relying on symptomatic treatment put an end to the medieval doctrines that had been in vogue until the late eighteenth century, which explains why these medical compilations were still disseminated throughout the 1700s while practically non-existent one century later (Bloch 1988: 229–32; Worboys 2011: 109–10).

The list of the corpus texts is available in the project's webpage, offering updated information about the author, title, year, text type and number of words of each item.[4] As far as theoretical treatises are concerned, the corpus contains the bulk of medical knowledge in the period in the different disciplines, some of them used as primary sources in universities and medical colleges. Among them, we could mention Thomas Short's *Medicina Britannica* (1746), Richard Mead's *Medical Precepts and Cautions* or G. Rees's *Observations on Diseases of the Uterus* (1805), etc. Surgical treatises, in turn, have been chosen to deal with various kinds of operations, the list including general handbooks such as John Pearson's *Principles of Surgery for the Use of Chirurgical Students* and more specific treatises such as William Cheselden's *The Anatomy of the Bones* (1733). Finally, recipe collections, include some well-known publications in the period, such as William Salmon's *Collectanea Medica* (1703), Mary Kettilby's *A Collection of Above Three Hundred Receipts* (1746) or Eliza Smith's *The Compleat Housewife of Accomplished Gentlewomen's Companion* (1773), among others. Some of them, however, are anonymous in view of their domestic use in eighteenth- and nineteenth-century England.

On another note, the corpus includes a number of texts of female authorship to allow further insight from the perspective of gender variation. Women are confirmed to have pioneered and led a number of linguistic changes in the history of English, not only phonological (Trudgill 1972: 179–95; Labov 2001: 282), but also morphosyntactic (Biber and Burges 2000: 21–37; Mondorf 2002: 158–80). This female leadership in linguistic change, according to Nevalainen, stems from the "women's openness to innovations, stylistic flexibility, contextual sensitivity, and variety of domestic roles – and with men's relative lack of these attributes" (2000: 53; 2002: 181–99). Bearing in mind the role of women in the evolution of Standard English, the corpus gives room to recipe compilations of male and female authorship in the assumption that they can be a reliable input to investigate linguistic changes in progress from the perspective of gender variation.

4 https://latemodernmss.uma.es/thecorpus.

2.2. The Tagging Process

The compilation of a tagged corpus of historical English is not a straightforward process, especially if pursued with an automatic tagger (Romero-Barranco 2020: 103–14). *CoLaMESP* has been tagged with the CLAWS, a part-of-speech tagging software for English texts developed by the UCREL team at the University of Lancaster (Garside 1987; Garside and Smith 1997).[5] The corpus makes use of CLAWS7, the current standard tagset, containing more than 160 tags which, if proficiently combined, become an added asset for the automatic retrieval of information from the corpus. In its current form, however, CLAWS has been especially designed for the processing of present-day English material, while the other forms of early English certainly require a pre-processing stage to satisfy this basic need.

It goes without saying that Jonathan Swift's language differs from present-day English in a number of ways. Even though most of these differences are found at the level of spelling, there are also discrepancies in terms of morphology and syntax. Among the former, a typical case at hand is the expression the possessive case, then rendered with and without the apostrophe in the period (i.e. *the kings men* vs *the king's men*), or the frequent use of the greengrocer's apostrophe in the plural nominative (i.e. *orange's*, *apple's*). Morphological differences also arise in the expression of the third-person singular present-tense inflection (i.e. *hath*) or the levelling of the past and participial forms in the paradigm of strong verbs (i.e. *give – gave – gave*). Syntactic differences, in turn, also come to light when we think of the use of, for instance, multiple negation, *them* as a demonstrative in subject positions, *you was*, *between you and I* or expletive *it* after the relativizer *which* in the period (Tieken-Boon van Ostade 2009: 86). These issues call for some sort of normalization prior to the process of automatic tagging itself.

Normalization is performed in two different stages. The first stage is a manual process consisting of the preparation of the electronic version of the corpus texts by means of Optical Character Recognition (OCR), which allows us to recognize them in scanned documents. The

5 See https://ucrel.lancs.ac.uk/claws for updated information about the latest version of the tagger.

OCR technology is not error-free, especially in the case of historical texts, and it is necessary to amend a number of errors arising from the machine's odd reading, such as the frequent use of <e> instead of <c>, <f> instead of <ſ> along with the misreading of particular symbols such as the ampersand and marks of punctuation, where commas and stops are confused with each other. In itself, it is a time-consuming process for the compiler leading to the graphemic transcription of the original, which is the input for the plain-text version of the corpus (.txt). These files hold the transcribed version of the text as found in the original sources, where spelling, punctuation and word division have been preserved as in the original witness. As shown in the following excerpt, the text features, for instance, the possessive case *a dead mans skull* without the apostrophe which is deemed necessary today, along with the different positions of the hyphen in the adverb together, following the author's original practice.

> A Medicine for the Falling-sickness.
>
> Take a penny weight of the powder of Gold, six penny weight of Pearl, six penny weight of Amber, six penny weight of Corral, eight grains of <notvariant>Bezoar</notvariant>, half an ounce of Peony seeds; also you must put some powder of a dead man's skull, that has been an Anatomy, for a Woman, and the powder of a Woman for a Man, compound all these together; and take as much of the powder of all these as will lie upon a two-pence for nine mornings together in Endive water, and drink a good draught of Endive water after it. (Elizabeth G. Kent, A Choice Manual, or Rare and Select Secrets in Physick and Chirurgery, 1726).

The second stage of normalization is a semi-automatic process using the software *Variant Detector 2* (VARD), also designed by the UCREL team at the University of Lancaster (Baron and Rayson 2008).[6] VARD was initially conceived to assist users of historical corpora in dealing with spelling variation, early Modern English in particular (Calle-Martín and Esteban-Segura 2020), but in our case it has also proved to be a valuable tool for the processing of late Modern English texts. The software is taken as a pre-processor to turn the late Modern English input into a present-day English output providing modern candidate

6 See https://ucrel.lancs.ac.uk/vard/about for further information about its most recent versions, a user guide and a list of related publications.

forms for the different spelling variants in early English with the inclusion of an XML-tag so that the original word can be consulted. Even though it is a fact that many of these variants are automatically processed (such as the nominal and adjectival suffix *-ick* > *-ic* or the apostrophe in the regular past morpheme *receiu'd* > *received*), others require the compiler's intervention to select the appropriate form in view of the list of candidates (such as proper names, technical terms and foreign words, among others). VARD uses machine-learning algorithms and can be trained to become more accurate with the use of an increasing number of texts, thus considerably reducing the user's commitment over time. The following excerpt then reproduces the modernized version of the original text where it can be observed that, among others, the genitive case is now rendered with the possessive apostrophe in *a dead man's skull* along with the modernized version of the third person inflection *hath* > *has* and spellings such as *Am-ber* > *Amber*, *to-gether* > *together*, etc. Although this version of the corpus has its own limitations for research purposes, it is also available in the project's webpage since it can be helpful to investigate particular cases of orthographic variation insofar as it allows the generation of all the spelling variants of a lemma through the use of its XML-tag.

> A Medicine for the Falling sickness.
>
> Take a penny weight of the powder of Gold, six penny weight of Pearl, six penny weight of Amber, six penny weight of Corral, eight grains of Bezoar, half an ounce of Peony seeds; also you must put some powder of a dead man's skull, that has been an Anatomy, for a Woman, and the powder of a Woman for a Man, compound all these together; and take as much of the powder of all these as will lie upon a two-pence for nine mornings together in Endive water, and drink a good draught of Endive water after it (Elizabeth G. Kent, *A Choice Manual, or Rare and Select Secrets in Physick and Chirurgery*, 1726).

This version is taken as the source data for the tagging of the corpus, an automatic process performed by CLAWS, which is a rule-based tagger that provides every running word with its corresponding POS-tag in view of its context. The added asset of CLAWS, as mentioned above, relies in the inventory of tags, since the latest version of the tagset incorporates more than 160 different tags, offering a number of possibilities in the handling of the major categories. When it comes to the verb, it displays more than 30 different tags, the list including finite and non-finite forms of lexical verbs, modal verbs, along with particular cases of morphological variation, such as the past and past participle forms of lexical verbs. The process, however, is not error-free as CLAWS achieves 96–97 per cent accuracy in PDE (Rayson et al. 2007),[7] which means that manual disambiguation is needed in order to correct the erroneous tags. This post-editing phase consists of two different stages, concerned with the ambiguous and the erroneous tags. When it comes to the former, on the one hand, CLAWS provides the candidate tags for each word, where the most likely tag is given in square brackets together with a percentage indicating its probability. It is then the compiler's responsibility to decide the correct one in view of context (Leech, Garside and Atwell 1983: 20–2; Romero-Barranco 2020: 109). When it comes to the erroneous tags, on the other hand, manual check is also required to make POS-tagging as accurate as possible (Garside 1987: 35). For instance, some nominal forms are erroneously interpreted as proper nouns (NP1) instead of common nouns (NN) due to the presence of an uppercase letter; while some verbs are also wrongly tagged in their base form rather than as an infinitive when two or more words appear between a modal verb and the infinitival form itself. In addition to this, the corpus gives room to a number of technical terms, most of them of classical origin, which are manually tagged as foreign words (FW). The following excerpt reproduces the final version of the corpus after the tagging process and its post-editing phase:[8]

> A_AT1 Medicine_NN1 for_IF the_AT Falling_JJ sickness_NN1 ._.
>
> Take_VV0 a_AT1 penny_NNU1 weight_NN1 of_IO the_AT powder_NN1 of_IO Gold_NN1 ,_, six_MC penny_NNU1 weight_NN1 of_IO Pearl_NN1 ,_, six_MC penny_NNU1 weight_NN1 of_IO Amber_NN1 ,_, six_MC penny_NNU1 weight_NN1 of_IO Corral_NN1 ,_, eight_MC grains_NN2 of_IO Bezoar_NN1 ,_, half_DB an_AT1 ounce_NNU1 of_IO Peony_NN1 seeds_NN2 ;_; also_RR you_PPY must_VM put_VVI some_DD powder_NN1 of_IO a_AT1 dead_JJ man_NN1 's_GE skull_NN1 ,_, that_DD1 has_VHZ been_VBN an_AT1

---

7 The error rate decreases to just 1.5 per cent when it comes to the tagging of the major categories (see https://ucrel.lancs.ac.uk/claws).

8 See https://ucrel.lancs.ac.uk/claws7tags.html for the complete list of CLAWS7 tagset.

Anatomy_NN1 ,_, for_IF a_AT1 Woman_NN1 ,_, and_CC the_AT powder_NN1 of_IO a_AT1 Woman_NN1 for_IF a_AT1 Man_NN1 ,_, compound_VV0 all_DB these_DD2 together_RL ;_; and_CC take_VV0 as_RG much_DA1 of_IO the_AT powder_NN1 of_IO all_DB these_DD2 as_CSA will_VM lie_VVI upon_II a_AT1 two-pence_NN for_IF nine_MC mornings_NNT2 together_RL in_II Endive_NN1 water_NN1 ,_, and_CC drink_VV0 a_AT1 good_JJ draught_NN1 of_IO Endive_NN1 water_NN1 after_CS it_PPH1 ._. (Elizabeth G. Kent, *A Choice Manual, or Rare and Select Secrets in Physick and Chirurgery*, 1726).

2.3. The Corpus in CQPweb

The CQPweb version of the corpus is also available for those users who prefer to make use of the corpus remotely.[9] In itself, it is a web-based corpus analysis system providing user-friendly interface for different collections of texts and it enables the processing of large corpora both with word-level annotation and rich text-level metadata (Hardie 2012: 380–1). Following the rationale of a standard CQPweb corpus collection, it allows standard and restricted queries, word lookups, frequency lists, keyword search and corpus analysis. Regardless of the typology of the query, these are allowed both as plain text and case-sensitive, the latter relying on the tagged version of the corpus to facilitate the retrieval of information making use of the CLAWS7 tagset. Figure 1 reproduces the abridged output generated for the past tense of lexical verbs in the recipe sub-corpus consisting of a total of 1,270 verbs, with a frequency of 2,440 instances per million words. CQPweb is user-friendly insofar as the results may be displayed in two different ways. When it comes to the list of instances, the user is bound to view them either in random order or in corpus order, the latter recommended only if the files have been named with an *ad hoc* label (i.e. author's name, year of composition, period, gender, etc.) and would therefore be generated in batches. The format of the results, in turn, is offered either in line view or KWIC view, the former recommended if interested in the preceding or the ensuing contexts as it facilitates any likely scanning or skimming of the results in search of a particular instance.

---

9 https://latemodernmss.uma.es/cqpweb.

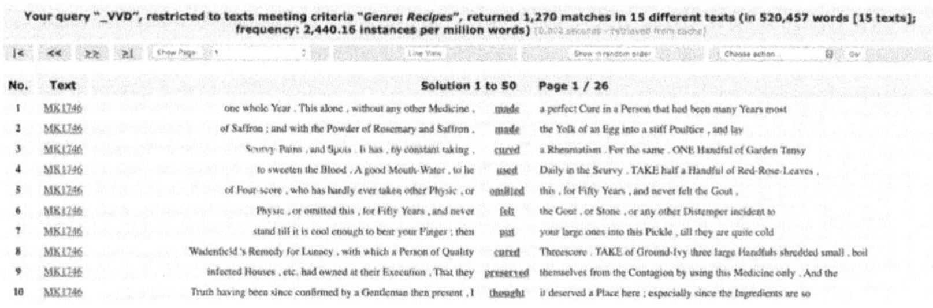

Figure 1: Standard query of the past tense of lexical verbs in CQPweb.

More importantly, however, the *analysis action* option is, in my opinion, the gist of CQPweb, housing a number of functionalities for the user both to specify the query or to undertake any subsequent statistical analysis. It does not simply allow to thin your query according to a specific number of instances or percentages, but it facilitates the sorting of the query by means of an intuitive sort control where the user selects the position (either the node or the pre- and post-contexts) along with the tag restrictions or a particular starting sequence. In addition to this, this option stands out as a statistical package providing some basic information about the frequency breakdown, the distribution and the dispersion coefficient values, which may be generated in tabulated form or in graphs. Figure 2, for instance, presents the bar chart of the past tense forms of lexical verbs in the corpus across text types, where it is shown that the past tense is more frequently used in theoretical and surgical treatises (n.f. 8,176.24 and 6,274.78 occurrences per million words, respectively) than in recipe collections (n.f. 2,440.16 occurrences). Finally, the application offers the possibility to save the current query results in CQPweb or to download them as a file for its subsequent treatment in a local device.

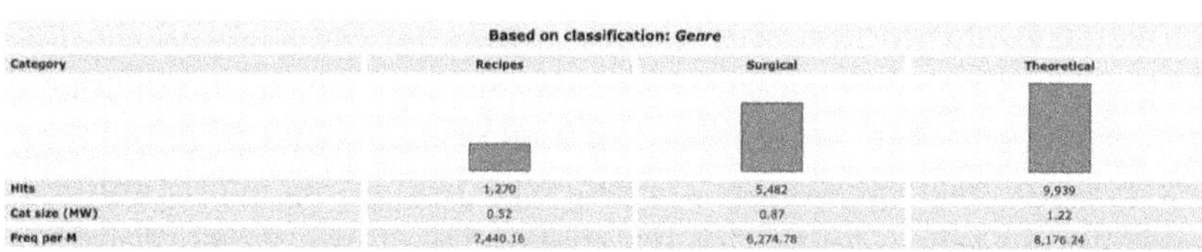

Figure 2: The past tense of lexical verbs across text types in CQPweb.

In light of all this, the CQPweb version of the corpus stands out as a potential resource for corpus handling in view of its flexibility, which makes it compatible with any corpus; its availability, processed with any device with internet connection; its accessibility, designed with an intuitive interface within reach of the average users of the platform; and its potential, able to process and generate results from different perspectives, from keywords and keytags to concordancing, collocations and distribution tables and charts.

3. Concluding Remarks

The present paper has presented the third component of *The Málaga Corpus of Early English Scientific Prose*, which has been especially conceived as a primary source for linguistic research in the period 1700–1900. *CoLaMESP* will surely become a landmark in the field in view of its representativeness, housing more than two-million words of late Modern English *Fachprosa*; of its chronology, organized into eight 25-year sub-periods for the study of linguistic changes in progress; of its practicality, containing material from the three types of medical writing; and of its versatility, offered for use either in your local device or online (Reppen 2010: 32). The tagging model is, in my opinion, the added asset of the proposal, incorporating more than 160 POS-tags which, if properly combined, show a great potential for research purposes on the levels of spelling and morphosyntax. Technical terms of foreign provenance have been provided with an *ad hoc* tag, thus allowing further introspection into the borrowing and development of these non-native terms in the history of English.

The corpus is still under development and the future updates will further consolidate it as a reference corpus for the study of the history of the English language. The collection is soon to incorporate a higher number of texts composed in both centuries and from the three text types of medical writing. The objective is to gather a three-million-word corpus which allows for the study of linguistic variation from a multi-faceted perspective. Bearing this in mind, the collection will also incorporate a higher number of works of female authorship to open doors for the analysis of gender variation in the assumption that it may become a test bed for the leading role of females in particular cases of linguistic change in the history of English.

The positive aspects of *CoLaMESP* are not only constrained to the late Modern English period itself, since it also constitutes an excellent resource for a wide variety of research studies in the history of the English language if used in combination with the earlier components of the *Málaga Corpus*, thus covering a time-span of approximately six hundred years. As of now, concluding that it is a valid source data for the analysis of late Modern English is a safe claim, even though users will surely have the last word about it.

Source

Calle-Martín, Javier, Miriam Criado-Peña, Verónica Hernández, Sinéad Linehan-Gómez and Juan Lorente-Sánchez, eds., *The Málaga Corpus of Late Modern English Scientific Prose* (Málaga: University of Málaga, 2016). Available at https://latemodernmss.uma.es.

References

Baron, Allistair and Paul Rayson, 'VARD 2: A Tool for Dealing with Spelling Variation in Historical Corpora', *Proceedings of the Postgraduate Conference in Corpus Linguistics* (Birmingham: Aston University, 2008).

Biber, Douglas and Jená Burges, 'Historical Change in the Language Use of Women and Men: Gender Differences in Dramatic Dialogue', *Journal of English Linguistics* 28/1 (2000), 21–37.

Bloch, Harry, 'Medicine and Science in the 19th and 20th Centuries', *Journal of the National Medical Association* 80/2 (1988), 229–232.

Calle-Martín, Javier and Antonio Miranda-García, 'From the Manuscript to the Screen: Implementing Electronic Editions of Mediaeval Handwritten Material', *Studia Anglica Posnaniensia* 46/3 (2011), 3–20.

Calle-Martín, Javier and Laura Esteban-Segura, 'The Málaga Corpus of Early Modern English Scientific Prose: fundamentación, implementación y desarrollo', in Soledad Díaz-Alarcón and Pilar Guerrero-Medina, eds., *Innovación metodológica para la investigación y docencia en filologías y traducción: casos prácticos* (Córdoba: Universidad de Córdoba – McGraw-Hill, 2020), 31–42.Garside, Roger, 'The CLAWS Word-Tagging System', in Roger Garside, Geoffrey Leech and Geoffrey Sampson, eds., *The Computational Analysis of English: A Corpus-Based Approach* (London: Longman, 1987), 30–41.

Garside, Roger and Nicholas Smith, 'A Hybrid Grammatical Tagger: CLAWS 4', in Roger Garside, Geoffrey Leech and Anthony Mark McEnery, eds., *Corpus Annotation: Linguistic Information from Computer Text Corpora* (London: Longman, 1997), 102–121.

Hardie, Andrew, 'CQPweb – Combining Power, Flexibility and Usability in a Corpus Analysis Tool', *International Journal of Corpus Linguistics* 17/3 (2012), 380–409.

Labov, Willliam, *Principles of Linguistic Change, Volume II: Social Factors* (Malden and Oxford: Wiley-Blackwell, 2001).

Leech, Geoffrey, Roger Garside and Eric Atwell, 'The Automatic Grammatical Tagging of the Brown Corpus', *ICAME Journal* 7 (1983), 13–33.

Miranda-García, Antonio and Javier Calle-Martín, 'Compiling the Malaga Corpus of Late Middle English Scientific Prose', in Nila Vázquez, ed., *Creation and Use of Historical English Corpora in Spain* (Newcastle upon Tyne: Cambridge Scholars Publishing, 2012), 51–65.

Mondorf, Britta, 'Gender Difference in English Syntax', *Journal of English Linguistics* 30/2 (2002), 158–180.

Nevalainen, Terttu, 'Gender Differences in the Evolution of Standard English', *Journal of English Linguistics* 28/1 (2000), 38–59.

Nevalainen, Terttu, 'Language and Woman's Place in Earlier English', *Journal of English Linguistics* 30/2 (2002), 181–199.

Pahta, Päivi and Irma Taavitsainen, 'Vernacularisation of Scientific and Medical Writing in Its Sociohistorical Context', in Irma

Taavitsainen and Päivi Pahta, eds., *Medical and Scientific Writing in Late Medieval English* (Cambridge: Cambridge University Press, 2004), 1–22.

Rayson, Paul, Dawn Archer, Alistair Baron, Jonathan Culpeper and Nicholas Smith, 'Tagging the Bard: Evaluating the Accuracy of a Modern POS Tagger on Early Modern English Corpora', *Proceedings of Corpus Linguistics 2007, University of Birmingham, UK, July 2007*.

Reppen, Randi, 'Building a Corpus. What are the Key Considerations', in Anne O'Keeffe and Michael McCarthy, eds., *The Routledge Handbook of Corpus Linguistics* (London and New York: Routledge, 2010), 31–7.

Romero-Barranco, Jesús, 'Spelling Normalisation and POS-Tagging of Historical Corpora: The Case of GUL, MS Hunter 135 (ff. 34r-121v)', in Miguel Fuster-Márquez, Carmina Gregori-Signes and José Santaemilia-Ruíz, eds., *Multiperspectives in Analysis and Corpus Design* (Granada: Comares, 2020), 103–14.

Thaisen, Jacob, 'Transparently Hierarchical: Punctuation in the Townshend Family Recipe Book', *International Journal of English Studies* 20/2 (2020), 11–30.

Tieken-Boon van Ostade, Ingrid, *An Introduction to Late Modern English* (Edinburgh: Edinburgh University Press, 2009).

Trudgill, Peter, 'Sex, Covert Prestige and Linguistic Change in the Urban British English of Norwich', *Language in Society* 1/2 (1972), 179–95.

Tyrkkö, Jukka, 'Early Modern Medicine in Manuscript and Print. A Triangulation Approach to Analysing Spelling Standardisation', *International Journal of English Studies* 20/2 (2020), 67–93.

Worboys, Michael, 'Practice and the Science of Medicine in the Nineteenth Century', *Isis* 102/1 (2011), 109–115.

Carla Suhr, Irma Taavitsainen and Turo Hiltunen

The Corpus of Late Modern English Medical Writing: Scientific and Social Change in the Eighteenth Century

1. Introduction

This chapter describes the corpus of Late Modern English Medical Texts (LMEMT) (Taavitsainen et al. 2019; see also Taavitsainen and Hiltunen 2019) and illustrates briefly some of the broad changes in medical writing taking place in the eighteenth century. LMEMT is the third instalment in a series of corpora, which altogether cover just over 400 years of the medical register of writing.

LMEMT is a specialized diachronic corpus that focuses on a single register of writing – medicine – of the eighteenth century. The corpus was compiled primarily for linguistic studies, but scholars in adjacent disciplines such as history will also find the corpus to be of use in their research. The long time-span of the corpus, especially when combined with the two earlier corpora (*Middle English Medical Texts*, 2005, and *Early Modern English Medical Texts*, 2010), makes it possible to identify patterns of change in language use and thought-styles.

We begin the chapter by describing the text-external compilation principles of LMEMT that aim to ensure the representativeness of the corpus. We then give an overview of the text categories of the corpus. Though many of these categories continue older traditions of medical writing, some of them represent new developments brought about by changes in society and scientific thinking. However, established text traditions also change to reflect contemporary interests and thought-styles. We end the chapter by giving examples of how texts in different corpus categories reflect the new mechanistic view of science and chemical medicine, the growing importance of societal concerns, and the rise of consumer society.

2. Compilation Principles and Categories of LMEMT[1]

For a register-specific corpus such as LMEMT and its sister corpora MEMT and EMEMT, text selection is of paramount importance to ensure that the corpus is an accurate representation of the textual reality. In the case of these three medical corpora, it was also considered important to make the corpora structurally compatible so that they can be used together for diachronic studies ranging from late Middle English to Late Modern English (see e.g. Taavitsainen, Schneider and Jones 2019; Tyrkkö 2019). The diachronic range can be extended beyond LMEMT by using it in combination with corpora such as ARCHER or Medicor or other present-day material such as PubMed (see e.g. Ratia and Suhr 2021; Schneider 2021). Figure 1 shows the text categories of the three medical corpora and illustrates the broad developments of the register over time: on the one hand, surgical texts and remedy books continue throughout the corpora, and, on the other hand, there is increasing specialization, which is most noticeable in the appearance of various journals, starting in the early modern period with the *Philosophical Transactions* (PT), a scientific journal published by the Royal Society, and the later additions of the specialized *Edinburgh Medical Journal* (EMJ) and the *Gentleman's Magazine* (GM), a general journal for lay audiences. A new category of texts focusing on public health emerges in LMEMT.

1 This section is based on the corpus description (Chapter 1) by Hiltunen and Taavitsainen and the category descriptions by Hiltunen, Lehto, Pahta, Ratia, Suhr, Taavitsainen, and Tyrkkö found in Chapter 11 of the LMEMT volume edited by Taavitsainen and Hiltunen (2019).

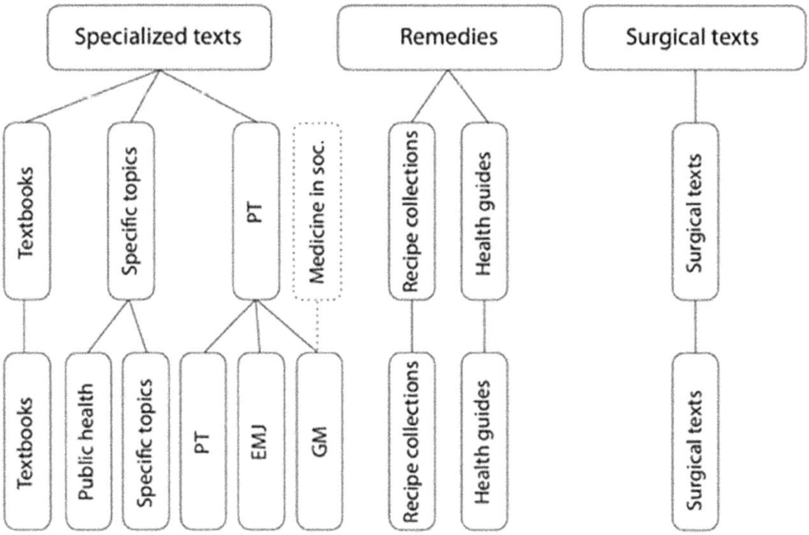

Figure 1: The text categories of the MEMT, EMEMT and LMEMT corpora.

In comparison to modern megacorpora of present-day English, the LMEMT corpus is not a very large corpus, as its size is just over two million words. However, the benefit of a smaller corpus is that we have been able to carefully curate the text selection according to text-external criteria that are based on knowledge of the historical context. The book accompanying the corpus also provides detailed information on the texts and their contexts as well as a manual for users of the corpus (see Taavitsainen and Hiltunen 2019; Taavitsainen et al. 2019). The corpus texts are provided in two formats: the digital edition is annotated using TEI-compliant XML, and the unannotated version consists of plain text files (see the manual in Hiltunen and Tyrkkö 2019) for more details on the two versions and suggestions for suitable corpus tools for linguistic analyses).

The LMEMT corpus aims to represent the full range of printed medical texts of the eighteenth century. Text selection was based on surveying available printed materials and statistics about book production, extensive background reading on medical writing of the period, as well as consultation with medical historians. The authors and audiences of the texts extend from lay people to educated elites, and the texts themselves are very heterogeneous. The topics cover everything from household recipe collections to discussions of vaccination as a public health measure. It should be noted, however, that the corpus does not represent handwritten texts such as letters, which continued to be a popular vehicle for consultation and transmitting medical advice in general (see e.g., Plastina 2022). Another important point is that the majority of the authors of texts included in LMEMT are male; female authorship was rare at the time, and the selection of authors represents this fact, too. Most of the corpus texts were accessed from the online repository *Eighteenth Century Collections Online* (ECCO) in XML format through collaboration with the ECCO Text Creation Partnership (TCP), but a number of texts were obtained from other repositories and keyed in manually.

Following the model set in the earlier corpora, LMEMT includes shorter texts in their entirety and approximately 10,000-word extracts of longer texts. This means that the corpus can be used to study common grammatical and discursive features (see e.g., Hiltunen 2022 on stance expressions and Ratia and Suhr 2021 on impersonal style). The corpus is useful also for studying mid-frequency lexical items (see e.g., Tyrkkö 2019 on medical signifier terms; Lehto 2019 and 2022 on representations of patients and practitioners). Studies on text structure should also take note of the fact that most extracts of longer texts are from the beginning of the text (but exclude prefatory material).

The corpus texts have been divided into seven broad categories on the basis of their topics: general treatises and textbooks; specialized treatises (divided into four sub-categories); medical recipe collections; regimens; surgical and anatomical texts; public health; and periodicals (scientific and general). The decision to form the text categories on the basis of the text-external criterion of topic was made for two reasons. First, it was important to continue with the principles adopted in the earlier corpora to ensure compatibility and comparability. At the same time, a fundamental premise underlying the compilation is that medical topics remain much the same over time, but what changes is how the topics are written about, including writing styles and argumentation patterns. Therefore, it is important to keep in mind that the text categories of LMEMT are not directly mapped onto specific registers or genres of writing. Importantly, we do not present our categorization as the only possible representation of the textual reality for all research tasks. Instead, corpus users are encouraged to move beyond the corpus categorization and flexibly form their own categories that better match their individual research questions. For example, medical case reports are found in several corpus categories, so a study of this text type requires the formulation of a new subcorpus that draws on all the corpus categories (see Lehto and Taavitsainen 2019). Book reviews in periodicals form a different subcorpus (see Taavitsainen 2021). A study on the stylistic differences in texts for diverse kinds of audiences is based on another subcorpus (see Taavitsainen 2019). It is also possible to use the text selection of the corpus as a starting point for extracting a representative selection of full texts from relevant databases (see e.g., Varila, Suhr and Tyrkkö forthcoming).

Figure 2 shows the diachronic distribution and word counts of the text extracts in each of the seven main text categories (specialized treatises are collapsed into one category). Some categories consist mainly of longer texts that are represented by 10,000 word extracts, whereas the articles in periodicals are much shorter. Texts in the categories of Public health and Specialized treatises are made up more evenly of a mixture of shorter and longer texts. There are more texts from the latter half of the century to reflect the general increase in the volume of published books in general. The relative sizes of the categories (in the number of texts) is also an indication of their ratio of all published medical books in the period.

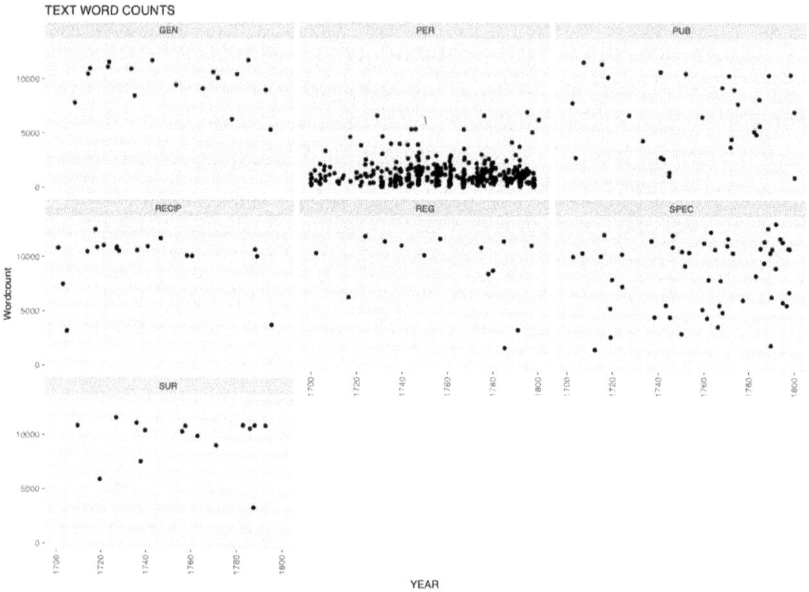

Figure 2: The diachronic distribution and word counts of text extracts in LMEMT by text categories. GEN=general treatises and textbooks; PER=periodicals (scientific and general); PUB=public health; RECIP=medical recipe collections; REG=regimens; SPEC=specialised treatises; SUR=surgical and anatomical texts.

Texts in the category of General treatises and textbooks (20 texts) were mainly written by medical professionals and aimed at non-specialist readers – including women – and medical students. The texts cover a wide range of current topics, such as the ethics of medical practitioners. New theories and thought-styles, for example the mechanistic view of the human body, can be found alongside older traditions.

The category of Specialized treatises consists of four sub-categories: diseases (20 texts), methods (17 texts), therapeutic substances (14 texts), and midwifery (13 texts). The mix of diseases discussed include both old and new diseases, though familiar diseases such as the scurvy are often given new explanations and treatments based on contemporary medical practice. The sub-category of methods focuses on new treatments for preventing and treating illnesses, such as inoculation and electrical and magnetic therapies, whereas specific medical substances – raw materials or finished products – are discussed in a sub-category of their own. Finally, midwifery texts range from theoretical discussions of reproductive biology to practical guidebooks on childbirth. As a whole, the texts in this category demonstrate the changes taking place in medical thinking in the eighteenth century, with new theories and an expansive view of health as both a public concern and an individual responsibility.

Medical recipe collections (23 texts) and Regimen texts (14 texts) deal with topics found already in classical medical texts. The medical recipes come from both popular printed collections of household remedies and several institutional compendia of medical recipes. These texts reflect mostly the interests of the middle class and elite. Regimen texts had the same readership, but they focused on preventative medicine. In addition to their long traditions, texts in these two categories also incorporated new theories such as mechanistic and chemical medicine and spread the knowledge about them to non-specialists.

The Surgical and anatomical texts category (17 texts) covers a wide spectrum ranging from overviews of the field to short works on a specific surgical operation or part of anatomy. Contrary to many other categories, the texts are mainly intended only for medical professionals, as they are concerned with anatomical and physiological descriptions and surgical procedures. The emphasis is firmly on first-hand observations, thus continuing a trend first emerging in the early modern period.

The category of Public health (30 texts) is a completely new one. Its addition is justified by the number of texts discussing the role of various medical practitioners, organizations and new institutions, such as hospitals, in medicine and in society in general. Furthermore, demographics and statistics, legislature and other measures to improve the health and hygiene of the public as a whole are novel aspects of the texts first found in this category.

Finally, the category of Periodicals consists of samples of articles on medical topics found in periodicals, which are divided into scientific and general publications in the corpus. Periodicals were an increasingly important type of publication in the eighteenth century. The scientific periodicals are represented by the *Philosophical Transactions*, established already in 1665, and the *Edinburgh Medical Journal*

(1733–).[2] The former journal combined medical topics with other scientific topics, whereas the latter focused strictly on medicine. *The Gentleman's Magazine*, on the other hand, is an example of a periodical magazine aimed at the educated lay person, who also wanted and even needed to know about medical matters.

3. Scientific and Social Change in LMEMT

Medical thinking in the eighteenth century continued many of the trends of earlier periods, and it is also reflected in the medical writing found in LMEMT. For example, the early modern turn towards empiricism and its reliance on first-hand experiences and observation as the source of knowledge continues in both the more theoretical treatises and texts aimed for educated lay readers. Chemical medicine, that is, medicines made from metals and minerals by distillation and other chemical processes, originated from Paracelsus but was in wide use by the eighteenth century. Chemical medicines are found in many learned collections of recipes, including the 1721 *Dispensatory of the Royal College of Physicians in London*. We see an increasing specialization within medicine, with the advent of texts about dentistry, sleep disorders, and melancholy, to name a few examples. At the same time, medieval and classical ideas such as astrological medicine and humoral theory are combined with new scientific discoveries in texts pitched for more general audiences. The empirical method combined with new tools such as the microscope that enabled much more detailed observations of the human body also led to new therapeutic approaches and novel ways of describing the functioning of the body and the effects of various diseases, treatments and therapeutic substances on the body. Thus the corpus contains texts about the use of, for example, magnetism

2 The term *Edinburgh Medical Journal* (EMJ) actually refers of a series of six journals by different names published in Edinburgh from 1733 to the present day. The first four of these journals cover the eighteenth century.

(Boerhaave 1743)[3], electricity (Wesley 1760) and pneumatic medicines (e.g. Beddoes 1795) to treat patients. Inoculation as a preventative for smallpox was the subject of heated disputes, which are represented by several texts in the corpus (e.g. Jurin 1724; Jenner 1798). Authors such as Boerhaave conceived the body as made up of moving solids and fluids connected by muscles, veins and fibres, whose distempers are the root condition for medical problems (Boerhaave 1714, 1715). The emerging mechanistic worldview can be seen in texts that describe the human body as "a most perfect Machine" (Rudd 1742: 4).

Case studies are often used as evidence of successful experiments and cures, and we can see the beginnings of statistical considerations when the validity of a treatment or medicine is considered in terms of large numbers rather than individual cases. This reflects not only an incipient interest in keeping track of statistical data, but also an increasing ability to acquire that kind of demographic data from institutions such as hospitals or various registers. Writing for "the benefit of the poor" or "the greater good" is a common trope in medical texts from the medieval period onwards, but in the eighteenth century public health is often explicitly discussed as an issue of the state and a matter that requires regularization and legislation. For example, the multitude of medical practitioners, ranging from learned physicians to apothecaries and self-taught charlatans, is seen as a problem in many texts that call for more state regulation. The ethics and roles of various medical practitioners are discussed – sometimes heatedly – in texts from several corpus categories, such as textbooks, periodicals and especially the texts in the new category of public health. Irregular practitioners, that is, practitioners without official medical credentials, are accused of fraudulent or even dangerous treatments, whereas the learned physicians are accused of using obfuscating language and inflating their prices. These types of accusations are, naturally, countered in defensive texts written by members of the targeted groups of practitioners. The founding of institutions such as hospitals, infirmaries and dispensatories can be seen as one attempt to regulate health care, but they are also a reflection of another strand of the discourses about public health, namely charity, as many of

3 All the eighteenth-century texts cited in this chapter are found in the LMEMT corpus, so they are not cited individually in the list of references.

these institutions relied on donations. Several texts target practices they consider to be detrimental to public welfare, such as the consumption of alcohol (Hales 1733) or the overindulgence of food (e.g. Cheyne 1724). Others advocate general measures for improving public health, such as municipal planning and cleanliness (Borthwick 1784) or regulating the price of medical services (Anon., *Essay for reforming the modern way of practising medicine in Edinburgh* 1727).

The general concern about public health was not considered to be the responsibility of the state alone, as many corpus texts show that their authors assume that patients take an active role in the treatment of their illnesses. The multitude of different levels of medical practitioners gave patients plenty of alternatives from which to choose a treatment, medicine or supplier (see Porter 1995). This was one of the contributing factors to the fierce competition between practitioners and the resulting debates about the roles of various medical practitioners. The number of medical texts written by and for lay audiences in LMEMT indicates an increasing interest in medical matters, not only in understanding medical theories and fashionable treatments (such as magnetism or electricity) but in self-diagnosing and self-medicating ailments. A member of polite society was expected to be able to converse also about medical matters, as revealed by the articles found in the *Gentleman's Magazine*, but lay readership was not limited to the middling and higher classes, but extended even to the lowest levels of society, thanks to increasing literacy. At the same time, we can see the beginnings of increasing specialization within medicine with the advent of medical journals such as the *Edinburgh Medical Journal*, which were aimed for medical professionals.

Finally, the LMEMT corpus texts reflect the rise of the consumer society in the eighteenth century. Medicines and medical services were a commodity offered to consumers, who sought help for real and perceived ailments concurrently from different sources (Porter 1995). Dozens of proprietary medicines for all kinds of ailments were available at a multitude of outlets not just in the capital but around the country. These medicines, which were produced by well-known physicians as well as apothecaries and self-styled "students of physick", were marketed quite aggressively in pamphlets and treatises, many of which can be found in LMEMT.

4. Conclusion

This chapter has briefly outlined the compilation principles and text categories of the LMEMT corpus and summarized some of the scientific and social changes that are reflected in the corpus texts and that have guided the text selection. In-depth analyses of the language of a particular register require a balanced and representative set of material, and this is what LMEMT, along with its sister corpora MEMT and EMEMT, aims to provide.

Medical writing has been an important part of scientific writing in English since the late medieval period, not least because of the significance of health and medicine for the lives of people from all walks of life. The developments in this domain, such as the processes of vernacularization and popularization – and gate-keeping – of medical knowledge and changes in scientific thinking, go hand in hand with social changes. By the eighteenth century, medical knowledge was considered the right and responsibility of everyone, regardless of wealth, occupation or social rank, as illustrated by Lewis Robinson in his *Every patient his own doctor*:

> For the benefit of mankind, we here furnish the public with some of the best and easiest methods of recovering and securing health, and of preserving life, which comprehend the greatest discoveries in the Medical Art. These will equally suit all ranks of people; the Poor, because the Remedies may be cheaply obtained; and the Rich, because they may be easily put in practice. Hence Health may be recovered with Facility, and a Knowledge of the powers of medicine obtained without Difficulty. So that our readers may at once cease to be Patients themselves, or, if they please, become Practical Physicians to others (Robinson 1785: iv).

References

Hiltunen, Turo, 'Towards a Local Grammar of Stance Expression in Late Modern English Medical Writing', in Turo Hiltunen and Irma Taavitsainen, eds., *Corpus Pragmatic Studies on the History of Medical Discourse* (Amsterdam and Philadelphia: John Benjamins, 2022), 127–52.

Hiltunen, Turo and Irma Taavitsainen, 'Towards New Knowledge: The Corpus of *Late Modern English Medical Texts'*, in Irma Taavitsainen and Turo Hiltunen, eds., *Late Modern English Medical Texts: Writing Medicine in the Eighteenth Century* (Amsterdam and Philadelphia: John Benjamins, 2019), 1–16.

Hiltunen, Turo and Jukka Tyrkkö, 'Manual to the LMEMT Corpus', in I. Taavitsainen and T. Hiltunen, eds., *Late Modern English Medical Texts: Writing Medicine in the Eighteenth Century* (Amsterdam and Philadelphia: John Benjamins, 2019), 337–54.

Lehto, Anu, 'Changing Portrayals of Medicine and Patients in Eighteenth-Century Medical Writing: Lexical Bundles in Public Health, Methods, and Case Studies', in Irma Taavitsainen and Turo Hiltunen, eds., *Late Modern English Medical Texts: Writing Medicine in the Eighteenth Century* (Amsterdam and Philadelphia: John Benjamins, 2019), 145–72.

——, '*Unhappy Patients and Eminent Physicians*. The Representation of Patients and Practitioners in Late Modern English Medical Writing', in Turo Hiltunen and Irma Taavitsainen, eds., *Corpus Pragmatic Studies on the History of Medical Discourse* (Amsterdam and Philadelphia: John Benjamins, 2022), 203–28.

Lehto, Anu and Irma Taavitsainen, 'Medical Case Reports in Late Modern English', in Irma Taavitsainen and Turo Hiltunen, eds., *Late Modern English Medical Texts: Writing Medicine in the Eighteenth Century* (Amsterdam and Philadelphia: John Benjamins, 2019), 89–111.

Plastina, Anna Franca, 'The Discursive Dynamics of Personal Experience Narratives and Medical Advice in 18th-Century British Consultation Letters: The Case of Dr. William Cullen', in Turo Hiltunen and Irma Taavitsainen, eds., *Corpus Pragmatic Studies on the History of Medical Discourse* (Amsterdam and Philadelphia: John Benjamins, 2022), 229–49.

Ratia, Maura and Carla Suhr, 'Interpreting the World of Late Modern English Medical Writing: From "I examined" to "ratios were obtained"', in Anna Čermáková and Markéta Malá, eds., *Variation in Time and Space. Observing the World through Corpora* (Berlin and Boston: De Gruyter, 2021), 113–32.

Schneider, Gerold, 'Medical Topics and Style from 1500 to 2018: A Corpus-Driven Exploration', in Turo Hiltunen and Irma Taavitsainen, eds., *Corpus Pragmatic Studies on the History of*

Medical Discourse (Amsterdam and Philadelphia: John Benjamins, 2021), 49–78.

Taavitsainen, Irma, 'Professional and Lay Medical Texts in the Eighteenth Century: A Linguistic Stylistic Assessment', in Irma Taavitsainen and Turo Hiltunen, eds., *Late Modern English Medical Texts: Writing Medicine in the Eighteenth Century* (Amsterdam and Philadelphia: John Benjamins, 2019), 173–97.

——, 'Medical Book Reviews 1665–1800: From Compliments to Insults', *Journal of Historical Pragmatics* 22/2 (2021), 245–62.

Taavitsainen, Irma and Turo Hiltunen, eds., *Late Modern English Medical Texts: Writing Medicine in the Eighteenth Century* (Amsterdam and Philadelphia: John Benjamins, 2019).

Taavitsainen, Irma, Turo Hiltunen, Anu Lehto, Ville Marttila, Päivi Pahta, Maura Ratia, Carla Suhr and Jukka Tyrkkö, comp., *Late Modern English Medical Texts: The Corpus* (Amsterdam and Philadelphia: John Benjamins, 2019).

Taavitsainen Irma, Gerold Schneider and Peter Murray Jones, 'Topics of Eighteenth-Century Medical Writing with Triangulation of Methods: LMEMT and the Underlying Reality', in Irma Taavitsainen and Turo Hiltunen, eds., *Late Modern English Medical Texts: Writing Medicine in the Eighteenth Century* (Amsterdam and Philadelphia: John Benjamins, 2019), 31–74.

Tyrkkö, Jukka, 'The *Symptom* Comes of Age: Sign Semantics from the Late Middle to Late Modern English', in Irma Taavitsainen and Turo Hiltunen, eds., *Late Modern English Medical Texts: Writing Medicine in the Eighteenth Century* (Amsterdam and Philadelphia: John Benjamins, 2019), 199–227.

Varila, Mari-Liisa, Carla Suhr and Jukka Tyrkkö, 'Visual Representation of Information in Medical Texts, 1500–1700', in Matti Peikola, Jukka Tyrkkö and Mari-Liisa Varila, eds., *Graphic Practices and Literacies in the History of English* (Turnhout: Brepols, forthcoming).

María F. García-Bermejo Giner and Javier Ruano-García

Investigating Variation and Change in Late Modern English Dialects: *The Salamanca Corpus*

1. Introduction

As is known, *The Salamanca Corpus* (*SC*) is an ongoing project conceived as a digital archive of diachronic dialect material that might bridge some of the gaps still existing in the history of English dialects (1500–1950). The *SC* seeks to refine our historical knowledge of regional varieties of speech by recovering and digitizing older and hardly accessible texts that comprise dialect writing and provincial glossaries. These are the most numerous sources that have come down to us where provincial speech is documented, and they offer useful data to explore dialect variation and change during Early and Late Modern English (LModE).

This chapter reports on recent work on the *SC* and focuses on what it can tell us about variation and change in LModE dialects. It describes the eighteenth- and nineteenth-century materials so far available, providing an overview of their distribution as regards text type, chronology and varieties documented. Our aim is to outline the major challenges that this compilation may entail while pointing to some recent findings that add to the body of historical documents representative of dialect speech. At the same time, this chapter highlights that, despite those pitfalls and widespread criticism about its use for linguistic research, the data of the *SC* offers useful insight into the history of forms that remain little explored, while it can prove beneficial in reconstructing linguistic ideas about dialects over time. To do so, we summarize selected case studies that illustrate the potential contribution of the *SC* to the study of variation and change in LModE dialects, including periphrastic DO in south-western varieties and the enregisterment of provincial speech.

2. *The Salamanca Corpus*

The *SC* project was launched in February 2011. Initially, its ambitious aim was the gathering of a digitized corpus of texts representative of English dialect literature (DL) and the English literary use of dialect (LD) written in the Early and LModE periods (see further García-Bermejo Giner 2010, 2012). They are transliterated, in Word format, following a double blind procedure. From the beginning, these texts were made freely available to the scholarly community in the University of Salamanca digital archive GREDOS (https://gredos.usal.es/handle/10366/82515). These types of texts represent our most important source of information about regional English variation in centuries from which we have very little contemporary information.[1] They are especially relevant for the centuries before an interest in the topic began in earnest in the late nineteenth century: we are referring to the publications of the *English Dialect Society* (1873–1896) and the *English Dialect Dictionary* (1898–1905) (*EDD*) edited by Joseph Wright (1855–1930). The *SC* allows for an unprecedented type of empirical research. In 2013 it was decided to create a third section in the *SC* devoted to early descriptions of the different varieties, regional dictionaries and glossaries. All in all, at present, the *SC* contains 571 digitized works, amounting to 14,342,545 words. As is to be expected (see further García-Bermejo Giner 2010), the period 1800–1950 contains the highest number of works: 334 novels, short stories, poetry collections and plays. LD is better represented than DL, as is prose rather than poetry and drama. There are eighty-eight glossaries. On the other hand, the period 1700–1799

1 Letters, diaries and journals are also very relevant to historical dialectology but are more scarce and harder to come by. See García-Bermejo Giner and Montgomery (1997, 2003), and Auer et al. (2023), among others.

only contains twenty-five literary works, none of which correspond to LD drama. DL prose is better represented than LD whereas LD verse is more abundant than DL. There are eighteen glossaries and collections of words. Finally, the earlier section, 1500–1699, includes ninety-seven texts. Most of them are LD drama, fiction and poetry. None of them are DL prose or plays, poems are scarce. There are only ten glossaries and dictionaries. The gradual increase of interest in regional variation and its literary repesentation across genres through the centuries can be perceived in the corpus. The *SC* is an ongoing project, many more texts are being digitized.

2. Gathering the Corpus: Some Challenges and Recent Findings

As a starting point we used Joseph Wright's monumental list of primary sources for *EDD*. Digital repositories such as archive.org, hathitrust.org or the digital collections of the British Library or the Bodleian Library have tremendously facilitated the task of finding copies of relevant texts. Also local archives and libraries are a most fruitful tool.[2]

The main challenge behind the compilation of the *SC* has been, and remains, to gather a representative number of texts of each one of the dialects, as well as of the three periods represented in the corpus. Just as dialect is not represented as often across genres, not all varieties were as frequently depicted in literary texts or described by contemporary glossarists, agriculturalists or historians. This can be clearly seen in the *EDD* bibliography. Whereas there are 300 references for Lancashire, 309 for Yorkshire (which Wright divides in five different sections: General, East Riding, North Riding, Mid Yorkshire and West Yorkshire), 113 for Devonshire or 94 for Cornwall, there are only 2 for Buckinghamshire or Rutlandshire, 4 for Bedforshire (one of which is

2 We greatly appreciate the generous help of many archivists and librarians who take a personal interest in the corpus and kindly answer our queries.

a lost manuscript), 4 for Cambridgeshire (of which 2 are agricultural surveys, 2 is a magazine and another a lost manuscript glossary), 5 for Leicestershire (four of which are works on the history of the county), 6 for Herefordshire (one of which belonged to the manuscripts collection of Prince Louis Lucien Bonaparte (1813–1891)), 6 for the Isle of Wight, 7 for Hertfordshire (six of which are agricultural surveys or works on the history of the county), or nine for the Isle of Man.

Exhaustive as *EDD*'s *Bibliography* is, at times we have been able to locate and transcribe works Wright did not have access to or, perhaps, for different reasons, decided not to use. For instance, a source for Devonshire dialect is a letter published in a local paper in September 1885. The author is a Roger Giles about whom we have been unable to find any information. Probably he used a pseudonym. *EDD online* now allows us unprecedented searches and a compelling insight into the nooks and crannies of the dictionary. Although not recorded in the *Bibliography*, other letters by Giles were indeed used for quotations in *EDD*, published in August, October, November and December of that same year. A search of *The British Newspaper Archive* has allowed us to locate thirty-eight more letters, published between 1870 and 1914, some of which are now available in the corpus.

Another interesting recent finding pertains to the Yorkshire dialect. Among Wright's sources for eighteenth-century Yorkshire dialect we find a short section in *The History and Antiquities of the Parish of Halifax, in Yorkshire* (1775) by Rev. John Watson (1725–1783). He devoted twenty pages to "Remarks on the Dialect of Halifax Parish" and "Vocabulary of Uncommon Words Used in Halifax Parish". Joseph Hunter (1783–1861) also used them for his *Hallamashire* Glossary (1825). Both were reproduced almost verbatim in 1789 by William Bentley (1747–1811) in *History of the Town and Parish of Halifax*. He did not acknowledge Rev. Watson as his source (and is not found in *EDD*'s *Bibliography*). Rev. Watson is apparently the author of two letters in the Halifax dialect published in 1759 in *The Union Journal* or *Halifax Advertiser* of which he was the editor. They were not recorded in *EDD* and antedate by sixteen years the above mentioned chapters. Given the scarcity of eighteenth-century sources (compared to later ones), findings such as this are of the utmost importance. The same can be said about a few Lancashire pantomimes that, despite their widespread social appeal and popularity during the 1800s, have gone unnoticed in dialect bibliographies, basically because some of them remain in manuscript in local archives or at the Lord Chamberlain's Plays collection in the British Library. Recent work on such texts shows their potential to examine questions of dialect enregisterment and stylization in historical contexts (see Ruano-García 2021).

3. Webpage: *thesalamancacorpus.com*

The *SC* has a periodically updated webpage available at: www.thesala mancacorpus.com. The menu bar includes:

- Catalogues of the relevant texts for each variety where those which have already been uploaded to GREDOS are highlighted.
- Galleries of paintings and/or photographs of writers and glossarists.
- Information about research on the corpus and related topics.
- News about the texts uploaded at each update.
- Three different sections devoted to Glossaries, DL and LD.

The Index for each of these displays the different time periods. The early section, 1500–1699, is broadly subdivided for each of the English geographic regions: North, South, East Midlands and West Midlands, plus a subsection, loosely termed *Various,* for works that contain information about several varieties. For instance, within the *Various* section in the *Glossaries* menu we can find William Caxton's (c.1415–1492) "Prologue" to *Eneydos* (1490), the chapter "Dialects: and A Word about Improper Diphthongs" in Alexander Gill's (1565–1635) *Logonomia Anglica* or both editions of John Ray's (1642–1705) celebrated *A Collection of English Words Not Generally Used* (1674, 1691). It is worth noting that the *Various* section index of DL and LD is further subdivided in *Northern General* and *South Western* with further subdivisions for *Drama, Prose* and *Verse*. For instance, the *Literary Dialects 1500–1699 – Various – Northern – Verse* contains links to *Broadside Ballads*; *An Eglogue betweene Billie and Iockie called Mushrome*

(1615) by Richard Brathwaite (1588–1673); *A Joco-Serious Dicourse* by George Stuart.

For the other two time periods, 1700–1799 and 1800–1950, it has been possible to specify the counties within each region. We follow the traditional pre-1974 county name and region assignment, as found in *The Survey of English Dialects* (1962–71) (SED), given that those corpus texts belong in that time span. In the *Glossaries* menu there is also a further *Various* subsection for works that contain information on different varieties. For instance in 1700–1799 – *Glossaries – Various* can be found *A Provincial Glossary, with a Collection of Local Proverbs and Popular Superstitions* (1787) by Francis Grose (1731–1791) or *Observations on Popular Antiquities* (1777) by John Brand (1744–1806), among others. In the DL and LD menus there are subdivisions for text genre: Prose, Verse, Drama.

Clicking on a county name opens a page with a listing of the authors and texts. We have created individual pages for each author. There we gather biographical information, a listing of their works relevant for the corpus, and any bibliograhical data. Most of these writers and glossarists were minor figures and, as such, very little is known about them.[3] They seldom appear in *The Oxford Dictionary of National Biography.* When they do, it is almost always because of other activities unrelated to regional variation. The uncovering of relevant data is often a case of true detective work. Genealogical databases such as familysearch.org or myheritage.es allow us to discover relevant biographical information. Also the online census records at nationalarchives.gov.uk provide us with much interesting information about individuals that seemed to have vanished into thin air. Information is also given about personal papers, letters, wills, etc. kept at local archives. The above mentioned *British Newspaper Archive* is a treasure trove not only for unknown publications but also for biographical data. For instance, almost nothing was known about John Drummond Robertson (1857–1934) who compiled *A Glossary of Dialect and Archaic Words Used in the County of Gloucester* (1890). A search of the relevant databases produced a plethora of details about his life in England, in Gloucester, London and

3 Canonical writers have been excluded from the corpus as their works have already been digitized due to their relevance for literary studies.

Torquay, his migration and return from South Africa, his publications on different topics in *The Bristol and Gloucestershire Archaelogical Society* and *The Gloucester School of Science Philosopical Society,* etc. Because of his stay in Johannesburg, Lord Moreton was in charge of the edition of his Gloucester Glossary.

Sometimes our search of these databases allows us to clarify and correct the existing information about some writers. Such is the case of Georgiana Verral (c.1837–?) who, under the pseudonym Elfin, published a DL poem *A Cornish Ghost Story. A Night's Adventures at the Devil's Stile, of Jacky Revose and Mary Trevean* (1862). William Prideaux Courtney and George Clement Boase say about her in their *Bibliotheca Cornubiensis* (1878. II: 822) "(dau. of Will. Verrall of Lewes, Sussex b. Worthing. Mistress of the Endowed sch. Crowan; Governess to the family of the rev. Vernon Page, R. of St. Tudy)". However, we have found out that the daughter of Mr. (William) Verrall of Lewes was not born in Worthin but in Lewes, in 1831. She married Mr. Parker George Synot in 1856. Courtney and Boase refer to her as Miss but at the time her poem was published she had already been married for six years. However, we have found a Georgiana Verral, born in Worthing, Sussex, c.1837, who, indeed, is recorded in the 1861 census as unmarried, twenty-four years old, National School Teacher, living in Crowan, Cornwall, where she is Head of the Churchtown School. In the Census records for 1871 and 1881, still unmarried, she is living in St. Tudy, Cornwall, at the home of Rev. Vernon Page (1818–1885).

On occasion, our search for information has allowed us to get in touch with descendants of the writers. An example is Mary Hartier (Harriet Mary Russ) (1861–1936). Mr. Michael Thompson's great-grand-father's third wife was a first cousin of the author's mother and confirmed to us that Harriet Mary Russ was indeed the person behind the *nom de plume* Mary Hartier. A descendant of John Ellett Brogden (1837–1875), the glossarist responsible for *Provincial Words and Expressions Current in Lincolshire* (1866), provided us with his photograph, from his private family archive.

4. Variation and Change in Late Modern English Dialects: Some Research Avenues

The evidence furnished by the *SC* can contribute to the history of LModE dialects. Despite the dearth of data representative of specific varieties and criticism about the use of inauthentic representations of speech (see Schneider 2013; Wolfram and Schilling 2016: 346), the information preserved in dialect writing offers useful insight into the history of forms that remain little explored, whilst it can prove beneficial in reconstructing ideas about dialects over time. Indeed, it provides us with largely untrodden records of speech where the structural and ideological dimensions of dialects intersect, and thus give valuable information about their past and how they were evaluated. In this section, we report on recent case studies based on the *SC* in order to outline some avenues of research, while pointing to some areas that await further investigation.

4.1. Grammar: Periphrastic do

Unlike other fields such as lexis and phonology, the representation of dialect grammar has gained little scholarly attention, largely because morphosyntactic features are often less noticeable than distinct sounds and thus get represented less frequently (see Honeybone 2020). Besides, the scarcity of materials from some dialects has complicated our endeavour to shed light on the historical frequencies, distribution and patterns of use of specific grammatical features. In fact, what little research has been done so far has been chiefly concerned with isolated samples of dialect speech or the works of specific authors (see García-Bermejo Giner 1991; Asprey 2020). Yet the increasing availability of data from less-investigated dialects is opening windows into uncharted aspects of grammar that can be explored through bigger samples of speech. Such is the case of DO-periphrasis, which Ruano-García (2023) has analysed in nineteenth-century representations of south-western dialects.

Periphrastic DO is one of the distinctive grammatical features of traditional south-western speech, which, according to Ihalainen

(1994: 225), refers to the use of "unstressed – *do* in affirmative" declarative sentences, as in examples (1) and (2):

(1) You mine how yer zister *da* read (Somerset).
(2) Doctur Chaarles Probum (. . .) com'd ower to Black Peppur Mine wheear I *ded* work tha Ingun (Cornwall).

As (1) shows, periphrastic DO was not inflected for third-person singular subjects, while, as Ihalainen (1994: 225) notes, it was unstressed, here suggested by <a> and <e> in *da* "do" and *ded* "did". At the same time, it was not only confined to present contexts, as example (2) indicates. Wagner (2004: 171) points out that this feature was employed as a tense carrier and marker of habitual aspect, i.e. to mark "an event that takes place repeatedly" (Godfrey and Tagliamonte 1999: 105). Indeed, some of the nineteenth-century accounts of this south-western characteristic remark on such functions. For example, Barnes (1886) underlines that in Dorset forms like *they did break* and *did vind* (i.e. find) were employed to indicate that they "broke and found several times" (23). Similarly, Elworthy (1877: 49) notes that in the Somerset dialect "the use of the periphrastic form with *do* (. . .) is so much the rule that (. . .) the tense, state, etc. are formed by the auxiliaries". Even though such early remarks are historically valuable for what they tell us about the presence of this grammatical feature, "nothing can be concluded from that alone" (Wagner 2007: 263). As a matter of fact, these statements cannot be taken to suggest that periphrastic DO was employed with the same frequency across south-western dialects, nor that it occurred in all declaratives with simple present and past verbs.

As expected, evidence from twentieth-century materials like the SED and the FRED corpus offers more refined insight into the frequency and distribution of this feature. On the one hand, Klemola's (2018: 271) analysis of the SED Basic Material confirms the south-western use of DO and distinguishes between a core area that covers the dialects of West Cornwall, Dorset, East Somerset and West Wiltshire, and a peripheral area including Central Cornwall, West Somerset and East Wiltshire, where periphrastic *did* is not recorded. On the other hand, de Both's (2019) findings from the FRED corpus largely tie in with the SED data as Somerset, Wiltshire and Cornwall show higher frequencies of periphrastic *do*. At the same time, the twentieth-century data explored thus far points that it was used to mark habitual aspect, though not exclusively, being likewise employed to encode punctual and continuous meaning, that is: "an event (hypothetical or otherwise) understood to have occurred once" and "an event or process that extends in time or a state that exists continuously", respectively (Godfrey and Tagliamonte 1999: 105). Kortmann (2004: 256) adds that in the FRED corpus "*do* is most frequently used as an analytic tense marker, again however mostly in habitual contexts" and especially "in temporal or conditional clauses".

In view of the scarcity of alternative records of LModE dialect speech, evidence from the *SC* can provide us with a missing link in the history of periphrastic DO, mainly in relation to its distribution and function. Drawing on thirteen nineteenth-century representations of the dialects of Cornwall, Devon, Dorset, Somerset and Wiltshire (c.37200 words), Ruano-García (2023) has analysed the distribution and uses of perverbal DO in a sample of 1,810 tokens of positive declarative sentences with present and past verbs. The analysis takes a frequentist approach and thus quantifies instances of periphrastic DO in relation to all the possible cases in which *do*/*did* may have potentially occurred (see Ruano-García 2023 for further details about the methodology of this case study).

Quantification of the data shows, on the one hand, that periphrastic DO was a low-frequency feature, with 15.5 per cent (281/1810) of all possible cases recorded, instances of DO being more common in present than in past contexts (184 vs. 97; 25.5 per cent vs. 8.9 per cent). Interestingly, the data concurs with de Both's (2019) findings, who reports on 4.1 per cent of occurrences in a dataset of 2048 tokens. The *SC* data yet points to variation across the representations scrutinized, as displayed in Table 1.

Table 1: South-western distribution of periphrastic do (per cent) (adapted from Ruano-García 2023)

	Cornwall (N = 511)	**Devon (N = 321)**	**Dorset (N = 268)**	**Somerset (N = 232)**	**Wiltshire (N = 478)**	**Total (N = 1810)**
do	30.1 (53/176)	4.6 (6/130)	28.9 (39/135)	75.7 (56/74)	14.5 (30/207)	25.5 (184/722)
did	8.9 (30/335)	1 (2/191)	26.3 (35/133)	15.2 (24/158)	2.2 (6/271)	8.9 (97/1088)
Total	16.2 (83/511)	2.5 (8/321)	27.6 (74/268)	34.5 (80/232)	7.5 (36/478)	15.5 (281/1810)

As we can see, *do* is most frequently represented in the case of Somerset, while it is rare in Wiltshire and nearly absent in the representations of Devonshire, which, according to Klemola (2018: 271), was a *do*-less dialect. When it comes to past contexts, DO-periphrasis was comparatively less common in all the south-western dialects, with Dorset showing the highest frequency of *did*, which is virtually unattested in Devon. Comparison with the SED thus shows some continuity over time. While Somerset seems to have been one of the focal areas of *do* and *did* during the 1800s, Dorset featured amongst the core dialects where *did* was employed, and Devon showed a gap in the nineteenth-century distribution of this grammatical feature.

On the other hand, the *SC* data suggests that during the nineteenth century periphrastic DO was favoured to encode habituality, though not exclusively. Indeed, it is found to mark a single event in narration contexts, as in examples (3a–b), whereas it encodes continuous aspect in (4) and is employed as tense carrier in temporal clauses like example (5):

(3a) They *did* call I a witch, along o' my havin' tied my handkercher over my head (Dorset).
(3b) Well, taakin about he da bring inta me yead wat I promised var ta tell ee about (Wiltshire).
(4) [. . .] but law *do* mean money, win or lose, an' so there was no fear o' that (Somerset).
(5) [. . .] they were too weak, d'ye see, to keep wosses off when they *did* come a-fightin' of 'em (Dorset).

Figures 1 and 2 show, however, that such uses are comparatively uncommon in all the dialects considered, both in present and past contexts.

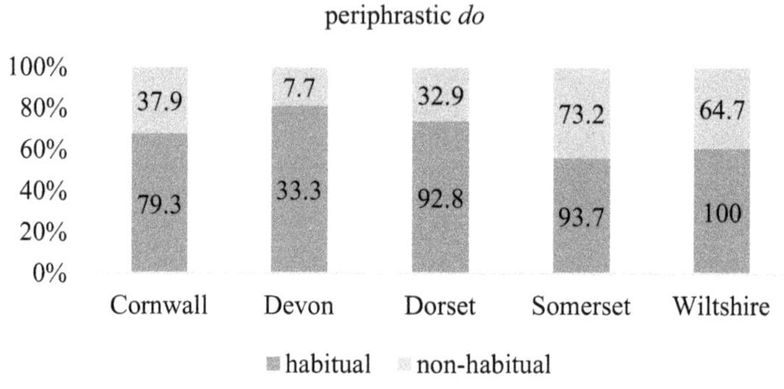

Figure 1: Aspect: cases of periphrastic *do* (per cent).

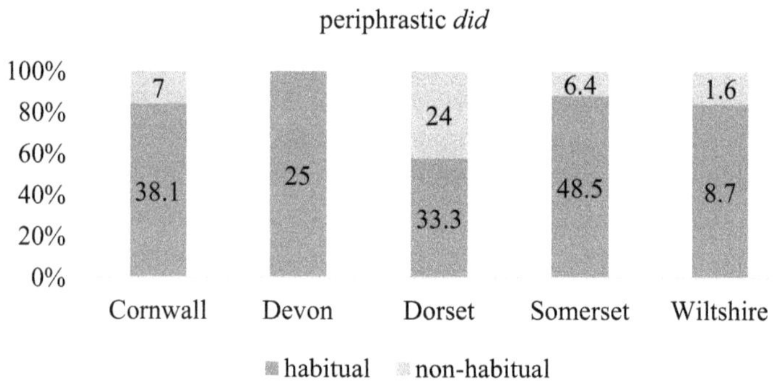

Figure 2: Aspects: cases of periphrastic *did* (per cent).

Although the data is not large enough for robust generalizations, the evidence preserved in representations of dialect can prove useful to investigate the history of this feature. Seen from this angle, the *SC* can inform our understanding of some aspects of grammatical variation in LModE dialects, which, as already noted, remains understudied in representations of regional speech.

4.2. Phonology and Spelling: Sociolinguistic Approaches

Over the past few years, the analysis of the phonological characteristics of dialect reproduced through non-standard spelling has shifted away from traditional descriptions of linguistic traits (see e.g. García-Bermejo Giner 2008; Sánchez-García 2012) to sociolinguistic approaches which treat respellings as variables that are quantified to determine the relative salience of the phonological features they represent (see Honeybone and Watson 2013). As such, respellings are taken as indexical resources because, in the words of Clark (2020: 105), "orthography not only depicts a representation of a sound pattern, but also links to a framework of social identity in much the same way". That is, conscious spelling choices are analysed as indexes of identity insofar as they signal salient features and social meanings linked with the dialect represented.

In this context, recent research has suggested that the uneven deployment of specific pronunciation respellings not only responds to the writer's representational skills and knowledge of the dialect. Rather, the extent to which they are combined with their corresponding standard forms seems to mirror the localizedness and salience of certain features. In the case of LModE Lancashire speech, Ruano-García (2020) shows that the variable representation of the GOAT (e.g. *waistcooat* "waistcoat"), MOUTH (e.g. *dreawnt* "drowned") and PRICE (e.g. *droyve* "drive") diphthongs corroborates Honeybone and Watson's (2013) localizedness criterion, whereby the more localized a feature is, the more salient it is and is thus respelt in dialect writing. As illustrated in Figure 3, the *SC* data suggests that the cline of salience of these forms may have been MOUTH > GOAT > PRICE, which metalinguistic remarks documented in grammars and glossaries confirm.

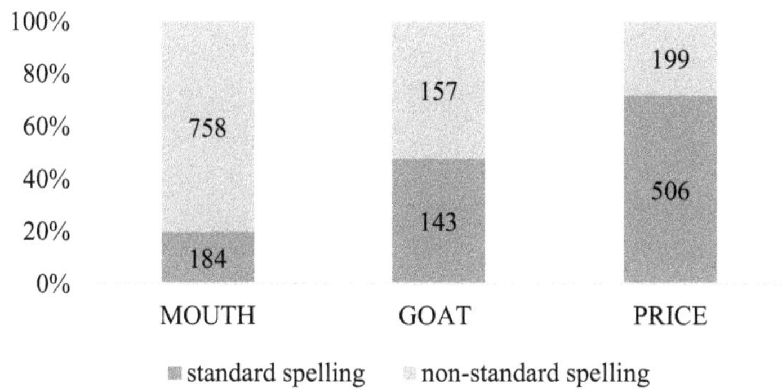

Figure 3: (Non-)standard spellings in LModE Lancashire texts (raw data) (adapted from Ruano-García 2020).

As in other studies (e.g. Honeybone and Watson 2013), this approach allows us to gain some insight into how these phonological features are evaluated as well as into their enregisterment as distinctive characteristics of the dialect represented. As a matter of fact, the third-wave sociolinguistic models of enregisterment (Agha 2003) and indexicality (Silverstein 2003) have proved particularly useful in this regard, basically because they provide an adequate framework to explore dialect awareness as well as shared ideas about the meanings associated with the use of specific dialects and/or linguistic features over time.

Drawing on seven fictional representations of the Derbyshire dialect from 1850–1900 (c.267400 words), Schintu (forthcoming) demonstrates that they relied on a stable repertoire of phonological forms employed "in order to evoke social meaning linked to place" (19). Her data points that the STRUT vowel and the GOAT, MOUTH and FACE diphthongs feature prominently, though with marked differences concerning the respellings whereby they were represented. As shown, variation in spelling choices lies in the type of representation (either LD or DL) and thus on the type of readership. For example, as displayed in Figure 4, instances of DL show preference for <u> over <oo> to represent STRUT (e.g. *suns* "sons"), which LD largely signals by means of the digraph (e.g. *roon* "run") along with <i>, e.g. *sich* "such". Similarly, <ei>/<ey> (e.g. *mey* "make") is virtually the norm in representations of FACE in cases of DL, whereas LD commonly relies on <e> and <a> followed by a consonant, as in *tekken* "taken" and *mak* "make"; these are rarely attested in representations of DL.

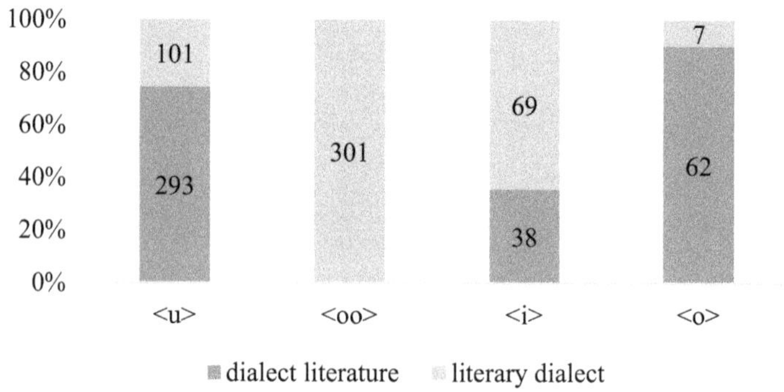

Figure 4: Respellings for STRUT in LModE Derbyshire texts (raw data) (adapted from Schintu forthcoming).

Schintu argues that variation in this sense reflects "discrepancies in the degree of perceived localness of the features reflected" (12), while pointing more generally "not only [to] the mutable nature of indexicality and enregisterment, but also [to] the fact that they are inherently dynamic processes, as remarkable indexical shifts have been found to operate over type of dialect representation" (20) (see also Schintu 2020, 2022).

Such indexical shifts are also found over time, as verse and fictional representations of the Lancashire dialect for example reflect. Here, Definite Article Reduction (e.g. *t'mon* "the man"), instances of *l*-vocalization (e.g. *aw* "all") along with <eaw/u> respellings for the MOUTH diphthong and realizations of the PRICE and GOAT vowels, as we have seen, feature as emblems of the dialect (Ruano-García 2020: 17). Their quantification yet shows that they were employed with varying frequencies over the eighteenth and the nineteenth centuries, thus pointing at shifting indexicalities during LModE and at the fact that individuals may experience such links "with varying degrees of intensity, durational constancy and force over the course of a life span" (Agha 2007: 154). Such an asymmetrical modelling of the Lancashire repertoire is further supported by theatrical representations, where similar reworkings are observed. They are especially visible in those plays that were written for out-group audiences and thus performed outside Lancashire (Ruano-García 2021). Their modified repertoire commonly includes identifiable Lancashire features (e.g. *l*-vocalisation) alongside generic northern and non-standard forms like uninflected *be* (e.g. *she be*) and the lack of FOOT-STRUT split (e.g. *Lunnon* "London") in response to external constraints like the type of audience and/or the place of the performance.

4.3. *Other Areas*

Just as the increasing availability of sources is broadening the scope of research into some grammatical features and third-wave sociolinguistic theories offer new readings for the respellings found in dialect writing, we may refer to other areas of linguistic interest that await scholarly attention. Most of them are catalogued by Ihalainen (1994: 213–15) as distinctive characteristics of late eighteenth- and early nineteenth-century dialects, which he classifies on the basis of isolated examples documented in contemporary sources and compares with later evidence such as that of the SED. Our list of selected understudied features does not attempt to be comprehensive, but rather to give an overview of what the available data of the *SC* can offer for future historical investigation.

- *same*/*seem* switch, or /ei/ > [i:], /i:/ > [ei]
  - (6a) Mr Lyons told a lot of other things about *Haygypt* and other furrin pairts (Devon).
  - (6b) tha Squires zon zeed un prowlin about in tha river cloas ta withy bade, *neaked* as a wur barn'd (Wiltshire).
  - (6c) You orkerd *crayter*! You shall pay for ahl a them geese, if you 'urts one on 'um (Worcestershire).
- otiose *of*
  - (7a) Yer dussn't lay a vinger on a bouoy now, if er's iver zo, or e'll 'ave 'ee up vur'saltin' *ov* un (Gloucestershire).
  - (7b) I lightened *ov* 'im anonst 'is 'ovel (Worcestershire).
  - (7c) atter sheaken hands wie tha Yankee an wishen *on* un good bye (Wiltshire).
- negation
  - (7a) Aw mun*na* buey th' muckfork, an aw mun*ner* buey th' peykil (Cheshire).
  - (7b) Well, he could*n't* say *naun* agin that ye see, so he did*n't* say *no more* about de Persians (Sussex).
  - (7c) I *never* shaa*nt* varget it (Wiltshire).
- relativization
  - (8a) poor wold Ann Kerley *what* was born and bred here (Dorset).
  - (8b) an' there's nowt [ø] maks one moore sleepy than to yer 'em come hummin o'er th' hedge (Lancashire).
  - (8c) There was summat stealed I know, but James Sneaker war the man *as* did it (Leicestershire).
- interjections / pragmatic markers
  - (9a) *By gum*! hoo's getten th' kink i' th' smaw o' her back (Cheshire).
  - (9b) *Ses*, E, my gud Mon greets o wunderous merry (Lancashire).
  - (9c) *Lokamussy*, whativver's put that in yer 'ed? (Leicestershire).

5. Concluding Remarks

This chapter has been concerned with a description of some recent advances and difficulties faced in the compilation of the *SC*, while it has reported on some ongoing work that offers compelling data about the history of LModE dialects. Even though the scarcity of texts representative of some varieties remains a challenging fact that looks hard to overcome, recent textual findings encourage us to believe that samples of dialect speech from specific counties and/or time periods await to be found and investigated. Indeed, the increasing availability of texts that have gone unnoticed, either because they were not listed in bibliographies of LModE dialects or because they have not been printed, are broadening the scope of investigation on specific linguistic levels and dialect features. Such is the case of third-wave sociolinguistic approaches to older dialect speech as well as of provincial grammar. We expect that future work on unexplored *SC* texts and others that will be soon added to the corpus might continue to add to the historical record of dialect speech, one that remains fragmented and poorly understood.

Source

García-Bermejo Giner, María F., Pilar Sánchez-García and Javier Ruano-García, eds., *The Salamanca Corpus: A Digital Archive of English Dialect Texts* (Salamanca: University of Salamanca, 2011). Available at http://www.thesalamancacorpus.com.

References

Agha, Asif, 'The Social Life of Cultural Value', *Language and Communication* 23/3 (2003), 231–73.

——, *Language and Social Relations* (Cambridge: Cambridge University Press, 2007).

Asprey, Esther, 'Black Country Dialect Literature and What it Can Tell us about Black Country Dialect', in Patrick Honeybone and Warren Maguire, eds., *Dialect Writing and the North of England* (Edinburgh: Edinburgh University Press, 2020), 29–50.

Auer, Anita, Anne-Christine Gardner and Mark Iten, 'Patterns of Linguistic Variation in Late Modern English Pauper Petitions from Berkshire and Dorset', in Markus Schiegg and Judith Huber, eds., *Intra-Writer Variation in Historical Sociolinguistics* (Lausanne: Peter Lang, 2023), 133–56.

Barnes, William, *A Grammar & Glossary of the Dorset Dialect* (London: Trübner & Co, 1886).

de Both, Fiona, 'Nonstandard Periphrastic DO and Verbal -*s* in the South West of England', *Journal of Historical Sociolinguistics* 5/ 1 (2019), 1–35.

Clark, Urszula, 'Enregistering Dialect Representation in Staffordshire Potteries' Cartoons', in Patrick Honeybone and Warren Maguire, eds., *Dialect Writing and the North of England* (Edinburgh: Edinburgh University Press, 2020), 103–25.

Courtney, William Prideaux and George Clement Boase, *Bibliotheca Cornubiensis, A Catalogue of the Writings, Both Manuscript and Printed, of Cornishmen, and of Works Relating to the County of Cornwall, with Biographical Memoranda and Copiousliterary References*, 2 Vols (London: Longmans, Greeen, Reader and Dyer, 1878).

Elworthy, Frederick Th., *An Outline of the Grammar of the Dialect of West Somerset* (London: Trübner & Co, 1877).

FRED = *Freiburg English Dialect Corpus*, 2000–2005. B. Kortmann et al. (eds.), http://www2.anglistik.uni-freiburg.de/institut/lskortmann/FRED/

García-Bermejo Giner, María F., 'Personal Pronouns in Derbyshire as Reflected in Sheridan Le *Fanu's Uncle Silas* (1864)', in Santiago G. Fernández-Corugedo, Juan Emilio Tazón-Salces, María Socorro Suárez-Lafuente, César Luis Alas-García and Virginia Prieto López, eds., *Studia Patriciae Shaw Oblata* (Oviedo: Universidad de Oviedo, 1991), 225–39.

——, 'Early Sixteenth-Century Evidence for [ɪə] < OE /ɑː/ in the North?' In María. F. García-Bermejo Giner, María Pilar Sánchez-García,

María Consuelo Montes-Granado, Elvira Pérez-Iglesias and Juan Andrés Jurado Torresquesana, eds., *Multidisciplinary Studies in Language and Literature: English, American and Canadian* (Salamanca: Ediciones Universidad de Salamanca, 2008), 59–63.

——, 'Towards a History of English Literary Dialects and Dialect Literature in the 18th and 19th Centuries: The Salamanca Corpus', in Barry Heselwood and Clive Upton, eds., *Papers from Methods XIII* (Frankfurt am Main: Peter Lang, 2010), 31–41.

——, 'The Online Salamanca Corpus of English Dialect Texts', in NilaVázquez-González, ed., *Creation and Use of Historical English Corpora in Spain* (Newcastle upon Tyne: Cambridge Scholars Publishing, 2012), 67–74.

García-Bermejo Giner, María F. and Michael Montgomery, 'Regional British English from the Nineteenth Century: Evidence from Emigrant Letters', in Alan S. Thomas, ed., *Issues and Methods in Dialectology* (Bangor: Department of English Linguistics, University of Wales Bangor, 1997), 167–83.

——, *The Knaresborough Workhouse Daybook: Language and Life in 18th-Century North Yorkshire* (York: Quacks Books in association with the Yorkshire Dialect Society, 2003).

Godfrey, Elizabeth and Sali Tagliamonte, 'Another Piece for the Verbal *-s* Story: Evidence from Devon in Southwest England'. *Language Variation and Change* 11 (1999), 87–121.

Honeybone, Patrick, 'Which Phonological Features Get Represented in Dialect Writing? Answers and Questions from Three Types of Liverpool English Texts', in Patrick Honeybone and Warren Maguire, eds., *Dialect Writing and the North of England* (Edinburgh: Edinburgh University Press, 2020), 211–42.

Honeybone, Patrick and Kevin Watson, 'Salience and the Sociolinguistics of Scouse Spelling: Exploring the Phonology of the Contemporary Humorous Localised Dialect Literature of Liverpool', *English World-Wide* 34/3 (2013), 305–40.

Ihalainen, Ossi, 'The Dialects of England since 1776', in Robert Burchfield, ed., *The Cambridge History of the English Language,* Vol. 5 (Cambridge: Cambridge University Press, 1994), 197–274.

Klemola, Juhani, 'The Historical Geographical Distribution of Periphrastic *do* in Southern Dialects, in Laura Wright, ed., *Southern English: Then and Now* (Berlin: Mouton de Gruyter, 2018), 262–92.

Kortmann, Bernd, '*Do* as a Tense and Aspect Marker in Varieties of English', in Bernd Kortmann, ed., *Dialectology Meets Typology: Dialect Grammar from a Cross-Linguistic Perspective* (Berlin: Mouton de Gruyter, 2004), 245–75.

Markus, Manfred, ed., *EDD Online 3.0.* http://eddonline-proj.uibk.ac.at/edd/terms OfUse.jsp.

Ruano-García, Javier, 'On the Enregisterment of the Lancashire Dialect in Late Modern English: Spelling in Focus', *Journal of Historical Sociolinguistics* 6/1 (2020), 1–38.

——, ' "Aw'm Lancashire, owd cock, and gradely hearty": Enregistered Lancashire Voices in the Nineteenth-Century Theatre', in Donatella Montini and Irene Ranzato, eds., *The Dialects of British English in Fictional Texts* (London: Routledge, 2021), 108–29.

——, '"Well, taakin taakin about he da bring inta me yead wat I promised var ta tell ee about": Representations of South-Western Speech in Nineteenth-Century Dialect Writing', *English Language and Linguistics* 27/3 (2023), 1–30.

Sánchez-García, Pilar, 'Depicting Northern English Dialects through Spelling: A Study Based on The Salamanca Corpus', in Nila Vázquez-González, ed., *Creation and Use of Historical English Corpora in Spain* (Newcastle: Cambridge Scholars Publishing, 2012), 433–62.

Schintu, Paula, '"Theers gud stuff amung uz Darbysher foaks": Dialect Enregisterment in 19th-Century Derbyshire', *Token* 10 (2020), 109–28.

——, *The Enregisterment of Late Modern Derbyshire Dialect (1850–1950)*. Ph.D. dissertation, Universidad de Salamanca, 2022.

——, 'Dialect on the Making: A Third-Wave Sociolinguistic Approach to the Enregisterment of Late Modern Derbyshire Spelling', *International Journal of English Studies* 23.2 (2023), 65–87.

Schneider, Edgar W., 'Investigating Historical Variation and Change in Written Documents: New Perspectives', in J. K. Chambers and Natalie Schilling, eds., *The Handbook of Language Variation and Change* (Oxford: Wiley, 2013), 57–82.

Silverstein, Michael, 'Indexical Order and the Dialectics of Sociolinguistic Life', *Language and Communication* 23/3 (2003), 193–229.

Wagner, Susanne, 'English Dialects in the Southwest: Morphology and Syntax'. In Bernd Kortmann, Kate Burridge, Rajend Mesthrie, Edgar W. Schneider and Clive Upton, eds., *A Handbook of Varieties of English*. Vol. 2 (Berlin: Mouton de Gruyter, 2004), 154–74.

——, 'Unstressed Periphrastic *do* – from Southwest England to Newfoundland?' *English World-Wide* 28/3 (2007), 249–78.

Wolfram, Walt and Natalie Schilling, *American English: Dialects and Variation* (Oxford: Wiley Blackwell, 2016).

Wright, Joseph, ed., *English Dialect Dictionary*, 6 Vols. (Oxford: Henry Frowde, 1898–1905).

David Denison, Nuria Yáñez-Bouza and Tino Oudesluijs

Editing *The Mary Hamilton Papers* (c.1740–c.1850)[1]

1. Introduction

In recent decades, the number of digital editions and linguistic corpora containing ego-documents such as diaries and private letters has seen a significant increase, both in English and in other languages (see e.g. Denison 1994; Meurman-Solin 2007; Baillot 2013; van der Wal et al. 2021). Since ego-documents include relatively detailed socio-historical information about the individuals involved, as well as shedding light on the broader socio-economic, cultural and political landscape of the region and period in which they were created, they provide a wealth of data for scholars from various disciplines, most notably (historical) sociolinguistics, literary studies and history (see e.g. Elspaß et al. 2007; van der Wal and Rutten 2013). For research covering the Late Modern English period in particular, developments in the fields of corpus linguistics and the digital humanities have led to significant progress in compiling and making available such editions and corpora. There remains, however, a shortage of socio-demographically informed data

1 *Unlocking the Mary Hamilton Papers* is an AHRC-funded project (AH/S007121/1) based at the University of Manchester and in collaboration with the universities of York and Vigo (2019–2023), which has also benefited from student internships at Manchester and York. The project builds on the *Image to Text* project (2011–2019), which received various modest grants for research assistance from sources at the University of Manchester, the John Rylands Research Institute and Library and the Universidade de Vigo. Nuria Yáñez-Bouza would also like to acknowledge Grant ED431C 2021/52 (Xunta de Galicia, Spain).

sources based on original manuscript material (rather than printed editions), which offer essential insights into the authors' individual language use, their social circles and cultural and literary practices more generally.

To address this, the *Unlocking the Mary Hamilton Papers* project set out to create both a digital edition and a linguistic corpus of ego-documents related to Mary Hamilton (1756–1816) based on transcriptions of original manuscript material. This material is mostly held at the John Rylands Research Institute and Library (JRRIL), with further material added from other repositories in the UK and US (see Section 2). Because of the time-span covered by the documents (c.1740–c.1850) and the wide range of topics discussed (e.g. court life, literary interests, women's education, courtship and romance), *The Mary Hamilton Papers* provide a unique opportunity to exploit an almost untouched archive and answer questions about literary practice, letter-writing and everyday language use in Georgian England. Furthermore, the rich material collected allows us to examine Mary Hamilton's social networks and potentially to consider how topics of research including reading practices, forms of address and the auxiliary verb system operate within and across those networks.[2]

This chapter constitutes a report on the creation of *The Mary Hamilton Papers* as a digital edition and a linguistic corpus. First, we describe the data sources with a brief summary of Mary Hamilton's life and of the core contents of the *Papers*. Section 3 turns to the editorial practices for the transcriptions, and Sections 4 and 5 introduce, respectively, the key features of the digital edition hosted in Manchester Digital Collections and of the linguistic corpus hosted in CQPweb. Section 6 closes the paper with some concluding remarks. This new resource not only adds to the growing body of resources in the field of digital humanities[3] but also helps to launch an exciting new wave

2 See the project website for more information on the four research strands.

3 Other ongoing projects constructing digital editions based on ego-documents include *Elizabeth Montagu Correspondence Online*, *The Letters of Hannah More: A Digital Edition*, *The Collected Letters of Robert Southey* and the *Darwin Correspondence Project.*

of studies on the Georgian period in general and on Mary Hamilton in particular.

2. Source Material

2.1. Mary Hamilton

Mary Hamilton (1756–1816) was the only child of Mary Catherine Hamilton (née Dufresne, d. 1778) and Charles Hamilton (1721–1771), who died when Mary Hamilton was fifteen. She spent much of her adolescence between the homes of her mother and of various relatives and guardians, and started working for the royal household as a sub-governess to the daughters of Queen Charlotte in 1777. Hamilton retired from Court five years later, as she found her duties too exhausting and needed to pursue "independence & Liberty" (GEO/ADD/3/83/39). From 1782 onwards, she kept in touch with some of the other royal governesses, both through correspondence and visits, and became a member of the Bas Bleu (Bluestocking) circle. There she counted Elizabeth Montagu, Hannah More, Frances Burney, Elizabeth Carter and Mary Delany among her literary friends. Despite not being a published writer like many of the others, Hamilton was an integral part of this network on both a social and literary level, and she frequently dined at the residences of Sir Joshua Reynolds and Horace Walpole, with whom she also corresponded. In 1785, Hamilton married John Dickenson (c. 1757–1842), the only son of John Dickenson Senior of Birch Hall (near Manchester), and in 1787 they had one child, Louisa Dickenson (later Anson). Together they lived in Taxal, Leighton Buzzard and London. Hamilton fell ill and died on 25 May 1816, aged sixty. As illustrated in various accounts of Hamilton's life, she was one of the most well-connected and highly cultured women in eighteenth-century British society, a fascinating figure "who moved in the same circles as many of the social, economic and intellectual elite of the period and left evidence of her life through the letters she retained and from the journals she kept" (Crawley 2014: 28; see also Anson and Anson 1925).

2.2. The Mary Hamilton Papers *Archive and Added Material*

Like many literate women in the eighteenth century, Hamilton was a seasoned letter-writer. She also kept detailed diaries and commonplace books in which she recorded various of her and others' daily activities and conversations, as well as her private thoughts. Hamilton was a meticulous archivist and preserved a substantial set of in-letters she and her husband received, as well as her own copies and drafts of out-letters. She furthermore compiled volumes of letters and other writings sent to her by friends, and the *Unlocking the Mary Hamilton Papers* project has taken the eponymous archive, held at the JRRIL at the University of Manchester, as its primary source material for both edition and corpus. The JRRIL archive contains 2,600 items from the period 1743–1826 and has been fully catalogued into three series: "correspondence", "manuscript diaries" and "manuscript volumes"; our edition characterizes some items differently. These sources have so far been complemented by 587 additional items related to Hamilton from eleven other repositories in the UK and US, raising the total number of items in the edition to 3,201 (17,865 images), of which 3,048 are private correspondence (letters, notes, journal-letters and volumes of journal-letters), thirty-eight are diaries and travel journals, and 114 are manuscript volumes containing a variety of different texts, e.g. anthologies of verse and prose, memoranda and account books plus miscellaneous wrappers, lists and other small items. Roughly 1,600 of these items have been manually transcribed (c. 875,500 words) and the transcriptions have been made available in the digital edition hosted in Manchester Digital Collections, in both diplomatic and normalized versions together with high-resolution images of the material (see Section 4), as well as in the linguistic corpus hosted in CQPweb, here tagged for parts of speech and semantic categories (see Section 5). The transcriptions are also freely available as plain-text files for non-profit use to anyone who registers for access via the project website. Table 1 gives an outline of the core contents at the time of writing (September 2023), using our disposition of materials rather than that of the catalogues.

Table 1: Overview of contents in *The Mary Hamilton Papers*

	Digital edition		**Transcribed**		
	items	**period**	**items**	**period**	**words**
Correspondence	3,048	1750–1826	1,537	1758–1819	659,722
Diaries/Journals	38	1776–1841	17	1776–1797	213,897
Other	115	1742–1853	44	1754–1799	1,807
Total	3,201	1742–1853	1,598	1754–1819	875,426

The correspondence collected in the edition is divided among a rich variety of sets including letters and journal-letters. These range from John Dickenson's letters to his wife and correspondence from Hamilton's family (e.g. Hamilton's uncle Sir William Hamilton, her cousin Lady Frances Harpur), the Dickenson family and other relatives (e.g. the Grevilles, the Murray sisters), to letters from the royal family (e.g. Queen Charlotte, George, Prince of Wales). Many are letters between friends, including members of the Bluestocking circle (e.g. Frances Burney, Hannah More, Horace Walpole), friends at Court (e.g. Charlotte Gunning, Martha Goldsworthy) and various other friends (e.g. the Clarke sisters), the majority in-letters. The diaries in the edition include seventeen autograph diaries by Mary Hamilton held at the JRRIL and twenty-one autograph diaries by Hamilton's husband John Dickenson and by her father-in-law John Dickenson Senior, these from the collection "Dickenson family of Birch Hall" held at Lancashire Archives in Preston. The materials classified as "other" in the edition come from various repositories and include a wide range of sources, from manuscript volumes written in Hamilton's hand and items written by friends or acquaintances which she annotated, to catalogues, memoranda and account books, as well as lists of letters, illustrations, signatures, wrappers. etc.

The material can be divided into seven different time periods, five of which cover Mary Hamilton's lifetime: 1742–1756 (before she was born); 1756 to mid-1777 (until she joined Court); mid-1777 to late 1782 (her time at Court); from late 1782 to mid-1785 (the period after Court and before she married John Dickenson – this is the shortest period yet richest in terms of surviving material); from mid-1785 to early 1797 (her married life as Mrs Dickenson, with marital home in the north of England); from early 1797 to her death in 1816 (marital home in the south); and finally 1816–1841, from which period there is correspondence addressed to John Dickenson (d. 1842), diaries and journals written by Dickenson, and other material concerning the Dickenson family. The very last item, an account book of Manchester property of Mary Parkin (née Dickenson), was written in 1853.

3. Editing Practices

In this section we provide a summary of the editorial practices we adopted in preparing the transcriptions in *The Mary Hamilton Papers*; full documentation is available on the project website. Certain details of procedure evolved over the ten-year period of editing as we grew more experienced with TEI, or when novel textual situations were encountered, and sometimes after consulting external advisers. From 2014 the transcriptions and images were displayed on the website of the precursor project (*Image to Text*, 2011–2019), which in 2019 was incorporated into the current project, *Unlocking the Mary Hamilton Papers*. As of 2020, the transcriptions and images began to be presented on the Manchester Digital Collections website, which in 2022 became the sole and permanent home of the edition.

Each item, whether a letter, diary or other kind of document, is represented by a file consisting of a header for metadata (e.g. title, archival information, author, date, location, summary) and a body containing the transcription of the text with XML mark-up in-line. Untranscribed items have a full header but only a token, one-line body. The files were created with the XML editor Oxygen in XML format following TEI P5 guidelines, and are subject to a schema created for the project by Denison, which prompts users in Oxygen with legitimate options for tags and values, flags invalid mark-up and helps reduce inconsistency. These files are the canonical repositories of information about an item, allowing different selections of that information to be retrieved or displayed as the purpose demands. Once completed, the transcriptions are checked by at least one of the editorial team members, and most by two.

An abridged list of the different elements documented in the editorial schema and employed in the XML mark-up is provided in the Appendix, covering (1) elements in the TEI header; (2) structural elements of the text in the body; (3) specific mark-up for opening and closings in correspondence; (4) other content-based mark-up such as person and place names, direct speech, foreign words and customized tags for research analysis; (5) elements concerning manuscript features like underlining, hyphenating, word spacing, additions and deletions; (6) elements to do with editorial intervention, like non-modern spelling and sic-forms, gaps and footnotes; (7) practice in the dating of letters; (8) our use of the element attribute @rend; and (9) mark-up for person references.

4. Digital Edition: *The Mary Hamilton Papers* in Manchester Digital Collections

Manchester Digital Collections (MDC) is an image-centred site that offers high-resolution images of an ever-increasing range of collections, including *The Mary Hamilton Papers*. There are tools for zooming or rotating images, as well as Mirador, a configurable image viewer that can be used to modify brightness, contrast, colours and so on. *The Mary Hamilton Papers* is one of the first collections in MDC to offer transcriptions of images and has served as a testing-ground for their presentation, adopting – and sometimes enhancing – the display features pioneered on the project website. On a desktop screen, the site provides two panels side by side, with an image on the left and a choice of different text-based data on the right. On first access, the right-hand panel displays by default some comprehensive metadata for the whole item, but users can choose instead to see thumbnails of all the pages for that item, or – where available – a diplomatic or normalized transcription of the image on the left. The user's selection for the right-hand panel is "sticky", i.e. it becomes the new default for the browser. There are buttons for moving forwards or backwards through the pages of multi-page items (users can also jump straight to any page), and there are similar buttons for moving through the items in a subseries of correspondence or diaries. The home page of the collection offers thumbnails with summary metadata of all the items, with filters for classmark, word(s) in the title, date range, author, recipient, and whether or not the item is transcribed. Clicking on the selected thumbnail opens the item. Access to individual items direct from CQPweb is also possible. By way of illustrative example, Figure 1 displays the first page of a letter from Queen Charlotte to Mary Hamilton (HAM/1/1/2/9) with the image and the diplomatic transcription, and Figure 2 the parallel visualisation with the normalised transcription.

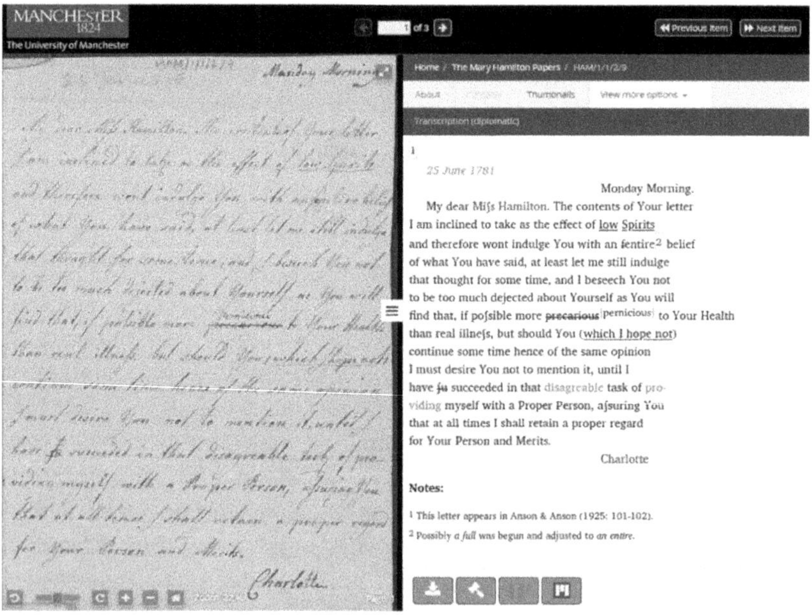

Figure 1: MDC display of the edition: image and diplomatic transcription (HAM/1/1/2/9).

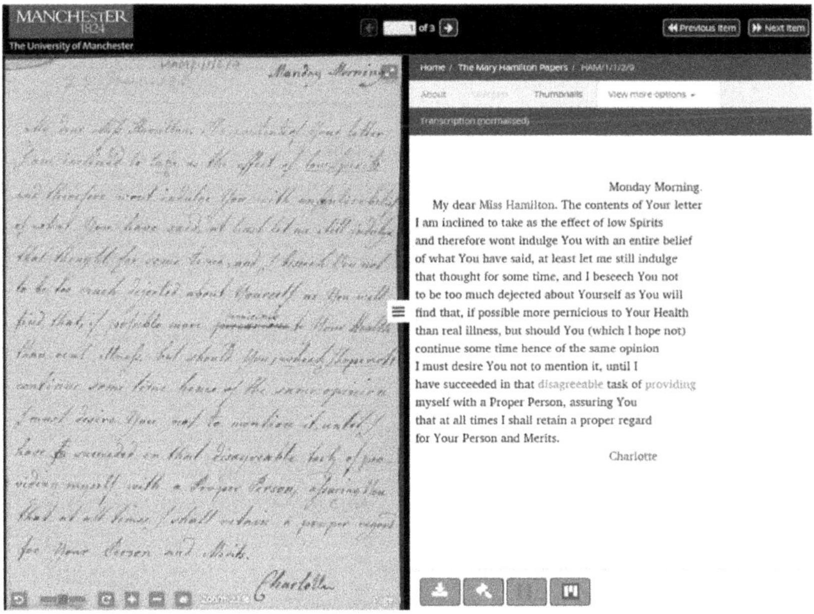

Figure 2: MDC display of the edition: image and normalised transcription (HAM/1/1/2/9).

Thanks to the mark-up in the body of the files, transcriptions can be displayed in either diplomatic or normalized form; the former recreates the contents of the item in question as close as possible to the original, whereas the latter offers an unformatted version of the final wording left by the author before any subsequent annotations, corrections or additions by others. The original purpose of the normalized form was to act as basis of a linguistic corpus and to facilitate part-of-speech tagging for CQPweb (see Section 5), but it has proved helpful for other content-based research and is convenient too for non-expert readers, as spellings and verbal morphology are modernized to standard British English forms, including the replacement of long-s <ſ> by rounded-s <s>, while author errors are corrected and abbreviations and suppressed ("blanked") parts of words are expanded. However, there is no regularization of initial capitalization of words, punctuation or, crucially, marking of possessives with or without (*e*)*s* or apostrophes, all of which appear identically in diplomatic and normalized transcriptions. As we shall see in the next section, linguists using the corpus in CQPweb have easy access to the original forms of the diplomatic text.

Some differences between the two transcriptions are coded in the mark-up of a single XML text stream: abbreviated forms are tagged with an <abbr> element, obsolete forms acceptable at the time (as judged by the *OED*) are tagged with <orig>, and idiosyncratic or erroneous forms are tagged with <sic>. These elements are in turn wrapped in a <choice> element whose second daughter is a corresponding <expan>, <reg> or <corr> element (expanded, regularized or corrected, respectively). All such normalization mark-up was done manually. The scripts which produce the transcriptions on-screen or the plain-text files select the first daughter of <choice> for the diplomatic display or file, and the second daughter for the normalized. Red-coloured text on-screen alerts users where diplomatic and normalized transcriptions differ. Other differences come from differential treatment by the scripts of particular tags. Thus, for example, text deleted by the author and tagged with a <del> element is displayed in the diplomatic transcription on-screen with a strike-through line and a tooltip which specifies whether the deletion is by erasure, cancellation and/or overwriting; however, in the normalized transcription on-screen and in both diplomatic and normalized plain-text files, the deleted text is silently omitted. There is similar differential treatment of <gap> elements used where text cannot (safely) be transcribed, which are solely displayed in the on-screen diplomatic transcription as hyphen characters within square brackets, the reason for the gap and its extent displayed in a tooltip. To take another example, the diplomatic transcription reproduces formatting such as underline, super- or subscripted letters, or position of text above or below the line, but there is no sign of it (apart from red colouring) in the normalized transcription on-screen, and none at all in the plain-text files.

Some of the maximal information encoded in the XML text stream is never visible in the transcriptions, for example, project-specific tags used to classify passages significant for research in the reading practices and sociolinguistic strands (see Section 1). Another example is the <emph> tag used for underlining, which actually discriminates between single, double, triple and dotted underlining, but all are displayed on-screen in the diplomatic transcription as single underline. Apart from project-specific mark-up, all the additional detail encoded in the texts will become available to researchers when the XML files are released after the conclusion of the project team's research.

A convention used in the transcriptions is that blue colouring indicates stretches of text that have a tooltip available on mouseover or touch-screen equivalent. Tooltips give information on persons mentioned, on authorial additions, on writers of annotations, on sources of quotations, and so on. In the normalized transcription only the person tooltips appear.

Both the diplomatic and normalized transcriptions reproduce the lineation and the pagination or column breaks of the original, except that words split across a line-end are reconstituted at the end of the earlier line in the normalized transcriptions. Retaining lineation provides users with an easy visual correspondence between image and transcribed text. The exception to that correspondence is where logical continuity of the text conflicts with physical position on the page, which can arise for various reasons. Thus, before the general use of envelopes, the "direction" or address of a letter could be written in the middle of a sheet in order to be on the outside after folding and sealing; however, blank space around the address was often filled up with writing, as paper was expensive for the author and postage was usually payable by the recipient. Likewise, the final few lines or an afterthought or postscript might get crammed into any available space on the last page of a letter or indeed another page altogether. The edition prioritizes continuity of text where it conflicts with actual placement, and such stretches of text are moved to their logical position. The transcriptions on-screen mark the original position of moved text with a ▼ symbol and a tooltip, while the moved text itself usually has an explanatory footnote in the diplomatic transcription, so the correspondence between image and text can in such cases be figured out relatively simply.

As previously noted, the normalized transcriptions are intended as the basis of a linguistic corpus. Continuity is enhanced not just by moving stretches of text where necessary but by taking the final version left by the author after any changes of mind (deletions, additions, substitutions), and by omitting subsequent annotations by recipients, archivists and others. The resulting dataset is tagged for part of speech by the CLAWS tagger, for semantic analysis by the USAS tagger, and it is then indexed for CQPweb, on which see the next section.

The project has identified well over 2,600 different persons mentioned in the *Papers*, though some of them have not been traced in records, a few (often servants) are known only by forename or by their employment, and a couple merely by their initials. The vast majority have been entered in a "personography", an XML file containing information on birth and death dates (with indications of certainty where necessary), variant names and titles (sometimes with a date range), relationships, occurrence in authority files, and more. The editing of this file is controlled by its own schema and represents a great deal of research in its own right. Selected data from all the entries is listed in alphabetical order on a page on the project website, showing canonical name, life dates, alternative names, occurrence in authority files if available (or a short biography for those persons who are correspondents) and project ID. The full personography powers the tooltips for person mentions in MDC, and it is hoped to add reverse links from transcriptions back to the fuller information in the personography.

Access to the 3,200-plus items in the edition is provided in a number of ways apart from the filtered search on its home page in MDC, described above. The project website offers an Excel file for download which lists every item and provides a selection of metadata on each, as well as a hyperlink to items published in MDC. All the currently published items of correspondence are indexed in correspSearch (Dumont, Grabsch and Müller-Laackman 2014), an international search engine hosted at the Berlin-Brandenburgischen Akademie der Wissenschaften which uses the <correspDesc> elements in suitable TEI-XML editions, allowing searches across multiple editions by sender, recipient, date range, place of sending and/or place of receipt, as well as place-names coded geographically in the GeoNames database for location on a map. Searches in correspSearch provide hyperlinks to letters and notes in their respective editions. Lastly, when a stretch of text in the corpus has been located by CQPweb search (see also following section), users who wish to see it *in situ* in MDC are offered instant access via hyperlink.

5. Linguistic Corpus: *The Mary Hamilton Papers* in CQPweb

The program CQPweb (see Hardie 2012) is a web-based search engine whose default syntax allows easy word or string search in a corpus or subpart, and – with only a little more knowledge of the search syntax – proximity search, part-of-speech search, alternative search terms and combinations thereof. Switching from "simple" to "CQP syntax" allows for additional and potentially very elaborate search strategies. A dedicated server hosted by Lancaster University offers dozens of corpora in various languages indexed for CQPweb, including *The Mary Hamilton Papers* in the "Historical English" section. What is indexed and how carefully it is done varies somewhat among the different corpora.[4]

Search hits in CQPweb are arranged by default as a concordance, with the search term in the centre and (for *The Mary Hamilton Papers*) ten words of context on either side. A quick scan of the concordance is often enough to show which hits are of interest. The hits can be processed as a set for sorting, thinning or download, or to reveal frequencies, distribution, collocations, etc. For an individual hit, users can jump to the context within CQPweb, with some five lines (which can be extended) displayed above and below. The default display resembles the normalized text of the edition minus its line-breaks, while the "alternative view" is a simplified version of the diplomatic text. Alternatively, users can click the open-book symbol against any hit, which then opens in MDC the exact page of the item in which the search string occurs.

The accuracy of part-of-speech tagging by the CLAWS4 tagger is improved by its being fed the normalized and tokenized text. However, unnormalized possessives pose a problem, as many could be wrongly identified, for instance as non-possessive plurals. Hoffmann has mitigated this by a series of *ad hoc* scripts which pre-process the text before

4 We are hugely grateful to Sebastian Hoffmann of the University of Trier for tokenizing the corpus and carrying out the POS-tagging, semantic tagging and CQPweb indexing, starting from reduced versions of the canonical XML files that Denison had supplied. Hoffmann's attention to detail and the ensuing dialogue between us has improved not only the CQPweb corpus but the consistency and accuracy of the MDC edition as well.

tagging. The corpus has also been tagged with the USAS semantic tagger, and searches incorporating USAS tags such as *Health and disease*, *Farming & Horticulture* or *Crime, law and order* can be carried out in CQPweb.

Foreign words and phrases and place-names are not highlighted as such in the MDC transcriptions, but we have used the elements <foreign> and <placeName> for their mark-up. These elements have been retained in the CQPweb indexing, meaning that place-names can be searched for, as can foreign words in any or in a specific language. In principle, all mentions of persons have been tagged in the edition with a project ID. Pronouns are not tagged, but they necessarily occur in proximity to reference by a fuller noun phrase anyway. CQP syntax allows users to search for all occurrences of a particular individual by project ID, whether referred to in the text by name (however spelled), by title, by nickname or codename, or when abbreviated or even "blanked" by the writer. Other aspects of mark-up can be searched for too, such as abbreviations, regularized forms, dates, salutations, and more.

6. Concluding Remarks

It will be evident that this long-term endeavour has had multiple ambitions which have generally turned out to be mutually beneficial. The early transcriptions by students in the *Image to Text* project (2011–2019) proved a remarkable success in bringing the history of English alive. The online edition that grew out of this research-led teaching exercise (and now hosted in MDC) is intended to be what might traditionally have been published in book form: both a scholarly edition and a complete facsimile. It combines accurate transcriptions, copious indexing, helpful footnotes and cross-referencing, together with high-resolution images. This is further enhanced by all the advantages of hyperlinking that online publishing permits, and on open access. The edition allows scholars and the interested public to browse this fascinating archive with ease and to use it in literary and linguistic research, as we have. We furthermore see great potential for work in fields including political, royal, social, medical, economic and postal history, art and music history, and no doubt others, and it is beginning to be exploited (see Coulombeau, Denison and Yánez-Bouza, in prep).

With the corpus in CQPweb we have produced a resource for historical linguists such as ourselves that comes directly from manuscript sources with minimal editorial intervention, which is in addition more carefully proofread and more consistent than most corpora can be, and which includes named writers operating in some cases over four decades. The search engine is oriented towards linguistics, but it offers a flexible way into the edition for any researcher. The rather full indexing of persons will be widely useful: there are over 38,000 tagged mentions of persons other than author or recipient. This in turn has led us to a robust and innovative method of constructing social networks (Denison and Oudesluijs in prep.), which play an important role in diachronic linguistic theory and sociolinguistics.

The use of a structured TEI schema has enhanced the consistency of transcription and mark-up, to the benefit of both edition and corpus. The schema, available on the project website, includes a lengthy discursive section, which means that the instructions agreed among the editing team are open to inspection. The pipeline that led from canonical XML files to an indexed corpus in CQPweb went through a number of refinements, and problems encountered on the way could sometimes be traced back to typos or inconsistencies in the original files, again to the benefit of the edition.

Some of the research produced by the project team is in preparation or in press, a few pieces already published. Preliminary work on the literary strand has been presented in Ulph (2021), addressing the relevance of the material for the study of the Romantic period in literary practices, and Coulombeau (2021), who offers new insights into the relationship between Mary Hamilton and a seventeen-year-old George, Prince of Wales (later George IV). From a linguistic perspective, Denison and Oudesluijs (2022) look into verb changes in the auxiliary system with a focus on the verb *be* and those other verbs (principally *have* and full modals) that it commutes with in its various uses. Wallis (forthcoming) explores intra-speaker variation in the correspondence from Francis Napier to Mary Hamilton, with special attention to his use of Scottish English, and Oudesluijs (forthcoming) examines Hamilton's writings in light of eighteenth-century copying practices. Taking a sociopragmatic approach, Yáñez-Bouza (forthcoming a, forthcoming b), Yáñez-Bouza and Oudesluijs (this volume) and Oudesluijs and (forthcoming) Yáñez-Bouza investigate the use of nominal forms of address in the form of author-oriented and self-oriented expressions, as a means to construct the author's social identity in relation to values of relative power/status, social distance and politeness. For up-to-date lists of publications and talks, please see the project website.

References

Anson, Elizabeth G. and Florence H. Anson, eds., *Mary Hamilton: Afterwards Mrs. John Dickenson, at Court and at Home. From Letters and Diaries, 1756 to 1816* (London: J. Murray, 1925).

Baillot, Anne, ed., *Briefe und Texte aus dem intellektuellen Berlin um 1800* (2011–2017), <http://www.berliner-intellektuelle.eu/>

Coulombeau, Sophie, 'This is Not a Love Story', *History Today* 71/10 (2021), 64–75.

Coulombeau, Sophie, David Denison and Nuria Yáñez-Bouza, eds., *Mary Hamilton and her Circles: An Edited Collection* (Manchester: Manchester University Press, in preparation).

Crawley, Lisa, 'A Life Recovered: Mary Hamilton 1756–1816', *Bulletin of the John Rylands University Library of Manchester* 90/2 (2014), 27–46.

Denison, David, 'A Corpus of Late Modern English Prose', in Merja Kytö, Matti Rissanen and Susan Wright, eds., *Corpora across the Centuries: Proceedings of the First International Colloquium on English Diachronic Corpora, St Catharine's College Cambridge, 25–27 March 1993* (Amsterdam and Atlanta: Rodopi, 1994), 7–16.

Denison, David and Tino Oudesluijs, 'Tracking Verb Changes in a Corpus of Non-Printed Manuscript Materials', *Grammar & Corpora 2022 Conference*, University of Ghent, 30 June–2 July 2022.

Denison, David and Tino Oudesluijs, 'Reconstructing Mary Hamilton's Social Networks', in Sophie Coulombeau, David Denison and

Nuria Yáñez-Bouza, eds., *Mary Hamilton and Her Circles: An Edited Collection* (Manchester: Manchester University Press, forthcoming).

Dumont, Stefan, Sasha Grabsch and Jonas Müller-Laackman, eds., (2014–). *correspSearch – Connect Scholarly Editions of Correspondence* (2.1.0) [Webservice], *Berlin-Brandenburg Academy of Sciences and Humanities* (2022), <https://correspSearch.net>, accessed 21 April 2023.

Elizabeth Montagu Correspondence Online. <https://emco.swansea.ac.uk/home/>

Elspaß, Stephan, Nils Langer, Joachim Scharloth and Wim Vandenbussche, eds., *Germanic Language Histories 'from Below' (1700–2000)* (Berlin: Mouton de Gruyter, 2007).

Hardie, Andrew, 'CQPweb – Combining Power, Flexibility and Usability in a Corpus Analysis Tool', *International Journal of Corpus Linguistics* 17/3 (2012), 380–409.

Manchester Digital Collections. <https://www.digitalcollections.manchester.ac.uk/>

Meurman-Solin, Anneli, 'The Manuscript-Based Diachronic Corpus of Scottish Correspondence', in Joan C. Beal, Karen P. Corrigan and Hermann L. Moisl, eds., *Creating and Digitizing Language Corpora*, Vol. 2 (London: Palgrave Macmillan, 2007), 127–47.

OED = *Oxford English Dictionary*, 3rd ed. online. <www.oed.com>

Oudesluijs, Tino, '"No criticism or remarks & pray burn it as fast as you read it" – Exploring Copying Practices in Mary Hamilton's Private Correspondence', in Luisella Caon, Thijs Porck and Mo Gordon, eds., *Proceedings of ICEHL-21, 7–11 June 2021, Leiden* (Amsterdam and Philadelphia: John Benjamins, forthcoming).

Oudesluijs, Tino and Nuria Yáñez-Bouza, 'Constructing Identities and Negotiating Relationships in Late Eighteenth-Century England: Mary Hamilton and her Correspondents at Court', *International Journal of English Studies* 23.2 (2023), 15–40.

The Collected Letters of Robert Southey. <https://romantic-circles.org/editions/southey_letters>

The Darwin Correspondence Project. <https://www.darwinproject.ac.uk>

The Letters of Hannah More: A Digital Edition. <http://hannahmoreletters.co.uk/Letters>

The Mary Hamilton Papers (c.1740–c.1850). Compiled by D. Denison, N. Yáñez-Bouza, T. Oudesluijs, C. Ulph, Ch. Wallis, H. Barker and S. Coulombeau, University of Manchester. 2019–2023. <https://doi.org/10.48420/21687809>

Ulph, Cassandra, 'Intimacy, Creativity and Networks: Reading Practices in *The Mary Hamilton Papers*', *GOTH 1st Annual Research Symposium*, The Open University, 20–21 May 2021.

van der Wal, Marijke and Gijsbert Rutten, eds., *Touching the Past. Studies in the Historical Sociolinguistics of Ego-Documents* (Amsterdam and Philadelphia: John Benjamins, 2013).

van der Wal, Marijke, Gijsbert Rutten, Judith Nobels and Tanja Simons, *The Letters as Loot / Brieven als Buit-Corpus*. Compiled with the assistance of volunteers of the Leiden-based Wikiscripta Neerlandica transcription project, and lemmatised, tagged and provided with search facilities by the Institute for Dutch Lexicology (INL) (Leiden University, 2021), 3rd release. <http://hdl.handle.net/10032/tm-a2-s4>

Wallis, Christine, 'Like Father, like Son? Scots and Intra-Writer Variation in *The Mary Hamilton Papers'*, in Samantha M. Litty and Nils Langer, eds., *Historical Interplays between Language Ideology, Language Policy, and Language Practices* (Bern: Peter Lang, forthcoming).

Yáñez-Bouza, Nuria, ' "By Miranda, Mary Hamilton, Mrs Dickenson" – Self-Reference in Late Modern English Private Correspondence', *Neuphilologische Mitteilungen* 124.2 (2023), 220–254.

——, ' "My dearest Clara ... my dear friend" – Personal Names and Direct Address in Mary Hamilton's Private Correspondence', *Journal of Historical Sociolinguistics*, forthcoming.

Yáñez-Bouza, Nuria and Tino Oudesluijs, ' "My dearest friend ... ever yours – Mary Hamilton': Exploring Forms of Address in the Late Georgian Period", in Javier Calle-Martín and Jesús Romero-Barranco, eds., Corpora and Language Change in Late Modern English (Bern: Peter Lang, 2024).

Appendix. Overview of Features Documented in the Editorial Schema of *The Mary Hamilton Papers*

TEI header	– Acknowledging funders. – Contributions by project team and others. – Date of writing. – File history. – Hands. – Number of sheets. – Number of words. – Responsibility for editing. – Responsibility for sets of files. – Sending and receipt of letters. – Title and language in MDC. – Title in repository catalogue. – Title of item in the edition. Documents written on behalf of another.
Structural elements of the text	– Column begins. – Divisions. Diaries and journal-letters, multiple letters or notes in a single item, addresses (and frank signatories), self-embedded divisions. – Line begins. – Page begins. – Paragraphs.
Opening and closing elements of a letter	– Closers. Signatures. – Datelines. – Dates. – Openers. – Postscripts. – Salutations in opener and closer.
Other content-based mark-up	– Direct speech. – Foreign words and text. Accents and spelling in French. – Indications by author for recipient. – Names. Names of people, names of places, spelling variation in names. – Passages marked for research analysis (project strands). – Quotations. – Verse line.

Manuscript features	– Additions. Addition vs. annotation, addition vs. continuation. – Ampersands, etc. – Annotations on manuscript. Which shelfmarks to transcribe. – Apostrophes. – Authorial lines and flourishes. – Censorship. – Change of hand. – Deletions. Substitutions. – Hyphens, dashes and lines for suppression. – Parentheses. – Quotation marks. Double, single. – Superscript, subscript, italics, etc. – Underlining. – Word spacing. Horizontal spacing between items.
Editorial intervention	– Cautious transcription. – Diplomatic vs. normalized. Correction; regularization, word separation at line-end, self-embedded tags; expansion of abbreviations, macron, *tho* and *tho'* ("though"), *thro* and *thro'* ("through"). – Footnotes. Links and cross-references, bibliographic citations. – Moved text. – No transcription. – Redundant words. – Supplied text. – XML comments (internal editorial notes).
Overview of dating of letters	– Date from catalogue, date sent/received, dates in journal-letters.
Overview of attribute @rend	– Cancellation of midline linebreak. – Rightwards movement. – Style.
Overview of person references	– <salute> vs. <seg>. – Referring to persons in <closer>: addressee, author. – Referring to persons in <opener>. – Referring to persons in <p>: addressee, author, other people.

Section 2. Empirical Studies

Zeltia Blanco-Suárez

Ridiculously Well or *Madly Ambitious*: Some Diachronic Notes on the Intensifying Adverbs *Ridiculously* and *Madly*[1]

1. Introduction

The notion of "stance" is an umbrella term which is often used interchangeably in the literature with similar concepts such as "evaluation" (Swan 1988; Hunston and Thompson 2000), "affect" (Ochs 1989) and "point of view" (Stubbs 1986; Smith 2002). In this study, however, "stance" is taken, in line with Lewis (2020: 2), to refer to "all manner of speaker comment on some event or situation or entity, including epistemic judgements, degree judgements, value judgements and affect". Cross-linguistically, a number of lexico-grammatical categories can be used to express speaker stance, among them adverbs (e.g. *certainly*, *apparently*, *surprisingly*), modal verbs (*might*, *will*, *ought to*) and complement clauses controlled by stance verbs (e.g. *doubt* or *claim*) or adjectives (e.g. *certain*, *interesting*, or *unlikely*) (see Biber 2006).

The present chapter focuses on one such strategy to express speaker stance, specifically the use of evaluative adverbs. In particular, it sets out to explore the history of two *-ly* adverbs: *madly* and *ridiculously*, from their origins in the thirteenth and sixteenth centuries, respectively, up to the Late Modern English period (henceforth LModE). From their initial uses as manner or evaluative adverbs, *ridiculously* and *madly* eventually

1 For generous financial support, I am grateful to the following institutions: the Ministry of Science and Innovation (ref. PID2020-114604GB-I00) and the regional government of Galicia (grant ED431B 2020/01).

developed an intensifying or degree reading ("very, extremely"), as illustrated in (1) and (2):

(1) Season 7 of Game of Thrones has been nothing short of *ridiculously* awesome (NOW Corpus. 2021. "The best memes and tweets so far from Game of Thrones season 7").
(2) It was a *madly* ambitious idea to launch right away, but we knew we had to do it (GloWbE Corpus. 2012).

The objective of this study is therefore twofold: on the one hand, it seeks to explore the diachronic evolution of these adverbs and, on the other, to account for the mechanisms and processes involved in their development. To this end, a collocational analysis of *ridiculously* and *madly* will be conducted, which takes into consideration three main variables:

(1) the types of words modified by these forms (e.g. adjectives, verbs, etc.);
(2) the semantic types: in this variable, three main categories were distinguished: (i) literal meanings, as recorded in the *Oxford English Dictionary* (OED) ("in a ridiculous manner, to a ridiculous degree" in the case of *ridiculously* and "in a mad or foolish manner" in that of *madly*) (see Section 4.1 below); (ii) ambiguous (degree) interpretations, i.e., those cases of these adverbs which admit both a literal and a degree interpretation; (iii) purely intensifying readings of *ridiculously* and *madly*.
(3) the function performed by *ridiculously* and *madly*: (i) as manner adjuncts, i.e., as an optional element with scope over the verb phrase; (ii) as premodifiers,[2] in those cases in which

2 Note that, although premodifiers and intensifiers occur both in the premodifier slot, I have opted for keeping these two distinct categories apart in this research in order to highlight the purely intensifying uses of these adverbs. In a collocation such as *ridiculously dressed*, e.g., *ridiculously* is considered as a premodifier, since it contextually admits a literal interpretation. By contrast, in a collocation such as *ridiculously awesome*, e.g., it is counted as an intensifier, as it only admits a degree reading.

ridiculously and *madly* function as modifiers of the following word and that collocation only admits a literal or an ambiguous reading; (iii) as intensifiers, i.e., those examples in which the adverbs can be counted as an adverb of degree; (iv) as disjuncts, i.e., as a type of speaker's comment on the accompanying clause (Quirk et al. 1985: 440), having scope over the whole sentence.

Furthermore, in order to examine more closely the collocational behaviour of these forms, and in line with other studies on intensifiers (Tagliamonte 2008; Méndez-Naya 2019), I have resorted to Dixon's (2004) taxonomy of adjectives to classify the adjectival collocates of *ridiculously* and *madly*. The occurrence of these adverbs with a wider range of adjective types would be indicative of a higher degree of grammaticalization (Hopper and Traugott 2003) and hence, of their greater productivity as intensifiers. Dixon (2004: 3–5) distinguished four core categories: DIMENSION (e.g. "big", "long", "tall"), AGE (e.g. "new", "young", "old"), VALUE (e.g. "good", "atrocious", "lovely") and COLOUR (e.g. "red", "black"), together with three peripheral semantic types: PHYSICAL PROPERTY (e.g. "hard", "strong", "clean"), HUMAN PROPENSITY (e.g. "jealous", "clever", "generous") and SPEED (e.g. "quick", "slow"). Dixon (2004: 3–5) included six additional types, which may be distinguished in several languages: DIFFICULTY (e.g. "easy", "difficult", "hard"), SIMILARITY (e.g. "similar", "different"), QUALIFICATION (e.g. "true", "likely", "normal"), QUANTIFICATION (e.g. "many", "some", "enough"), POSITION (e.g. "high", "low", "northern") and CARDINAL NUMBERS (e.g. "first", "last").

This chapter is organized as follows: Section 2 introduces some terminological issues concerning the expression of stance and intensification and provides an overview of the key processes involved in the development of intensifiers. Section 3 presents the different sources of evidence used in this research; the development of *ridiculously* and *madly* over time traced in the light of the data collected is shown in Section 4 and, finally, some concluding remarks and suggestions for further research are outlined in Section 5.

2. Stance Adverbs and Intensifiers

Stance or evaluative adverbs are used to mark the speaker's stance, i.e., "to indicate the degree of strength of the meaning of a proposition as a whole or in part, by way of signaling evidence, certainty, confidence and insistence" (Rhee 2016: 398). From a diachronic perspective, the inventory of stance adverbs has been considerably expanded, not only with the development of these forms into sentence adverbs and their increasing adverbialization (see Swan 1988, 1997), but also as a result of the evolution of certain of these adverbs into intensifiers, most notably within the booster class (Peters 1994; Nevalainen 2008). Early Modern English (EModE), in fact, has been a particularly fruitful period for the development of intensifiers, as noted by Peters (1994: 271).

One characteristic of *–ly* adverbs in English, as opposed to other Germanic languages, is their multifunctionality and ability to combine with different constituent types (Hoye 1997: 203; Lewis 2020: 3–4). Examples (3)–(7) thus serve to illustrate the ambivalence of *madly* and *ridiculously* specifically: in (3), for example, *madly* functions as a manner adjunct modifying a verb phrase (*to make fortune the maister of thine happynesse*), but it may likewise serve an intensifying function with scope over the following adjective, as in the case of the collocation *madly curious* in (4). In like manner, *ridiculously* may function as a manner adjunct, as in (5), in which it modifies a verb phrase (*call wicked policies, wisdom, and their success, happiness*), but also as an intensifier, as in example (6), in which it combines with the adjective *awesome*. In addition, it may be used as a disjunct or sentence adverb, as in (7). In this last example *ridiculously* is found in initial position, has scope over the whole sentence and is used to convey the speaker's or writer's attitude towards the proposition.

(3) What fond conceit (therefore) moueth thée (thou foolish man) thus *madly* to make fortune the maister of thine happynesse (EEBOCorp 1.0. 1585. John Norden. A sinfull mans solace most sweete and comfortable).

(4) He's totally irrelevant in every way, and I'm *madly* curious about him (BYU-BNC Corpus. 1990. Alison Leonard. Gate-crashing the dream party).

(5) And yet lewd men, most *ridiculously* and absurdly, call wicked policies, wisdom, and their success, happiness (EEBOCorp 1.0. 1660. Richard Younge. A Christian library).
(6) Last summer, Steve and I went to Vegas and got upgraded to a *ridiculously* awesome suite in the Four Seasons (COCA Corpus).
(7) *Ridiculously*, the sky seems too blue not to imagine that perhaps this might be Italy (BYU-BNC Corpus. 1985–1994. [Scotsman]).

As noted by Swan (1987: 519), quoted in Hoye (1997: 203), the direction of shift from word to sentence modifier or vice versa may differ according to each form, since adverbs are often at different stages in their development. As shown in examples (3)–(7) above, this seems to be the case of the two forms under study here: while *ridiculously* has progressed further to sentence adverb functions, *madly* seems to be restricted in Present-day English (PDE) to modifier at word level. Moreover, the multifunctionality of these adverbs in English results in polysemy and homonymy (Traugott 2010: 32) and, in fact, it entails a considerable degree of overlap between speaker assessment or evaluation, degree and manner. For instance, the adverb *really* in *John was really ill* can be interpreted both as an intensifier ("very") and as an epistemic adverb ("in fact, actually") (Lewis 2020: 5).

The diachronic evolution of stance adverbs reveals that many of these forms originated as manner adverbs and came to express "the speaker's normative judgment respecting degree or conditions of truth" and as adverbs of modality which may "act preemptively to inform and to persuade a hearer of the nature and importance of the speaker's evaluation" (Powell 1992: 76). Their development, therefore, clearly implies subjectification, "a pragmatic-semantic process whereby meanings become increasingly based in the speaker's subjective belief state/attitude toward the proposition, in other words, towards what the speaker is talking about" (Traugott 1995: 31) (see also Traugott 2003, 2010). (Inter)subjectification, then, implies a change along a cline of subjectivity from less to increasingly more subjective and eventually intersubjective meanings (non-/less subjective > subjective > intersubjective meanings) (Traugott 2010: 34). This is the case, for instance, of the adverb *lovely* (see Adamson 2000): in Old English (OE), *lovely* denoted a relatively objective quality ("loving, amiable"), but came to acquire increasingly subjective or affective meanings in Middle English (ME) ("physically beautiful") and finally developed an intensifying reading in the nineteenth century. The development of a degree meaning of *lovely* was triggered by its possibility to co-occur with other adjectives in the pre-modifier slot (e.g. in *lovely long legs*), which led to the reinterpretation of the construction as [adverb + adjective] rather than [adjective + adjective]. The development of increasingly subjective meanings of *lovely* and its eventual reanalysis as an intensifier led Adamson to propose the following cline of evolution for intensifiers: descriptive adjective > affective adjective > intensifier (2000: 55).

In addition to subjectification, the development of stance and degree adverbs or intensifiers often implies semantic bleaching or desemanticization (Hopper and Traugott 2003), since these forms have their origin in lexical sources, but eventually acquire more grammatical meanings over time. This is the case of the prototypical intensifier *very*, which originally meant "true", but also of other forms such as *terribly* ("very severely or painfully"), which can co-occur in PDE with positive collocates, as in *terribly good*, owing precisely to this desemanticization or bleaching.

Moreover, many stance and degree adverbs have developed disjunct uses over time in a cline from manner or degree adverb to disjunct adverbial (see Swan 1991; Brinton 2017). Among such examples we find *admittedly*, *surely* and *strangely*. In the case of *ridiculously*, as shown in example (7) above, the adverb also seems to have developed disjunct uses. The pathway of change into a disjunct, however, remains to be discussed on the basis of the data consulted.

3. Sources of Data

In order to trace the history of *ridiculously* and *madly* in British English, for this qualitative and quantitative study I have drawn on various historical sources, specifically the OED, the *Early English Books Online Corpus 1.0* (EEBOCorp 1.0) and the online collections *Eighteenth Century Fiction* (ECF) and *Nineteenth Century Fiction* (NCF), thereby covering from their earliest records up to LModE.

EEBOCorp 1.0 is based on Early English Books Online (EEBO), a database which was originally published by Chadwick Healey in 1998. EEBOCorp 1.0, however, is a corpus compiled by Peter Petré in 2013, which contains approximately 525 million words and features a wide variety of genres, among them historical, philosophical, religious and literary texts from 1473 to 1700. In turn, ECF and NCF are not corpora strictly speaking, but rather online collections of English prose works. Their choice here serves to overcome a gap in the existing records for the eighteenth and nineteenth centuries, respectively. As with the original EEBO collection, ECF and NCF were also produced by Chadwick Healey and include about 11 and 37.5 million words. However, these two databases are just restricted to prose works by British and Irish writers from 1700 to 1903, including those by major novelists of the period, such as Austen, the Brontës, Dickens, Shelley, Scott or Defoe.

Table 1 below provides a broad overview of the main features of these data sources, in addition to the total number of occurrences of *ridiculously* and *madly* in each:

Table 1: Data sources used and absolute frequencies for *ridiculously* and *madly*

Corpus	**Abbreviated title**	**Period**	**Size**	**Tokens of *ridiculously***	**Tokens of *madly***
Early English Books Online Corpus 1.0	EEBOCorp	1473–1700	525 million w.	798	729
Eighteenth Century Fiction	ECF	1700–1780	11 million w.	22	19
Nineteenth Century Fiction	NCF	1782–1903	37.5 million w.	53	204

4. *Ridiculously* and *Madly*: A Diachronic Overview

4.1. Ridiculously *and* Madly*: A Preliminary Overview*

According to the OED, *ridiculously* is formed on the adjective *ridiculous*, a Latin borrowing whose earliest records date from the sixteenth century, with the meaning "in a ridiculous manner or to a ridiculous degree; absurdly", as in example (8), in which *ridiculously* modifies the verb *seek*. As evinced by the OED, it later developed a degree reading, as in the case of the collocations *ridiculously incorrect* and *ridiculously cute*, in (9) and (10), respectively.

(8) So foolishly and *ridiculously* seeking holes and corners to hyde them selues in (1563. OED, s.v. ridiculously adv. α.).
(9) He has written what is *rediculously* incorrect (1823. OED, s.v. ridiculously adv. β.).
(10) You half expect a bereted Parisian to saunter out of one of the *ridiculously* cute, Euro-themed bistros (2009. OED, s.v. ridiculously adv. α.).

As with *ridiculously*, *madly* is also formed by derivation on the adjective *mad*, although *madly* is a native form. The adverb was first documented in the first half of the thirteenth century meaning "in a mad or foolish manner", as shown in example (11). Over time, however, it came to denote passionate feelings, most frequently to refer to somebody who was in love, as in (12). Later on, *madly* came to be used as an intensifier ("very, extremely"), hence its co-occurrence with the positive adjective *interesting* in (13).

(11) Hwi motestu so *medliche* ("why do you speak so madly?") (c. 1225. OED, s.v. madly adv.).
(12) I was so *madly* in love as to think of marrying her (1767. OED, s.v. madly 2a).
(13) It is a *madly* interesting place (1902. OED, s.v. madly 2a).

In addition, in PDE *ridiculously* may function as a stance adverbial (Biber et al. 1999) or attitudinal disjunct (Greenbaum 1970), as shown in example (14). In these cases, *ridiculously* indicates the writer's or speaker's attitude towards the proposition and typically expresses judgements or evaluations, thus having scope over the whole sentence. In this function, the adverbial may occupy different positions in the sentence, as reflected in (14) and (15), with initial and medial positions, respectively.

(14) *Ridiculously*, a song that had been popular in her childhood flooded her mind (BYU-BNC Corpus. 1993. Quinn Wilder. One shining summer).
(15) As though, *ridiculously*, he could blot out the misery in his mind by destroying a picture (BYU-BNC Corpus. 1989. Gillian Cross. On the edge).

The information from the OED and the examples retrieved from the BNC Corpus, therefore, suggest that both *ridiculously* and *madly* developed degree readings over time and that *ridiculously* can be used additionally as a disjunct or stance adverbial. In the remainder of Section 4 the results from the corpus and online collections will be presented, so as to supplement the preliminary information about these adverbial forms and, hence, corroborate the degree of productivity of *ridiculously* and *madly* as intensifiers, as well as their evolution and usage across time.

4.2. Ridiculously*: A Look into the EModE and LModE Period*

Concerning the first of the three variables analysed, the type of words modified, the data show an evolution in the types of collocates favoured by *ridiculously* (see Table 2 and Figure 1). Thus, in EModE *ridiculously* shows a preference for verbal elements (66.7 per cent of its collocates), followed by adjectival (19.4 per cent), participial forms (13.5 per cent) and, much more marginally, by prepositional phrases (0.4 per cent of the occurrences). In turn, in the subsequent periods *ridiculously* co-occurs mostly with adjectives and participles. In fact, in the eighteenth century it functions as a modifier of adjectives and participles in over 70 per cent of the cases, with 36.4 per cent each, yet it can also modify verbal elements (27.2 per cent of the total). This same trend is also noticed in the nineteenth century, since modification of adjectives accounts for 62.3 per cent of the occurrences, followed by participial and verbal elements (17 per cent each) and by prepositional phrases (3.7 per cent).

Table 2: Types of words modified by *ridiculously* in the data

	EEBOCorp 1.0	*ECF*	*NCF*
A[3]	155	8	33
P	108	8	9
V	532	6	9
PP	3	0	2
Total	798	22	53

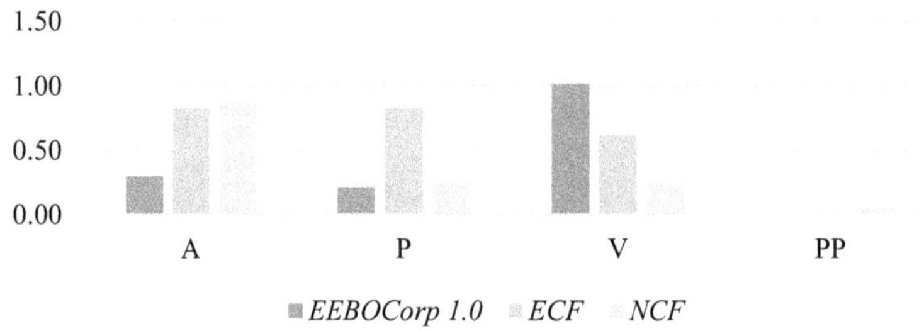

Figure 1: *Types of words modified by ridiculously in the data.*[4]

Examples (16)–(19) illustrate the types of collocates of *ridiculously* in the data: it is attested as a modifier of verbs such as *affirm* ((16)), of prepositional phrases such as *out of fashion* (17), as well as of participles and adjectives like *cloathed* and *vain* in (18) and (19), respectively:

(16) And this fasting vvas not fasting from sinne, nor moral or Christian temperance, as the Protestants *ridiculously* affirme, for such fasting they vvere bound euer to keepe (EEBOCorp 1.0. 1582. Gregory Martin. The Nevv Testament of Iesus Christ).

(17) Let the fare bee such as may neither impaire the health of it, nor the devotion; the apparell neat, not chargeable, not

3 In the remainder of this chapter, the following abbreviations will be used to refer to the different types of words modified: A (adjectives), P (participles), PP (prepositional phrases) and V (verbs).

4 Normalized frequencies per million words (pmw) are provided in all figures.

mimically in, nor *ridiculously* out of fashion (EEBOCorp 1.0. 1637. Joseph Henshaw. Meditations miscellaneous, holy and humane).

(18) They are for the most part *ridiculously* cloath'd, and all, generally, great Hypocrites (EEBOCorp 1.0. 1684. Jean-Baptiste Tavernier. Collections of travels through Turky into Persia).

(19) She is *ridiculously* vain of her family, and has taught Sir George to be so too (ECF. 1761. Frances Chamberlaine Sheridan. Memoirs of Miss Sidney Bidulph).

As regards its function (see Table 3 and Figure 2), the first records of *ridiculously* as an intensifier are recorded in the eighteenth century. In EModE, by contrast, it functioned mostly as a manner adjunct, modifying verbs or participles, in 79.9 per cent of the attestations, and as a premodifier of other adjectives and participial elements (20.1 per cent of the cases). Intensifying uses clearly increase over time, accounting for 45.5 per cent and 67.9 per cent of the total in the eighteenth and nineteenth centuries, respectively.

Table 3: Functions of *ridiculously* in the data

	EEBOCorp 1.0	*ECF*	*NCF*
Manner adjunct	638	8	13
Premodifier	160	4	4
Intensifier	0	10	36
Total	798	22	53

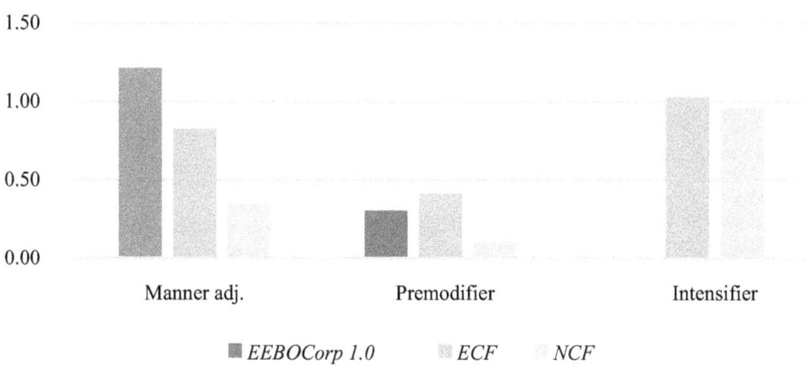

Figure 2: Functions of *ridiculously* in the data.

The last of the variables examined concerns the different semantic types (cf. Table 4 and Figure 3). As the data suggest, the percentage of literal meanings of *ridiculously* has decreased considerably over time: from 79.9 per cent in EModE down to 24.5 per cent in the nineteenth century. In turn, degree readings of the adverb have clearly increased, from 45.4 per cent in the eighteenth century up to 67.9 per cent in the nineteenth-century data. Likewise, ambiguous interpretations have become less prominent across time, from 20.1 per cent in EModE to 7.6 in the last period examined. Semantic types are closely related to the function of the adverb. Thus, degree readings correlate with an intensifying function of the adverb, whereas literal meanings correspond to those in which *ridiculously* functions either as a manner adjunct or as a premodifier of other adjectives or participles with a literal or an ambiguous reading.

Table 4. Semantic types of *ridiculously* in the data

	EEBOCorp 1.0	***ECF***	***NCF***
Literal	638	8	13
Ambiguous	160	4	4
Degree	0	10	36
Total	798	22	53

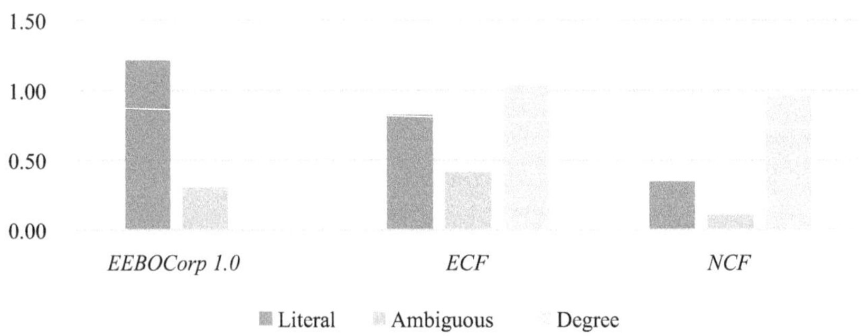

Figure 3. Semantic types of *ridiculously* in the data

Examples (20)–(25) serve to illustrate the different semantic types found in the corpus data. In (20), *ridiculously* functions as a manner adjunct with a literal meaning ("foolishly"), describing the unwise behaviour of the bishops of Rome. In (21) and (22), in turn, it is a pre-modifier of the adjectives *ignorant* and *superstitious* and shows instead an ambiguous reading: on the one hand, it could be argued that *ridiculously* can be taken literally ("ignorant in a ridiculous manner" and "superstitious in a manner which is ridiculous"); on the other, it could also be felicitously interpreted as expressive of degree in this context ("greatly, very ignorant" and "greatly, very superstitious"), coerced by the collocates *ignorant* and *superstitious*, both of which are gradable adjectives. In examples (23) to (25), instead, *ridiculously* acts as an intensifier or degree adverb, equivalent to "extremely, very". A literal interpretation in these cases seems unlikely, especially in (24) and (25), given the positive semantic prosody (see Stubbs 1995) of the collocates *well* and *grand*, clearly incompatible with the original negative meaning of the adverb.

(20) Therefore the Bishops of Rome go about foolishly and *ridiculously* to defende their supremacie by this place (EEBOCorp 1.0. 1571. Rudolf Gwalther. An hundred, threescore and fiftene homelyes or sermons).

(21) Touching our Iudgement which we haue of others, either in esteeming, or contemning them, it is most vaine, and *ridiculously* ignorant (EEBOCorp 1.0. 1624. Pierre Du Moulin. Heraclitus).

(22) The Curds in general are a brutish sort of people; neither does any one dare to cur an Onion with a Knife in their presence; but it must be squeez'd between two Stones by him that intends to make use of it; so *ridiculously* superstitious they are (EEBOCorp 1.0. 1684. Jean -Baptiste Tavernier. Collections of travels through Turky into Persia).

(23) Shall I give you the particulars of a *ridiculously* spiteful conversation that passed between my brother and me (ECF. 1748. Samuel Richardson. Clarissa).

(24) In fact, I got so *ridiculously* well that I had no occasion to drink any of the coltsfoot wine that Lady Drum was good enough to send me (NCF. 1871. William Black. A Daughter of Heth).

(25) She knew, from the surprised expression on Dixon's face, how *ridiculously* grand she herself must be looking (NCF. 1855. Elizabeth Gaskell. North and South).

If we consider the adjectival collocates of *ridiculously* in the light of Dixon's (2004) taxonomy, the data actually reveal no changes over time concerning the number of adjectival categories. Thus, throughout the EModE and LModE data *ridiculously* co-occurs with six different adjective types: DIMENSION (e.g. "long"), HUMAN PROPENSITY (e.g. "jealous, idle"), PHYSICAL PROPERTY (e.g. "ill"), POSITION (e.g. "low"), QUALIFICATION (e.g. "true") and VALUE (e.g. "odious", "silly"). The latter is in fact the most numerous category across all periods, accounting for 41.5 per cent of the total in EModE, 57.1 per cent in the eighteenth century and 42.3 per cent in the nineteenth century. Moreover, *ridiculously* shows a wider variety of adjectival collocates in EModE than in the eighteenth- and nineteenth-century data. This, however, owes to the number of collocations with just one token and, in fact, it does not correlate with a greater number of adjective categories.

4.3. Madly*: A Look into the EModE and LModE Period*

The first variable analysed concerns the type of words modified by *madly*. As shown in Table 5 and Figure 4 below, *madly* has modified the same range of words across time, although it shows a clear preference for verbal collocates, which account for over half? of the occurrences in all the periods: 83.1 per cent in EModE, 52.6 per cent in the eighteenth century and 69.1 per cent in the nineteenth century). In addition to verbal elements, *madly* may modify adjectival and participial collocates, as well as prepositional phrases. In this case, however, the only example attested in the data is that of the collocation *madly in love* (*with*). Unlike *ridiculously*, however, which combines mainly with adjectives in the most recent data, adjectival collocates are not the preferred choice of *madly* in any of the periods examined.

Table 5: Types of words modified by *madly* in the data

	EEBOCorp 1.0	***ECF***	***NCF***
A	41	4	20
P	76	1	16
V	606	10	141
PP	6	4	27
Total	729	19	204

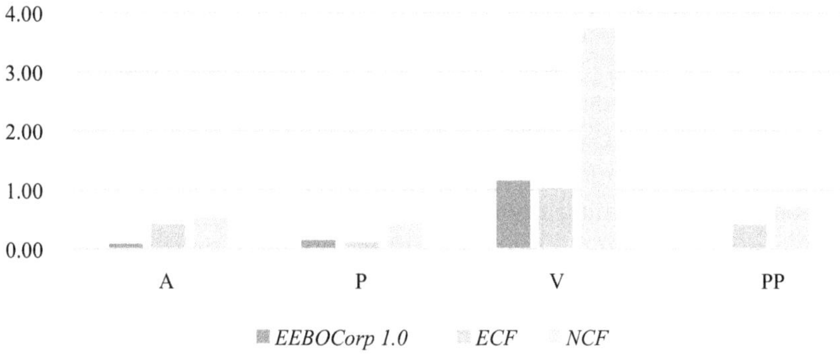

Figure 4: Types of words modified by *madly* in the data.

The types of collocates of *madly* in the data are illustrated in examples (26)–(29). Thus, *madly* may modify verbs such as *to run* in (26), participles such as *enraged* in (27), adjectives, as in the case of *disproportionable* in (28), and prepositional phrases such as *in love with* in example (29):

(26) So also in this, men direct the doings and deuices of their whose life [...] and neglect the commaundementes & heauenly doctrine of God, running blyndly and *madly* into al sin (EEBOCorp 1.0. 1576. Arthur Golding. The vvarfare of Christians).

(27) Thus forward the Christians departed, [...] but were no sooner reentred but Mutafier came, who when he missed Meruine he became *madly* inraged, and with the llust of his anger set all the City on fire, [...] (EEBOCorp 1.0. 1612. Gervase Markham. The most famous and renowned historie, of that woorthie and llustrious knight Meruine).

(28) That London, the Metropolis of England, is perhaps a Head too big for the Body, and possibly too strong: [. . .] That our Parishes are now grown *madly* disproportionable (EEBOCorp 1.0. 1662. John Graunt. Natural and political observations).

(29) I wish the foolish girl was not so *madly* in love with him, for I long to torture his proud heart (ECF. 1765. Frances Brooke. The history of Lady Julia Mandeville).

As regards function, the second variable of analysis (see Table 6 and Figure 5), the cases of *madly* as a manner adjunct in the data (87 per cent of the total) clearly outweigh its pre-modifier (10.3 per cent) and intensifier (2.7 per cent) functions. In its function as manner adjunct and premodifier, *madly* is attested from the earliest data and across all periods examined. In turn, its role as an intensifier first emerged in the nineteenth century and it has always been more marginal (12.7 per cent of the total of cases in the nineteenth century).

Table 6: Functions of *madly* in the data.

	EEBOCorp 1.0	*ECF*	*NCF*
Manner adjunct	674	10	144
Premodifier	55	9	34
Intensifier	0	0	26
Total	729	19	204

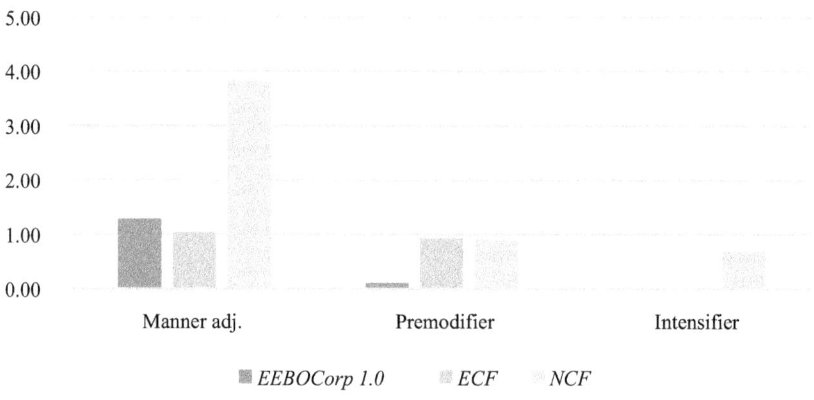

Figure 5: Functions of *madly* in the data.

Examples (30)–(32) below serve to illustrate the different functions of *madly* in the data, specifically as a manner adjunct modifying the verb *to defend* in (30), as a pre-modifier of the participle *enraged* in (31), and as an intensifier expressing degree in the collocation *madly indulgent* in (32). Although in (31) and (32) *madly* has scope over the following word and occupies in both cases the pre-modifying adjective slot, it should be reminded here that in this research the premodifier and intensifier functions have been considered separately so as to highlight specifically the uses of *madly* and *ridiculously* as a degree adverb or intensifier (for further details on the variable "function" in the data, see Section 1 and footnote 1 above).

(30) If he be not a malignaunt me~bre of Antichrist, that so malicyously and *madlye* defendeth hys noughtye quarell (EEBOCorp 1.0. 1552. John Bale. An expostulation or com-playnte agaynste the blasphemyes of a franticke papyst of Hamshyre).

(31) then retired the Pagans, but were no sooner reentred but Mutafier came, who when he missed Meruine he became *madly* inraged, and with the frenzi of his anger set all the City on fire (1612. Gervase Markham. The most famous and renowned historie, of that woorthie and illustrous knight Meruine).

(32) I lay them both to the charge of his harsh yet careless father and his *madly* indulgent mother (NCF. 1901. George Douglass Brown. The House with the Green Shutters).

Finally, as far as semantic types are concerned (see Table 7 and Figure 6), the data reveal that the number of literal readings of *madly* has decreased dramatically over time, from 91.4 per cent in EModE to 22.1 per cent in the nineteenth century. By contrast, the percentage of ambiguous meanings of *madly* has risen exponentially, from 8.6 per cent in the EModE period up to 66.2 per cent in the nineteenth-century records. In line with the ambiguous examples, the number of attesta-tions of *madly* with a degree reading has also increased over time, since these are only recorded in the nineteenth century. This degree meaning is clearly associated with the intensifier function of the adverb, which was also firstly attested in this century.

Table 7: Semantic types of *madly* in the data

	EEBOCorp 1.0	*ECF*	*NCF*
Literal	666	10	45
Ambiguous	63	9	135
Degree	0	0	24
Total	729	19	204

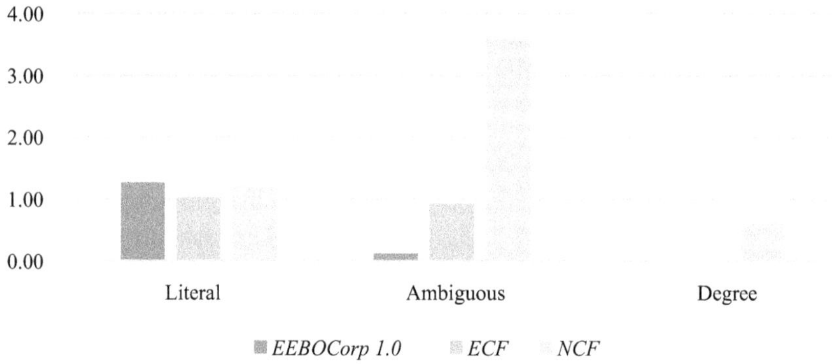

Figure 6: Semantic types of *madly* in the data.

Examples (33)–(38) show the different types of meanings of *madly* in the corpus data. In (33) *madly* has a literal meaning, since it refers to men who do not follow God's precepts and commandments. For this reason, their behaviour is claimed to be foolish and will inevitably result in committing terrible sins. Examples (34) and (35) are considered here as ambiguous: in (34), for instance, men are described as obstinate and stubborn. This quality may be considered as mad or stupid in itself, i.e., to a degree which the writer considers mad or foolish, in which case we could argue that *madly* is to be taken in a literal sense. At the same time, however, it could be argued that this stubbornness is taken to a limit and hence expresses an extreme degree, an interpretation which is facilitated by the gradability of the quality of obstinacy. In this case, *madly* could be simply paraphrased as "extremely, very obstinate". This same ambiguity can also be applied to the collocation *madly in love* in (35). The behaviour of the female character is claimed to be foolish and mad, which would correspond to a literal reading of *madly*, and yet, at the same time, *madly in love* can also be taken to mean in such a context "to be very much in love with someone", hence functioning as an intensifier. Interestingly, the ambiguous uses of *madly* are also present in the data in combination with verbs, as in (36). In this case, *madly* can be interpreted literally, but it can also refer to an action (in this case circling the arms) that is done passionately or intensely, thereby functioning as an intensifier. In contrast, examples (37) and (38) are cases of intensifying *madly* ("very"). In (37) the narrator is describing the character of the lieutenant, who is also said to be a very courageous person and in search of recognition. Moreover, the positive polarity of the collocate makes it hardly compatible with a literal interpretation of *madly*. This is also the case of the combination of *madly* with the positive adjective *delighted* in (38), for which the intensifying reading is the only one allowed. In these cases, therefore, *madly* is better interpreted as "greatly desirous" and "greatly delighted", respectively.

(33) So also in this, men direct the doings and deuices of their whose life, cheefly by the iudgement of the world, and neglect the commaundementes & heauenly doctrine of God, running blyndly and *madly* into al sin (EEBOCorp 1.0. 1576. Arthur Golding. The vvarfare of Christians).

(34) And because some such people have been cast on our Shore, [...] They are (saith Hee) swelled with pride, *madly* obstinate (EEBOCorp 1.0. 1654. Richard Whitlock. Zootomia).

(35) I wish the foolish girl was not so *madly* in love with him, for I long to torture his proud heart (ECF. 1765. Frances Brooke. The History of Lady Julia Mandeville).

(36) But he looked sad, and Evan was sorry for him, and thinking that he had been rather sharp at parting, turned halfway down the street to wave his hand, and lo, John Raikes was circling both arms in air *madly* (NCF. 1861. George Meredith. Evan Harrington).

(37) My lieutenant, for instance, is a man of wonderful courage and enterprise; he is *madly* desirous of glory (NCF. 1831. Mary Shelley. Frankenstein: Or, The Modern Prometheus).

(38) In the beginning of the winter you left me just engaged in another business, a business with which I was *madly*

delighted, and fully persuaded I should be enchanted for ever (NCF. 1782. Frances Burney. Cecilia).

Finally, if we consider the different collocates of *madly* according to the classification proposed by Dixon (2004), the adverb has barely changed its distribution across the different adjectival categories. In the EModE data it is attested with four possible categories HUMAN PROPENSITY (e.g. "ambitious") (62.1 per cent), PHYSICAL PROPERTY (e.g. "hot") (17.2 per cent), QUALIFICATION (e.g. "erroneous") (13.8 per cent) and VALUE (e.g. "stupid") (6.9 per cent). HUMAN PROPENSITY is still the most frequent category in the ensuing centuries (75 per cent and 62.5 per cent in ECF and NCF, respectively). However, in the LModE data there are no collocations which can be subsumed under the QUALIFICATION category and there are no records of adjectival collocates which may qualify as PHYSICAL PROPERTY in the eighteenth-century data. Finally, the category VALUE increases over time, from 6.9 per cent of the total of collocations in the EModE data to 25 and 18.7 per cent in the eighteenth- and nineteenth-century records, respectively.

4.4. Ridiculously *and* Madly*: Historical Development*

The development of the adverbs *ridiculously* and *madly* is best viewed in the light of the grammaticalization and subjectification theories. The different historical sources consulted (see Sections 4.1, 4.2 and 4.3 above) have shown that they are first attested with literal readings, functioning as manner adjuncts (see, for instance, examples (20) and (33) above). Next to these literal examples, *ridiculously* and *madly* are recorded in the earliest data with ambiguous uses, i.e., in cases which admit both a more literal reading and a coerced interpretation as degree adverbs, given the inherent semantics of the participial or adjectival collocate. These ambiguous uses already show incipient subjectivity and are speaker- rather than event-oriented, since they can be paraphrased as "to a degree which I consider ridiculous/mad". This is the case, for instance, of the collocations *ridiculously ignorant*, *ridiculously superstitious* and *madly obstinate* in (21), (22) and (34) above. These examples thus show incipient subjectivity and behave similarly to *lovely*, which developed subjective readings over time via subjectification (see

Adamson 2000). The gradualness of the subjectification process, however, is not so evident in the data for *ridiculously* and *madly*, given the coexistence of literal and more subjective examples already from the earliest records in the sixteenth century.

As evinced by the data, the actual intensifying function of *ridiculously* and *madly* arose centuries later, in the eighteenth and nineteenth century, respectively. In this regard, the findings from the evidence consulted are in line with the preliminary evolution of *madly* identified by Rhee on the basis of the OED: "mad manner" > "passionately" > "extremely" (2016: 404), both in terms of the dates and of the actual cline of development. The data consulted for this research thus suggest that the intensifying roots of *madly* are most likely associated with highly marked emotional states, in collocations such as *madly in love*, which contextually admit a degree interpretation. Moreover, the co-occurrence of *madly* with verbs denoting an action that is done passionately or emphatically, as in the case of *circle the arms* in (36) above, seem to have reinforced and paved the way for the subsequent emergence of unambiguous degree uses of the adverb (see (37) and (38)). Similarly, although purely intensifying uses of *ridiculously* first emerged in the eighteenth century, from the 1590s onwards the corpus data record certain combinations of *ridiculously* with adjectives and participles that felicitously admit a degree reading. This is the case of collocates such as *absurd*, *false*, and *superstitious* (see (22) above), which indicate negative personality traits. These examples, therefore, admit two potential interpretations: "absurd/false/superstitious to a degree which I consider ridiculous" and "to a degree which I consider very absurd/false/superstitious".

The evolution of *ridiculously* and *madly* presented above suggests that these evaluative or stance adverbs have been increasingly semantically bleached and have developed more abstract and grammatical meanings over time. In other words, they came to be reanalysed as degree markers in the course of their history. Their progressive bleaching is most obvious in combinations with positive collocates (see, for instance, *ridiculously well* in (24), *ridiculously grand* in (25) and *madly delighted* in (38)), which are incompatible with negative origin of these forms and clearly attest to a wider collocational expansion. The corpus data have also revealed that *ridiculously* is more productive as an intensifier than *madly*, given the actual frequencies, the larger variety of collocates, and the wider number of adjective types in Dixon's (2004) taxonomy. In addition to increasingly grammatical meanings, *ridiculously* and *madly* became more subjectivized over time. Nonetheless, the evidence from the corpora and collections consulted does not record any occurrences of *ridiculously* as a disjunct, unlike the contemporary examples shown in (7) and (14). The development of intersubjective uses and its role as sentence disjunct, therefore, seems to be a more recent phenomenon.

Ridiculously and *madly* also seem to behave along the lines of other evaluative or stance adverbs such as *strangely* and *luckily*. According to Lewis (2020), the roots of the intensifying function of *strangely* and *luckily* are found in passive constructions. This origin, however, is slightly problematic in the case of *ridiculously* and *madly*, given that they are recorded from very early on with adjectival and participial collocates alike. In this case, the EModE data do not seem to support an expansion from originally participial into non-deverbal or adjectival elements. The evolution of *ridiculously* and *madly*, however, does mirror that of *strangely* and *lovely* in their rise of intensifying uses. Furthermore, just like *strangely*, *ridiculously* can also be used as a disjunct, although this function seems to have arisen more recently. The pathway of development from a manner or degree adverb into a disjunct (see Brinton 2017) remains to be explored considering more contemporary data.

In addition to grammaticalization and subjectification, the evolution of these intensifiers can be associated with metonymization, as well as with metaphor. Thus, qualifying something as "ridiculous" and "mad" implies an inherently superlative component, which in the case of these forms is eventually generalized to express high degree. Metaphor is also at play in the development of these adverbs, given that a negative evaluation comes to be interpreted as high degree eventually.

5. Concluding Remarks

This study has traced the diachronic evolution of the adverbs *madly* and *ridiculously* in British English, from their earliest attestations back in the thirteenth and sixteenth century, respectively, up to the LModE period. From their original uses as manner adverbs conveying stance or evaluation, *madly* and *ridiculously* have progressively risen in subjectivity and eventually developed intensifying uses, which are most conspicuous in the case of *ridiculously*. In addition, *ridiculously* has evolved from word to sentence modifier, as suggested by the more recent uses as disjunct shown in the preliminary overview in Section 4.1 above. Moreover, in line with other adverbial forms, these adverbs may serve several functions synchronically, which results in homonymy and polysemy. For this reason, the intensifying readings of *madly* and *ridiculously* may coexist with the literal ones in the same periods.

To conclude, this research focused mainly on the individual histories of *madly* and *ridiculously* throughout the EModE and LModE periods. In order to obtain the most comprehensive picture of the development of these forms from a diachronic perspective, however, it would be necessary to look into more contemporary data so as to examine their behaviour and productivity in the most recent stages of the language. Considering their frequencies, as well as their uses and collocational patterns in view of Dixon's (2004) taxonomy, may provide important insights into the distribution and usage of these adverbs in PDE. Furthermore, a contrastive analysis of the uses of *ridiculously* and *madly* in British and American English, the other major reference variety, would also be of interest. These, of course, remain issues for future research.

Sources

Davies, Mark, *Brigham Young University-British National Corpus* (based *on the British National Corpus* from Oxford University Press) (Brigham Young University, 2004–2023). Available at https://www.english-corpora.org/bnc/.

——, *Corpus of Contemporary American English* (Brigham Young University, 2004–2023). Available at https://www.english-corpora.org/coca/.

——, *Global Web-Based English* (Brigham Young University, 2004–2023). Available at https://www.english-corpora.org/glowbe/.

——, *News on the Web* (Brigham Young University, 2004–2023). Available at https://www.english-corpora.org/now/.

Healey, Chadwyck, *Eighteenth Century Fiction* (Proquest, 1996–2023). Available at http://collections.chadwyck.co.uk/home/home_c18f.jsp.

——, *Nineteenth Century Fiction* (Proquest, 2000–2023). Available at http://collections.chadwyck.co.uk/home/home_c19f.jsp

Oxford English Dictionary (Oxford University Press, 2023). Available at http://www.oed.com/.

Petré, Peter, *Early English Books Online Corpus 1.0* (Leuven: KU Leuven, 2013). Available at https://lirias.kuleuven.be/handle/123456789/416330/.

References

Adamson, Sylvia, 'A Lovely Little Example: Word Order Options and Category Shift in the Premodifying String', in Olga Fisher, Anette Rosenbach, and Dieter Steins, eds., *Pathways of Change: Grammaticalization in English* (Amsterdam and Philadelphia: John Benjamins, 2000), 39–66.

Biber, Douglas, Stig Johansson, Geoffrey Leech, Susan Conrad and Edward Finegan, *Longman Grammar of Spoken and Written English* (Harlow: Pearson Education Limited, 1999).

Biber, Douglas, 'Stance in Spoken and Written University Registers', *Journal of English for Academic Purposes* 5/2 (2006), 97–116.

Bolinger, Dwight, *Degree Words* (The Hague and Paris: Mouton, 1972).

Brinton, Laurel J., *The Evolution of Pragmatic Markers in English: Pathways of Change* (Cambridge: Cambridge University Press, 2017).

Dixon, R.M.W., 'Adjective Classes in Typological Perspective', in R.M.W. Dixon and Alexandra Y. Aikhenvald, eds., *Adjective Classes: A Cross-Linguistic Typology* (Oxford: Oxford University Press, 2004), 1–49.

Greenbaum, Sidney, *Studies in English Adverbial Usage* (Cambridge: Cambridge University Press, 1970).

Hopper, Paul J., and Elizabeth Closs Traugott, *Grammaticalization*, 2nd edition (Cambridge: Cambridge University Press, 2003).

Hoye, Leo, *Adverbs and Modality in English* (London: Longman, 1997).

Hunston, Susan, and Geoffrey Thompson, eds., *Evaluation in Text: Authorial Stance and the Construction of Discourse* (Oxford: Oxford University Press, 2000).

Lewis, Diana. 2020, 'Speaker Stance and Evaluative *–ly* Adverbs in the Modern English Period', *Language Sciences* 82 (2000), 101332.

Méndez-Naya, Belén, 'The Intensifier System of the Ormulum and the Interplay of Micro-level and Macro-level Contexts in Linguistic Change', in Kristin Bech and Ruth Möhlig-Falke, eds., *Grammar – Discourse – Context: Grammar and Usage in Language Variation and Change* (Berlin: Mouton de Gruyter, 2019), 93–124.

Nevalainen, Terttu, 'Social Variation in Intensifier Use: Constraint on –*ly* Adverbialization in the Past?', *English Language and Linguistics* 12/2 (2008), 289–315.

Ochs, Elinor, *The Pragmatics of Affect* (Berlin: Mouton de Gruyter, 1989).

Peters, Hans, 'Degree Adverbs in Early Modern English', in Dieter Kastovsky, ed., *Studies in Early Modern English* (Berlin: Mouton de Gruyter, 1994), 269–88.

Quirk, Randolph, Sidney Greenbaum, Geoffrey Leech, and Jan Svartvik. *A Comprehensive Grammar of the English Language* (London: Longman, 1985).

Powell, Mava-Jo, 'The Systematic Development of Correlated Interpersonal and Metalinguistic Uses in Stance Adverbs', *Cognitive Linguistics* 3/1 (1992), 75–110.

Rhee, Seongha, 'On the Emergence of the Stance-marking Function of English Adverbs: A Case of Intensifiers', *Linguistic Research* 33/3 (2016), 395–436.

Smith, Carlotta, 'Accounting for Subjectivity (Point of view)', in Bruce E. Nevin, ed., *The Legacy of Zellig Harris. Language and Information into the 21st Century, 1: Philosophy of Science, Syntax, and Semantics. Festschrift für Zellig Harris* (Amsterdam: John Benjamins, 2002), 137–63.

Stubbs, Michael, 'A Matter of Prolonged Fieldwork: Notes towards a Modal Grammar of English', *Applied Linguistics* 7 (1986), 1–25.

——, 'Collocations and Semantic Profiles: On the Cause of Trouble with Quantitative Studies', *Functions of Language* 2/1 (1995), 23–55.

Swan, Toril, *Sentence Adverbials in English: A Synchronic and Diachronic Investigation* (Tromsø: University of Tromsø, 1987).

——, 'The Development of Sentence Adverbs in English', *Studia Linguistica: A Journal of General Linguistics* 42/1 (1988), 1–17.

——, 'Adverbial Shifts: Evidence from Norwegian and English', in Dieter Kastovsky, ed., *Historical English Syntax* (Berlin: Mouton de Gruyter, 1991), 409–38.

——, 'From Manner to Subject Modification: Adverbialization in English', *Nordic Journal of Linguistics* 20/2 (1997), 179–95.

Tagliamonte, Sali, 'So Different and Pretty Cool! Recycling Intensifiers in Toronto, Canada', *English Language and Linguistics* 12/2 (2008), 361–94.

Traugott, Elizabeth Closs, 'Subjectification in Grammaticalisation', in Dieter Stein and Susan Wright, eds., *Subjectivity and Subjectivisation: Linguistic Perspectives* (Cambridge: Cambridge University Press, 1995), 31–54.

——, 'From Subjectification to Intersubjectification', in Raymond Hickey, ed., *Motives for Language Change* (Cambridge: Cambridge University Press, 2003), 124–39.

——, 'Intersubjectivity and (Inter)subjectification: A Reassessment', in Kristin Davidse, Lieven Vandelanotte, and Hubert Cuyckens, eds, *Subjectification, Intersubjectification and Grammaticalization* (Berlin: Mouton de Gruyter, 2010), 29–71.

Cristina Blanco-García

Ephemeral Causal Adverbial Subordinators: Their Emergence and Decline in Modern English[1]

1. Introduction

Adverbial subordinators are an intriguing word class. From a historical point of view, their inventory has undergone a series of changes over time and it is far from being stable nowadays. It was in the Late Middle English period and particularly in the Modern English period when the language witnessed an enrichment in the field of adverbial connectives followed by a rapid decline in the use of those new coined subordinators, to the point of dying out or becoming highly restricted. Those subordinators were labelled as "ephemeral subordinators" by Kortmann (1997: 301).

Ephemeral subordinators were particularly common in the CCC group (causal, conditional, concessive; cf. Kortmann 1997: 80). This paper will focus on the causal domain and will trace the history of seven selected ephemeral causal subordinators, namely *for as much as*, *for because*, *for why*, *in as much as*, *in so much as*, *sin* and *sithen* assessing their ephemeral nature.

My aim is to offer a historical analysis of the set of ephemeral causal subordinators focusing on the following issues: (i) the patterns of distribution of the seven selected subordinators across time with regard to their frequency; (ii) their combination with "pleonastic" *that* (cf. Beal 1988; Rissanen 1997); (iii) the position of causal clauses in

1 I am grateful to Programa Estatal de Generación de Conocimiento, Ministerio de Ciencia e Innovación (grant PID2020-114604GB-100).

the sentence; and (iv) distribution across text-types. To this end, data have been extracted from the *Penn-Helsinki Parsed Corpus of Middle English*, the *Penn-Helsinki Parsed Corpus of Early Modern English* and the *Penn-Helsinki Parsed Corpus of Modern British English*.

The paper is structured as follows. Section 2 provides the catalogue of causal subordinators across history and the criteria followed to select the seven ephemeral causal subordinators at issue. Section 3 outlines the structure and characteristics of the corpora used. The main results obtained are presented in Section 4, and finally Section 5 offers some preliminary conclusions.

2. The Catalogue of Causal Subordinators in the History of English

The catalogue of causal subordinators in English has always been far from being fixed. In fact, over the course of the history of the language there has been a continuous increase and renewal among subordinators belonging to this domain. When describing the history of adverbial subordinators, Rissanen (2011: 2) refers to Middle English (henceforth ME) as the time of enrichment and to Early Modern English (henceforth EModE) as the time of establishment and innovation, the Renaissance bringing a large number of loanwords and new stylistic ideas. Table 1, adapted from different sources consulted, accounts for the various ephemeral, rare or even obsolete connectives available in the causal domain in ME, EModE and Late Modern English (henceforth LModE) where the prototypical have been underlined. The selection of the seven ephemeral adverbial subordinators at issue in this study has followed the criteria summarized below:

(i) The subordinator is only attested in EModE.
(ii) The subordinator is attested in both EModE and in ME.
(iii) The subordinator is attested in both EModE and in PDE but it is characterized for being archaic or obsolete or for not having a CCC meaning as its primary one.

Table 1: Causal subordinators in ME, EModE and LModE

Sources	ME	EModE	LModE/PDE
Kortmann	*now (that)*	*now (that)*	*now (that)*
(1997: 331)	*for (that)*	*for (that)*	***(be)cause***
	þæt / that	***(be)cause (that)***	*in that*
	by (the)	*in that*	*since*
	cause (that)	*since*	*as*
	in that	***sith (that)***	***for as much as*** [arch]
	sith(en)/sin (that)	***for as much as***	*seeing (that, how)*
	for as much as	***in asmuch as***	
	in as much as	***in somuch as***	
	in so much as	*as*	
	þurh þæt	*seeing (that)*	
		being (that/as)	
		for because	
		in respect (that)	
		whiles (that)	
CHEL (ME)	***because***	***for (that)***	***for (that)***
(Fischer	***by (the)***	***because (that)***	***because***
1992: 207–408)	***cause that***	*that*	***because (that)***
CHEL (EModE)	*for the*	*now (that)*	*being (as/that)*
(Rissanen	*cause (that)*	*since*	*as*
1999: 187–331)	***by-cause (that)***	***sith***	*seeing (as/that)*
CHEL (LModE)	***for (that)***	***forbecause***	
(Denison	*for…for-thi/*	*as*	
1998: 92–329)	*therefore*	***for why***	
		in that	
Görlach		*as*	
(1993: 122)		***sith***	
		since	
		because	
		for	
		now	
		for why	
		in that	

(*Continued*)

Table 1: *Continued*

Sources	ME	EModE	LModE/PDE
Visser (1963–1973: 936–37)[2]	*for ðon (ðe)* *for ðæm (ðe)* *for ðæm (þæt)* *for þy ðe* *for ðy ðy* *mid ðy ðe* *ðy* *ðe* ***for-why***		

As shown in Table 1, adverbial subordinators which can express causality in English have continually increased. At the same time, causal conjunctions have proved to be continually in need of replacement. These ephemeral subordinators are characterized by their polyfunctionality, the subordinating function not being the primary one. On the other hand, most of them are composite in nature as well as complex in formation. Moreover, many of these subordinators are phrasal and their degree of grammaticalization differs. Some of them mirror their composition, as is the case of *for as much as* and *in as much as*. Not surprisingly, the connective *for*, which was the prototypical causal subordinator before the establishment of *because* (Rissanen 1998: 392–400; 2007: 199–201; Uchida and Iyeire 2017), is present in three out of the seven subordinators under study (*for as much as*, *for because* and *for why*). Additionally, the ephemeral causal subordinator *sithen* is also found in combination with *for* in the data analysed, as shown in example (1) below, which coincides with one of the earliest attestations of the subordinator in the corpus:

(1) So sholde an housbonde eek be to his wyf. *For sith that* al the body is the housbondes, so sholde hire herte been, or

2 Surprisingly, Visser (1963–1973) does not include in his monumental work on the history of English syntax an account of causal subordinators beyond ME and the relevance given to this adverbial relation is more limited than that given to conditionals, concessive or other relations such as manner, comparison or result.

elles ther is bitwixe hem two, as in that, no parfit mariage (CMCTPARS-M3,321.C2.1439).[3]

This phenomenon is known as hypercharacterization (Lehmann 2005) or accretion (Kuteva 2008), which López-Couso (2019: 336) describes as follows: "tendency towards increased complexity through the accumulation of apparently "redundant" linguistic material in the marking of one category within the same structure, which brings about multiple determination of form and function."

In Present-Day English, *because*, as well as its variants, is the prototypical causal subordinator, as shown in Table 2, which contains the lists of causal adverbial subordinators included in the three standard grammars of English but other causal connectives are also used to mark this adverbial relation, although the number of possibilities is more restricted than in previous stages of the language.

Table 2: Causal adverbial subordinators in different grammars of English

Quirk et al. (1985: 1104–6)	Huddleston and Pullum et al. (2002: 731)	Biber et al. (1999: 842–44)
as	***as***	***as***
as long as	***because***	***because/cos***
because / 'cause	***for***	***for***
because of the fact that	*inasmuch as*	*in that*
by virtue of the fact that	*seeing*	***since***
due to the fact that	***since***	*with*
for		
in (the) light of the fact that		
inasmuch as		
in case		
in that		
in view of the fact that		
on account of the fact that		
owing to the fact that		
seeing (that)		
since		
while		

3 A modernized version of this example would read: 'So should a husband also be to his wife. Because all the body is the husband's, so should her heart be, or else there is between them two, as in that, no perfect marriage' (my translation).

3. Structure and Characteristics of the Corpora

Three corpora have been used for data retrieval: the *Penn-Helsinki Parsed Corpus of Middle English*, the *Penn-Helsinki Parsed Corpus of Early Modern English* and the *Penn-Helsinki Parsed Corpus of Modern British English*, thus covering the time span from 1150 to 1914, which is the flourishing period of ephemeral subordinators (EModE) as well as the previous and the subsequent periods (ME and LModE, respectively).

The *Penn Helsinki Parsed Corpus of Middle English, second edition* (PPCME2) amounted to a total of roughly 1.2 million words of running text, coming from 56 text samples dating from 1150 to 1500. The corpora are subdivided into eighteen different subregisters. The text categories included in the corpus are the following: Bible, biography (life of saints), fiction, handbook (astrology, medicine and other), history, homily, religious treatise, philosophy, romance, rule, sermon and travelogue.

Table 3 provides the number of words per period as well as the overall word count of the PPCME2.

Table 3: PPCME2 word count per period and overall[4]

Period	Word count
ME1 (1500–1569)	284,345
ME2 (1570–1639)	146,575
ME3 (1640–1710)	491,413
ME4 (1640–1710)	272,030
Total	1,194,363

The *Penn-Helsinki Parsed Corpus of Early Modern English* (PPCEME) includes texts totalling over 1.7 million words. Table 4 provides the number of words per period and the overall word count of the PPCEME.

4 The information has been taken from the corpus webpage (https://www.ling.upenn.edu/hist-corpora/PPCME2-RELEASE-4/index.html)

Table 4: PPCEME wordcount per period and total

Period	Word count
EME1 (1500–1569)	571,385
EME2 (1570–1639)	629,214
EME3 (1640–1710)	541,647
Total	1,742,246

It must be noted that for the present study, 10 files from subperiod EME3 (1640–1710) dating from over 1700 were eliminated to avoid overlapping with the texts from the *Penn Parsed Corpus of Modern British English*, which contains material dating from 1707 to 1914. The files which have been discarded and the total number of words eliminated (21,543 words in all) are given in Table 5:

Table 5: Files discarded from the EME3 (1640–1710) subperiod in the *Penn Helsinki Parsed Corpus of Early Modern English* (PPCEME)

File name	Number of words	Section	Date	Text-type
nhadd-1700-e3-h	257	Helsinki	1706	Letters, private
nhadd-1700-e3-p1	521	Penn1	1706	Letters, private
farquhar-e3-h	5,646	Helsinki	1707	Drama comedy
farquhar-e3-p1	6,192	Penn1	1707	Drama comedy
farquhar-e3-p2	5,470	Penn2	1707	Drama comedy
spencer-1700-e3-p1	973	Penn1	1708	Letters, non-private
spencer-1700-e3-p2	826	Penn2	1708	Letters, non-private
rhaddsr-1710-e3-p2	187	Penn2	1712	Letters, private
rhaddsr-1700-e3-h	1,007	Helsinki	1702–1703	Letters, private
nhadd-1710-e3-p2	464	Penn2	1718–1719	Letters, private
TOTAL:	21,543			

Once these files were discarded, the number of words in subperiod EME3 (1640–1710) amounts to 520,104.

The *Penn-Helsinki Parsed Corpus of Modern British English* (PPCMBE2) consists of almost 2.8 million words, coming from 275 text samples dating between 1707 and 1914. For the convenience of the analysis and the presentation of the data, the corpus has been divided into three subperiods of roughly 69 years each, as shown in Table 6.

Table 6: PPCMBE2 word count per period and overall

Period	Word count
LME1 (1700–1769)	799,213
LME2 (1770–1839)	926,181
LME3 (1840–1914)	1,041,570
Total	2,766,964

The examples of the ephemeral adverbial subordinators were extracted from the corpora with WordSmith (version 6.0) by searching for all the different spellings, which were obtained from wordlists from the corpora themselves and the *Oxford English Dictionary*.

For the analysis of the results, the data were stored in an Excel spreadsheet and coded for the linguistic variables: (i) presence of a pleonastic marker; (ii) the occurrence of a correlative element; and (iii) position of the subordinate clause in relation to the main clause and extralinguistc variables: (i) subperiod and (ii) text-type.

4. Results

Tables 7 and 8 display the occurrences of the seven ephemeral causal subordinators under study per subperiods in the *Penn Helsinki Corpora*, both in absolute figures and in normalized frequencies per 1,000,000 words in brackets, as well as the total numbers of examples per subordinator in the corpora.

Table 7: Ephemeral causal subordinators in the *Penn Helsinki Corpora*: Absolute and normalized frequencies

Subperiod	N° of words	Ephemeral causal subordinators		
		for as much as	***for because***	***for why***
ME1 (1150–1249)	284,345	–	–	–
ME2 (1250–1349)	146,575	–	–	1 (6.82)
ME3 (1350–1419)	491,413	33 (67.15)	18 (36.63)	7 (14.24)
ME4 (1420–1499)	272,030	4 (14.7)	3 (11.03)	–
EME1 (1500–1569)	571,385	15 (26.25)	17 (29.75)	2 (3.50)
EME2 (1570–1639)	629,214	7 (11.12)	2 (3.18)	0
EME3 (1640–1700)	520,104	3 (5.77)	1 (1.92)	1 (1.92)
LME 1 (1700–1769)	799,213	3 (3.75)	–	–
LME 2 (1770–1839)	926,181	–	–	–
LME3 (1840–1914)	1,041,570	4 (3.84)	–	–
Total	5,682,030	69 (12.14)	41 (7.22)	11 (1.93)

Table 8: Ephemeral causal subordinators in the *Penn Helsinki Corpora*: Absolute and normalized frequencies

Subperiod	N° of words	Ephemeral causal subordinators			
		in as much as	***in so much as***	***sin***	***sithen***
ME1 (1150–1249)	284,345	–	–	–	–
ME2 (1250–1349)	146,575	–	–	–	–
ME3 (1350–1419)	491,413	–	–	–	15 (30.52)

Continued

Table 8: *Continued*

Subperiod	Nº of words	Ephemeral causal subordinators			
		in as much as	*in so much as*	*sin*	*sithen*
ME4 (1420–1499)	272,030	10 (36.76)	–	–	10 (36.76)
EME1 (1500–1569)	571,385	9 (15.75)	3 (5.25)	11 (19.25)	13 (22.75)
EME2 (1570–1639)	629,214	2 (3.18)	6 (9.53)	–	17 (27.02)
EME3 (1640–1700)	520,104	1 (1.92)	10 (19.23)	–	1 (1.92)
LME 1 (1700–1769)	799,213	1 (1.25)	7 (8.76)	–	–
LME 2 (1770–1839)	926,181	4 (4.32)	1 (1.08)	–	–
LME3 (1840–1914)	1,041,570	14 (13.44)	1 (0.96)	–	–
Total	5,682,030	41 (7.22)	28 (4.93)	11 (1.93)	56 (9.86)

As shown in these tables, the seven ephemeral causal subordinators are characterized by their low frequency, ranging from 12.14 in the case of *for as much as* to 1.94 and 1.93 for *sin* and *for why*, respectively.

Figure 1 below provides an overview of the occurrence of the ephemeral causal subordinators under examination in the three main historical periods analysed in this paper. The figure reveals an uneven distribution of the connectives over the three stages. It is not until the first subperiod of EModE (1500–1569) that the seven subordinators are represented in the corpus, although five of them, namely *for as much as*, *for because*, *for why*, *in as much as* and *sithen*, are already attested in the ME material. In addition, two connectives occur for the first time in EModE. These are *in so much as* and *sin*, the latter being found only in this period. Moreover, LModE also witnessed the disappearance of three ephemeral causal connectives, namely *for because*, *sin* and *sithen*, while the other four decreased considerably over this period.

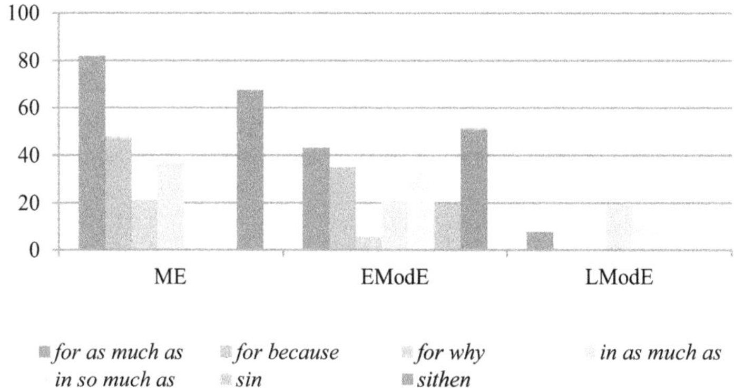

Figure 1: Ephemeral causal subordinators in ME, EModE and LModE in the *Penn Helsinki Corpora* (Normalized frequencies per 1,000,000 words).

Figure 2 summarizes the diachronic development of the seven subordinators per subperiod and clearly shows that most of them originated in Late ME, around 1350, although their peaks differ greatly.

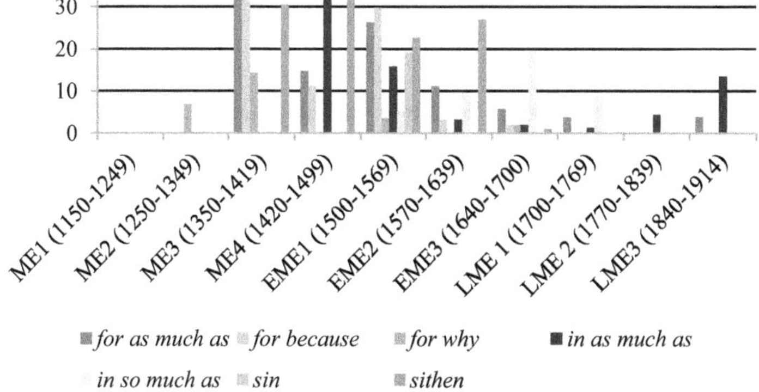

Figure 2: Ephemeral causal subordinators per subperiods in ME, EModE and LModE in the *Penn Helsinki Corpora* (Normalized frequencies per 1,000,000 words).

The causal subordinator *for why* is the only connective out of the set under study to be traced in the corpus as early as ME2 (1250–1350), approximately in 1349, which roughly coincides with the first quotations of this subordinator provided in both the MED and the OED. (2) below is the first occurrence of this subordinator in the corpus:

(2) Sothely þay sall Ioye nowe, be in- ȝettynge of grace, and in tym to come be syghte of Ioye, and thare-fore þay sall Ioye, *for why* Ioy comes of lufe (CMROLLTR-M2 4,4.105, 4.105).[5]

The corpus yields earlier attestations of the sequence *for why*, but not functioning as a causal subordinator, but as a complementizer. In example (3), for instance, *for why* is a complementizer which introduces a [+*wh*-] complement clause, whereas in (4) we find an example of a so-called "minor complementizer"[6], which resembles the default declarative complementizer *that*:[7]

(3) ȝet wile icc shæwenn ȝuw *forrwhi* | | Goddspell iss Goddspell nemmnedd | (CMORM-M1,PREF.L81.92).[8]

(4) & all þe follc þær ute abad, | & þuhhte mikell wunnderr | | *Forrwhi* þe preost swa lannge wass | | þatt daȝ ȝ att Godess allterr | (CMORM-M1,I,4.160).[9]

It is in the third subperiod of ME (ME3; 1350–1419) when three subordinators of the set, namely *for as much as*, *for because* and *sithen*, first occur as causal subordinators in the corpus. However, their frequency

5 A modernized version of this example would read: 'Truly they should be joyful now, being in grace, and in the future seek happiness, and therefore they should feel happy because happiness comes from love' '(my translation)'.

6 For further details on minor complementizers, see López-Couso and Méndez-Naya (2020).

7 Interestingly, all the instances retrieved from the first subperiod of the corpus (1150–1249) are from the same text, *The Ormulum*, which may indicate that the origin of the connective is related to religious prose.

8 A modernized version of this example would read as follows: 'I will show you yet why the Gospel is named the Gospel' '(my translation)'.

9 A modernized version of this example could be: 'And all the folk stayed out there, and it seemed a great wonder that the priest was so long that day at God's altar' '(my translation)'.

of occurrence differs: whereas *for because* and *sithen* have a similar normalized frequency (36.63 and 30.52, respectively), *for as much as* reached its peak in this period, with a normalized frequency of 67.15.

Examples (5) – (7) illustrate the earliest attestations of *for as much as*, *for because* and *sithen* in the corpus. The dates are similar to those given in the etymological dictionaries, except for the subordinator *for because*, for which the dictionaries provide later occurrences. While the earliest MED example is from 1425 (see example (8)) and the example from the OED dates from a century later (see example (9)), the first examples of *for because* in my data date back to circa 1400.

(5) After þe deth of Cassibalam, *for-asmiche as* he hade none heire of his body, þe lordes of þe lande, by commune assent, cronede Androgen, Erl of Cornewaile, and made him kyng (CMBRUT3-M3,33.1018).
(6) Good men and woymen, þys day ys called yn holy chyrch þe Sonenday yn þe Passyon; *for bycause þat* our Lord Ihesu Cryst began hys passyon þys day (CMMIRK-M34,110.3013).
(7) A doumb prelat is not a very prelat, *sithen* he vsith not the offis of a prelat (CMPURVEY-M3,I,31.1535).
(8) *For bycause* al is corrumpable...Ne were ther generacioun, Oure sectis stren for to save (a1425(?a1400), RRose (Htrn 409)4856; MED s.v. bicause (conj.) 1a).
(9) *For bicause* I was in her presence, I toke acquaintaunce of her excellence (1509, S. Hawes *Pastime of Pleasure* 147; OED s.v. because, adv., conj., and n., B 1a).

It was in the last subperiod of ME (ME4; 1420–1499) when the causal subordinator *in as much as* is attested in the data for the first time. Consider example (10):

(10) Dowtyr, I am wel plesyd wyth þe *in-as-meche as* þu beleuyst in alle þe Sacramentys of Holy Chirche & in al feyth þat longith þerto, & specialy for þat þu beleuyst in manhode of my Sone & for þe gret compassyon þat þu hast of hys bittyr Passyon (CMKEMPE-M4,86.1938).

The first attestation of the subordinator *in so much as* is found as late as the first subperiod of EModE (EME1; 1500–1569). This is given as (11).

(11) Wherfore, she is to me more better lady then ever she was before, *in so much that* she hath promysed me hir good ladyship as long as ever she shall lyve (DPLUMPT-E1-H,202.5).

The low number of examples in the corpus is clearly insufficient to draw any tentative conclusions on the diachronic development of the subordinators at issue, given that their normalized frequencies per 1,000,000 words range from 12.14 (highest) to 1.93 (lowest). By contrast, it can safely be claimed that it is in Late ME (1350–1499) and EModE, particularly in its first subperiod (1500–1569), when most of the ephemeral causal subordinators flourished. Furthermore, after that time of expansion, there was a marked period of decline in the use of these ephemeral adverbial subordinators and most of them died out or became rarely used. The three subordinators that are attested in LModE are *for as much as*,[10] *in as much as* and *in so much as*.[11] Illustrations of the last examples attested for these connectives in the data are given in (12) to (14).

10 It is remarkable that four out of the seven LModE examples of this subordinator in the data, representing 57.14 per cent of the total, are from two different versions of the Bible, one by Anthony Purver (1764) and a second one from the English Old Testament Revisers (1885). Additionally, the causal subordinator *for as much as* appears in *The Bible Word-book: A Glossary of Archaic Words and Phrases in the Authorised Version of the Bible and the Book of Common Prayer* (1884) by William Aldis Wright. However, this causal subordinator does not have an entry of its own in the aforementioned glossary, but is given as a synonym of *forsomuch as*. The entry reads as follows: "Forsomuch as (Luke xix.9). Forasmuch as, because."

11 Moskowich and Monaco (2016: 36) have also accounted for the presence of these three ephemeral causal subordinators, *in as much as*, *in so much as* and *for as much as*, in the *Coruña Corpus of English Scientific Writing*, which covers the period 1700–1900. Interestingly, their study, which is based on women's writings, does not report any occurrences of these ephemeral causal subordinators in their data, only of the prototypical causal subordinator *because*.

(12) The learner can be made to understand the obvious truth, that language, and literature are the great exercise ground of thought, and mind; *in as much as* all thought passes through language (THRING-1883-2,159.61).

(13) I swear by my self, says the Lord, *for as much as* thou hast done this Thing, and not with-held thy own only Son; That I will thoroughly bless thee, and multiply thy Offspring abundantly, to be like the Stars of Heaven, and the Sand which is upon the Sea-shoar: and they shall inherit the Gates of their Enemies (PURVER-OLD-1764-1,22,1G.401).

(14) Do you not perceive that the manners and customs of different nations widely vary; *in so much*, that what is thought to deserve praise in one country, is in another deemed worthy of punishment? (BOETHRI-1785-2,69.532).

In the light of the data in the corpus, it can be concluded that these seven connectives are low-frequency forms and that, as suggested by Kortmann (1997: 331–5), they gained momentum in the last subperiods of ME and in the course of EModE.

4.1. Pleonastic that

Adverbial subordinators were commonly followed by the so-called "pleonastic" *that* in earlier English. Combinations of the type subordinator + *that* (e.g., *oþ þat*) can be traced as early as the OE period. In ME, this tendency became stronger and *that* came to function as an indicator of the subordinating role of multifunctional forms. The phenomenon increased considerably in Late ME, declining rapidly in the seventeenth century, to such an extent that it virtually disappeared towards the end of the same century (Rissanen 1997: 303–4).[12]

In this section devoted to the pleonastic *that* two objectives are pursued:

(a) To analyse its use and distribution in the corpus.

12 The use of pleonastic *that* has also been examined by other scholars, among them Kivimaa (1966), Beal (1988), Rissanen (1997; 1999) and Calle-Martín (2017).

(b) To assess its decline with the different ephemeral causal subordinators at issue.

As shown in Table 9, pleonastic *that* is a rather sporadic feature with the ephemeral causal subordinators at issue, since only three them, namely *for because*, *sin* and *sith*, are attested in the data with the appended *that*. Interestingly, most of the few attestations of pleonastic *that* are found in the ME period and it no longer occurs after the early seventeenth century.

Table 9: Pleonastic *that* with ephemeral causal subordinators in the *Penn Helsinki Corpora*. Absolute figures and percentages in brackets

Subperiod	**Ephemeral causal subordinators**						
	for as much as	***for because***	***for why***	***in as much as***	***in so much as***	***sin***	***sith***
ME1 (1150–1249)	–	–	–	–	–	–	–
ME2 (1250–1349)	–	–	–	–	–	–	–
ME3 (1350–1419)	–	14 (77.78)	–	–	–	–	6 (54.54)
ME4 (1420–1499)	–	1 (5.55)	–	–	–	–	–
EME1 (1500–1569)	–	3 (16.67)	–	–	–	1 (100)	2 (18.18)
EME2 (1570–1639)	–	–	–	–	–	–	3 (27.27)
EME3 (1640–1700)	–	–	–	–	–	–	
LME 1 (1700–1769)	–	–	–	–	–	–	
LME 2 (1770–1839)	–	–	–	–	–	–	
LME3 (1840–1914)	–	–	–	–	–	–	

For because is the ephemeral causal subordinator which shows the highest number of instances in combination with the appended *that*

(18/41; 43.9 per cent). The greatest majority of the examples (14/18; 77.8 per cent) date from the ME3 period (1350–1419) and, what is even more remarkable, those 14 examples are found in only two texts. On the one hand, 10 instances occur in *Mirk's Festial*, a collection of homilies by John Mirk.[13] Consider examples (15) and (16) below:

(15) þen **for bycause þat** Sonday ys no day of fastyng, þerfor ȝe schull begyn your fast at Aske-Wanysday, and þat day com to holy chyrche, and take askes at þe prestys hond, and ber forth in your hert þat he sayth to you, when he layth askes on your hedys (CMMIRK-M34,82.2193).

(16) But **for bycause þat** þe seruyce of þys day[14] is so long, I woll schortly tell you whi þys day is called soo (CMMIRK-M34,114.3126).

On the other hand, the remaining four examples are from *Mandeville's Travels*, by an unknown author; see (17) as an illustration:

(17) And *for because þat* he was so wel with god þerfore þei worschipe him (CMMANDEV-M3,109.2679).

The remarks provided in the corpus regarding the philological information of this text read as follows:

> [. . .] an anonymous translation of a French work written by Jehan de Bourgogne in 1356/7 under the penname of Sir John Mandeville. The work is based on authentic travelogues, Guiollaume de Boldensele (1336) and Odoric de Pordenone (1330), but is essentially a work of fiction. The translator writes very good English, but often misunderstands the French text.

---

13 The corpus provides the following philological information about this text:
A free reworking of the Legenda Aurea (a sermon cycle written in Latin about 1260–1270 by Jacobus a Voragine), with many additions from the Gesta Romanorum and comments, as well as two sermons from local sources. It is a full festival sermon cycle with many narrations, much of it apparently from local oral tradition.
Given that this text is a reworking of a text originally written in Latin, we can tentatively say that the subordinator *for because that* was maintained here or chosen instead of the prototypical causal subordinator *because* on account of the text's origin (Latin influence).

14 The day that is being referred to is Palm Sunday.

The fact that these four examples of *for because* come from a text translated from French cannot be overlooked, given that they date from subperiod ME3 (1350–1419), a time that witnessed the decline of *for* as a causal subordinator and the rapid establishment of *because* borrowed from French.

Examples of the combination *for because that* from the subsequent periods, i.e. ME4 (1420–1499) and EME1 (1500–1569), are shown in (18) and (19), respectively:

(18) And *for because that* kynge Arthure lay by hys wyff and gate on her sir Mordred, therefore kynge Lott helde ever agaynste Arthure (CMMALORY-M4,58.1917).

(19) And *for bycause that* honours, that the people do gyue to men, can not make men worthye such honours: it appereth that honours haue no proper beautie, or similitude of dignytie of it selfe (BOETHCO-E1-P2,61.121).

It is worth commenting that the use of *for because* with the subordinating particle *that* is sometimes reinforced by the presence of the correlative adverb *therefore* in the main clause (5/41; 12.20 per cent), as shown in examples (15) and (18). There are also two examples in the corpus in which the correlative item is *yet*, rather than *therefore*. However, in those examples, the adverb appears before the subordinate clause. Consider example (20):

(20) But *ȝet, for bycause þat* he was a knyȝt, and saw þe lyon, þat ys kyng of all bestys, yn destres, he drogh out his swerde, and smot þe edyr yn two pecys (CMMIRK-M34,119.3201).[15]

As seen in the previous examples, the subordinator *for because* frequently occurs in the corpus with the appended *that* and is sometimes also reinforced by the correlative adverbs *therefore* or *yet* in the main clause. This is not at all surprising, given that *for because* had to be accompanied by other elements which indicated in a straightforward

15 A modernized version of this example would read: 'But yet because he was a knight, and had seen a lion, which is the king of all beasts, in distress, he drew his sword and tarnished the snake into two pieces' (my translation).

way that it functioned as a subordinating conjunction, since this subordinator is the result of the combination of the old prototypical causal connective *for* and the new causal subordinator *because*.

In addition to *for because*, only two other ephemeral causal subordinators sporadically appear accompanied by the particle *that*. These are *sin* (1/11; 9.09 per cent) and *sith* (11/56; 19.64 per cent), illustrated in (21) and (22), respectively.

(21) Wherfore frendes, quod the duke, *sins that* we parceiue it is al your hole mindes to haue this noble man for your king whereof we shall make his grace so effectuall reporte, that we doubte not but it shall redounde vnto your great weal and commoditye: we require ye that ye to morow go with vs and wee with you vnto his noble grace, to make our humble request vnto him in maner before remembred (MORERIC-E1-H,77.143).

(22) Now *sith that* Jhesu Crist took upon hymself the peyne of alle oure wikkednesses, muchel oghte synful man wepen and biwayle, that for his synnes Goddes sone of hevene sholde al this peyne endure (CMCTPARS-M3,295.C1.281).

Out of the 11 examples of *sith* followed by *that*, six of them (54.54 per cent) are from the ME3 subperiod (1350–1419), which corresponds with the time in which the first occurrences of this subordinator are found in the data. Therefore, the use of the appended *that* seems to correlate or have a stronger presence in the earliest attestations of the connective, i.e. during the period of its establishment as a causal connective.

The ephemeral causal subordinators *sin* and *sithen* are also found in combination with *that* in the OED and the MED quotation databases (cf. examples (23), (24), (25) and (26)).

(23) *Syn that* a knyght is capitayn of a batayll the lyf of them..lyeth in his hand (1474, W. Caxton tr. Game & Playe of Chesse (1883) ii. iv. 44; OED s.v. sin, adv., prep., and conj. C2b).

(24) *Sen that* he is turnyd away fra the vnrest of this life..he heris what the haly gast spekis priuely in him (a1500 (c1340), Rolle Psalter (UC 64)84.8; MED s.v. sin (conj.) 1a).

(25) Jeremye..as anentis þe hebrues is seen to ben booistousere þan þe sermoun of isaie & of osee: & þan oþere prophetis, but in wittis he is euene: *siþen* [L. *quippe*] *þat* in þe same spirit he propheciede (a1382, *Bible (*Wycliffite, E.V.*)* (Bodl. 959) (1969) Jer. Prol. l. 4; OED s.v. sithen, adv., conj., and prep. B2b).

(26) Can they be said not to come therefore voluntarily, *sithen that* where there is a chose, there is a kinde of freedome? (1610, R. Bernard *Plaine Evid.* 130; OED s.v. sithen, adv., conj., and prep. B2b).

Additionally, the MED dictionary provides an example given below as (27) in which *sithen* is used in combination with *as*, rather than with *that.*

(27) *Sithen as* we may not to-geder spek, be writynge we shall oure hertes breke (c1500, I pray you M (BodLMisc c.66)25; MED s.v. sitthen (conj.) 5b).

The appended particle *as* is not found in the corpus with ephemeral causal subordinators. The absence of this marker with the connectives *for as much as*, *in as much as* and *in so much as* can be justified on the grounds that these three causal subordinators are already too complex in nature and all of them already feature *as*. Although in my data there are not any examples of pleonastic *that* in combination with the three aforementioned subordinators, the MED dictionary provides an instance of *in so much as* with appended *that* (cf. example (28)), where *as* has been dropped.

(28) Noþer he noþer hys men oony sute oftyd to þat myll, *Insomoch that* A quiteclayme þay had of þat maner of sute afore þe sayde Reynolde whas y-ffeffyd of þe sayde Mylle (c1460, Oseney Reg. 203/6; MED s.v. in sō muche, in sō muchel (adv.) 1c).

As we have seen, pleonastic *that* frequently cooccurs with the adverbs *yet* and *therefore* in the main clause (see, e.g., examples (15) and (20) above for the subordinator *for because*). However, some instances in my data show the use of these correlative adverbs in sentences introduced by ephemeral causal subordinators without pleonastic *that.* Consider in this respect example (29), which features the correlative element *therefore* introducing the main clause and the subordinator *for why* without the appended *that*.

(29) Sothely þay sall Ioye nowe, be in- ȝettynge of grace, and in tym to come be syghte of Ioye, and *thare-fore* þay sall Ioye, *for why* Ioy comes of lufe (CMROLLTR-M2 4,4.105).

By way of summary, it can be said that despite the low frequency of occurrence of pleonastic *that* with the seven causal subordinators at issue, the data clearly indicates that the subordinating particle *that* is more likely to be appended in the earliest attestations of the subordinators, which frequently date from the last subperiods of ME. Moreover, the subordinator which more commonly appears in combination with pleonastic *that* is *for because*, particularly in its first occurrences in the corpus. In view of this, it could tentatively be said that pleonastic *that* was a requirement to reinforce its function as a subordinating conjunction given that this connective is formed by the combination of the old and the new causal subordinators *for* and *because*. Furthermore, the multiword subordinators which have *as* in their formation (*for as much as*, *in as much as* and *in so much as*), do not have pleonastic *that* appended. Moreover, the correlatives *yet* and *therefore* are sometimes found in the main clause of those sentences in which the causal subordinate clause is introduced by one of the ephemeral causal subordinators under study. The motivation for the use of such correlatives is to reinforce the semantics of the subordinate clause, in this case causality, particularly in those cases where the subordinator may not suffice.

4.2 Position of the Subordinate Clause

This section is devoted to the study of the position of the sub-clauses in relation to the main clause, i.e., initial, medial or final position of the subordinate clauses introduced by the seven ephemeral subordinators under examination. Table 10 and Figure 3 show the distribution of initial, medial and final position of adverbial clauses introduced by the ephemeral causal connectives in the corpus.

Table 10: Position of adverbial clauses introduced by ephemeral causal subordinators in the *Penn Helsinki Corpora*. (Absolute figures; percentages in brackets)

Subordinator	Initial	Medial	Final	Total
for as much as	40 (57.97)	–	29 (20.01)	69 (100)
for because	26 (63.41)	1 (2.44)	14 (20.29)	41 (100)
for why	3 (27.27)	–	8 (72.73)	11 (100)
in as much as	4 (9.75)	1 (2.44)	36 (87.8)	41 (100)
in so much as	6 (21.43)	–	22 (78.57)	28 (100)
Sin	4 (36.36)	2 (18.18)	5 (45.45)	11 (100)
sith	28 (50)	–	28 (50)	56 (100)
Total	111 (43.19)	4 (1.56)	142 (55.25)	257 (100)

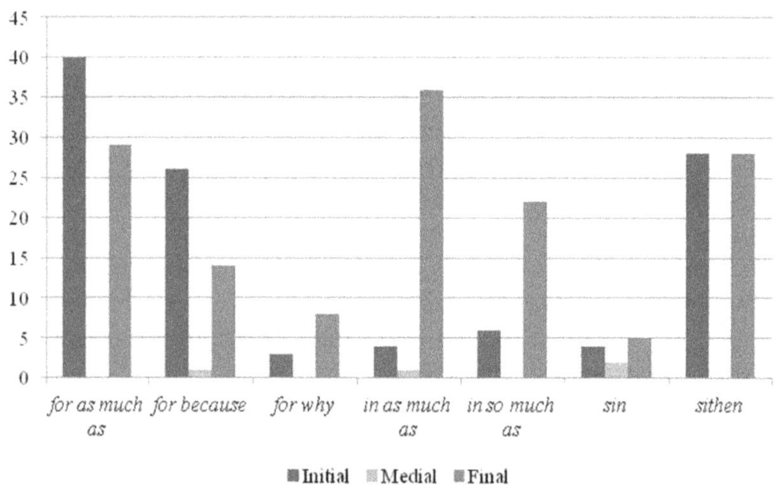

Figure 3: Position of subordinate clauses introduced by ephemeral causal subordinators in the *Penn Helsinki Corpora* (Absolute figures).

As shown here, although the three possible positions are attested in the data, final position is the most common one (55.25 per cent), followed by initial position (43.19 per cent), while medial position is clearly a very marginal choice (1.56 per cent). Final position is the predominant position with the connectives *for why* (consider example (30)), *in as much as* (see (31)), *in so much as* (cf. (32) = (11)) and *sin* (see (33)). By contrast, initial position is the preferred choice with the subordinators *for as much as* (cf. example (34) = (13)) and *for because* (see example (35)). Medial position, in turn, is only found with three of these subordinators, namely *for because*, *in as much as* and *sin*, though only scarcely. Consider example (36) as an illustration of this position with *in as much as*. In the case of causal clauses introduced by *sithen*, initial and final positions are evenly distributed.

(30) And al be it so that thise thinges ben diverse, yit natheles hangeth that oon of that oother; *forwhi* the ordre destynal procedith of the simplicite of purveaunce (CMBOETH-M3,451.C2.472).

(31) I am wel plesyd wyth þe *in-as-meche as* þu beleuyst in alle þe Sacramentys of Holy Chirche (CMKEMPE-M4,86.1938).

(32) = (11) Wherfore, she is to me more better lady then ever she was before, *in so much that* she hath promysed me hir good ladyship as long as ever she shall lyve (DPLUMPT-E1-H,202.5).

(33) Also Plini the yonger saith, He that is nat enuironed with charite, in vaine is he garded with terrour; *sens* armure with armure is stored (ELYOT-E1-P1,155.98).

(34) = (13) I swear by my self, says the Lord, *for as much as* thou hast done this Thing, and not with-held thy own only Son; That I will thoroughly bless thee, and multiply thy Offspring abundantly, to be like the Stars of Heaven, and the Sand which is upon the Sea-shoar: and they shall inherit the Gates of their Enemies (PURVER-OLD-1764-1,22,1G.401).

(35) *For because* thou art confounded with the Oblivion of thy self, thou complainest of thy Banishment, and of the Loss of thy Estate (BOETHPR-E3-P1,38.175).

(36) We are compelled to admit, *in as much as* the barbarous elements are still wofully {COM:sic} rife among us, that there must be present an equally woful misconception or disregard of the parental duties (ELLIS-1851-2,24.144).

4.3. Text-Type

In this section, I discuss the distribution of ephemeral causal subordinators over time in the different text-types represented in the corpus, given that previous studies have shown that variation is evident among conjunctions in terms of their frequency and their occurrence in a variety of genres; see, for example, Peterson (2009), Lenker (2010) and Grund and Smitterberg (2014).

Although all the texts included in the *Penn Helsinki Corpora* belong to the written medium, some texts are clearly closer to the spoken language than others. In order to facilitate the analysis of the results, the 18 registers represented in these corpora have been arranged into subcategories following the classification established by Culpeper and Kytö (2010: 17–18):

Table 11: Register distribution in the *Penn Helsinki Corpora* according to the dimension of (in)formality and the dichotomy speech-like vs. written

		Informal		**Formal**
Speech-related	Speech-like	Diaries		
		Letters, private		
	Speech-based	Trial proceedings		
	Speech-purposed	Drama Fiction		Sermons
Writing-based and writing-purposed		Romance	(Auto)biography Travelogue	Bible Educational treatise Handbook History Law Letters, non-private Medicine Philosophy Religious treatise Science

As shown in Table 11, they distinguish two major groups of texts: (1) speech-related texts and (2) writing-based and writing-purposed texts. The former group can be further subdivided into three different subgroups: (1) speech-like texts (e.g. personal letters and diaries), which are defined in terms of a scale consisting of features of communicative immediacy; (2) speech-based texts (e.g. trial proceedings), based on real-life speech events; and (3) speech-purposed texts, designed to be articulated orally, either reproducing real-time interaction (drama) or monologues (sermons). It must be noted, however, that this classification is not a clear-cut one, but rather contains interrelated and overlapping groups (Culpeper and Kytö 2010: 18). Additionally, the registers in the corpora can also be situated along a formal-informal continuum, with texts such as diaries at the informal end and scientific texts at the formal one.

In what follows, I provide the diachronic distribution of the seven ephemeral causal subordinators according to the dichotomy speech-related texts vs. writing-based and writing-purposed texts (normalized frequencies per 100,000 words).

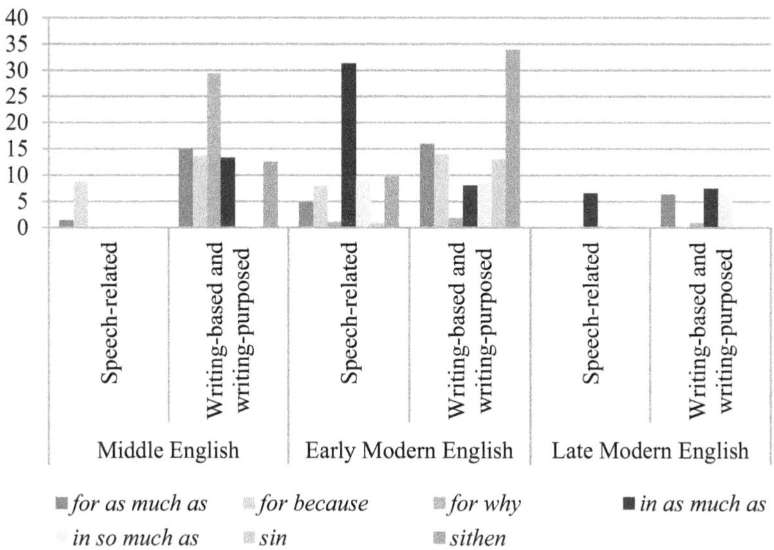

Figure 4: Distribution of the ephemeral causal subordinators per period and register (normalized frequencies per 100,000 words).

As Figure 4 illustrates, all the ephemeral causal subordinators under study show in the three periods a marked preference to appear in writing-based and writing purposed texts rather than in speech-related texts. However, it is worth noting that the ephemeral causal subordinator *in as much as* frequently appears in trial proceedings, a speech-based text-type, particularly in the EModE period, with a normalized frequency of 31.19 per 100,000 words, the highest across period and register. Consider (37) and (38) in this respect:

(37) For nowe was the time, *in as much as* the Londoners would take his part, if the matter were presented unto them (THROCKM-E1-H,I,67.C1.222).

(38) Did you go immediately from that room up stairs? – I did, *in as much as* there was no egress to the back yard, the door being blockaded, as I have described (FROST-1840-1,195.1236).

The ephemeral causal subordinator *for because* is somewhat frequent in the ME period in sermons, a formal register belonging to the speech-purposed group, as shown in example (6) above, repeated here for convenience as (39). The preference of this causal subordinator to occur in this text-type may be justified by the eloquent nature of this register as well as by the influence of Latin and French on liturgical texts.

(39) = (6) Good men and woymen, þys day ys called yn holy chyrch þe Sonenday yn þe Passyon; *for bycause þat* our Lord Ihesu Cryst began hys passyon þys day (CMMIRK-M34,110.3013).

The data shows that the subordinator *for as much as* frequently appears in history texts. In fact, in the ME period, 29 out of the 37 examples of this subordinator are found in this text-type. An illustration is provided in (40) below:[16]

16 In addition to the ephemeral causal subordinator *for as much as*, which is part of the set of connectives discussed in this paper, this example also shows the ocurrence of another ephemeral causal subordinator, namely *for the cause that* (cf. Table 1 above), with dropping of the article *the*.

(40) ffor þe gode Erle Cuthbert of Lyndeseye, and al þe peple of Northumberlond, & almost al þe grete of Engeland, helde with Swyne þat was Kyng of Dennemarc, *for-asmiche as* þai louede nouȝt Kyng Eldrede, *ffor cause þat* gode broþer Edward was slayn falsely for enchesoun of him (CMBRUT3-M3,118.3585).

These findings are in line with those by Claridge and Walker (2001). Their study, devoted to the development of various causal subordinators in written and speech-related genres in EModE, proves that at that time *for*, the obsolete causal subordinator, was still commonly used in written (treatises and law) and speech-related texts (sermons and trials). They tentatively conclude that "written language is more conservative in that it uses obsolescent items", although they acknowledge that the number of instances is too low to draw definitive conclusions. The same holds for my study, but it is undeniable that ephemeral causal subordinators are clearly more common in written texts than in speech-related ones, and among those, in formal, learned genres than in informal text-types. Furthermore, it is in the EModE period, the flourishing period of ephemeral causal subordinators, when the connectives at issue in this piece of research happen to occur in a wider variety of texts, whereas in both ME and LModE their textual distribution is less varied.

5. Conclusions

To conclude, in view of the results from this study, it can be argued that the seven ephemeral causal connectives are low-frequency items and that they had momentum in the EModE period.

The behaviour of the ephemeral causal connectives regarding the linguistic variables studied in the present paper (the combination with pleonastic *that*, the position of the subordinate clause and the distribution across registers) show the following tendencies: (i) pleonastic *that* appears more recurrently in the earliest examples of the subordinators, which frequently date from the last subperiods of ME. Additionaly, this pleonasm is also observed to appear more commonly with the causal subordinator *for because*, which may respond to a need to reinforce its function as a subordinating conjunction given that this connective is formed by the combination of the old and the new causal subordinators *for* and *because*. Furthermore, the multiword subordinators which have *as* in their formation (*for as much as*, *in as much as* and *in so much as*), do not have pleonastic *that*, probably due to their complex nature; (ii) there is a general tendency for the causal adverbial clauses introduced by the seven ephemeral causal subordinators to be placed in final position, whereas medial position is scarcely attested; and (iii) ephemeral causal subordinators are more prone to appear in written texts than in speech-related texts and formal registers hold the vast majority of examples of the ephemeral causal subordinators.

Sources

Kroch, Anthony and Ann Taylor, eds., *The Penn-Helsinki Parsed Corpus of Middle English*, 2nd edition, release 4 (Department of Linguistics: University of Pennsylvania, 2000). Available at http://www.ling.upenn.edu/hist-corpora/PPCME2-RELEASE-4/index.html

Kroch, Anthony, Beatrice Santorini and Lauren Delfs, eds., *The Penn-Helsinki Parsed Corpus of Early Modern English*, CD-ROM, 1st edition, release 3 (Department of Linguistics: University of Pennsylvania, 2004). Available at http://www.ling.upenn.edu/ppche/ppche-release-2016/PPCEME-RELEASE-3

Kroch, Anthony, Beatrice Santorini and Ariel Diertani, eds., *The Penn Parsed Corpus of Modern British English*, CD-ROM, 2nd edition, release 1 (Department of Linguistics: University of Pennsylvania, 2016). Available at http://www.ling.upenn.edu/ppche/ppche-release-2016/PPCMBE2-RELEASE-1

Kurath, Hans et al., eds., *Middle English Dictionary* (Ann Arbor, MI: University of Michigan Press, 1952–2001). Available at http://quod.lib.umich.edu/m/med/.

Oxford English Dictionary (Oxford University Press, 2023). Available at http://www.oed.com/.

WordSmith 6.0 for Windows (Lexical Analysis Software and Oxford University Press, 1996–2017). Available at: http://lexically.net/wordsmith/

References

Beal, Joan, ' "Goodbye to all 'that"? The History and Present Behaviour of Optional "that"", in Nixon Graham and John Honey, eds., *An HistoricTtongue. Studies in English Linguistics in Memory of Barbara Strang* (London and New York: Routledge, 1988), 49–66.

Biber, Douglas, Stig Johansson, Geoffrey Leech, Susan Conrad, and Edward Finegan, *Longman Grammar of Spoken and Written English* (London: Longman, 1999).

Calle Martín, Javier, '"When that wounds are evil healed": Revisiting Pleonastic *that* in Early English Medical Writing', *Studia Anglica Posnaniensia* 51/1 (2017), 1–16.

Claridge, Claudia and Terry Walker, 'Causal Clauses in Written and Speech-related Genres in Early Modern English', *ICAME Journal* 25 (2001), 31–63.

Culpeper, Jonathan and Merja Kytö, *Early Modern English Dialogues. Spoken Interaction as Writing* (Cambridge: Cambridge University Press, 2010).

Denison, David, 'Syntax', in Suzanne Romaine, ed., *The Cambridge History of the English Language. Vol. IV: 1776–1997* (Cambridge: Cambridge University Press, 1998), 92–329.

Fischer, Olga, 'Syntax', in Richard M. Hogg, ed., *The Cambridge History of the English Language. Vol. II: 1066–1476* (Cambridge: Cambridge University Press, 1992), 207–408.

Görlach, Manfred, *Introduction to Early Modern English* (Cambridge: Cambridge University Press, 1993).

Grund, Peter and Erik Smitterberg, 'Conjuncts in Nineteenth-Century English: Diachronic Development and Genre Diversity', *English Language and Linguistics* 18 (2014), 157–81.

Huddleston, Rodney, Geoffrey K. Pullum et al., *The Cambridge Grammar of the English Language* (Cambridge: Cambridge University Press, 2002).

Kivimaa, Kirsti, *þe and þat as Clause Connectives in Early Middle English with Especial Consideration of the Emergence of the Pleonastic þat* (Helsinki: Societas Scientiarum Fennica, 1966).

Kortmann, Bernd, *Adverbial Subordination: A Typology and History of Adverbial Subordinators Based on European Languages* (Berlin and Boston: Mouton de Gruyter, 1997).

Kuteva, Tania, 'On the "Frills" of Grammaticalization', in María José López-Couso and Elenea Seoane, eds., *Rethinking Grammaticalization: New Perspectives for the Twenty-first Century* (Amsterdam and Philadelphia: John Benjamins, 2008), 189–217.

Lenker, Ursula, *Argument and Rhetoric. Adverbial Connectors in the History of English* (Berlin and Boston: Mouton de Gruyter, 2010).

López-Couso, María José, 'Grammar in Context: On the Role of Hypercharacterization in Language Variation and Change', in Kristin Bech and Ruth Moehlig-Falke, eds., *Grammar – Discourse – Context: Grammar and Usage in Language Variation and Change* (Berlin and Boston: Mouton de Gruyter, 2019), 335–66.

López-Couso, María José and Belén Méndez-Naya, 'Masked by Annotation: Minor Declarative Complementizers in *Parsed Corpora of Historical English'*, *Research in Corpus Linguistics* 8/2 (2020), 133–158. <https://doi.org/10.32714/ricl.08.02.07>, accessed 9 April 2022.

Moskowich Isabel and Leida María Monaco, 'Linking Ideas in Women's Writing: Evidence from the Coruña Corpus', *Revista de Lingüística y Lenguas Aplicadas* 11 (2016), 335–49.

Peterson, Peter G., 'Commas and Connective Adverbs', in Pam Peters, Peter Collins and Adam Smith, eds., *Comparative Studies in Australian and New Zealand English: Grammar and Beyond* (Amsterdam and Philadelphia: John Benjamins, 2009), 277–92.

Quirk, Randolph, Sidney Greenbaum, Geoffrey Leech, and Jan Svartvik, *A Comprehensive Grammar of the English Language* (London: Longman, 1985).

Rissanen, Matti, 'Optional *that* with Subordinators in Middle English', in Raymond Hickey and Puppel Stanislaw, eds., *Language History and Linguistic Modelling: A Festschrift for Jacek Fisiak on his 60th Birthday* (Berlin and Boston: Mouton de Gruyter, 1997), 373–83.

Rissanen, Matti, 'Towards an Integrated View of the Development of English: Notes on Causal Linking', in J. Fisiak and K. Marcin, eds., *Advances in English Historical Linguistics*. Trends in Linguistics, 112 (Berlin and Boston: De Gruyter Mouton, 1998), 389–406.

Rissanen, Matti, 'Syntax', in Richard. M. Hogg, ed., *The Cambridge History of the English Language. Vol. III: 1476–1776* (Cambridge: Cambridge University Press, 1999), 187–331.

Rissanen, Matti, 'The Development of Adverbial Subordinators in Early English', in Matti Rissanen, Leena Kahlas-Tarkka, Marianna Hintikka and Rod McConchie, eds., *Change in Meaning and the Meaning of Change: Studies in Semantics from Old to Present-Day English* (Helsinki: Société Néophilologique, 2007), 173–210.

Rissanen, Matti, 'On the Long History of English Adverbial Subordinators', in Anneli Meurman-Solin and Ursula Lenker, eds., *Connectives in Synchrony and Diachrony in European Languages* (Helsinki: The Research Unit for Variation, Contacts and Change in English (VARIENG) (Studies in Variation, Contacts and Change in English), 2011), <http://www.helsinki.fi/varieng/journal/volumes/08/rissanen/>, accessed 5 October 2019.

Uchida, Mitsumi and Yoko Iyeire, '*For* and *Because*: A Comparative Study of Causal Conjunctions in Caxton's *Paris* and *Vienne* and Three French Versions of the Same Text', in Mitsumi Uchida, Yoko Iyeiri and Lawrence Schourup, eds., *Language Contact and Variation in the History of English* (Japan: Kaitakusha, 2017), 61–79.

Visser, Frederik Theodor, *An Historical Syntax of the English Language*, Vol I–III. (Leiden: E. J. Brill, 1963–1973).

Wright, Aldis William, *The Bible Word-Book: A Glossary of Archaic Words and Phrases in the Authorized Version of the Bible and the Book of Common Prayer* (London: Macmillan and Co., 1884).

Miriam Criado-Peña

Demonstrative *them* in American English over Two Centuries (1820–2020)[1]

1. Introduction

The English demonstrative paradigm has traditionally distinguished four different forms according to the context shared by speakers in terms of proximity to the referent, be it either near (*this*, *these*) or distant (*that*, *those*). Grammatically speaking, these demonstratives can function as pronouns when they act as self-standing noun phrases (1) or as determiners when they precede the head of a noun phrase (2). When it comes to the use of plural determiners, however, the neutral form *them* is sometimes employed as a substitute of the plural forms *these* and *those*, especially in the case of the latter, as shown in (3).

(1) *Those* are interesting books
(2) *Those books* are interesting
(3) *Them books* are interesting

The use of modern *them* in these particular contexts goes back to Old English, more specifically, to Old English singular and plural dative forms *þaem*/*þam* (Maček 1995a: 225; 1995b: 243). Dialectal *them* as a variant of *these*/*those*, in turn, is thought to have its origin in the medieval period, when it was rendered in a wide array of forms. This is exemplified, for instance, in Yokota's (2006: 637) comparative study of *these*

1 The present research has been funded by the Spanish Ministry of Economy and Competitiveness (grant number PID2021-126496NB-I00). This grant is hereby gratefully acknowledged.

and *those* in three different texts of *Pricke of Conscience*, where manifold variants of *them*, including *þem*, *hem* and *þaim*, among others, were found in place of *those* in the three fourteenth-century texts surveyed. The first occurrence of demonstrative *them* before a plural noun, however, is not witnessed until the early Modern period. According to the *Oxford English Dictionary* (OED; Simpson and Weiner 1989), this variant is first recorded in 1596 ("To Samaria and *them* partes"), and thus it is deemed as a fairly late development in the history of the English language (Hazen, Hamilton and Vacovsky 2011: 77).

The substitution of plural *these*/*those* for *them* in Present-day English is considered to be a dialectal feature that is found in a broad range of vernacular dialects, including those spoken in the United Kingdom, the United States and the Caribbean (see, for example, Beal 2004; Schneider 2004; Hazen, Hamilton and Vacovsky 2011). In this respect, Pabst (2022: 136–7) gathered a collection of works where demonstrative *them* is attested in different varieties of English, as illustrated in Table 1.

Table 1: Demonstrative *them* across varieties (Retrieved from Pabst 2022: 136–7)

Geographic location	Variety	Author(s)
Suffolk, England	Suffolk English	Claxton (1981: 9)
North of England	Northern (England) English	Beal (2004: 119)
East Anglia, England	East Anglian English	Trudgill (2004: 148)
Glamorgan, Wales	Glamorgan English	Lewis (1990: 115)
Belfast, Northern Ireland	Belfast English	Henry (1995: 34)
New England, USA	New England English	Kurath et al. (1939: 620–5)
Texas and Louisiana, USA	African American English and Southern White Vernacular English	Cukor-Avila (2001:114)
Southern USA	Southern (US) English	Schneider (2003: 29)
USA	Urban African American English	Wolfram (2004: 333)
West Virginia, USA	Appalachian English	Hazen, Hamilton and Vacovsky (2011)
Newfoundland, Canada	Newfoundland English	Clarke (2004: 311)
New Brunswick, Canada	New Brunswick English	Kinloch (1985: 70)
North America and the Caribbean	"Most colloquial varieties"	Schneider (2004: 1114)

As gleaned from Table 1, *them* seems to be a widespread form within the demonstrative paradigm in many varieties of English worldwide. Its distribution has been explored by some scholars who have highlighted the scarce frequency of plural distal *those* among vernacular speakers as a result of the popularity of *them*. Wright (1905: 279) endorses this idea as he states that "[*t*]*hose* is seldom or never heard in genuine dialect speech. Its place is supplied by [*t*]*hem* in all the dialects of Sc[otland], Irel[and] and Eng[land]". The widespread use of demonstrative *them*, however, is not restricted to the United Kingdom inasmuch as it is also acknowledged to be "almost universal in North America and the Caribbean" (Schneider 2004: 1114). The other side of the coin is seen in standard British and American English, where this variant is not as common today on account of its high social stigmatization, although it appears to enjoy greater popularity among working-class speakers (Pabst 2022: 136). It therefore seems to be the case that the use of demonstrative *them* in place of *those* is "socially marked rather than regionally distinctive" (Schneider 2003: 27) and that speakers are aware of its function as a style marker and may even sometimes employ it in order to imitate an illiterate voice (Hazen, Hamilton and Vacovsky 2011: 82).

While the use of demonstrative *them* in some dialectal varieties of English has received some attention in the scholarly literature, no studies have focused on the diachronic development of the construction in American English from a corpus-based approach. In view of this gap in the literature, the present piece of research presents results from an analysis of a selection of the twenty most frequent constructions containing demonstrative *them* in American English so as to shed some light on the diachronic evolution of this variable and the influence that some linguistic and extralinguistic factors may have had upon the choice of demonstrative over the two centuries under study. In this vein, a threefold objective is pursued: (a) to analyse the historical development of demonstrative *them* in the period 1820–2020; (b) to investigate its use and distribution across text types in order to assess whether text typology is related to the selection of the demonstrative; and (c) to ascertain the contribution of a series of linguistic conditioning factors in the use of this variable. The following linguistic factors are considered: animacy (animate vs. inanimate); recoverability of antecedent (recoverable vs. unrecoverable); direction of reference (anaphoric vs. cataphoric); syntactic function (subject vs. object); and impact of quantifiers (quantified vs. non-quantified).

2. Methodology

The data used as source of evidence come from *The Corpus of Historical American English* (COHA). COHA, compiled by Mark Davies (2010) at Brigham Young University, is the largest structured corpus of historical English, covering a period of 200 years (1820–2020). This collection of texts is composed of more than 475 million words divided into more than 100,000 individual texts and it encompasses material from five different genres, namely TV/movies, fiction, popular magazines, newspapers and non-fiction books. The corpus has been carefully lemmatized and tagged for part-of-speech, allowing the user to search by words, phrases, lemmas, wildcards and more complex constructions such as a "most + ADJ + NOUN" (Davies 2010). Considering its size and interface, COHA enables researchers to investigate a wide range of linguistic changes that could not be explored with smaller corpora (Davies 2012: 258). This may be the case of low-frequency phenomena, making it an ideal tool for the study of demonstrative *them* in American English.

Table 2: *COHA* corpus word count

TV/Movies	Fiction	Popular Magazines	Newspapers	Non-fiction books	Total
40,035,257	222,380,834	106,238,951	45,203,769	61,173,020	475,031,831

As far as the methodological procedure is concerned, the complete set of instances was retrieved automatically using the web interface with the prompt "them + NOUN". The first step was to select the twenty most frequent constructions containing the demonstrative *them*. In this fashion, the following pairs have been selected, enumerated from the most to the least frequent one: *them things*; *them days*; *them boys*; *them people*; *them fellers*; *them guys*; *them horses*; *them folks*; *them men*; *them words*; *them kids*; *them fellows*; *them niggers*; *them children*; *them dogs*; *them clothes*; *them women*; *them places*; *them books*; and *them girls*. Next, a process of manual disambiguation was needed so as to rule out those instances beyond the scope of the study, that is, those cases where *them* does not act as a demonstrative, as shown in (4–5). All in all, the present work is based on a total of 2,299 instances.

(4) We're not supposed to call *them* boys, but that's what they are [COHA, 1987, FIC, BonfireVanities]
(5) While he spoke to *them* words of kindness and consolation [COHA, 1846, FIC, FactFictionACollection]

3. Analysis

3.1. Demonstrative Them *over Time*

This section is devoted to the historical development of demonstrative *them* in the period 1820–2020 on the basis of the data provided by the twenty most frequent noun phrases containing *them* as demonstrative. According to the *Dictionary of American Regional English* (DARE; Hall 2012), the earliest instance of the phenomenon is not found in American English until 1850 ("*Them* folks cum al the ways to help Me"). The diachronic study, however, demonstrates that this usage is an earlier innovation that can be traced back to previous decades. This variant is first recorded in COHA in the year 1822, as shown in (6–8):

(6) *Them* things did not seem to lay on her mind [COHA, 1822, FIC, New-EnglandTale]
(7) have got a book that treats upon hydrostatics and *them* things [COHA, 1822, FIC, New-EnglandTale]
(8) but he knew *them* words as well as the catechism [COHA, 1822, FIC, New-EnglandTale]

Figure 1 reproduces the distribution of demonstrative *them* over time in terms of normalized frequencies per million words and regardless of text typology. The results exhibit a proliferation of variant *them* that is observed throughout the entire nineteenth century. This variable appears to diffuse steadily from its emergence in 1822 until it reaches its peak at the beginning of the following century, rising from 4.78 to 14.49 occurrences. Since then, a different state of affairs with regard to the use of dialectal *them* is observed. In this respect, the data display a sharp decline in its popularity in the course of the twentieth century that is especially noteworthy towards the second half of the century to such an extent that its occurrence drops to 4.54 in the last twenty years.

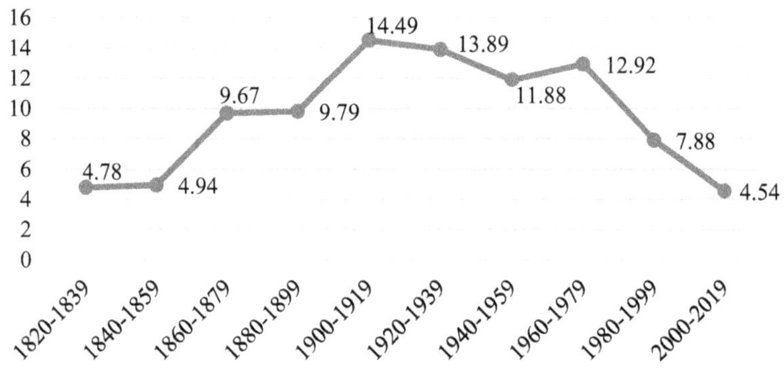

Figure 1: Demonstrative *them* over time (n.f.).

In spite of its use among vernacular speakers, the employment of *them* has been continuously stigmatized and categorized as vulgar or illiterate from its late start in the history of English. This is especially true for the twentieth century as a result of an upsurge in the publication of grammars, where this practice was censured, and of institutional indoctrination insofar as pupils were instructed to replace *them* for standard *those* in the written domain. In line with this, Maček (1995b: 241–242) argues that most descriptive standard English grammars do not even mention this use of *them*, which is neither included in relevant studies dealing with American usage that were published during the century. This absence might be interpreted as an indicator of its status as an uneducated or even a nonexistent form, whereas the use of *those* was the only option offered to the readers (Maček 1995b: 242). Demonstrative *them* is solely mentioned in a few standard grammars of English and, although it is not marked as ungrammatical, it is censored as vulgar in all of them. The phenomenon received attention for the first time in Murray's *English Grammar* (1824: 136) where he refers to it as a "fault"[2] and after that, it was categorized as a signal of illiteracy or vulgarity in both *Webster's Dictionary of English Usage* (Webster 1898: 897–8)[3] and *The American Language: An Inquiry into the Development of English in the United States* (Mencken 1949: 451)[4]. At the time, some publications focused instead on the "irregular" aspects of the language and, among them, this usage of *them* is mentioned in *The Vulgarities of Speech Corrected* (1829), also regarded as vulgar and even as ungrammatical:

> Among grammatical mistakes, I may mention the use of one little word, which occurs so often, that if it be improperly introduced, is a certain mark of vulgarity, I mean the word "them," when it is used instead of "these," or "those;" as when you say, "I have done *them* things now," instead of "those things;" or when you say, "*them* colours are very pretty," for "those colours are very pretty." The only way in which you can discover this error, and correct it, is to try whether you can put "those" or "these" instead of *them*, and always do so when you can (Anonymous 1829: 210–11).

In light of this negative attitude towards the use of demonstrative *them* over time, it seems evident that its decline in the course of the twentieth century is surely associated with the impetus received from grammarians, who systematically claimed for the use of the standard form *those* in these particular contexts, together with the influence that

2 "Many persons are apt, in conversation, to put the objective case of the personal pronouns, in the place of *these* and *those*: as, 'Give me them books;' instead of 'Give me those books.' We may sometimes find this fault even in writing" (Murray 1824: 136).

3 "[T]he demonstrative *them* is now largely restricted to the speech of the uneducated and to the familiar speech of others" (Webster 1989: 898).

4 "Of demonstrative pronouns, there are but two in Standard English, *this* and *that*, with their plural forms, *these* and *those*. To them, vulgar American adds a third, *them*, which is also the personal pronoun of the third person" (Mencken 1949: 451).

schoolmasters exerted in favour of the standard plural form. The fact that the new generations were taught to restrict or even eliminate this usage of *them* in schools was probably a decisive factor contributing to its wane in popularity, and consequently to its drastic drop towards the second half of the twentieth century. In this regard, Allen (1976: 1977) investigated the use of dialectal *them* in New England English during the late 1940s and the early 1950s. The results of his study point to a shift in attitude towards its usage that is manifested in its popularity among the different age groups. Among them, 60 per cent of the oldest group of informants used *them*, whilst only 22 per cent of the middle-aged speakers employed the word in these environments. Curiously enough, none of the youngest informants preferred this variant form (Allen 1976: 58–9; 1977: 10–11), hence corroborating its rejection among the different generations over time (see also Hazen, Hamilton and Vacovsky 2011: 93–4). It can be therefore tentatively concluded that the use of demonstrative *them* was growing in popularity in the vernaculars during the nineteenth century, but its censorship in grammars and school textbooks resulted in an increase of social stigma and in a consequent denial from speakers, who increasingly opted for the plural standard forms.

3.2. Demonstrative Them *across Text Types*

The present section delves into the distribution of demonstrative *them* across text types. In this respect, five different genres have been analysed so as to evaluate whether or not its use is related to text typology: fiction books; magazines; popular newspapers; non-fiction/academic books; and TV/movies.

The results displayed in Figure 2 point to the twentieth century as a key period in the development of vernacular *them*, with a gradual decrease in its usage regardless of text typology. This period therefore marks off the beginning of a more conservative attitude towards the employment of plural demonstratives in the United States, a practice that progressively became the standard in both the spoken and written domains. Some differences in its use, however, can be noted across text types. In her study of demonstrative *them*, Maček suggested that even though it emerged in the nineteenth century in order to indicate non-standard speech, "[a] century and a half later it seems to be spreading 'up market' in spoken varieties" (1995b: 245). The findings, however, refute the idea of this variant becoming more reputable among society in view of the low incident of the phenomenon seen in magazines, newspapers and academic books, being its usage almost negligible throughout the two centuries under study. Bearing in mind that these three genres represent the more formal styles of writing, it is then not surprising that the use of the non-standard form is found to be more constrained within them.

A different picture is observed in the case of "speech-like" genres (see Culpeper and Kytö 2010: 17), depicted in both fiction books and TV/movies, as they manifest a significantly higher occurrence of *them* in their datasets. Interestingly enough, these two genres seem to follow the same trend observed in the diachronic development of the variant, exhibiting a progressive decrease of the non-standard usage in the course of the twentieth century, even though evolving at a different rate in each text type. The higher proportion of *them* in these two genres may be explained if its usage as a style marker is considered since, as mentioned above, it has been acknowledged that speakers often make use of the variant in an effort to put on an uneducated voice. In fact, a closer look at the evidence reveals that a substantial number of instances attested in fiction books and TV/movies corresponds to the use of reported speech and to the portrayal of fictional characters belonging to certain socioeconomic or academic backgrounds, as demonstrated in (9) and (10), respectively. It is in this respect that Webster affirmed that the use of demonstrative *them* today is largely restricted to the speech of illiterate speakers and that, consequently, it is mostly detected in the same places as other words of a similar status, that is, in speech-like genres as well as "in the familiar usage of educated people when they are being humorous", especially in the twentieth century (1989: 898).

(9) "*Them* fellers ain't fooling away their time," Milton said gravely. [COHA, 1912, FIC, ElkanLublinerAmerican]

(10) They's some places whur it iz ez *them* folks o' oum kin move around free as frogs in a muddy pond. [COHA, 1993, FIC, ShiningOnes]

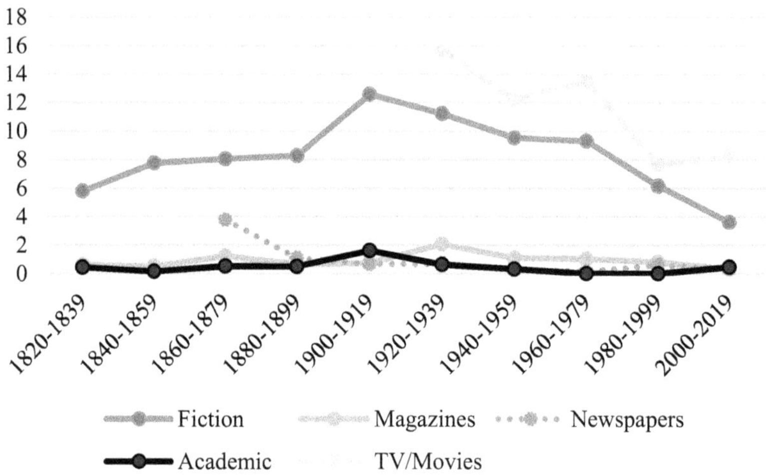

Figure 2: Demonstrative *them* across text types (n.f.).

Given the fact that fiction books are mostly taken as a representation of the written domain and TV/movies represent oral communication, the different rate of vernacular *them* observed in these two fictional genres suggest an opposite trend in the usage of singular and plural demonstratives in terms of the dichotomy speech-based vs. written-based text types. A higher proportion of *them* as a variant of standard distal *those* is found in the TV/movies dataset (in contrast to its lower frequency in fiction books), these results contrasting those obtained by Halliday and Hasan in their investigation of the patterns of anaphoric usage of *this* and *that* across text types. In their work, they argue that "in narrative of a traditional kind [. . .] we often find *that*, where in conversational narrative, a speaker would tend to use *this*, conveying a sense of immediacy and also of solidarity with the hearer, of shared interest and attention" (1976: 61). Following this rationale, fiction books would be expected to be more prone than television to the employment of *them*, although the numbers point to the opposite. This may, however, be partly explained considering the fact that TV/movies are scripted and therefore conversations are not spontaneous.

As far as the usage of the non-standard form *them* in TV/movies is concerned, Hazen, Hamilton and Vacovsky (2011) comment on the effect of broadcast media on speakers in the Appalachian region indicating that its presence in the media mostly consists of "parodies and stereotypes of Appalachian speakers, and [that] it is with this metalanguage that [they] have become more aware of what dialect features are stigmatized" (2011: 99). The stigmatization of vernacular features on television may therefore be correlated with its decline as a variant of *those* in the country as it made speakers cognizant of the social stigma that it carried.

3.3. Linguistic Conditioning Factors

Previous studies have confirmed the contribution of a number of linguistic factors in the choice of demonstratives in English, including some such as recoverability of antecedent, antecedent type, phoric type, proximity and syntactic environment, among others (see, for example, Maček 1995a; Botley and McEnery 2001; Hazen, Hamilton and Vacovsky 2011). In line with this, this section evaluates the influence of a series of linguistic factors so as to cast some light on their participation with regard to the use of demonstrative *them* in American English. The following factors have been considered: (a) animacy; (b) recoverability of antecedent; (c) direction of reference; (d) syntactic function; and (e) influence of quantifiers. Importantly enough, the present analysis does not consider proximity as a factor (i.e. proximal/distal semantic contexts) despite having been traditionally regarded as influential in the selection of demonstratives in English. Scholars have generally agreed upon the fact that demonstrative *them* can be used in lieu of both *these* and *those*, however, evidence has demonstrated that it functions as a demonstrative substituting standard distal *those* in the vast majority of the cases. In fact, Map 624 of the *Linguistic Atlas of New England* proves that while 45.7 per cent of participants would replace *these* with vernacular *them* in the phrase "these fellows", 88.6 per cent of the informants who would use the variant in the phrase "those boys" (Kurath et al. 1939; Pabst 2022: 137). The instances obtained from the corpus exhibit an overwhelming proportion of *them* as a substitute of *those* in these syntactic environments and, consequently, the proximal/distal distinction has not been taking into consideration.

The selection of some of the linguistic factors that have been assessed is partly based on two previous works dealing with the distribution of demonstratives in English, namely Botley and McEnery's (2001) work on the standard demonstrative pronouns *this*, *that*, *these* and *those* and Hazen, Hamilton and Vacovsky's (2011) article on demonstrative *them* in Appalachian English. The first linguistic factor that has been considered is the *animacy* of the complement, divided into two groups according to whether they are animate or inanimate entities, as exemplified in (11) and (12), respectively.

(11) She tells *them men* anything they want to hear [COHA, 1969, FIC, ChosenPlaceThe]
(12) That's what you have to pay for in *them places* [COHA, 1931, FIC, XXXYYY]

The second potential conditioning factor is *recoverability of antecedent*, that is, the relationship between a particular demonstrative expression and its referent (Botley and McEnery 2001: 9). In this fashion, the referent can be *recoverable* when it occurs in the preceding or the following textual context (13) or *unrecoverable* (14) when there is no other mention to the item in the discourse.

(13) And the way he could talk about things and the way he had of saying hello to everybody like he was giving away something. That's what you was crazy about, and that ain't changed. I don't know. *Them things* couldn't change in Johnny, not even if he tried [COHA, 1945, TV/MOV, San Antonio]
(14) "It shows a curve in the drive, with one of them green motor busses goin' by, the top loaded, and off in the background to one side the Palisades loomin' up against a fair-weather sunset, while in the middle you can see clear up to Yonkers. Honest, it's almost as good as some of *them things* on the insurance calendars, and I'm standin' gawpin' at it when Brooks Bladen and Marjorie drifts along" [COHA, 1914, FIC, WithTorchy]

The third factor under evaluation is the *direction of reference*, which can be either anaphoric (15) or cataphoric (16). *Reference* can be defined as a type of cohesion that indicates the fact that a particular piece of information needs to be retrieved from elsewhere (Halliday and Hasan 1976: 31). Two different types of references can be distinguished according to whether or not the item that is being alluded to is mentioned within the text. The term *exophora* is employed for those cases where the item is missing in the textual context, while *endophora* is used in the opposite contexts. The present study, however, is only concerned with endophoric reference and further categorizes it into anaphoric (backward pointing to a preceding textual unit) or cataphoric (forward pointing to a following element), illustrated in (15) and (16), respectively.

(15) Nasty zombie meths up there. *Them boys* were chewing their faces off. [COHA, 2017, TV/Movies, Snatch]

(16) I was fishin' in *them days*, when you go to New York [COHA, 1912, FIC, DepotMaster]

Syntactically speaking, a demonstrative can function as a *subject* or as an *object* in a sentence, as shown in examples (17–18). Bearing this in mind, the *syntactic function* of vernacular *them* is also investigated in order to determine if this factor is related to its usage.

(17) *Them* fellers was made to travel [COHA, 1887, FIC, AdriftsInWilds]

(18) I reckon *them* fellers is pretty sure to git one of us yit [COHA, 1906, FIC, BobHamptonPlacer]

Finally, the *impact of quantifiers* on the use of non-standard *them* is also taken into consideration insofar as it has been deemed as influential in some previous discussions on demonstratives (see Yokota 2006; Hazen, Hamilton and Vacovsky 2011). Two different categories are therefore distinguished: the first including the instances where demonstrative *them* is modified by a preceding quantifier (i.e. *quantified*) and the second containing those cases where there is no quantifier present (i.e. *non-quantified*), as illustrated in (19) and (20), respectively.

(19) But *all them* days is past and gone [COHA, 1866, FIC, DiversViewsOpinions]

(20) But why didn't you never come home *them* days? [COHA, 1920, FIC, Play:AnnaChristie]

Table 3: Assessment of linguistic factors (per cent)

Animacy	Animate	60.99
	Inanimate	39.01
Recoverability of antecedent	Recoverable	58.63
	Unrecoverable	41.37
Direction of reference	Anaphoric	86.20
	Cataphoric	13.80
Syntactic function	Subject	26.05
	Object	73.95
Impact of quantifiers	Quantified	18.23
	Non-quantified	81.77

Table 3 presents the frequency of demonstrative *them* in American English in light of the five linguistic factors analysed. As gleaned from the data, the use of *them* when it modifies an animate entity substantially outnumbers the instances where it is followed by an inanimate complement, with a rate of 60.99 per cent and 39.01 per cent, respectively. Curiously enough, this pattern does not account for some vernaculars, as in the case of the English spoken in the Appalachian region, where the non-standard form is, on the contrary, more widely disseminated when it accompanies inanimate complements (Hazen, Hamilton and Vacovsky 2011: 88–9). Hence, the influence of animacy may not be interpreted in relation to a specific phenomenon, but as a factor triggering alternative forms across varieties.

Among the different linguistic factors evaluated, the recoverability of the antecedent is the least influential when it comes to the use of *them* in these particular environments. Notwithstanding this, the vernacular form appears to be somewhat preferred when the referent occurs within the preceding or following textual context, with a percentage of 58.63 per cent in comparison with the other 41.37 per cent of the instances where it is unrecoverable. A systematic diffusion of the phenomenon is, in turn, witnessed when the referent precedes the substitute to such an extent that it amounts up to 86.20 per cent of the instances containing recoverable elements. According to Botley (1999: 156), "it has been observed already that cataphora is less common than anaphora" and therefore, "[t]he general preference for anaphora is no surprise". Botley and McEnery (2001: 18–19) endorse this tenet as they identify a striking preference for anaphoric reference as regards the use of standard demonstratives in English. Their analysis show a general consensus among informants on the use of this type of reference with a total amount of 1,456 instances in opposition to only 19 instances where cataphora is favoured. This is particularly the case of plural distal *those* since no instances of cataphora are found after it, a practice that is possibly also adopted by users of *them*.

In terms of its syntactic function, the use of *them* predominates when it acts as the object of a sentence, showing a rate of 73.95 per cent. One possible explanation that has been suggested for this tendency is the fact that variants can sometimes develop syntactic trends on the basis of certain lexical collocations (Hazen, Hamilton and Vacovsky 2011: 92). In view of this assumption, the five most frequent noun clauses containing *them* are compared with the five least frequent ones in light of its function within the sentence so as to discern whether or not this is the reason for the unequal distribution of the variable.

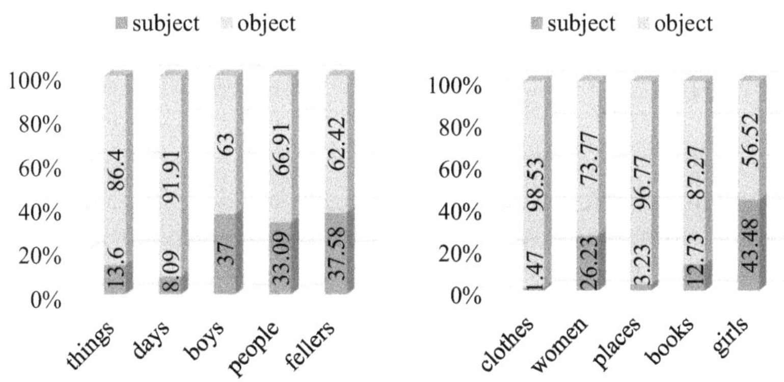

Figure 3: Demonstrative *them* according to its frequency and syntactic function (per cent).

The results displayed in Figure 3 do not corroborate this tenet in the particular case of vernacular *them* insofar as the frequency of lexical collocations do not seem to contribute to a higher use of the variable. Interestingly enough, however, the data suggest a correlation between the syntactic function of *them* and the animacy of the complement. In this fashion, a more widespread employment of the variant when it acts as the subject of the sentence is exhibited when it precedes animate entities (i.e. *boys*, *people*, *fellers*, *women* and *girls*) as opposed to the lower frequencies noted in combination with inanimate complements (i.e. *things*, *days*, *clothes*, *places* and *books*). The animate-inanimate dichotomy is therefore taken as a contributing factor that plays a pivotal role in the syntactic function of variants, at least in the particular case of demonstrative *them*.

Finally, the impact of quantifiers is the most influential factor considering that it presents a sharp contrast in terms of the dissemination of the phenomenon, which diffuses more widely when it is not modified by a quantifier, representing 81.72 per cent vs. 18.2 per cent in the presence of these words. The contexts where a demonstrative is not premodified are then considered to favour the use of the non-standard form, thus following the same trend as other varieties of English, such as Appalachian English (Hazen, Hamilton and Vacovsky 2011: 88–9).

4. Conclusions

The present paper has investigated the diachronic development of *them* as a demonstrative in American English paying attention to its distribution over time in the period 1820–2020 and its variation across text types. A number of conditioning linguistic factors have also been examined to ascertain whether or not its dissemination is the result of the particularities of the linguistic context. The study has led me to the following conclusions.

Firstly, the diachronic analysis has corroborated the deployment of demonstrative *them* as a nineteenth-century phenomenon. The variant grew significantly in popularity since its emergence in the 1820s until the beginning of the following century, when a shift of attitude towards its usage is witnessed. The results point to grammars, school textbooks and television programmes as the leading forces behind the fall of *them* in the United States, a practice that progressively became the standard in the course of the twentieth century. In this regard, the stigmatization and censorship of vernacular features in both the written and the oral sources examined are surely associated with the steady decline of the variant.

Secondly, text typology has also proved to be a decisive factor contributing to the choice of the form in American English. The data reveal a conservative practice in the more formal genres, namely magazines, newspapers and academic books, in light of the low incidence of demonstrative *them* manifested in these types of texts, which is found to be almost negligible throughout the two centuries under study. A different state of affairs, however, is observed in the case of speech-like genres (i.e. fiction books and TV/movies), as they exhibit a wider dissemination of the non-standard form. The higher proportion of *them* in these two genres can be explained on account of its usage as a style marker, being commonly employed in an effort to put on an illiterate voice. This usage is represented in fiction books, mostly in the expression of reported speech, and in the media with the portrayal of fictional characters from particular socioeconomic or academic backgrounds with a tendency towards the use of the non-standard form.

Thirdly, a selection of potential conditioning linguistic factors has also been evaluated in terms of their influence upon the use of vernacular *them*. Among them, the factors showing the sharpest contrast as regards the presence/absence of the variable are the direction of the reference in the case of recoverable items, the syntactic function of *them* in the sentence and the impact of quantifiers on its use. Overall, the study has demonstrated that demonstrative *them* is preferred in the following linguistic environnments: (a) when it accompanies an animate entity; (b) when the referent it alludes to is followed in the preceding textual context, that is, when it is recoverable and the reference is anaphoric; (c) when it functions as the object of the sentence, especially when it is found in combination with inanimate entities; and (d) when it is not premodified by a quantifier.

Source

Davies, Mark, *Corpus of Historical American English* (Brigham Young University, 2010). Available at https://www.english-corpora.org/coha/.

References

Allen, Harold B., *The Linguistic Atlas of the Upper Midwest* (Minneapolis: University of Minnesota Press, 1976).

Allen, Harold B., 'The Linguistic Atlas of the Upper Midwest as a Source of Sociolinguistic Information' in James C. Raymond and I. Willis Russell, eds., *James B. McMillan: Essays in Linguistics by his Friends and Colleagues* (Alabama: The University of Alabama Press, 1977), 3–21.

Anonymous, *The Vulgarities of Speech Corrected: With Elegant Expressions for Provincial and Vulgar English, Scots and Irish; for the Use of Those Who Are Unacquainted with Grammar* (London: F. C. Westley, 1829).

Beal, Joan, 'English Dialects in the North of England: Morphology and Syntax', in Bernd Kortmann, Kate Burridge, Rajend Mesthrie, Edgar W. Schneider and Clive Upton, eds., *A Handbook of Varieties of English. Volume 2: Morphology and Syntax* (Berlin and New York: Mouton de Gruyter, 2004), 114–41.

Botley, Simon, 'Corpora and Discourse Anaphora: Using Corpus Evidence to Test Theoretical Claims', PhD thesis (Lancaster University, 1999).

Botley, Simon and Tony McEnery, 'Demonstratives in English: A Corpus-Based Study', *Journal of English Linguistics* 29/1 (2001), 7–33.

Clarke, Sandra, 'Newfoundland English: Morphology and Syntax' in Bernd Kortmann, Kate Burridge, Rajend Mesthrie, Edgar W. Schneider and Clive Upton, eds., *A Handbook of Varieties of English. Volume 2: Morphology and Syntax* (Berlin and New York: Mouton de Gruyter, 2004), 303–18.

Claxton, Alic O. D., *The Suffolk Dialect of the 20th Century* (Suffolk: Boydell Press, 1981).

Cukor-Avila, Patricia, 'Co-Existing Grammars: The Relationship between the Evolution of African American and White Vernacular English in the South', in Sonja L. Lanehart, ed., *Sociocultural and Historical Contexts of African American English* (Amsterdam and Philadelphia: John Benjamins, 2001), 93–127.

Culpeper, Jonathan and Merja Kytö, *Early Modern English Dialogues: Spoken Interaction as Writing* (Cambridge: Cambridge University Press, 2010).

Davies, Mark, 'The 400 Million Word Corpus of Historical American English (1810–2009)', in Irén Hegedüs and Alexandra Fodor, eds., *English Historical Linguistics 2010* (Amsterdam and Philadelphia: John Benjamins, 2012), 231–62.

Hall, Joan H., ed., *Dictionary of American Regional English*, Vol. 5 (Cambridge: Harvard University Press, 2012).

Halliday, M. A. K. and Ruqaiya Hasan, *Cohesion in English* (Hong Kong: Longman, 1976).

Hazen, Kirk, Sarah Hamilton and Sarah Vacovsky, 'The Fall of Demonstrative *them*: Evidence from Appalachia', *English World-Wide* 32/1 (2011), 74–103.

Henry, Alison, *Belfast English and Standard English: Dialect Variation and Parameter Setting* (Oxford: Oxford University Press, 1995).

Kinloch, A. Murray, 'The English Language in New Brunswick 1784–1984' in Reavley Gair, ed., *A Literary and Linguistic History of New Brunswick* (Fredericton: Fiddlehead Poetry Books and Goose Lane Editions, 1985), 60–75.

Kurath, Hans, Bernard Hanley, Julia Bloch, Guy S. Lowman and Marcus L. Hansen, eds., *Linguistic Atlas of New England (LANE),* Vols. 1–3 (Providence: Brown University for the American Council of Learned Societies, 1939).

Lewis, J. Windsor, 'Syntax and Lexis in Glamorgan English', in Nikolas Coupland and Alan L. Thomas, eds., *English in Wales: Diversity, Conflict, Change* (Avon: Multilingual Matters, 1990), 109–20.

Maček, Dora, 'The Development and Function of the Dialectal *them*', *Studia Romanica et Anglica Zagrabiensia* XL (1995a), 221–235.

Maček, Dora, 'The Continuity of the Dialectal *them*', *Studia Romanica et Anglica Zagrabiensia* XL (1995b), 241–6.

Mencken, H. L., *The American Language: An Inquiry into the Development of English in the United States*. 4th edition (New York: Alfred A. Knopf, 1949).

Murray, Lindley, *English Grammar, Adapted to the Different Classes of Learners. With an Appendix, Containing Rules and Observations for Assisting the More Advanced Students to Write with Perspicuity and Accuracy* (Bridgeport: Josiah B. Baldwin, 1824).

Pabst, Katharina, 'Putting "the Other Maine" on the Map: Language Variation, Local Affiliation, and Co-Occurrence in Aroostook County English', PhD thesis (University of Toronto, 2022).

Schneider, Edgar W., 'Shakespeare in the Coves and Hollows? Towards a History of Southern English', in Stephen J. Nagle and Sarah L. Sanders, eds., *English in the Southern United States* (Cambridge and New York: Cambridge University Press, 2003), 17–35.

Schneider, Edgar W., 'Synopsis: Morphological and Syntactic Variation in the Americas and the Caribbean', in Bernd Kortmann, Kate Burridge, Rajend Mesthrie, Edgar W. Schneider and Clive Upton, eds., *A Handbook of Varieties of English. Volume 2: Morphology and Syntax* (Berlin and New York: Mouton de Gruyter, 2004), 1104–15.

Simpson, John A. and Edmund Weiner, eds, *Oxford English Dictionary*, 2nd edition [CD-Rom] (Oxford: Oxford University Press, 1989).

Trudgill, Peter, 'The Dialect of East Anglia', in Bernd Kortmann, Kate Burridge, Rajend Mesthrie, Edgar W. Schneider and Clive Upton, eds., *A Handbook of Varieties of English. Volume 2: Morphology and syntax* (Berlin and New York: Mouton de Gruyter, 2004), 142–53.

Webster, Noah, *Webster's Dictionary of English Usage* (Springfield: Merriem-Webster Inc., 1898).

Wolfram, Walt, 'Urban African Vernacular English: Morphology and Syntax', in Bernd Kortmann, Kate Burridge, Rajend Mesthrie, Edgar W. Schneider and Clive Upton, eds., *A Handbook of Varieties of English. Volume 2: Morphology and Syntax* (Berlin and New York: Mouton de Gruyter, 2004), 319–40.

Wright, Joseph, *The English Dialect Grammar* (Oxford: Clarendon, 1905).

Yokota, Yumi, 'A Study of *these* and *those* in Three Different Texts of *Pricke of Conscience*', *English Studies* 87/6 (2006), 631–43.

Jesús Fernández-Domínguez

Tracking Down Marginal Productivity: The Suffix *-ment* between 1820 and 2019

1. Introduction

The term *available* is used in word-formation studies in reference to morphological processes which can be employed for productive coinage at a given time. *Availability* is often depicted alongside *profitability* – the number of lexemes that a process can coin –, and together they conform the hypernym *morphological productivity*. Availability is in this context the qualitative side of productivity, while profitability represents its quantitative side. The division of productivity into profitability and availability was not made explicit until Corbin (1987) and, in contrast to the assiduous attention directed at the former, the latter concept still stands as a slippery one (Bauer 2001: 49; Palmer 2015).

The notion of availability gets particularly equivocal in the area of language change because the fact that a morphological process is available at a given time in the history of the language does not necessarily mean that it will be available at a later stage. This involves not only that "statements of availability are temporally limited" (Bauer 2001: 205; see Bauer, Lieber and Plag 2013: 32), but also that there must exist a *locus* for the transition from availability to unavailability, and vice versa. If, as is widely agreed, availability is a non-gradable concept, word-formationists should be able to detect that transitional point and describe its nature. This need is perceived as growing in the light of accounts like Bauer, Lieber and Plag's (2013: 198–201), who refer in passing to morphological processes that allegedly stopped being productive in the past but where lexical activity seems to have revived. A case in point is that of *-ment*, a nominalizing suffix whose productive capacity peaked during the eighteenth and nineteenth centuries and which has been in progressive decline since (see Bauer 2001; Palmer 2015: 126). The suffix *-ment* creates deverbal nominalizations, very frequently expressing the category ACTION, and its status today is ambiguous between available and unavailable, given recent reports on occasional creations that make it impossible to catalogue *-ment* as obsolete (Kawaletz and Plag 2015; Kawaletz 2023).

With the above in mind, the aims of this paper are:

(i) to explore and contextualize the evolution of *-ment* actional derivation in the 1820s–2010s time frame, and
(ii) to assess the extent to which corpora and dictionaries can offer insights into the status of marginally productive processes.

In what follows, I first discuss the circumstances and factors surrounding the development of the suffix *-ment* and English nominalization in Section 2, while details on the data selection process are given in Section 3. The findings of the analysis are presented in Setion 4, and Section 5 offers the conclusions.

2. The Rise and Fall of the Suffix *-ment*

Morphological productivity is arguably one of the most contested areas of research in contemporary lexical morphology, a deep-rooted concept that can be traced back to the beginnings of modern linguistics. Prominent views of productivity are Schultink's (1961) understanding that it is the possibility for language-users to coin unintentionally an infinite number of new formations, or Bauer's (2001: 211) remark that productivity is "ambiguous between the sense 'availability' and the sense 'profitability'". The publication of works addressing productivity from a theoretical perspective is unceasing and takes place from all schools of morphology, the main difficulty being reconciling their different understanding of the phenomenon (Anshen and Aronoff 1988;

Dressler and Ladányi 2000; Bauer 2001; Gaeta and Ricca 2006). The tendency of most studies up to the mid-twentieth century was to concentrate on the synchronic description of morphological processes, and a subsequent turn was to broaden the scope of research on to the diachronic evolution of specific rules (Dalton-Puffer 1994; Cowie and Dalton-Puffer 2002; Palmer 2015).

The study of diachronic productivity necessarily means considering the very scope of word formation, in the sense that, even if studied synchronically, the target of this discipline is neologisms, i.e. words which exist at a given point but did not exist before then. This temporal component is inherent to word formation, but the delimitation of the discipline is partly shaped by the misleading boundary between synchrony and diachrony. We would for instance agree that the study of a phenomenon occurring between 1500 and 1900 would be a matter of diachrony, similarly also for the span 1700–1900. However, the more that temporal window is narrowed, the more complex it is to discern when we have moved out of diachrony into synchrony. Word-formation research between 1850 and 1900 would be probably regarded as synchronic, but would the analysis of a linguistic feature between 1800 and 1900 be a matter of one, or of the other? No answer is straightforward in this case, but it seems evident that the decisive factor distinguishing synchronic and diachronic word formation is a quantitative one, also because "diachronic changes leave synchronic traces in the morphology" (Bauer 2001: 26). For the purposes of this paper, I adhere to a *panchronique* (Tournier 1985: 65) or *synchronic-diachronic* (Marchand 1969: 8) conception of word formation, where a certain leeway is allowed for the impact of the output of derivation (see Bauer 1983: 64; Dressler and Ladányi 2000: 128; Cowie and Dalton-Puffer 2002: 417–21).

One pivotal matter in productivity studies is that concerning its measurement. The applied side of productivity has been the focus of numerous studies starting from Neuhaus (1973) neologism-based calculations and Aronoff's (1976) relativized approach, which lie at the root of essentially all subsequent models, be them dictionary- (Anshen and Aronoff 1999) or corpus-based (Baayen 1992, 2009; Gaeta and Ricca 2006).

One of the complexities in this sphere lies in the definition of productivity "not in terms of the number of existing forms, but rather in terms of the *likelihood* that new forms will enter the language" (Anshen and Aronoff 1988: 643, my emphasis; see also Dressler and Ladányi 2000: 104, 106). A fundamental paradox is found in the fact that only attested data – be it corpus or dictionary – can be used for the quantification of a phenomenon that is essentially all about potential. Kastovsky (1986: 593) was a forerunner in detecting such contradiction: "it is this frequency of rule application which we usually call productivity – and we tend to forget that this concept refers to both competence and performance at the same time". Both corpus and dictionary models are fraught with pros and cons, for example regarding how concepts like *new word*, *point in time*, or *neologism* are conceived, even more so because such models were originally devised for computations of synchronic productivity, and hence the diachronic component often implies forcing their manoeuvrability. In the case of English, however, lexicographic tools like the OED or textual corpora like *The Corpus of Historical American English* (COHA; Davies 2010) compensates some, not all, of the existing limitations (see Anshen and Aronoff 1999: 18–20; Cowie and Dalton-Puffer 2002: 418–21). Lieber (2014: 88) is clear in this regard:

> By their very nature, dictionaries look for a certain threshhold of usage before a word comes to be recorded, so the low frequency and item unfamiliar forms that stand to tell us the most about derivational patterns are often not to be found. Moreover, the more compositional the meaning of a derived word, the less it actually needs to be recorded in the dictionary.

Be that as it may, assumptions underpinning all productivity models are (i) that morphological productivity can be measured; (ii) that morphological processes can be ranked from more to less productive; and (iii) that the productivity index of a process may oscillate in time, be it upwards or downwards (see Dressler and Ladányi 2000: 127–31). These three factors converge in the case of *-ment*.

The suffix *-ment* is the archetypal example of a rule with a considerable past productivity degree but subsequent decline in morphological activity. The productive output of *-ment* was prominent from the twelfth century and peaked between the seventeenth and the nineteenth centuries by attaching especially to Romance (*abandonment*, *tracement*) and Germanic roots (*emboxment*, *fakement*). From that period on its lexical activity progressively diminished, to the point that the suffix has been already regarded as unproductive in Present-Day English (Anshen and Aronoff 1999: 24; Bauer 2001: 8; Lieber 2014: 88; Palmer 2015: 126). It is nevertheless noteworthy that new sporadic forms in *-ment* are reported in the same publications, frequently interpreted as inventive creations more than as the result of productive word formation (Bauer, Lieber and Plag 2013: 198–200; Kawaletz and Plag 2015: 293). Formations like those in (1) cast doubts on the current status of *-ment* and make it impossible to definitely declare it as unavailable:

(1) alertment, ambushment, approvement, divorcement, fakement

One of the alleged reasons for the decrease in the productivity of *-ment* is the emergence of competing nominalizers in the same morphological environment, which triggers a situation of rivalry. Morphological competition has been largely explored from the early 2000s and, in short, takes place when two or more word-formation patterns can express the same syntactic-semantic category, and hence contend with each other for coinage (see Štekauer 2017). In the case of *-ment*, frequent rivals are deverbal conversion and the affixes *-al* and derivational *-ing*. This study attempts to explain the diminished productivity of *-ment* precisely by monitoring not just its scope of action, but also that of its rivals. To that end, the study devises clusters of competing nominalizations (Section 3) and identifies and comments on their patterns of behaviour (Section 4).

3. Data Processing

For the purposes of tracking down the evolution of *-ment* from the nineteenth century up to the present day, the COHA was selected on account of its features: it contains c. 475 million words of American English texts covering the 1820s–2010s period, it is balanced for domains and sub-genres, and its part-of-speech (POS) tagging has an error rate of only 1.5 per cent[1]. The COHA was scanned for *-ment* coinages from

1 COHA uses the CLAWS tagger (https://ucrel.lancs.ac.uk/claws).

the 1820s–2010s time frame, each supplemented with information from the *Oxford English Dictionary* (Proffitt 2019). This makes it possible to detect changes in the historical behaviour of the process, and it also evidences that results of low productivity differ depending on the perspective and method adopted.

Because our objective is to account for the allegedly marginal productivity of *-ment*, it was crucial for the method to circumvent both derivatives with a high COHA frequency – because high corpus values are indicative of lexicalization, in turn irrelevant to productive word formation – and derivatives not attested presently – because that would imply that the unit does not exist as per the corpus standards. The focus was hence shifted towards *-ment* units attested once in the period 2015–2019. Two facts support this decision:

(i) *Hapax legomena* – frequency-1 entries in a corpus – are an oft-cited resource in corpus-based productivity measurements. Originally introduced by Baayen (Baayen 1992, 2009), hapaxes have become a benchmark for productivity models because they are interpreted as a sign of potential productivity. Baayen's reasoning is as follows: when a word-formation process A is very productive, it will create a high number of different types, while a less productive process B will create fewer new types. All the different units (*types*) of B will in principle be attested in a given corpus during sampling given their lower quantity, but the productive potential of A will cause a number of its types to pass unnoticed, or to be sampled in the corpus only once. In morphological processes like A, hapaxes reveal not only actual attestations, but also to what extent other derivatives of that process are expected to be coined, even if not attested yet. Hapax-based models have become an archetype for productivity measurement and their use is extensive (Gaeta and Ricca 2006), although concern over their theoretical foundations has been voiced too (Bauer 2001: 147–56). In particular, low frequency ranges abound in morphologically complex forms, but also in typos, misspellings and erroneous entries in general, so a strictly automatic or unfiltered handling of hapaxes will lead to inaccurate findings.

(ii) 2015–2019 is the most recent time range available in the COHA. By restricting searches to this period, it is possible to discover *-ment* hapaxes used then, independent of their (non-)attestation at an earlier stage. This procedure affords a snapshot of units with a very low usage today before considering whether such usage reflects an upwards or downwards productivity trend, i.e. whether *-ment* is dying out or whether it is recovering its lexical potential. In doing so, the bias is avoided of lexemes which entered the written language once and never completely left it – because written records are permanent. In this sense, Hohenhaus (2005: 362) stresses that overlooking the enduring nature of written texts “may have a distorting effect especially for corpus-based studies, unless frequency is overtly linked with specific time-spans”. Such dilemma is bypassed through the above temporal restriction, inspired by Gaeta and Ricca’s (2006) *variable-corpus approach*, whereby a corpus is internally sectioned in order to concentrate on specific subperiods.

The following stages were followed towards data collection:

(i) Search for hapaxes ending in *-ment* in the COHA in the 2015–2019 span. 318 entries were obtained which were then filtered by removing units that are not morphologically complex (*liniment*), derivatives of a process other than *-ment* (*self-appointment*, a prefixation of *self-*) and errors in general (*l’habillement*). The target of this stage is *-ment* derivatives which express an ACTION (e.g. *acquirement*, *allurement*, *confrontment*, etc.). The initial list was thus cut down to 52 units.

(ii) Identification of the lexical base of all *-ment* derivatives and use of each base as input in order to detect derivatives of other word-formation processes. For example, the hapax *engraftment* was collected in stage (i), and its lexical base (*engraft*$_V$) allows retrieving the forms *engraft*$_N$, *engrafting* and *engrafture* from the COHA. These four forms are here seen as rivals which compete for coinage and were set up as a cluster[2] of semantically-corresponding derivatives. As in stage (i), expression of the meaning ACTION was a condition for the inclusion of a derivative as a rival in the cluster. Because every *-ment* unit gives rise to one cluster, this stage results in 52 clusters.

(iii) Lookup of the full COHA frequencies of the derivatives in every cluster. One of the nominalizing processes attested during this stage was deverbal conversion, which presents the methodological challenge of homonymy, e.g. *engraft*$_V$ > *engraft*$_N$. Given the lack of a formal mark of derivation – as opposed to *-ance* or *-ing* –, the frequency of converted nouns was obtained by relying on the COHA's POS-tagging. For example, *engraft_nn* has a frequency of two, and two was noted down as the token frequency of *engraft*$_N$. This is so despite the risk of including mistaggings in the counts, which is counterbalanced by the estimated accuracy of the POS-tagging in COHA.

(iv) Addition of lexicographic information from the OED to every derivative: first attestation date, usage level and any relevant etymological details.

The data processing results in 129 nominalizations distributed across fifty-two clusters, each including information on lexical bases, corpus frequency for each period 1820s–2010s, attestation dates, usage status and any other relevant details.

4. Discussion

Section 3 has organized the study data and grouped derivatives into clusters, which are now available for examination. This section introduces a

2 The term *cluster* is hereafter used in reference to a group of synonymous derivatives morphologically related by their bases but formed with a different word-formation rule (see Fernández-Alcaina 2021).

model for the measurement of morphological competition (Section 4.1) and then analyses the evolution of the clusters, with particular emphasis on the suffix *-ment* (Section 4.2).

4.1. The Referenced Index of Competition

The (un)productive condition of *-ment* is assessed here in the context of morphological competition, not in vain productivity and competition are intimately related notions, even if the exact nature of this relationship is still unclear (for a diachronic insight into competition, see Fernández-Alcaina 2021). The clusters of rival units set up above are examined below through the *Referenced Index of Competition* (C*), a formula that measures to what extent the derivatives in a cluster may succeed in competition:

$$C^* = ((N / N_C) / V_C) / R_C$$

In C*, the higher the resulting figure, the greater the likelihood that the lexeme will prevail in that cluster. The maximum possible result for C* is one, and the values involved in the formula are the token frequency of the lexeme (N), the total? token frequency of all the competitors in the cluster (N_C), the number of different competitors in the cluster (V_C), and the *Reference C* (R_C). The purpose of R_C is to adjust the model's results by considering how many rivals occur in a given cluster, under the assumption that success in competition largely depends on the number of competitors – the more competitors, the more demanding the dominance. The highest possible R_C is one – when a cluster contains only one lexeme, and hence competition is resolved – and this value goes down as more lexemes stand as rivals. Accordingly, R_C is 0.5 for clusters with two competitors, 0.33 for three competitors, 0.25 for four competitors, 0.2 for five competitors, etc. The rationale behind C* is that the evolution of morphological competition is traced not just by the individual frequency of lexemes, but also by other variables which globally determine the fate of lexemes (for other applications of the model, see Fernández-Domínguez 2017; forthcoming).

For illustration, consider the results in the 2010s for the cluster *age*$_V$, consisting of the nominalizations *age*$_N$, *agement* and *aging*:

Table 1: C* values for the cluster age_V (2010s)

Lexeme	N	N_C	V_C	R_C	C*
age_N	6,448	6,667	3	0.33333	0.9671
agement	1	6,667	3	0.33333	0.0001
aging	218	6,667	3	0.33333	0.0326

Note that the values of N_C, V_C and R_C are identical to all the derivatives, since the function of these three factors is to modulate C*'s findings by making them comparable across clusters. At least two facts can be gathered from Table 1: one, that age_N is clearly dominant in the decade of the 2010s, as its C* index (0.9671) is close to one; and two, that its competitors have few chances of success at present, especially *agement* (0.0001), with a very low value. It is also remarkable that none of these nominalizations is attested in the OED, which can be interpreted as a sign of their lexical volatility and novel morphological nature.

As explained above, C* allows comparing the competitive potential both of a given word-formation process across different clusters in the same period (e.g. *agement* vs. *allurement*) and of the same process in different periods (e.g. *agement* in 1900, in 1950 and in 2000). For instance, we may explore the behaviour of the *-ment* derivatives in the clusters age_V (Table 1) and $abridge_V$ (Table 2) during the 2010s:

Table 2: C* values for the cluster $abridge_V$ (2010s)

Lexeme	N	N_C	V_C	R_C	C*
$abridge_N$	5	7	2	0.5	0.7142
abridgement	2	7	2	0.5	0.2857

The two word-formation rules featured in Table 2 are deverbal conversion and *-ment*, both present also in Table 1. In the two clusters, conversion is dominant and *-ment* displays a poorly competitive C* index. However, in contrast to the negligible potential of *agement* (0.0001, Table 1), the perspectives for *abridgement* (0.2857, Table 2) are not promising but leave a remote possibility of future prevalence. Each *-ment* derivative behaves differently in its own context. There are two causes for this divergence: one is that *agement* contends against two competitors, while *abridgement* competes against only one. It is no wonder that the more rivals stand in competition, the more challenging success is. The second cause is the disproportionate frequency gaps between *agement*'s rivals (one vs. 6,448 and 218) and *abridgement*'s rivals (two vs. five). In a nutshell, it is not only the qualitative but also the quantitative factor that plays a role in this model, and so units like age_N show overwhelming values that place them as indisputably prevalent. At any rate, and despite contextual factors, the two nominalizations by conversion (age_N and $abride_N$) are unambiguously dominant. This comparison corroborates that the model successfully captures quantitative nuances of cluster-internal and -external morphological competition, which has not been proposed elsewhere, to the best of my knowledge.

Let us next undertake a comparative analysis of derivatives at two discrete time intervals. The cluster $bewitch_V$ has three rival forms ($bewitch_N$, *bewitching* and *bewitchment*), inspected here for the 1880s (Table 3) and the 1890s (Table 4):

Table 3: C* values for the cluster $bewitch_V$ (1880s)

Lexeme	N	N_C	V_C	R_C	C*
$bewitch_N$	1	4	3	0.33333	0.25
bewitching	3	4	3	0.33333	0.75
bewitchment	0	4	3	0.33333	0

Table 4: C* values for the cluster $bewitch_V$ (1890s)

Lexeme	N	N_C	V_C	R_C	C*
$bewitch_N$	0	2	3	0.33333	0.5
bewitching	1	2	3	0.33333	0.5
bewitchment	1	2	3	0.33333	0

Besides variables which are common to both clusters (V_C and R_C), Tables 3 and 4 display a different N_C because this value depends on the individual token frequencies of the rivals. Regarding competition, the two clusters share the particularity that one of the three forms is unattested in the corpus: $bewitchment_N$ in the 1880s, *bewitch* in the 1890s. The opposite is the case with *bewitching*, which is attested in the two periods, although its performance in the 1880s (0.75) is higher than in the 1890s (0.5). The cause is that its token frequency is higher than that of its competitor in the 1880s (*bewitch*$_N$), while it is identical to that of its competitor in the 1890s (*bewitchment*). As for lexicographic information, *bewitch*$_N$ is unattested in the OED, *bewitching* is first attested in 1535 and *bewitchment* in 1610.

Examples like *bewitch*$_N$ are noteworthy because corpus data substantiates its competitive capacity, while lexicographic data simply does not contemplate the existence of the unit. This incongruity is explained by the different data sources and compilation criteria in the corpus and the dictionary; in my view, corpus attestedness is proof of the existence of a unit, regardless of what a different source – e.g. a dictionary or some other corpus – may indicate. In summary, the results suggest that both *bewitch*$_N$ and *bewitchment* show inconsistent patterns across the two time frames, while *bewitching* is relatively more stable. It is also noteworthy that the usage of *bewitching* was more prevalent in the 1880s than in the following period, and that the *-ment* derivative is poorly competitive in the two clusters.

4.2. Using C for Diachronic Competition*

The procedure followed for specific clusters in Section 4.1 was replicated for every cluster in every decade from 1820 to 2019. This allows applying C* to all the nominalizations in the sample and hence tracking down the development of competing word-formation rules throughout. What follows is a selection of the most interesting or challenging cases, given space limitations. Each figure below shows the evolution of a cluster by plotting the C* indices of its derivatives from 1820 to 2019 – the colour key at the bottom indicates the word-formation rules involved.

Figure 1 exemplifies relatively levelled rivalry in the cluster *bewitch*$_V$, which consists of three nominalizations by conversion, *-ing* and *-ment*. *Bewitching* shows an interesting behaviour, with sharp contrasts between stages of clear domination and stages of low lexical activity, often alternately (1980s–2010s). When *bewitching* does not prevail, there is either an evenly-matched contention between the three derivatives (1860–1900, 1920–1940) or dominance by *-ment* (1930, 1950–1990). This is the tendency until the 1980s, when *-ment* values drop and remain close to zero up to the present. The role of conversion in this cluster is limited: it displays a high index in the 1820s and in the 2000s, but it remains below 0.4 for the rest of the time range. The OED information backs up these results, as *bewitching* is first attested in 1535 and *bewitchment* in 1610, but *bewitch*$_N$ remains unattested as of today.

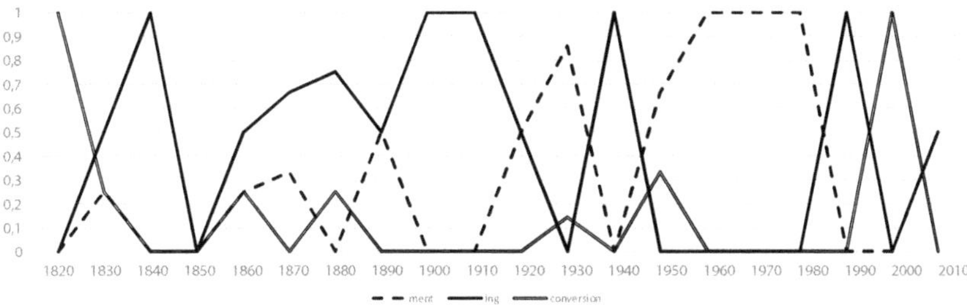

Figure 1: C* values for the cluster *bewitch*$_V$ (1820–2019).

Next, Figure 2 is a two-unit cluster: *allure*$_N$ (OED first attestation in 1534) vs. *allurement* (OED first attestation in 1548). It can be noticed that C* considers *allure*$_N$ as prevailing and *allurement* as non-prevailing for practically the full two centuries, with very clear values for both derivatives. The only exception is found in the gap between 1880 and 1920, when the roles are swapped and competition is more intense. The reason lies in the token frequencies of *allure*$_N$, which remain between twenty and twenty-four, while *allurement* rises from below ten to around twenty as well. This causes C* to reflect parallel values for the two units, thus resulting in a period of close dispute. Eventually, *allurement* drops after 1930 and *allure*$_N$ becomes the dominant form, as happens still today.

Figure 2: C* values for the cluster *allure*$_V$ (1820–2019).

A situation with more rival forms develops in the cluster *cajole*$_V$ (Figure 3), where four different nominalizations contend for survival. Their attestation dates in the OED are considerably distant from each other: 1649 (*cajolery*), 1719 (*cajole*$_N$), 1724 (*cajoling*) and 1816 (*cajolement*).

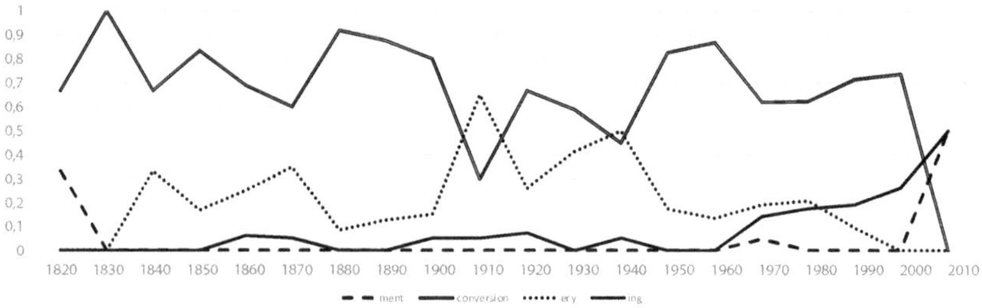

Figure 3: C* values for the cluster *cajole*$_V$ (1820–2019).

As in previous cases, the converted unit shows generalized dominance in all periods (C* values between 0.66 and 0.92), with only a significant drop in the 2010s, caused by the rise of *-ment* and *-ing*. These are on the whole two poorly competitive rules which very rarely display C* indices above 0.2. The fourth contending form in this cluster is *cajolery*, whose performance indicators range between 0.2 and 0.7, except for a clear fall in the 2010s. The interpretation of these findings is that *cajole*$_N$ is a well established and institutionalized nominalization which leaves narrow margin for the use of new forms, in which case *cajolery* seems to be the preferred option. The exceptional rise of the two least frequent forms (*cajoling* and *cajolement*) around the 2010s can be explained because their COHA occurrences are uses in fiction or magazine, two registers which favour creative and conscious coinage. *Cajoling* and *cajolement* are also the units with the latest attestation dates in the cluster.

We may also look at a case of clear dominance, as in the cluster *confront*$_V$:

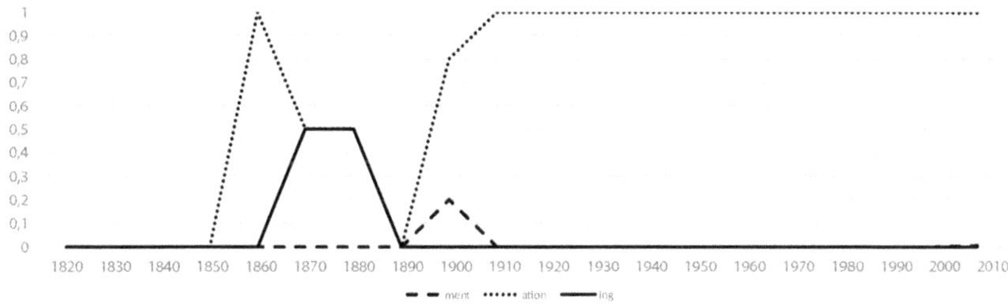

Figure 4: C* values for the cluster *confront*$_V$ (1820–2019).

Three rivals have been attested for this cluster (*confrontation*, *confronting*, *confronment*), although *confrontation* is evidently dominant by and large. Contrary to the cluster *cajole*$_V$ (Figure 3), the OED first attestation dates for the three units all happen within a narrow time range: 1618 (*confrontment*), 1642 (*confronting*) and 1665 (*confrontation*). It is worth noting that, in contrast, COHA contains no occurrences of *confrontation* and *confronting* until the 1860s, and of *confrontment* until the 1900s. This is due to the different criteria employed in the selection of documentary material in the corpus vs. the dictionary, and proves the importance of contextualizing and contrasting results from these two sources. In this case particularly, C* gives an unquestionable estimation of dominance for *confrontation*, whose value is one – the maximum possible – from 1910 on, with the only exception of a hapax by *-ment* in 2010, which implies a value of 0.0045 that brings *confrontation* minimally down to 0.9954. This is of course still indicative of maximal dominance.

Let us finally have an overview of the individual token frequencies of derivatives and their evolution in time. Figure 5 offers, for each decade, the mean token frequency of all the competing derivatives in opposition to the mean token frequency of *-ment* derivatives only. For example, for a cluster like *languish*$_V$, the former considers the frequencies of all its derivatives (*languish*$_N$, *languishing*, *languishment*) and the latter involves exclusively *languishment*:

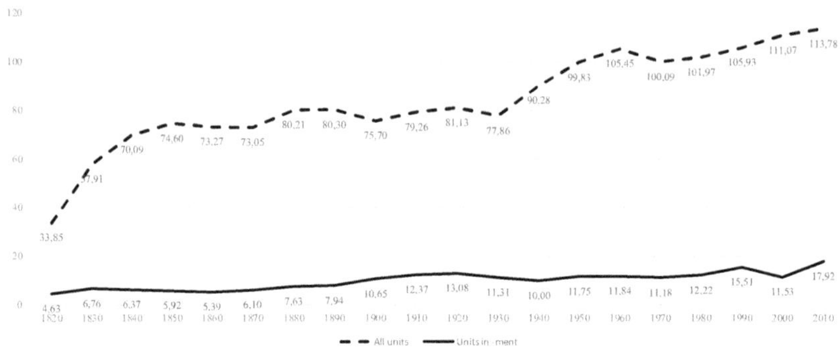

Figure 5: Mean token frequency per derivative (all units vs. units in *-ment*) (1820–2019).

The most apparent aspect is the vast difference between the mean token frequency of derivatives globally vs. derivatives in *-ment*. The frequencies of the *-ment* forms range between *N* 4.63 and 17.92, while the corresponding values for all forms jointly go up to even *N* 113.78. This is partly explained by the method of the study, where hapaxes in *-ment* play a central role. Another explanation is the limited competitive behaviour of *-ment* altogether which, as shown in the tables and figures above, is almost always surpassed by its rivals in the clusters. In addition, this discrepancy between the *N* frequencies is accentuated with the passage of time, and so the frequency gap between the orange and the blue line is of *N* 29 in the 1820s, it rises to *N* 51–66 between 1830s and 1930s, and shoots up to *N* 80–95 from 1940s to 2010s. This performance points towards a gradual decrease in the productive capacity of *-ment*, and it ties in with views that have seen the beginning of the end for this suffix in the twentieth century (Anshen and Aronoff 1999: 24; Bauer 2001: 8; Lieber 2014: 88; Palmer 2015: 126).

Note that, nonetheless, the token frequencies of *-ment* units remain relatively stable throughout these two centuries (i.e. between *N* 4.63 and 17.92), so the explanation of the decline of *-ment* should not be sought simply in suffix-internal factors, but in the surrounding context. In accordance with Figure 5, it is the frequency of the competitors of *-ment* that rises from the early twentieth century on, and this causes the frequencies of *-ment*, enough for prevalence previously, to become insufficient in competition. This account explains not only the high productivity of conversion or *-ing* to the detriment of *-ment* at present, but also the fact that occasional *-ment* coinages still get attested in the twenty-first century, as reported elsewhere (Bauer, Lieber and Plag 2013: 198–200; Kawaletz and Plag 2015: 293; Kawaletz 2023).

From the presented information, it can be concluded that there is a considerable degree of lexical productivity related to actional nominalization in the context of morphological competition. Typically, three or four rival forms are in contention simultaneously, and this has been the case since the 1820s, the starting point for this research. In such environment, the suffix *-ment* played an active role especially during the nineteenth century, when its frequency values and C* indices were on a par with those of rival patterns, and gradually fell behind the performance of processes such as conversion or *-ing* from the twentieth century. Today, corpus and dictionary data suggest that *-ment* is at a low productive capacity, but it is still able to coin forms at irregular intervals.

5. Conclusions

This study has tackled deverbal actional nominalization, in particular that involving the dubiously productive suffix *-ment*. In order to understand how the cognitive category ACTION is conveyed through word formation between 1820 and 2019, corpus and dictionary data were used. Based on the findings, certain conclusions can be drawn:

(i) The model C* offers a reliable insight into competition and makes it possible to evaluate the lexical capacity of word-formation processes both cluster-internally and -externally. In applying C*, corpus data proves fundamental, although with certain methodological precautions, e.g. keeping a balanced division of the corpus sections or avoiding units with very high frequency ranges (see Section 3). It has also been shown that the parallel exploitation of dictionary and corpus data offers an up-to-date picture of morphological rules whose productive status has been portrayed as uncertain.

(ii) Deverbal conversion and *-ing* are the morphological resources most frequently prevailing in competition, according to C*. For reasons beyond the scope of this paper, these seem to be versatile rules whose derivatives tend to have high token frequencies and show the ability to co-exist with each other. This makes them enduring alternatives and explains why they have been the preferred alternative for coinage, with rare exceptions, during the past two centuries.

(iii) The suffix *-ment* has displayed a generalized but steady decrease in its competitive potential since 1820. Even if COHA-derived evidence confirms that the token frequencies of *-ment* units *per se* have remained stable throughout, the capacity of their rivals has been expanded substantially. Because morphological competition is a matter of coexistence (Aronoff 2016, 2019), increase in the use of an affix for a given meaning tends to imply the decrease in the use of its rivals. In the case of the category ACTION, the evidence indicates that *-ment* has been cornered and that its present possibilities for coinage are few, although categorizing it as unavailable is at least risky, given occasional coinages in the twenty-first century.

The results of this study therefore point to an appraisal of *-ment* as poorly productive but *still* available. Indeed, other rival word-formation patterns are preferred in the creation of actional nominalizations, and hence display higher token frequencies and C* values. Nonetheless, the fact that *-ment* retains the capacity for occasional coinage is here taken to mean that it is still needed to fulfill naming needs. As I see it, the number and nature of *-ment* units are salient enough to consider them as something more than *ad hoc* formations. Even if such derivatives have been mostly regarded as anecdotal in the literature, their joint analysis has evidenced non-negligible quantities, which could be explained in terms of optimization, i.e. getting the most output from your input. This offers a new panorama on the development of *-ment*.

This viewpoint is backed up by corpus and dictionary data. Corpus evidence has returned low-frequency values for *-ment* units, which is customarily interpreted as indicative of potential productivity (Baayen 1992, 2009). Regarding lexicographical evidence, we take sides with Lieber (2014: 88) that "with affixes whose productivity is in dispute (e.g. *-al* or *-ment*) we might be more inclined to take absence from the dictionary as significant". Non-attestedness in the OED has been found for forms like *agement*, *ensoulment*, *escrowment* or *frazzlement* and this, together with a low corpus frequency, reveals such forms as novel creations with a future productive potential.

In 1999, Anshen and Aronoff declared: "Clearly *-ment* is not a productive affix in modern English as shown informally by the difficulty of thinking of a new word in *-ment*" (1999: 22). This statement, valid then, seems to have been turned today, as proved by the reference to novel *-ment* derivatives in recent work (Bauer, Lieber and Plag 2013: 198–9; Kawaletz and Plag 2015). The productive oscillations of *-ment* during the past two centuries seem to exemplify what Lipka calls *rediscovery* of linguistic phenomena, i.e. "that old 'facts' and old theoretical constructs reappear more or less well-adapted in modern theories" (1975: 198). The lexical activity of this suffix was dynamic for centuries before its progressive decline around the nineteenth century, in the light of late-twentieth century productivity models. Almost half a century after such assessments, newer lexicographic and corpus evidence shows that *-ment* is synchronically productive, if to a minimal degree. Reasons to include *-ment* among productive processes are:

(i) Its ability to coin derivatives,
(ii) The morphological analysability and semantic coherence of its derivatives,
(iii) The existence of a lexical base-derivative relationship parallel to other word-formation rules,
(iv) The integration of its derivatives in the nominal paradigm of English, thus acquiring all the inflectional and word-class features of nouns.

The suffix *-ment* is being *rediscovered* as a productive rule in Present-day English word formation, largely thanks to new research methods and more extensive datasets. For this reason, we should neither call for a case of *illusion of explanatory depth*, nor categorically deny the validity of works which previously declared *-ment* as unproductive, since they operated based on the tools and information available back then. As a matter of fact, new editions of those publications now omit *-ment* from the catalogue of unproductive processes. Lieber's (2014: 93) remark captures this idea neatly: "Methodolody and theory of course go hand in hand".

This paper has hopefully shown that dubiously productive processes like *-ment* are not only relevant synchronically, but that their understanding can shed light on the complex transition from productivity to non-productivity or vice versa. In van Marle's (1984: 66) words, "[b]y means of a careful and detailed investigation of the various stages of these historical changes – and, of course, of the structural properties of the "transitional" patterns –, the diachronic study of language may greatly add to our knowledge of synchronic structure".

Sources

Davies, Mark, *Corpus of Historical American English* (Brigham Young University, 2010). Available at https://www.english-corpora.org/coha/.

Oxford English Dictionary (Oxford University Press, 2023). Available at http://www.oed.com/.

References

Anshen, Frank and Mark Aronoff, 'Producing Morphologically Complex Words', *Linguistics* 26 (1988), 641–55.

——, 'Using Dictionaries to Study the Mental Lexicon', *Brain and Language* 68 (1999), 16–26.

Aronoff, Mark, *Word Formation in Generative Grammar* (Cambridge, MA: MIT Press, 1976).

——, 'Competition and the Lexicon', in Annibale Elia, Claudio Iacobini and Miriam Voghera, eds., *Livelli di Analisi e Fenomeni di Interfaccia. Atti del XLVII Congresso Internazionale della Società di Linguistica Italiana* (Roma: Bulzoni, 2016), 39–52.

——, 'Competitors and Alternants in Linguistic Morphology', in Franz Rainer, Francesco Gardani, Wolfgang U. Dressler and Hans Christian Luschützky, eds., *Competition in Inflection and Word-Formation* (Dordrecht: Springer, 2019), 39–66.

Baayen, R. Harald, 'Quantitative Aspects of Morphological Productivity', in Geert E. Booij and Jaap van Marle (eds), *Yearbook of Morphology 1991* (Dordrecht: Kluwer, 1992), 109–49.

——, 'Corpus Linguistics in Morphology: Morphological Productivity', in Anke Lüdeling and Merja Kytö, eds., *Corpus Linguistics. An International Handbook* (Berlin: Mouton De Gruyter, 2009), 900–19.

Bauer, Laurie, *Word-Formation in English* (Cambridge: Cambridge University Press, 1983).

——, *Morphological Productivity* (Cambridge: Cambridge University Press, 2001).

——, Rochelle Lieber and Ingo Plag, *The Oxford Reference Guide to English Morphology* (Oxford: Oxford University Press, 2013).

Corbin, Danielle, *Morphologie Dérivationelle et Structuration du Lexique* (Tübingen: Niemeyer, 1987).

Cowie, Claire and Christiane Dalton-Puffer, 'Diachronic Word-Formation and Studying Changes in Productivity over Time: Theoretical and Methodological Considerations', in Javier E. Díaz Vera, ed., *A Changing World of Words: Studies in English Historical Lexicography, Lexicology and Semantics* (Amsterdam: Rodopi, 2002), 410–37.

Dalton-Puffer, Christiane, 'Productive or Not Productive? The Romance Element in Middle English Derivation', in Francisco Fernández, Miguel Fuster and Juan José Calvo, eds., *English Historical Linguistics 1992* (Amsterdam and Philadelphia: John Benjamins, 1994), 247–60.

Dressler, Wolfgang U. and Mária Ladányi, 'Productivity in Word Formation (WF): A Morphological Approach', *Acta Linguistica Hungarica* 47/1–4 (2000), 103–44.

Fernández-Alcaina, Cristina, *The Competition of Word-Formation Processes in the Derivational Paradigm of Verbs* (Berlin: Peter Lang, 2021).

Fernández-Domínguez, Jesús, 'Methodological and Procedural Issues in the Quantification of Morphological Competition', in Juan Santana and Salvador Valera, eds., *Competing Patterns in English Affixation* (Bern: Peter Lang, 2017), 67–117.

——, 'Actional Nominalization in Present-Day English in the Light of The Referenced Index of Competition', in Alexandra Bagasheva, Akiko Nagano and Vincent Renner (eds.), *Competition in Word-Formation* (Amsterdam: John Benjamins, forthcoming).

Gaeta, Livio, 'How Lexical is Morphology? The Construction and the Quadripartite Architecture of Grammar', in Lívia Körtvélyessy, Pavol Štekauer and Salvador Valera, eds., *Word-Formation across Languages* (Cambridge: Cambridge Scholars Publishing, 2016), 109–46.

Gaeta, Livio and Davide Ricca, 'Productivity in Italian Word-Formation: A Variable-Corpus Approach', *Linguistics* 44/1 (2006), 57–89.

Hohenhaus, Peter, 'Lexicalization and Institutionalization', in Pavol Štekauer and Rochelle Lieber, eds., *Handbook of Word-Formation* (Dordrecht: Springer, 2005), 353–73.

Kastovsky, Dieter, 'The Problem of Productivity in Word Formation', *Linguistics* 24 (1986), 585–600.

Kawaletz, Lea, *The Semantics of* -ment *Nominalizations* (Berlin: Language Science Press, 2023).

Kawaletz, Lea and Ingo Plag, 'Predicting the Semantics of English Nominalizations: A Frame-Based Analysis of *-ment* Suffixation', in Laurie Bauer, Lívia Körtvélyessy and Pavol Štekauer, eds., *Semantics of Complex Words* (Dordrecht: Springer, 2015), 289–319.

Lieber, Rochelle, 'Methodological Issues in Studying Derivation', in Rochelle Lieber and Pavol Štekauer, eds., *The Oxford Handbook of Derivational Morphology* (Oxford: Oxford University Press, 2014), 84–94.

Lipka, Leonhard, 'Rediscovery Procedures and the Lexicon', *Lingua* 37 (1975), 197–224.

Marchand, Hans, *The Categories and Types of Present-Day English Word-Formation. A Synchronic-Diachronic Approach* (Munich: Beck, 1969).

Marle, Jaap van, *On the Paradigmatic Dimension of Morphological Creativity* (Berlin: De Gruyter, 1984).

Neuhaus, Heinz Joachim, 'Zur Theorie der Produktivität von Wortbildungssystemen', in Abraham P. ten Cate and Peter Jordens, eds., *Linguistische Perspektiven: Referate des VII Linguistischen Kolloquiums* (Tübingen: Niemeyer, 1973), 305–17.

Palmer, Chris C., 'Measuring Productivity Diachronically: Nominal Suffixes in English Letters, 1400–1600', *English Language and Linguistics* 19/1 (2015), 107–29.

Schultink, Henk, 'Produktiviteit als Morfologisch Fenomeen', *Forum der Letteren* 2 (1961), 110–25.

Štekauer, Pavol, 'Competition in Natural Languages', in Juan Santana-Lario and Salvador Valera, eds., *Competing Patterns in English Affixation* (Bern: Peter Lang, 2017), 15–32.

Tournier, Jean, *Introduction Descriptive à la Lexicogénétique de l'Anglais Contemporain* (Paris: Slatkine, 1985).

Juan Lorente-Sánchez

Past Participle Forms in Competition: *-ed* vs *-(e)n* in Historical British and American English[1]

1. Introduction

In comparison with Early Modern and present-day English, the verbal morphology of Late Modern English (LModE) is characterized by considerable levels of variation in terms of the use and distribution of past participle forms (Mondorf 2012: 843), especially of some verbs falling into the category of "irregular" in a recognizable number of grammars and dictionaries of the language over time. Whilst a regular verb is systematically reproduced with the suffix *-ed* appended to the base form so as to represent its past tense and past participle (e.g. *denote* > *denoted* [pt. and pp.]), an irregular verb is defined as "one where the shape of at least one inflectional form has to be specified for that particular verb" (Huddleston and Pullum 2005: 33–4); in other words, a verb whose past tense, past participle or both are structured in a rather distinct manner from the "regular" *-ed* ending (e.g. *write* > *wrote* [pt.], *written* [pp.]) (see *Collins COBUILD English Grammar* 1990: xx; Carter and McCarthy 2006: 421).

1 The present research has been funded by the Autonomous Andalusian Government (grant number UMA18-FEDERJA-129). This grant is hereby gratefully acknowledged. I would like to thank both the editors and the anonymous reviewers of the volume, whose valuable comments and feedback have helped me produce an improved version of the chapter. I am also deeply grateful to Prof. Javier Calle-Martín and Dr. Marta Pacheco-Franco for having provided me with the idea presented in the paper, as well as for their permanent support throughout all these years working together.

The morphological composition of irregular verbs is in itself variable as well – not only nowadays, but also in LModE – , mainly on account of the degrees of variation and/or similarity that may exist between the main parts of an irregular verb compared with other irregular verbs. In this context, this kind of verbs may be organized into seven major categories, which are distinguished from each other apropos of whether they adhere a suffix, whether they contain some alteration in the base vowel, and whether there are differences between the base form (or root), the past tense and the past participle (see Quirk et al. 1972: 109–10; 1985: 103; Greenbaum and Quirk 1990: 29). According to several sources for the study and learning of English, these classes of irregular verbs are characterized as follows (Quirk et al. 1972: 109–21; Crystal 1995: 204; Biber et al. 1999: 394–6):

- Class 1 verbs, such as *lend*, are fairly similar to regular verbs, excepting that they take a *-t* ending instead of *-ed* to mark out the preterite and the past participle (i.e. *lent*). There is, however, a subgroup of verbs within this category that admit the utilization of the two suffixes alternatively (e.g. *spoil* > *spoiled/spoilt* [pt. and pp.]; *dwell* > *dwelled/dwelt* [pt. and pp.]).
- Class 2 verbs are identical in their past tense and the past participle, formed either by a *-t* or *-ed* inflection, though with a change in the base vowel (e.g. *think* > *thought* [pt. and pp.]; *sell* > *sold* [pt. and pp.]).
- Class 3 verbs present the same past tense and participle as the base form (e.g. *set*, *cut*, *cost*).
- Class 4 verbs, like *dig*, also display the same consonants but a minor modification in the base vowel (i.e. *dug*).
- Class 5 features those verbs whose past tense is formed with *-ed*, whilst the past participle may be structured with the regular ending or by means of a nasal suffix (e.g. *show* > *showed* [pt.], *showed/shown* [pp.]).
- Class 6 verbs lack an inflection in their past tense but include -(*e*)*n* in their participle, with a vowel change in one of the other two parts or in both (e.g. *give* > *gave* [pt.], *given* [pp.]; *freeze* > *froze* [pt.], *frozen* [pp.]).[2]

2 The only exception to this is the verb *beat*, wherein no vocalic variation is found in either the past tense or the past participle (i.e. *beat* [pt.], *beaten* [pp.]) (Quirk et al. 1972: 118).

- Finally, class 7 verbs have different preterite and participle forms, they do not incorporate a suffix and the base vowel is changed (e.g. *begin* > *began* [pt.], *begun* [pp.]).[3] Note that these verbs vary from those of group 4 in that the latter have the same structure for both the preterite and the past participle.

Out of the irregular verbs enumerated, only a handful of these belonging to the first category and those from class 5 present more than one form for the rendering of their past participles. These include, as just shown, the alternative use between the regular *-ed* inflection and the suffixes *-t* and *-(e)n*, respectively.

As far as *-ed* and *-t* are concerned, the interchange of the two participle endings has been – for at least half of a century – a subject of special interest in the linguistic comparative study of British and American English (henceforth BrE and AmE). Clear proof of it resides on the availability of academic publications over time which mention the topic, including papers published in scientific journals such as Johansson's (1979: 205–6), chapters in books such as *The Cambridge History of the English Language* (see Lass 1999: 175) and *One Language, Two Grammars: Grammatical Differences between British and American English* (see Hundt 2009: 20; Levin 2009: 65–81; Schlüter 2009: 112–20; Elsness 2009: 244–5), as well as general and specialized volumes such as *The Cambridge Encyclopedia of the English Language* (Crystal 1995) and *British or American English? A Handbook of Word and Grammar Patterns* (Algeo 2006), among others.

From a historical viewpoint, the choice between the forms can be traced back to the eleventh century, when some verbs ending in *-nd* such as *send* or *lend* began to adopt the suffixes indifferently as participial forms (i.e. *send(e)/sent(e)* and *lēned/lent(e)*), a practice which became more frequent in the course of Middle English (ME). In the final stages of the fifteenth century and the beginning of the sixteenth, this trend was followed by some other verbs such as *spill* and *smell*, propagating

3 Quirk et al. remark that *go* might be considered as an exceptional and a "particularly irregular" verb herein, given that it exhibits a completely independent past tense structure, i.e. *went*, as opposed to its past participle form *gone* (1985: 105; also 1972: 111; Lass 1999: 138).

steadily throughout Early Modern English (EModE) and the first half of the LModE period (Lass 1999: 175; also *e-Middle English Dictionary*: s.v. senden, lēnen). At present, the phenomenon stands as "one of the most cited morphological differences between [AmE] and [BrE]" (Levin 2009: 60; also Schlüter 2009: 112), the former denoting an outstanding preference towards the regular *-ed* inflection and the latter towards *-t* (see Crystal 1995: 204; Lass 1999: 175; Hundt 2009: 20).[4]

Regarding the *-ed* and *-(e)n* shift, on the other hand, the topic has also been a matter of discussion in an array of dictionaries, grammars and academic studies. Overall, most of these references agree that it exists, at least with certain verbs, a bias towards employing *-ed* at the expense of *-(e)n* as participle markers and that this is more pronounced in AmE – as well as in other varieties such as Australian English – compared to BrE (Elsness 2009: 244; see Collins and Peters 2004: 595–6, quoted in Elsness 2009: 244; also Algeo 2006: 13–19). The present contribution seeks to address the *-ed*/*-(e)n* alternation in BrE and AmE in 1600–1900, the time when the major grammatical divergences between the two varieties of the language first take place (Beal 2012: 68; Mondorf 2012: 843).

Chronologically speaking, this morphological variation has also its origins in post-Old English (OE), at some point of ME, an era in which many strong verbs started to be conjugated as weak. Whilst a relatively small number of them have kept the weak as the unique participle structure – formed in most cases with an alveolar suffix – (e.g. *weep*: OE *wōpen* > ME *wep(p)ed*/*weppet* > ModE *wept*) (Lass 1992: 126; Wełna 2012: 425–9; also *e-Middle English Dictionary*: s.v. wẹ̄pen), others have accepted ever since both the strong *-(e)n* and the weak *-ed*. This has lead to a constant alternation between the suffixes

4 Hundt (2009: 20) identifies this tendency of AmE for regularizing the past participles of verbs like *spoil* or *burn* (i.e. *spoiled* and *burned*) as an evident case of "colonial innovation", a term understood here as the process whereby this variety of English is more advanced in the implementation and usage of the 'unconventional shape' of a particular linguistic feature – in opposition to its traditional structure. BrE is in this respect more unwilling than AmE to accept this sort of changes and, as such, more prone to employ the forms *spoilt* and *burnt*. Notwithstanding this, according to Crystal (1995: 204), it likewise enables a higher "deal of usage variation" depending on the context wherein these *-t* participles are used.

primarily determined by the specific verb under consideration (e.g. *sow*: OE *sāwen* > ME *sowen(e)*, *sowed* > ModE *sown/sowed*) (see *e-Middle English Dictionary*: s.v. souen; Simpson and Weiner 1989: s.v. sow; Wełna 2012: 429).[5]

Parallel to the above, there is another group of verbs, including among others *show*, which also allow for the *-ed*/-(*e*)*n* participial alternation, yet they have developed a completely opposite historical pathway, that is, from weak to strong (see Lass 1992: 126).[6] These verb-types, however, have been somewhat disregarded as to the distribution of their competing participles, probably based on the prevalence of -(*e*)*n* in BrE and AmE, as assumed by allusions to the issue found in well known dictionaries of the English language (Evans and Evans 1957: s.v. show; Simpson and Weiner 1989: s.v. show, among others).[7]

Belonging to the OE weak class 2, such verbs formed the past participles via the incorporation of the *-od*(*e*) marker to their stems, to which the prefix *ge-* could be likewise added (Lass 1987: 175; 1992: 127). Later evolving to *-ed*, the competition of this regular structure with -(*e*)*n* dates to the beginning of the ME period, when these OE weak class 2 verbs gradually started to implement the originally strong participle alongside it (Simpson and Weiner 1989: s.v. show; Wełna 2012: 423, 425). This practice continued increasing steadily in the succeeding centuries and has persisted well until the present day, as summarized below (see Bosworth and Toller [1898] 1964: s.v. show, strew; Simpson

5 Note that although they belong to the same historical category of OE strong class 7, verbs like *sow* and *mow* denote today contrasting preferences in the selection of a particular suffix (Wełna 2012: 429).

6 If compared with the number of verbs going from strong to weak, an evolution of this kind might be regarded, according to Lass (1992: 126), as rare in the transitional stage between OE and ME, "as is the borrowing of foreign verbs into the strong conjugation" (e.g. *strive*: Old French *estriver* > ME *strīven*, *strōve*/*strīved* [pt.], *striven(e)*/*(i)strīved* [pp.] > ModE *strive*, *strove* [pt.], *striven* [pp.]) (also Wełna 2012: 425; *e-Middle English Dictionary*: s.v. strīven).

7 A quantitative survey of the phenomenon by means of three large-scale corpora of contemporary BrE and AmE – the *British National Corpus* (*BNC*), the *Corpus of Contemporary American English* (*COCA*) and the *Global Web-Based English* corpus (*GloWbE*) to be specific – comes to justify this theory, since it has been found that -(*e*)*n* overwhelmingly outnumbers *-ed*, especially in BrE.

and Weiner 1989: s.v. show, strew; *e-Middle English Dictionary*: s.v. sheuen, streuen):

- *show*: OE *scēawod(e)* > ME *sheu(e)d(e)/shau(e)n* > ModE *shown/showed.*
- *strew*: OE *strēawod(e)* > ME *strewed(e)/strauen* > ModE *strewn/strewed.*

Even though -*(e)n* is today the predominant option to the detriment of -*ed* in both BrE and AmE, these participial suffixes have had a variable historical distribution. Indeed, a preliminary overview of the phenomenon has tentatively shown that this is particularly evident in the seventeenth century and the whole LModE period. Bearing this in mind, the paper pursues a twofold objective: (1) to analyse the distribution of these alternatives in the period under scrutiny; and (2) to shed some light on their uses in British and American English over time, determining its contrasts and similarities. To this purpose, six verbs belonging to the category of OE weak class 2 which later developed the strong -*(e)n* variant are considered, namely *awake*, *saw*, *sew*, *show*, *strew* and *wake* (see Wełna 2012: 425).[8]

2. Methodology

The evidence stems from a number of sizeable corpora representative of early BrE and AmE. As far as BrE is concerned, the data come from three different sources, including the seventeenth-century component

8 The verb *saw* might be regarded as an exception, as it has its provenance in Old Norse (ON) rather than in OE. Notwithstanding this, the verb has also been included in my study insofar as it was originally weak and, more importantly, it had a participle structure comparable to the other OE weak class 2 verbs before it incorporated the strong -*(e)n* marker throughout ME (*saw*: ON *sagaðr* > ME *(i)saued/sauen(e)* > ModE *sawed/sawn*) (see Wełna 2012: 423–5; also Simpson and Weiner 1989: s.v. saw; Barnes 2008: 151; *e-Middle English Dictionary*: s.v. sauen).

of the *Early English Books Online* corpus (*EEBO*) (Davies 2017), the *Eighteenth Century Collections Online* (*ECCO*) (Gale 2018) and the *Corpus of Late Modern English Texts* (*CLMET*) (De Smet et al. 2015).

First, *EEBO* is one of the largest corpora of early BrE, as it contains 755,078,402 words in 24,971 texts from the Early English Books Online. Its seventeenth-century component consist of 621,287,829 words in c. 22,000 texts of diverse types, which means that it constitutes more than three quarters of the whole material.[9]

Second, *ECCO* "is the most comprehensive dataset available in machine-readable form for eighteenth-century printed texts". This collection is rooted in the *English Short-Title Catalogue*, which facilitates its connection with similarly compiled online projects and corpora made up of written material from different historical periods, for instance, *EEBO* (Tolonen et al. 2021: 20; also 2022: 95–6).[10] The version of *ECCO* used to the purpose includes 80,654,998 of transcribed and annotated words out of 2,473 pieces from 1700–1799.[11]

Finally, *CLMET* is composed of approximately 35 million words from the period 1710–1920 and it is subdivided into three sections of 70 years each (that is, 1710–1780; 1780–1850; and 1850–1920), with a balanced distribution in terms of word count (De Smet 2005: 70; De Smet et al. 2015: 2). For this research, *CLMET3.1* has been used since, if compared with previous versions of the corpus, it contains a wider number of texts and authors along with some technical improvements and modifications.[12]

---

9 See https://www.english-corpora.org/corpora.asp and https://www.english-corpora.org/eebo/.

10 See https://www.gale.com/binaries/content/assets/gale-us-en/primary-sources/eighteenth-century-collections-online/ecco-roll-fold-2016-web.pdf.

11 See https://textcreationpartnership.org/tcp-texts/ecco-tcp-eighteenth-century-collections-online/ and https://app.sketchengine.eu/#dashboard?corpname=preloaded%2Fearly_english/.

12 These changes can be summarized in "(a) retokenization and retagging, (b) fixing of some systematic issues that come with historical data, and (c) enhancing annotation by adding lemmas and simplified part-of-speech class tags" (De Smet et al. 2015: 2). See also https://fedora.clarin-d.uni-saarland.de/clmet/clmet.html/.

Table 1: Subperiods and overall word count of *CLMET3.1* (adapted from the corpus manual; De Smet et al. 2015: 10)

Subperiod	**Word count**
1710–1780	10,460,119
1780–1850	11,473,445
1850–1920	12,942,471
Total	34,876,035

When it comes to AmE, the analysis relies on the information supplied by the *Evans Early American Imprints* collection (*EVANS*) (Readex 2018)[13] and the nineteenth-century component of the *Corpus of Historical American English* (*COHA*) (Davies 2010). The former consists of 5,007 titles listed in Charles Evans' *American Bibliography* of books issued in USA since the arrival of the printing press in 1639 until 1820 (see Evans 1903).[14] It holds 112,832,006 words compiled under the same principles and guidelines as the other TCP computerized collections. As reproduced in Table 2, the eighteenth century supplies the biggest portion of it, with 98,115,447 words, followed by the seventeenth with 8,884,679 and the nineteenth with 5,831,880.

13 Together with *EEBO* and *ECCO*, the *EVANS* corpus is a part of the major *English Historical Book Collection* of the TCP (see https://textcreationpartnership.org), which is at the same time included within the category of 'preloaded' and 'ready-for-use' corpora of the *Sketch Engine* tool (see Kilgarriff et al. 2004; also 2014: 8). Consequently, these three collections of historical English have been analysed via the online version of this piece of software, given the number of advantages its main functions offer. For example, the computational system "allows the user to view word sketches, thesaurally similar words, and 'sketch differences'". The first of them is completely unified with the program's concordancer, that is, "by clicking on a collocate of interest in the word sketch, the user is taken to a concordance of the corpus evidence giving rise to that collocate in that grammatical relation" (Kilgarriff et al. 2004: 108; also 2014: 9–14).

14 See https://textcreationpartnership.org/tcp-texts/evans-tcp-evans-early-american-imprints/ and https://www.sketchengine.eu/historical-collection-eebo-ecco-evans/.

Table 2: Centuries and overall word count of *EVANS* (adapted from https://app.sketchengine.eu/#dashboard?corpname=preloaded%2Fearly_english)

Century	Word count
Seventeenth	8,884,679
Eighteenth	98,115,447
Nineteenth	5,831,880
Total	112,832,006

On the other hand, *COHA* is a corpus of 475,031,831 words from 140,703 individual documents from the period 1820–2019, aimed to be an extensive and representative source of historical AmE (Davies and Chapman 2016: 132). The nineteenth century subset is made up of 129,254,741 words, approximately a 27.21 per cent of the entire corpus.[15]

On the whole, the five sources together amount to up to 978,905,609 words from a wide variety of documents, hence making them an appropriate input for both a synchronic and a diachronic study of the two participial forms in competition in historical BrE and AmE. Even though these pieces of evidence are annotated by means of POS-tags so as to simplify diverse forms of linguistic research, the retrieval of occurrences has been carried out without taking any grammatical labels into consideration. This is mainly due to the existence of a number of erroneously tagged units as a result of an automatic annotation process. Given that the *-ed* participial form of the verbs at hand coincides in shape with the past tense, there are certain occasions, as in (1), wherein the tag corresponding to the preterite of a lexical verb is inaccurately assigned to a participle. In addition to this, there are some other cases where the opposite situation is observed, as illustrated in (2), with a past tense wrongly labelled as a participle.

(1) [. . .] hee laboureth, to prooue the Proposition of this his Syllogisme. That hath beene oftener *showed*, than hee hath syllables in his Proper Balled: [. . .] (*EEBO*, A01042, 1627).

15 See https://www.english-corpora-org/coha/.

(2) But the good Bishop of Lincolne (for in him was then the office of Chancellor) in this *showed* himself a better Orator, then Prophet. (*EEBO*, 102454, 1640).

My study is thus based on the complete list of instances of the six verbs whose participles may be found structured with both the *-ed* and -(*e*)*n* endings (i.e. *showed/shown*, *strewed/strewn* and so on).[16] Disambiguation is a requisite to incorporate only those occurrences in which an actual participle is displayed and, as such, to provide an accurate representation of the alternation between the two variables in the historical period and the varieties of English under review. All in all, 69,393 participial instances have been gathered after disambiguation, 45,000 of which used with -(*e*)*n* and the remaining 24,393 with *-ed*.

3. Analysis

3.1. Diachronic Evolution of the Forms

Tables 3 and 4 below reproduce the distribution of the participial forms -(*e*)*n* and *-ed* in my data, where the figures presented have been normalized to 100,000,000 words.

16 Though archaic and constrained to dialectal usage in present-day English, the forms *shewed/shewn* and *strowed/strown* have also been considered in the analysis given their prominent recurrence in the period 1600–1900 (see Lowth 1763: 83; Fowler 1927: 531, 573; Quirk et al. 1985: 107; Simpson and Weiner 1989: s.v. show, strew).

Table 3: Distribution of the participial forms -(*e*)*n* and -*ed* in BrE (1600–1900) (n.f.)

BrE	***Awake***		***Saw***		***Sew***	
	-(e)n	***-ed***	***-(e)n***	***-ed***	***-(e)n***	***-ed***
1600–1699	0.64	132.14	33.16	23.02	1.29	38.63
1700–1799	1.1	107.56	42.8	43.9	6.59	141.58
1800–1900	–	49.15	61.44	8.19	151.54	86.01
	Show		***Strew***		***Wake***	
	-(e)n	***-ed***	***-(e)n***	***-ed***	***-(e)n***	***-ed***
1600–1699	2,456.99	2,923.44	5.47	117.18	0.64	17.71
1700–1799	6,939.57	321.57	49.39	192.06	–	108.65
1800–1900	8,768.87	45.05	524.25	221.17	16.38	131.06

Table 4: Distribution of the participial forms -(*e*)*n* and -*ed* in AmE (1600–1900) (n.f.)

AmE	***Awake***		***Saw***		***Sew***	
	-(e)n	***-ed***	***-(e)n***	***-ed***	***-(e)n***	***-ed***
1600–1699	–	33.77	33.77	11.26	11.26	67.53
1700–1799	–	121.29	41.79	107.02	2.04	112.11
1800–1900	2.22	57.01	37.75	76.25	62.18	148.05
	Show		***Strew***		***Wake***	
	-(e)n	***-ed***	***-(e)n***	***-ed***	***-(e)n***	***-ed***
1600–1699	866.66	1,463.19	11.26	33.77	–	45.02
1700–1799	6,170.28	1,225.09	21.4	125.36	–	64.21
1800–1900	10,073.54	210.98	587.03	209.5	1.48	299.81

The results reveal a general preference towards the use of -*ed* in the seventeenth and the eighteenth century in both BrE and AmE, as most verbs tend to render their participles with the conventionally regular weak form in almost the first two-thirds of the period under analysis. An exception to this is the participial form of the verb *saw*, more widely attested with -(*e*)*n* in 1600–1699, with almost a similar incidence in the varieties (33.16 occurrences in BrE and 33.77 in AmE), though more frequently rendered as *sawed* in 1700–1799, particularly in AmE (107.02 instances).

The data also show the opposite practice in nineteenth-century BrE, given that the majority of verbs – *saw*, *sew*, *show* and *strew* – are found to favour the irregular -(*e*)*n* at the cost of the other suffix. In AmE, by contrast, the shift seems to advance at a slower pace, since *-ed* is still in 1800–1900 the marker that predominates in the participle of these verbs, excepting *show* and *strew*, and even with these the regular ending is persistent to some extent (210.98 and 209.5 instances, respectively). This picture may lead us to gather, at least tentatively, that the change to the current state of affairs – where *-(e)n* prominently surpasses *-ed* in number and usage – took place later, presumably at some point of the twentieth century.[17]

While there are apparently no intra-linguistic reasons that may come to justify the retention of *-ed* in nineteenth century AmE for some of these verbs, the keeping of this participle might have been influenced by the sociocultural context of this variety at that specific stage of its history. Commonly referred to in the literature as the "National Period" or, as Algeo (2001: 4–5) has coined, "the childhood and adolescence of [AmE]", the dawn of this epoch takes us back to the last quarter of the eighteenth century, a moment marked by the historical episode of the American Declaration of Independence, which also brought the pursual of an autonomous and distinctive variety of the language in the following years, among other matters (Algeo 2001: 4–5; also Beal 2012: 68). Minkova (2014: 17) notes that "[t]he idea of a separate American language was widely accepted in the nineteenth century". Therefore, the preservation of *-ed* in opposition to *-(e)n* in 1800–1900 could be regarded as a way for AmE to linguistically distinguish itself from BrE. Despite this, she further states that the latter "continued to be admired and imitated well into the twentieth century" (2014: 17), which explains why participial structures such as that illustrated in (3) began to progressively predominate over those with *-ed* from 1900 onwards.[18]

---

17 See Hundt (2009: 20–4), Schlüter (2009: 112–20) and references therein for insights into the morphological distribution of irregular verbs in twentieth-century AmE.

18 The preference for *-(e)d* in 1800–1900 AmE could have also been due to the mass migrations that occurred in the United States throughout the nineteenth century, where a large part of the population from several regions of the East of the country moved towards the West. This social phenomenon "promoted a homogeneity of language" (Algeo 2001: 36), which, perhaps, might have played a role in the keeping of the regular participle marker at the time. Interestingly enough, however, the eventual irregularization of participles could have likewise been affected

(3) What her fingers searched for now were the small knots of thread that she had *sewn* into the lining of the left pocket: five of them, thick enough to [...] (*COHA*, ElusiveMrsPollifax, 1971).

Even though the analysis has shown relatively uniform distributions of *-ed* and -(*e*)*n* over time, there is some margin for variation inasmuch as certain verbs deserve, in my opinion, a separate mention, namely *show*, *awake* and *wake*. It seems that the first might have acted as the initiating element of the shift from *-ed* to -(*e*)*n*, a trend that was later followed by the rest of the verbs. The other two, in turn, stand out for maintaining the *-ed* participle over -(*e*)*n* throughout the whole 1600–1900 period.

3.1.1. The Verb Show as Initiating Element of the **-ed** *to* **-(e)n** *Change*

The eighteenth century witnessed the spread of a number of dictionaries and grammars, probably as a continuation of those issued in EModE in an attempt to standardize the language. Samuel Johnson's *A Dictionary of the English Language* (1755) outstandingly contributed to accomplish this goal, to such an extent that it also served as the main foundation in the production of subsequent paramount linguistic pieces, as it is the case of Robert Lowth's *A Short Introduction to English Grammar* (1763) (Auer 2012: 943; Finegan 2012: 969–70; Percy 2012: 1009).

As far as the verb *show* is concerned, Johnson (1755) mentions in his dictionary that the participle of this verb is formed by means of the -(*e*)*n* inflection, without making any reference to the other form, whereas with verbs like *saw* he explicitly suggests that both the *-ed* and -(*e*)*n* participial markers are feasible. Tables 5 and 6 below provide the distribution of the participles *shown* and *showed* in BrE and AmE throughout the different decades of the eighteenth century. As observed, the participial structure *shown* prevails over *showed* from the beginning to the end of the century in both varieties. The only exception to this general trend is attested in AmE in the 1700–1710 decade, where the regular suffix is found to slightly outnumber the -(*e*)*n* variant. Such evidence may come to justify the omission of *showed* in Johnson's work, as well as to corroborate that this verb is the

by the important portion of British migrants that arrived in America in the early twentieth century (see Algeo 2001: 49–50), who may have possibly exerted some influence in the manner participles were used.

first of its class in developing an early preference for -(*e*)*n* and in steadily neglecting *-ed*. This scenario seems to have remained consistent over time, with just some sporadic degrees of variation. According to the *OED*, the past participle *shown* is today "the usual form; [though] the older *showed* is still sometimes used in the perfect tenses active (chiefly with material object)" (Simpson and Weiner 1989: s.v. show; also Fowler 1927: 532).

Table 5: Distribution of the participles *shown* and *showed* in eighteenth-century BrE (n.f.)[19]

BrE	*Shown*	*Showed*
1700–1710	7,135.88	251.85
1710–1719	6,402.49	647.65
1720–1729	6,811.93	1,389.5
1730–1739	7,813.63	397.3
1740–1749	6,695.01	469.47
1750–1759	7,569.37	391.04
1760–1769	5,988.54	171.41
1770–1779	6,685.64	263.15
1780–1789	6,255.22	251.93
1790–1799	6,936.78	112.42

Table 6: Distribution of the participles *shown* and *showed* in eighteenth-century AmE (n.f.)

AmE	*Shown*	*Showed*
1700–1710	3,100.75	3,350.24
1710–1719	2,724.23	2,545.01
1720–1729	5,292.44	2,809.57
1730–1739	5,131.55	1,436.83
1740–1749	5,925.3	1,858.23
1750–1759	6,288.61	1,154.24
1760–1769	7,878.04	1,240.86
1770–1779	6,798.66	755.41
1780–1789	6,022.93	829.03
1790–1799	5,110.63	678.23

19 Note that the data presented in this specific context come uniquely from *ECCO*, as it is the only eighteenth-century BrE corpus used in this study which permits the classification of instances into decades.

On the other hand, the later *-ed* to *-(e)n* shift in the other verbs could have been triggered by the linguistic influence of Lowth's authoritative prescriptive grammar. While he shares Johnson's view as regards the past participle of verbs like *saw* or *strew*, he prioritizes the use of the structures *sawn* and *strewn*, yet noting – via asterisks – that the regular forms *sawed* and *strewed* are likewise possible and valid in use (see Lowth 1763: 82–3). Even though *saw* and *strew*, together with *sew*, still denote some inclination for *-ed* to form their participles in the second half of the period 1700–1799, a minute survey of these in my corpora has revealed that most instances with *-(e)n* in eighteenth century BrE and AmE appear after the publication of Lowth's grammar, such as those illustrated in (4–6).[20] This tentatively suggests that his work had indeed some responsibility in the progressive change from *-ed* to *-(e)n* participles that arises, sooner or later depending on the variety, with the course of the years. The historical codification of the English language is thus a moderate, gradual and non-neutral procedure, as "[h]owever descriptive it may aim to be, it necessitates prescriptivism, not in the sense of prescribing some and proscribing other usages but in selecting and promoting some variants over others" (Finegan 2012: 970).

(4) It may be *sawn* or cut with carpenter's tool, into any form whatever (*EVANS*, N18559, 1792).
(5) Their furies hither, ſo with wrecks and dead Had *ſtrewn* the floods, disfigur'd thus the ſtrands (*ECCO*, K078097.001, 1787).
(6) Some were nailed on crosses; others *sewn* up in the skins of wild beasts, and exposed to the fury of dogs (*CLMET*, 3_1_1_67, 1776).

3.1.2. **(a)waked** *and* **(a)woken** *in the 1600–1900 Period*

The different diffusion of the participles of *awake* and *wake* in 1600–1900 is based on the volatility of their uses since OE and ME, their

20 The rate of *-(e)n* participles after Lowth's piece with respect to the total of occurrences in eighteenth-century BrE and AmE is the following: (1) *sawn* (c. 66.67 per cent in BrE and 65.85 per cent in AmE); (2) *strewn* (c. 75.56 per cent in BrE and 100 per cent in AmE); (3) *sewn* (100 per cent in both varieties).

selection being contingent upon whether they were thought to pertain to the traditionally strong or weak classes of verbs. Even today, "the principal parts are still somewhat fragile and fluid, with much blending of forms and functions" (Burchfield 1998: 82).

In my data, however, the phenomenon seems to develop a straightforward tendency over time. The form *-ed* prevails from beginning to end, while those with -(*e*)*n* are erratic in the greatest part of the period, their higher frequencies mostly, and almost uniquely, observed in the nineteenth century. The change towards -(*e*)*n* occurred in the twentieth century, principally due to the appearance of a third participle form of these verbs, i.e. *(a)woke*, which began to compete in a recurrent manner against *(a)waked* in the second half of LModE. This variant possibly flourished from the preterite paradigm of the verb, where it could also be alternatively employed with *(a)waked* (see Johnson 1755).

Figures 1–4 present the distribution of -(*e*)*n* and *-ed* in *awake* and *wake* together with the forms *awoke* and *woke* in BrE and AmE in 1600–1900. Leaving aside the outstanding character of *(a)waked* in the seventeenth and eighteenth centuries, the results display different frequencies of appearance in the nineteenth century depending on the verb and the language variety. First, *awoke* is found to slightly outnumber *awaked* in BrE, with a total of 61.44 instances vs 49.15, whereas *awoken* is negligible. In AmE, on the contrary, *awaked* predominates, though the occurrence of *awoke* is relatively high (39.97 instances). When it comes to the verb *wake*, *-ed* leads the way in the two varieties, AmE in particular, followed at a distance by *woke* and the -(*e*)*n* form, both more regularly witnessed in BrE (45.05 and 16.38 occurrences, respectively).

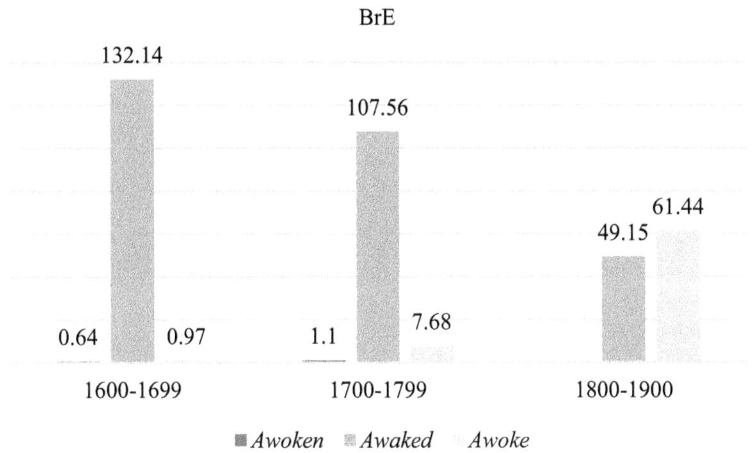

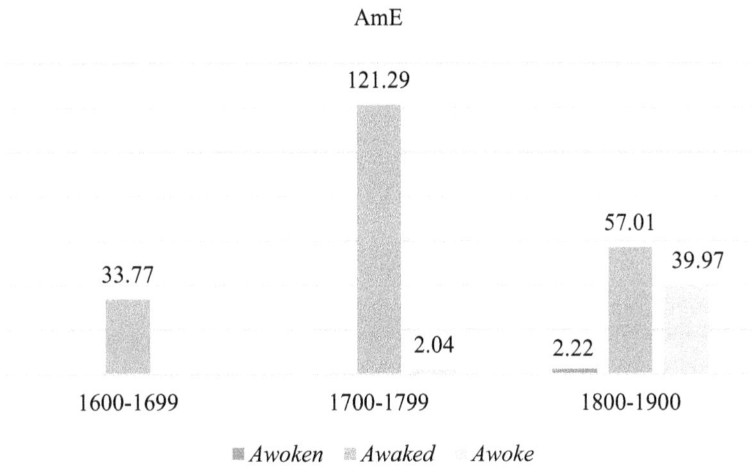

Figures 1 and 2: Distribution of the forms *awoken*, *awaked* and *awoke* in historical BrE and AmE, respectively (n.f.).

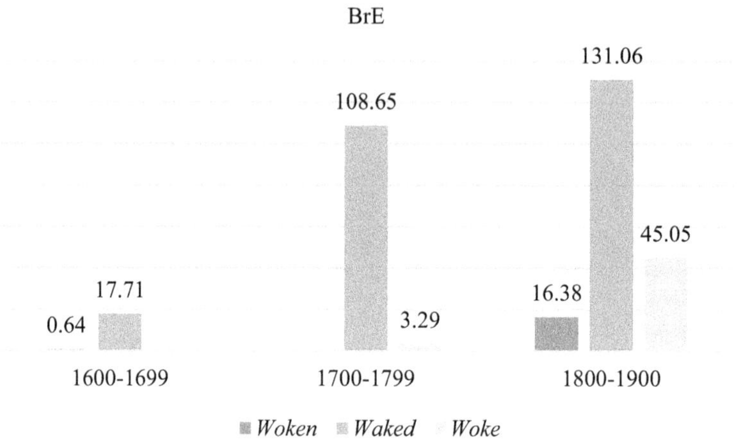

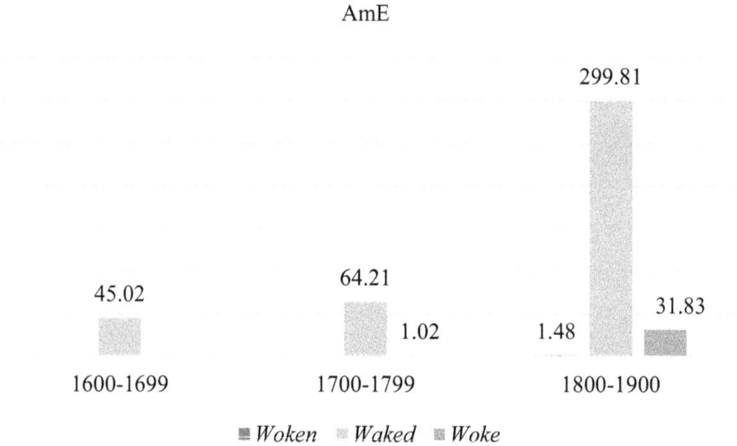

Figures 3 and 4: Distribution of the forms *woken*, *waked* and *woke* in historical BrE and AmE, respectively (n.f.).

The supremacy of -(*e*)*n* did not come up to the twentieth century, still at the beginning of it *-ed* was the commonest form and the other participle structures were viewed as rare alternatives (Fowler 1927: 39). It is probably not until the second half of the century, when *(a)woken* eventually absorbed *(a)woke*, that -(*e*)*n* became the participial marker par excellence. Today, this situation remains similar: *awoken* and *woken* predominate, while *awaked* and *waked* are "more likely to occur in English dialects (and also in the language of children) than in standard English" (Burchfield 1998: 82). Finally, Algeo (2006: 13, 18) remarks that the participial forms *awoken* and *woken* are also nowadays several times more recurrent in British than in American documents.

3.2. Functions of -ed *and* -(e)n *in the Period and across the Varieties*

The present section analyses the *-ed*/*-(e)n* alternation in terms of the main functions of participles. It aims to assess whether the different uses favour a specific participial form, as well as to determine any variation between early BrE and AmE. Following Crystal (1995: 204), four participial functions have been considered in this respect: (1) to indicate a past aspect, as in (7); (2) to indicate the passive voice, as in (8); (3) to operate as the initial constituent in some subordinate clauses, as in (9); and (4) to act as an adjective, as in (10).

(7) Christ himself suffered on this account (as we have already *shown*) and others of his servants have thought it their Glory to be called unto suffering for it (*EEBO*, A41202, 1692).

(8) [. . .] were in the act of tearing me to pieces, when I was *waked* by the stepping of Hall, my room-mate into bed (*COHA*, GeorgiaScenesCharacters,1835).

(9) The noble trunk itself is far from being valueless. *Sawn* into posts, it upholds the islander's dwelling; converted into charcoal, [. . .] (*COHA*, Omoo, 1847).

(10) The Wall of the Fortification is about thirthy foot high built of *sawed* Stone, such as they gett out of the sand between the Sea and the Sound (*EVANS*, N00716, 1699).

From a quantitative standpoint, both *-(e)n* and *-ed* are found more repeatedly employed with almost all the verbs to denote the passive voice and a past aspect. On a different note, the number of instances where they operate as an adjective is lower, with the only exception of *saw*, in which such a function is viewed to outnumber the indication of a past aspect. Finally, those cases where they stand as the initial element of a subordinate clause are rarer, comprising overall a handful of occurrences with respect to the totality.[21]

The data indicate that *show* is the verb presenting the most clear-cut trend of development of all.[22] As illustrated in Figures 5 and 6, the two principal functions of participles are witnessed to increase over time with *shown*. Such a chronological distribution is contrary to *showed*, which decreases as soon as the regular form is omitted as participle form in benefit of the irregular -(*e*)*n*. Concerning the variation between BrE and AmE, the main difference is that both the decline of *showed* and the boost of *shown* are more pronounced in BrE in almost all the subperiods. The only exception is in the transition from the eighteenth to the nineteenth century. At this point, the use of the -(*e*)*n* ending as an aid to indicate a passive rises more drastically in AmE, where the difference between the occurrences of *shown* in 1700–1799 and 1800–1899 is larger than in the other variety (1,069.28 vs 725.43 instances, respectively).[23]

21 An overview of this last function in the material seems to hesitantly point -(*e*)*n* as the favourite participial marker for such a purpose, still certain minor variations may be also observed depending on the verb.

22 See Appendix 1 to compare the diffusion of *shown/showed* as indicators of a past aspect and the passive voice with that of the other verbs under consideration.

23 Note that those cases where two functions overlap (e.g. *it had been shown*) have been left out in the analysis in order to avoid ambiguity.

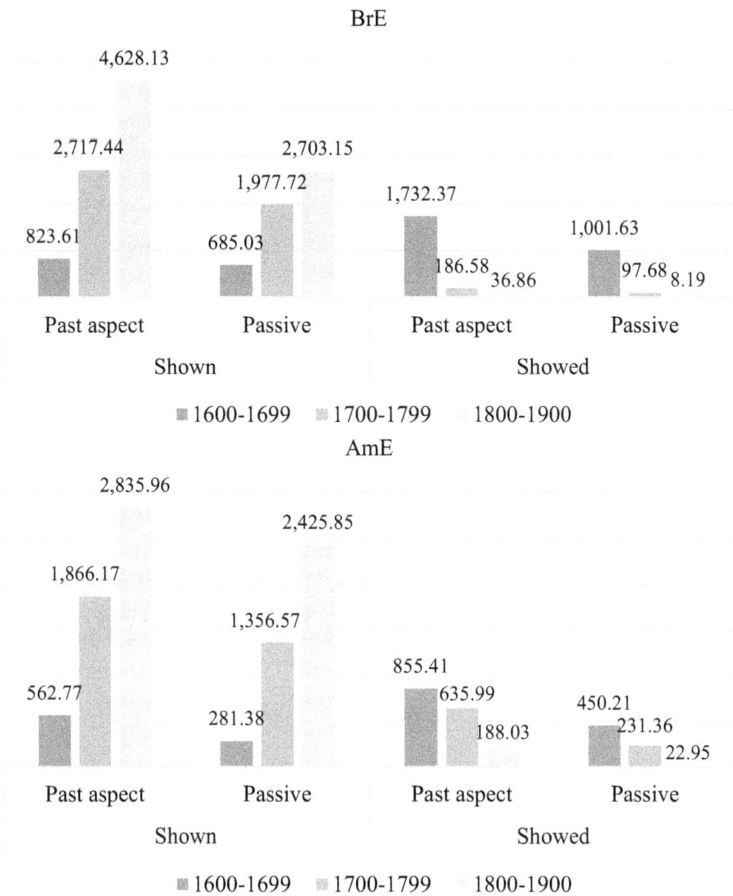

Figures 5 and 6: Distribution of *shown* and *showed* with respect to the main participial functions in historical BrE and AmE, respectively (n.f.).

On the other hand, the adjectival function of *shown* and *showed* is negligible compared, for instance, to the main participial functions, but, above all, in proportion to the complete distribution of the forms in the varieties. More specifically, they comprise less than 1 per cent of the whole set of occurrences of this verb in my data.[24] Adjectival participles

24 Note that most instances of *shown/showed* as participial adjectives have been attested with the -(*e*)*n* suffix (e.g. 'Whether we must take every Affirmer to have

are, in this vein, regarded with the rest of the verbs (see Levin 2009: 80–1; 85). Tables 7 and 8 then illustrate their diffusions in historical BrE and AmE.

Table 7: Distribution of adjectival participles in BrE (1600–1900) (n.f.)

Adjectival participles (AmE)	***Awake***		***Saw***		***Sew***	
	-(e)n	***-ed***	***-(e)n***	***-ed***	***-(e)n***	***-ed***
1600–1699	–	–	–	11.26	–	11.26
1700–1799	–	–	–	23.44	–	2.04
1800–1900	–	–	8.14	12.58	2.22	0.74
	Strew				***Wake***	
	-(e)n		***-ed***		***-(e)n***	***-ed***
1600–1699	–		11.26		–	–
1700–1799	–		2.04		–	1.02
1800–1900	8.88		3.7		–	1.48

Table 8: Distribution of adjectival participles in AmE (1600–1900) (n.f.)

Adjectival participles (BrE)	***Awake***		***Saw***		***Sew***	
	-(e)n	***-ed***	***-(e)n***	***-ed***	***-(e)n***	***-ed***
1600–1699	–	0.97	1.29	3.38	–	0.97
1700–1799	–	2.2	6.59	7.68	–	4.39
1800–1900	–	4.1	12.29	4.1	12.29	20.48
	Strew				***Wake***	
	-(e)n		***-ed***		***-(e)n***	***-ed***
1600–1699	1.29		3.38		0.16	–
1700–1799	8.78		7.68		–	–
1800–1900	53.24		–		–	–

The results reveal that the regular suffix *-ed* is the preferred marker in the first half of the period and that -(*e*)*n* has a major significance from 1800 onwards. Some variation, however, may be likewise observed

a Commission, if he shew it not? Or every shewn Commission to be current, and not surreptitious, though contrary to Law?', *EEBO*, A27006, 1696).

according to the verb and the variety. First, *(a)wake*, as expected, is an exception since *-ed* outnumbers -(*e*)*n* throughout the whole period. Second, the verb *strew* features some preference for -(*e*)*n* to the detriment of *-ed* already in eighteenth century BrE (8.78 vs 7.68 occurrences). Finally, despite the fact that the forms with -(*e*)*n* present a comparatively high frequency, the verbs *sew* and *saw* seem to be more inclined towards *-ed* in nineteenth-century BrE and AmE, respectively.

4. Conclusions

The morphological shape of the past participle of certain irregular verbs is found to have outstanding levels of fluctuation throughout LModE, OE weak class 2 verbs in particular. Some of these verbs adopted the strong participle ending -(*e*)*n* together with the original *-ed* in the transition to ME, offering the possibility of an alternative usage of the forms which has persisted with the passing of time. The present contribution has analysed the *-ed*/-(*e*)*n* alternation in BrE and AmE in the historical period 1600–1900, paying attention to six of these historically OE weak class 2 verbs.

The study has shown that most verbs have a preference for the *-ed* participial ending in the seventeenth and the eighteenth centuries in the two varieties. It has also revealed that an inversion of the trend takes place only in nineteenth-century BrE. This has led me to conclude that the movement towards the predominance of -(*e*)*n* in AmE occurs later, possibly throughout the twentieth century. In addition to this, special emphasis has also been put on the dissemination of *show* and *(a)wake*, since they exhibit different patterns of diffusion if compared with those of the other verbs. The former presents the earliest preference for -(*e*)*n*, while the latter has been found to keep *-ed* in the period.

The paper has additionally addressed the phenomenon on the basis of some different functions of participles. In this vein, the results have demonstrated that *show* presents the most straightforward and balanced trajectory, with *shown* rising significantly over time as indicator of a past aspect and the passive voice, and *showed* decreasing for the same purposes. Finally, the analysis has also considered the adjectival function of participles with the other five verbs under survey. Although some minor variation has been found across the verbs and the varieties, *-ed* seems to be the choice in the seventeenth and the eighteenth centuries, whilst *-(e)n* has gained substantial ground since the nineteenth.

Sources

Davies, Mark, *Corpus of Historical American English* (Brigham Young University, 2010). Available at https://www.english-corpora.org/coha/.

——, *Early English Books Online Corpus* (Brigham Young University, 2017). Available at https://www.english-corpora.org/eebo/.

De Smet, Hendrik, Susanne Flach, Jukka Tyrkkö and Hans-Jürgen Diller, eds., *The Corpus of Late Modern English, Version 3.1: Improved Tokenization and Linguistic Annotation* (KU Leuven, Freie Universität Berlin, University of Tampere, Ruhr-Universität Bochum, 2015). Available at https://fedora.clarin-d.uni-saarland.de/clmet/clmet.html.

Eighteenth Century Collections Online (Gale, 2018). Available at https://quod.lib.umich.edu/e/ecco/.

Evans Early American Imprints (Text Creation Partnership, 2011). Available at https://textcreationpartnership.org/tcp-texts/evans-tcp-evans-early-american-imprints/.

Kurath, Hans et al., eds., *Middle English Dictionary* (Ann Arbor, MI: University of Michigan Press, 1952–2001). Available at http://quod.lib.umich.edu/m/med/.

Simpson, John A. and Edmund S. C. Weiner, eds., *Oxford English Dictionary*, 2nd edition (Oxford: Clarendon Press, 1989).

References

Algeo, John, 'External History', in John Algeo, ed., *The Cambridge History of the English Language. Volume VI: English in North America* (Cambridge: Cambridge University Press, 2001), 1–58.

——, *British or American English? A Handbook of Word and Grammar Patterns* (Cambridge: Cambridge University Press, 2006).

Auer, Anita, 'Late Modern English: Standardization', in Alexander Bergs, and Laurel J. Brinton, eds, *English Historical Linguistics: An International Handbook* Vol. 1 (Berlin and Boston: Mouton de Gruyter, 2012), 939–952.

Barnes, Michael, *A New Introduction to Old Norse. Part I: Grammar.* 3rd edition (Exeter: Short Run Press Limited, 2008).

Beal, Joan C., 'Periods: Late Modern English', in Alexander Bergs, and Laurel J. Brinton, eds, *English Historical Linguistics: An International Handbook,* Vol. 1 (Berlin and Boston: Mouton de Gruyter, 2012), 63–78.

Biber, Douglas, Stig Johansson, Geoffrey Leech, Susan Conrad, and Edward Finegan, *Longman Grammar of Spoken and Written English* (Harlow: Longman, 1999).

Bosworth, Joseph, and Thomas Northcote Toller, *An Anglo-Saxon Dictionary* (London: Oxford University Press, [1898] 1964).

Burchfield, Robert, *The New Fowler's Modern English Usage* (Oxford: Oxford University Press, 1998).

Carter, Ronald, and Michael McCarthy, *Cambridge Grammar of English: A Comprehensive Guide. Spoken and Written English Grammar and Usage* (Cambridge: Cambridge University Press, 2006).

Collins COBUILD English Grammar (London: William Collins Sons & Co Ltd, 1990).

Collins, Peter, and Pam Peters, 'Australian English: Morphology and Syntax', in Bernd Kortmann, and Edgar W. Schneider, eds, *A Handbook of Varieties of English: A Multimedia Reference Tool. Volume 2: Morphology and Syntax* (Berlin and Boston: Mouton De Gruyter, 2004), 593–610.

Crystal, David, *The Cambridge Encyclopedia of the English Language* (Cambridge: Cambridge University Press, 1995).

Davies, Mark, and Don Chapman, 'The Effect of Representativeness and Size in Historical Corpora: An Empirical Study of Changes in Lexical Frequency', in Don Chapman, Colette Moore, and Miranda Wilcox, eds, *Studies in the History of the English Language VII: Generalizing vs. Particularizing Methodologies in Historical Linguistic Analysis* (Berlin and Boston: Mouton De Gruyter, 2016), 131–150.

De Smet, Hendrik, 'A Corpus of Late Modern English Texts', *ICAME Journal* 29 (2005), 69–82.

Elsness, Johan, 'The Present Perfect and the Preterite', in Günter Rohdenburg, and Julia Schlüter, eds, *One Language, Two Grammars: Grammatical Differences between British and American English* (Cambridge: Cambridge University Press, 2009), 228–245.

Evans, Charles, *American Bibliography: A Chronological Dictionary of all Books, Pamphlets and Periodical Publications Printed in the United States of America from the Genesis of Printing in 1639 down to and Including the Year 1820* (Chicago: The Blakely Press, 1903).

Evans, Bergen, and Cornelia Evans, *A Dictionary of Contemporary American Usage* (New York: Random House, 1957).

Finegan, Edward, 'Standardization: Prescriptive Tradition', in Alexander Bergs, and Laurel J. Brinton, eds, *English Historical Linguistics: An International Handbook,* Vol. 1 (Berlin and Boston: Mouton de Gruyter, 2012), 967–980.

Fowler, Henry Watson, *A Dictionary of Modern English Usage* (Oxford: Clarendon Press, 1927).

Greenbaum, Sidney, and Randolph Quirk, *A Student's Grammar of the English Language* (London: Longman, 1990).

Huddleston, Rodney, and Geoffrey K. Pullum, *A Student's Introduction to English Grammar* (Cambridge: Cambridge University Press, 2005).

Hundt, Marianne, 'Colonial Lag, Colonial Innovation or Simply Language Change?', in Günter Rohdenburg, and Julia Schlüter, eds, *One Language, Two Grammars: Grammatical Differences between British and American English* (Cambridge: Cambridge University Press, 2009), 13–37.

Johansson, Stig, 'American and British English Grammar: An Elicitation Experiment', *English Studies* 60/2 (1979), 195–215.

Johnson, Samuel, *A Dictionary of the English Language* (London: W. Strahan, 1755).

Kilgarriff, Adam, Pavel Rychlý, Pavel Smrz, and David Tugwell, 'The Sketch Engine', in Geoffrey Williams, and Sandra Vessier, eds, *Proceedings of the Eleventh EURALEX International Congress* (Lorient: Université de Bretagne Sud, 2004), 105–115.

Kilgarriff, Adam, Vít Baisa, Jan Bušta, Miloš Jakubíček, Kovář Vojtěch, Jan Michelfeit, Pavel Rychlý, and Vít Suchomel, 'The Sketch Engine: Ten Years on', *Lexicography. Journal of ASIALEX* 1 (2014), 7–36.

Lass, Roger, *The Shape of English: Structure and History* (London: J. M. Dent & Sons Ltd, 1987).

——, 'Phonology and Morphology', in Norman Blake, ed., *The Cambridge History of the English Language. Volume II: 1066–1476* (Cambridge: Cambridge University Press, 1992), 23–155.

——, 'Phonology and Morphology', in Roger Lass, ed., *The Cambridge History of the English Language. Volume III: 1476–1776* (Cambridge: Cambridge University Press, 1999), 56–186.

Levin, Magnus, 'The Formation of the Preterite and the Past Participle', in Günter Rohdenburg, and Julia Schlüter, eds, *One Language, Two Grammars: Grammatical Differences between British and American English* (Cambridge: Cambridge University Press, 2009), 60–85.

Lowth, Robert, *A Short Introduction to English Grammar: With Critical Notes* (London: A. Millar, R. and J. Dodsley, 1763).

Minkova, Donka, *A Historical Phonology of English* (Edinburgh: Edinburgh University Press, 2014).

Mondorf, Britta, 'Late Modern English: Morphology', in Alexander Bergs, and Laurel J. Brinton, eds, *English Historical Linguistics: An International Handbook,* Vol. 1 (Berlin and Boston: Mouton de Gruyter, 2012), 842–869.

Percy, Carol, 'Standardization: Codifiers', in Alexander Bergs, and Laurel J. Brinton, eds, *English Historical Linguistics: An International Handbook,* Vol. 1 (Berlin and Boston: Mouton de Gruyter, 2012), 1006–1020.

Quirk, Randolph, Sidney Greenbaum, Geoffrey Leech, and Jan Svartvik, *A Grammar of Contemporary English* (London: Longman, 1972).

——, *A Comprehensive Grammar of the English Language* (London and New York: Longman, 1985).

Schlüter, Julia, 'Phonology and Grammar', in Günter Rohdenburg, and Julia Schlüter, eds, *One Language, Two Grammars: Grammatical Differences between British and American English* (Cambridge: Cambridge University Press, 2009), 108–129.

Tolonen, Mikko, Eetu Mäkelä, Ali Ijaz, and Leo Lahti, 'Corpus Linguistics and *Eighteenth Century Collections Online* (ECCO)', *Research in Corpus Linguistics* 9/1 (2021), 19–34.

Tolonen, Mikko, Eetu Mäkelä, and Leo Lahti, 'The Anatomy of the Eighteenth Century Collections Online (ECCO)', *Eighteenth-Century Studies* 56/1 (2022), 95–123.

Wełna, Jerzy, 'Middle English: Morphology', in Alexander Bergs and Laurel J. Brinton, eds, *English Historical Linguistics: An International Handbook,* Vol. 1 (Berlin and Boston: Mouton de Gruyter, 2012), 415–434.

Appendix 1: Distribution of -(*e*)*n* and -*ed* participles excepting "show" as indicators of past aspects and the passive voice in historical BrE and AmE (n.f.)

Past aspect (BrE)	***Awake***		***Saw***		***Sew***	
	-(e)n	***-ed***	***-(e)n***	***-ed***	***-(e)n***	***-ed***
1600–1699	0.16	19.96	1.13	1.77	0.16	4.99
1700–1799	–	27.44	1.1	2.2	–	10.98
1800–1900	–	16.38	–	4.1	28.67	4.1
	Strew				*Wake*	
	-(e)n		*-ed*		*-(e)n*	*-ed*
1600–1699	0.16		14.16		–	6.44
1700–1799	5.49		13.17		–	35.12
1800–1900	32.77		20.48		16.38	90.11
Passive voice (BrE)	***Awake***		***Saw***		***Sew***	
	-(e)n	***-ed***	***-(e)n***	***-ed***	***-(e)n***	***-ed***
1600–1699	0.48	108.16	28.81	17.38	1.13	31.39
1700–1799	1.1	72.44	29.63	30.73	6.59	124.02
1800–1900	–	24.57	40.96	–	102.39	61.44
	Strew				*Wake*	
	-(e)n		*-ed*		*-(e)n*	*-ed*
1600–1699	4.02		98.83		0.16	11.11
1700–1799	35.12		167.92		–	66.95
1800–1900	421.86		188.4		–	36.86
Past aspect (AmE)	***Awake***		***Saw***		***Sew***	
	-(e)n	***-ed***	***-(e)n***	***-ed***	***-(e)n***	***-ed***
1600–1699	–	22.51	–	–	11.26	11.26
1700–1799	–	24.46	1.02	8.15	–	12.23
1800–1900	–	29.61	–	11.84	2.96	25.17
	Strew				*Wake*	
	-(e)n		*-ed*		*-(e)n*	*-ed*
1600–1699	–		11.26		–	11.26
1700–1799	3.06		19.36		–	18.35
1800–1900	27.39		12.58		0.74	179.14
Passive voice (AmE)	***Awake***		***Saw***		***Sew***	
	-(e)n	***-ed***	***-(e)n***	***-ed***	***-(e)n***	***-ed***
1600–1699	–	11.26	33.77	–	–	45.02
1700–1799	–	93.77	36.69	74.4	2.04	73.38
1800–1900	–	25.91	23.69	39.23	52.56	119.18
	Strew				***Wake***	
	-(e)n		***-ed***		***-(e)n***	***-ed***
1600–1699	11.26		11.26		–	33.77
1700–1799	17.33		100.9		–	40.77
1800–1900	541.13		190.99		0.74	102.9

Marta Pacheco-Franco

Webster's Spelling Reform: From *-our* to *-or* in *Colour*-Type Words[1]

1. Introduction

There exist in Present-day English (henceforth, PdE) two orthographic renderings for words like *colour* and *honour*: the one hereby adopted, which is characteristic of British English (BrE), and *color* and *honor*, which tipify American English (AmE) (Gramley et al. 2021: 278). These are but two spelling variants of the very same suffix, which, though no longer productive, would form abstract nouns of condition like those above. The affix was introduced into English in the form of lexical borrowings from Anglo-Norman, spelled *-our*, and from Latin, spelled *-or* (*OED* s.v. *-our*, *-or*, suffixes). For most of the nouns concerned, however, the etymological source is unclear and the two origins are contemplated in sources like *OED*, as in *colour*, which is "[p]artly a borrowing from French [and] [p]artly a borrowing from Latin" (*OED* s.v. *colour*, n.). Although their etymons ultimately go back to the Latin term, the truth is that the emergence of the *-or* spelling seems to have been a fifteenth-century development that was never prevalent in BrE usage (Pacheco-Franco and Calle-Martín 2020: 174). To answer the question of how this variant survived into the PdE configuration, in spite of its low incidence over time, we have to consider the figure of Noah Webster.

Historical accounts of AmE orthography often pay much attention to the role played by Webster and his spelling reform in the configuration

1 The present research has been funded by the Spanish Ministry of Universities (grant number FPU19/05104). This grant is hereby gratefully acknowledged.

of the system. Although he opposed the simplification of spelling at first (Upward and Davidson 2011: 302), Webster's beliefs had changed by the publication of his *Dissertations on the English Language* (1789) and later – and more aggressively – in *A Compendious Dictionary of the English Language* (1806). His proposal at reform was based on the principles of simplification and uniformity, whereby he promoted many of the orthographic renderings that characterize AmE today (see Trudgill and Hannah 2017: 85–7). The shift from *-our* to *-or* is, in fact, illustrative of both of these principles, as the latter is not only a simplified version of the former, but it also regularizes the spelling of word-final /ər/ , as also found in agentive nouns like *doctor* and *emperor*. Needless to say, these forms were not of the lexicographer's own invention. Instead, he selected some variants from the pool that had been available in the Early Modern period and which – to a certain extent – survived into Late Modern English (Burchfield 1989: 120; Algeo 2000: 598; Horobin 2013: 140–1).

According to the literature, his regulatory endeavours were largely accepted by the population of the time. This turn of events is particularly interesting in view of Webster's precedents. Indeed, the English language was not unfamiliar to calls for spelling reform throughout history, since these have been a constant ever since the Early Modern period (see Upward and Davidson 2011; Horobin 2013). As evinced by the very nature of the system, however, they remained largely unsuccessful. Even in America's short history, there had already been a failed attempt at reform, Benjamin Franklin's *Scheme* (1779). Though unsuccessful, it seems that the founding father paved the way for Webster, whose rationale for the re-spelling of AmE was profoundly distinct. Other than entailing some linguistic "improvement" in orthography, the proposal was ideologically loaded (Horobin 2013: 194–5). It seems that, ever since the War of Independence, "the very notion of American English itself was strongly tied to nationalism" (Wolfram and Schilling-Estes 1998: 17), an idea that Webster exploited to his success. Indeed, his reform became substantially more influential on the political level as he succeeded in "promoting a sense of pride in distinctively American language variants" (Algeo 2000: 599). His objective was clear: "a national language is a band of national union" (Webster 1789: 397, original emphasis) and spelling opened the way to achieve it more plainly.

The socio-historical context of nineteenth-century AmE is crucial for understanding why a proposal such as Webster's would take root in the language. The 1800s saw an ever-growing sentiment of nationalism throughout the United States, caused by various historical events and influencing attitudes towards the variety and its use. For many, the War of 1812 has been regarded as "the [true] war of independence" (Cooper 1991: 546), since "the spirit of national self-confidence emerging in literature and elsewhere" after that suggests that the "mental bondage" still linking the United States to Great Britain had finally come to an end (Simpson 1986: 122–3; Cooper 1991: 546). The general election of 1828, marked by Andrew Jackson's victory, helped advance these ideas of self-assurance. Jackson, who had been known as the "Indian fighter" since 1815, centred on promoting nation-internal policies, such as fostering westward expansion and solving territorial disputes (Simpson 1986: 139). These led to a sense of "endonormative orientation" that translated directly into the language and, in terms of Schneider's Dynamic Cycle, Phase 4 was thus set in motion (2007: 283). Indeed, pride in the nation ultimately equated with pride in the national language and vice versa. Essentially, the linguistic forms promoted by lexicographers like Webster and Bartlett – the latter in his *Dictionary of Americanisms* (1848) – were widely celebrated. The United States had thus shifted from exonormativity to endonormativity by the mid-nineteenth century.

It is within this context that Webster put forward his proposal, which was, by all accounts, successful. Notwithstanding the mass of literature supporting the lexicographer's prominence in the creation of the American orthographic system, empirical studies assessing his influence are still lacking. This state of affairs raises questions regarding the mechanisms of standardization that operated towards the success of this spelling reform. Linguistic forms must undergo selection, diffusion and codification before being considered standard and it is still unclear how Webster fits into this process. The present paper thus presents a state-of-the-art study aimed at reviewing the role(s) played by the lexicographer in the configuration of AmE spelling. This will be accomplished by means of a corpus-based case study focusing on the *-our*/*-or* variation exemplified by *colour*-type words.

2. Methodology

This paper puts forward a corpus-based study that draws information from two sources, the *Evans* corpus (Text Creation Partnership 2011) and the *Corpus of Historical American English* or *COHA* (Davies 2010). The corpora have been chosen in light of their quantitative and qualitative features. Containing 140 and 475 million tokens, respectively, they currently sample language use in America during the periods 1640–1800 and 1820–2010. Their research design is similar inasmuch as the texts conforming them cover a wide variety of genres, including – but not limited to – literature, academic works, social and historical documents and, in the case of the latter, also TV and film scripts. Despite their apparent comparability, two issues arise in working with *Evans* and *COHA*. The first relates to the genre division of the corpora. The latter, housed in Mark Davies's *English Corpora* website, enables searches by genre, a functionality that will prove extremely useful in the upcoming analysis. *Evans*, however, is available for download and the files are presented in bulk. Since genre is not coded into the headers, such an analysis would require manual classification of the more than 5,000 files conforming the corpus, which is unfeasible.

The second issue concerns the historical coverage of *Evans* and *COHA*, as there are 20 years left unsampled in the history of American English, the period 1800–1819, which coincidentally correspond with the publication of Webster's *A Compendious Dictionary* (1806). For the purpose of bridging this gap, two measures have been taken. First, the files produced in *Evans* in the year 1800 have been taken to represent, albeit with limitations, the entire decade 1800–1809. Secondly, the files pertaining to the decade 1810–1819 have been re-incorporated into this study. These were discarded in the most recent update of *COHA* because they "had fairly poor genre balance and there were only about one million words of data" (Davies 2021). While not entirely representative, these will, nevertheless, provide invaluable insight into the selection of the spelling variants *-our* and *-or* in the early nineteenth century.

Once the shortcomings of the study were considered, the absolute frequency of the twenty-five topmost frequent items allowing for *-our*/

-*or* variation in Present-day English were retrieved.[2] The processes certainly differed for each corpora. In the case of *Evans*, the software *AntConc* (Anthony 2020) was employed for retrieving the results, whereas *COHA* was consulted online (Davies 2010). In the end, over 600,000 instances of these *colour*-type words were retrieved, 205,883 with the spelling -*our* and 413,620 with -*or*. The tokens were then normalized to a common base of 100,000 words to enable their comparison diachronically and across genres in *COHA*. The relative frequencies are thus presented in the analysis, though always bearing in mind the statistical significance of the variants. The chi-square test and Cramér's *V* were calculated for this.

For the purpose of comparing usage to Webster's precepts, the present paper also puts forward what has been called a precept corpus analysis. A precept corpus is a collection of works that actively engage with linguistic codification and, to a certain extent, with prescriptivism, such as grammars, dictionaries and usage guides (see Auer and González-Díaz 2005; Yáñez-Bouza 2008; Auer 2009 for previous precept studies). Table 1 presents the works considered in this study, which – while focusing on the figure of Webster – also includes authors like Worcester in the mid-nineteneth and Funk and Wagnall in the late 1800s. The data retrieved from the precept corpus pertains to the headword of each entry. The occurrences of each spelling variant were then copied on a file, which would calculate the percentage of -*our* and -*or* for each subperiod in the corpus. These data are presented, alongside the normalized frequencies of usage, in the upcoming analysis. Finally, it should be noted that there is a 20-year lag in the representation of the precept data with respect to usage, since it is impossible to measure the influence of codification on the language of the time (Auer and González-Díaz 2005: 323). Their success, if so, would not have been either immediate nor simultanenous.

2 Most specifically, the linguistic input for the study includes the following words: *ardour*, *armour*, *behaviour*, *candour*, *clamour*, *colour*, *demeanour*, *endeavour*, *favour*, *fervour*, *harbour*, *honour*, *humour*, *labour*, *neighbour*, *odour*, *rigour*, *rumour*, *savour*, *splendour*, *succour*, *tumour*, *valour*, *vapour* and *vigour*.

Table 1: Works conforming the precept corpus

Author	Year	Title
Webster	1790 (1783)	*The American Spelling Book*
Webster	1806	*A Compendious Dictionary of the English Language*
Webster	1828	*An American Dictionary of the English Language*
Worcester	1830	*A Comprehensive Pronouncing and Explanatory Dictionary*
Worcester	1846	*A Universal and Critical Dictionary*
Webster	1848 (1847)	*An American Dictionary of the English Language* (Enlarged edition)
Worcester	1860	*Dictionary of the English Language*
Webster	1865 (1864)	*An American Dictionary of the English Language*, Royal Quarto Edition (Webster-Mahn)
Webster	1898 (1890)	*Webster's International Dictionary*
Funk and Wagnall	1893	*A Standard Dictionary of the English Language*

3. Data Analysis

Figure 1 illustrates the distribution of *-our* and *-or* in *colour*-type words in the period 1640–1800 as sampled by *Evans*. The data show the overall dominance of *-our* all throughout the period, which confirms that the American variety relied on the exonormative model of usage stemming from Britain during its early years. Nevertheless, instances of *-or* start growing in the 1750s, which coincides with the progressive decline of its counterpart *-our*. In the following 50 years, the former would increase 278.4 per cent, while the latter would drop around 44 per cent. Although these trends are not completely parallel, the distribution of the variants check for statistical significance in the corpus (χ^2 (3) = 9,984.2, p = 0.001), with a medium-to-large effect size (Cramér's V = 0.23), which suggests that the initially stable pattern of usage might have been changing. Indeed, the lines in the figure seem to be converging at the onset of the nineteenth century, a development that the data from *COHA* corroborate.

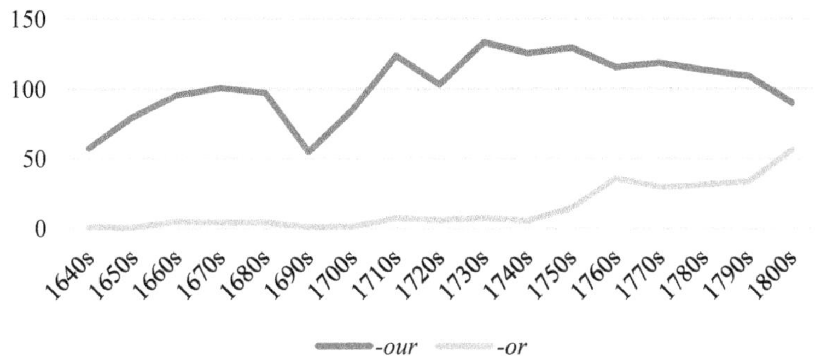

Figure 1: Distribution of *-our* vs. *-or* in the period 1640–1800 in *Evans* (n.f.).

In turn, Figure 2 depicts the selection of the aforementioned variants in the period 1810–1969, as covered by *COHA*. The pattern seems to pick up where *Evans* left off. Although *-our* is the dominant rendering at the beginning of the period, it soon crosses paths with its analogue, *-or*, in the 1820s. Then, the BrE variant progressively loses ground over the nineteenth century, until it virtually disappears from usage in this variety in the twentieth.[3] The changing paradigm among the speakers is reflected in the statistical significance of the forms (χ^2 (3) = 28,792, p = 0.001), which continue to feature a large effect size (Cramér's $V = 0.27$).

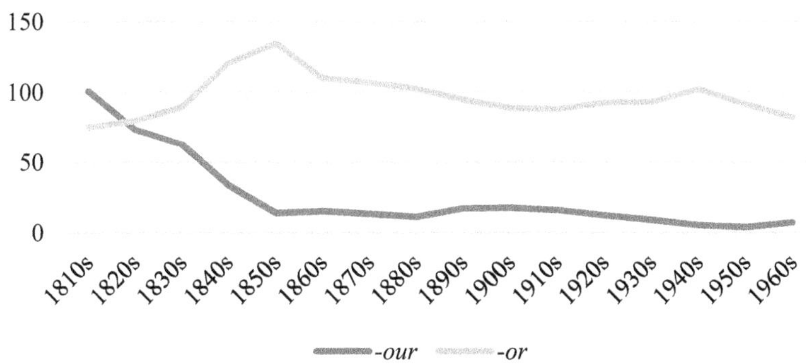

Figure 2: Distribution of *-our* vs. *-or* in the period 1810–1989 in *COHA* (n.f.).

3 While the period sampled by *COHA* is 1810–2019, the figure only includes data for 1810–1960, since instances of *-our* are negligible after the 1930s.

The development in Figures 1 and 2 is worth considering in the light of the historical progression of *-our* and *-or* in BrE as well. Pacheco-Franco and Calle-Martín (2020: 174) highlighted that the *-or* form was on its way to extinction in the domain of *colour*-type words, a pattern that was also observable in *Evans* down to the mid-eighteenth century. Nevertheless, *-or* was somehow revitalized in AmE and its extinction was reverted. Instead, this form became the standard spelling in this variety. From the lens of linguistic competition, the form seems to have specialized on the grounds of diatopic variation (Pacheco-Franco and Calle-Martín 2020: 180; Aronoff 2019: 44). That is, *-or* found an available niche in *colour*-type words within the American variety, which, for whatever sociolinguistic reasons, coveted orthographic differentiation from BrE. It is the underlying rationale for this demarcation that ultimately safeguarded the continuation of *-or* in this linguistic domain. The development of this variant in the English orthographic system may thus be considered a story of survival. Still, it is unclear why a differentiation between AmE and BrE in terms of spelling was ever considered necessary.

As discussed in the introduction, Webster has often been credited with playing a significant role in the creation of AmE orthography. The lexicographer certainly had strong opinions regarding the spelling of *colour*-type words, which he made clear all throughout his work. His attitudes towards spelling reform, however, changed over time. Whereas he first considers that maintaining the *-u-* in *-our* is absurd but is willing to concede its use (Webster 1790: x), *A Compendious Dictionary of the English Language* promotes a fully-fledged reform of the orthographic system, which includes quite a vehement endorsement of the form *-or*. In the preface, Webster (1806: ix) refers to this re-spelling as an attempt to "purify our orthography from corruptions and restore to words their genuine spelling". His views on *-our* would not change by the publication of *An American Dictionary*, where he argues with regards to this rendering that "[n]othing in language is more mischievous than the mistakes of a great man" (Webster 1828: xxxiii). The belief that there was something inherently wrong about the *-our* spelling – which he adduced to requiring etymologization, as it had previously happened with *doctor*-type nouns (*OED*, s.v. *-or*, suffix) – was passed on to his disciple and, later competitor, Worcester, who also favoured the *-or* rendering. This author, however, followed the rationale of usage, arguing that "the omission of the *u*, in many words in which it was retained by Johnson, has now become the established usage" (1830: xvii), and he was just right.

Nevertheless, the question of usage brings to light a major issue regarding the present day conceptualization of Webster. Figure 1 elucidated the growing use of *-or* from the mid-eighteenth century onwards, around 40 years before the publication of his *Dissertations* (1789). This mismatch between the initial spread of the form and the release of Webster's work is brought into light in Figure 3, which illustrates the distribution of the spelling variants in the precept corpus alongside usage. In the first place, there seems to be some correlation between the speakers' practices and Webster's recommendations in the first few decades of the period. In both cases, *-or* seems to be growing in frequency while *-our* declines, virtually disappearing from dictionaries soon after. Although this might be taken as an indicator of Webster's influence on the orthographic system, it should be emphasized that the simplified variants were already on the rise by the time his blue-back speller was published in 1783. As discussed above, the trend dates back to the mid-eighteenth century. The overall dominance of *-or* in the precept corpus also stems from Worcester's recommendations over time. While this author would oppose other instances of spelling reform discussed by Webster – such as the spelling *-er* for words like *theatre* –, the acceptance and promotion of this variant on his behalf illustrates that the form was, indeed, already becoming widespread. In the end, the data suggest that the role of American lexicography in the standardization of *-or* in *colour*-type words was not in the selection and diffusion of this rendering, but rather in its maintenance and codification.

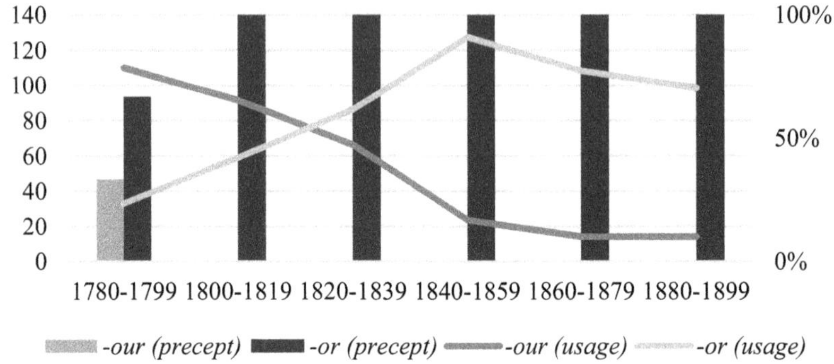

Figure 3: Distribution of *-our* vs. *-or* in the period 1780–1899 in the precept corpus and in usage (%, n.f.).

Bearing in mind that BrE had discarded this spelling long ago, the questions of how exactly these forms came back into usage in eighteenth-century AmE and how they permeated the standard are still unanswered. Although Algeo (2000: 598) argues that *color* was an "already existing option [of a less orthographically rigid age]" in an attempt to account for its origin, the seventeenth-century frequencies of *-or* in Figure 1 disprove his claims. The negligible frequencies of *-or* at the onset of the period suggest that it must have been systematically revitalized in some other way. Nevertheless, the unfeasibility of a genre variation study in *Evans* ultimately contributes to this confusion, which means that the question of selection remains unanswered.

The data in *COHA*, however, do shed light on the dissemination and maintenance of the form across genres, even if the findings are somewhat conflicting. First, the period 1810–1819 attests to the preference for *-our* across fiction, non-fiction and magazines. In the following decade, the trend would drastically change in the latter genre, with instances of *-or* becoming dominant and its counterpart rapidly falling into disuse. The same cannot be said of fiction and non-fiction. While these genres seemed to have adopted the *-or* spelling by the mid-nineteenth century, their orthography was slightly more conservative inasmuch as the decline of *-our* was more progressive. Although the data thus seem to point towards the genre of magazines as the main advocate of reform, there is a problem with how the variants are distributed in the 1810s, especially as this configuration is so clearly different from the pattern of usage in the next decade. The issue most likely lies in the representativity of this decade in the corpus.

Table 2: *-our* and *-or* by genres in *COHA* (n.f.)

	1810s		1820s		1830s		1840s		1850s	
	-our	*-or*	*-our*	*-or*	*-our*	*-or*	*-our*	*-or*	*-our*	*-or*
Fict.	102.1	76.8	94.85	48.3	82.63	58.58	37.08	92.31	12.34	108.91
Non-f.	130.4	20.16	98.79	49.87	72.03	73.33	58.84	126.5	43.48	137.76
Mag.	92.8	84.66	9.01	159.8	9.88	165	11.32	167.8	4.41	177.15

As discussed in the methodology, the latest version of *COHA* removed the texts produced in the period 1810–1819 due to their limited representativity of genres. In particular, magazines barely added up to 85 thousand tokens, which only constitutes 7.48 per cent of the total wordcount for the decade. This obviously creates a problem for the data, thereby suggesting that the normalized frequencies in Table 1 may not entirely correspond to the reality of usage, where *-or* might have been far more frequent. Though illustrative, these results are better understood in the light of the data from the 1820s onwards, which suggest that magazines might have diffused this distinctly AmE spelling. This theory would also conform with the qualitative analysis of such publications.

Indeed, magazines and other type of periodicals were designed for the purpose of drawing and emphasizing differences between the English and the American in any and all aspects of public life. Haveman (2015: 6) argues that magazines are "excellent platforms for oppositional stances on many issues", such as the promotion of nationalistic feelings.[4] At the same time, the characteristics of these periodicals make them an excellent vehicle for the diffusion not only of ideas, but also of linguistic forms, as they enable the "develop[ment of] rich reciprocal interactions with their readers", thus making them an "important source

4 This notion is most clearly depicted in the introduction to *The United States Democratic Review*, where the concepts of Englishness and antidemocracy are opposed to what is American and democratic (O'Sullivan 1838: 15).

of social cohesion in this era" (Haveman 2015: 6–7). In the end, the locality of periodicals – which, at their most, were supraregional within the United States – was a more appropriate venue for the promotion of distinctly American features than other publications with a wider circulation, such as fiction. While the question of the revival and selection of *-or* in AmE remains unresolved, the mechanisms working towards its diffusion and maintenance are manifest. Printing – more specifically, magazines – and lexicography joined in the endeavour to produce an American spelling for words like *colour*, the latter of which also contributed to its codification.

4. Discussion

The literature has paid much attention to the figure of Noah Webster as the leader of spelling reform in the United States (see Algeo 2000; Venezky 2001; Upward and Davidson 2011; Horobin 2013). Most accounts of orthography in AmE highlight the relevance of his works towards the codification of the variety, but more so as the main actor of change when it comes to spelling. Nevertheless, the data from the standardization of *colour*-type words in AmE showed that the *-or* form was already on the rise by the time that Webster first wrote about reforming spelling. Although this obviously casts doubts on what role Webster played in the configuration of AmE spelling, the findings may also be reconciled with the claims in the literature.

While Webster did not initially agree with the spelling reform that Franklin had attempted (Upward and Davidson 2011: 302), his views about the inappropriateness of certain forms still slipped in *The American Spelling Book* (1790). More particularly, the lexicographer referred to the rendering *-our*, perhaps prompted by the growth and spread of *-or* during his time. This variant had, in fact, gained much ground in mid-eighteenth-century AmE, while there did not seem to be a parallel development in Britain. It is highly likely that this trend in American usage caught the lexicographer's attention, who might have become aware of how a spelling reform targeting minor changes was not only feasible – as it was already taking place –, but also necessary for the United States to achieve complete independence (Webster 1789: 397). Indeed, Webster (1789: 397) primarily aimed at "mak[ing] a difference between the English orthography and the American", which may be considered a crucial step towards linguistic independence following the Declaration of 1776.

These claims have crucial implications when it comes to evaluating the role played by the lexicographer. The claim that "his influence ... was not innovative, but regulatory" (Algeo 2000: 598) may now be interpreted in a different light. Webster did not simply select one of the spelling variants available at the time, but rather one that was already in vogue among his countrymen. In doing so, however, he might have amplified its already growing frequency and contributed towards its maintenance and codification. However, attention must be paid to his participation in infusing the form with prestige, here in the shape of the distinct sense of Americanness that the new spelling conveyed. After all, Webster imbued his proposal with the political connotations that ultimately led to its triumph, while the linguistic concepts of etymology and uniformity that seemed to support the re-spelling of *colour*-type words were relegated to the background (Webster 1789: x; 1806: vii–ix). Indeed, the new spelling soon became a signpost of Americanness, thus illustrating the scope of his policy. The sentiment underlying these spelling variants might have facilitated their diffusion through the aforementioned channels, i.e. through magazines and other publications of the like.

The differences between the perceived and the real timeline of the AmE spelling reform are also accounted for from a theoretical perspective, i.e. by means of Schneider's Dynamic Cycle. Although Webster's reform was initially conceived as an instantiation of the endonormative orientation that characterized nineteenth-century AmE, the re-spelling is most likely a product of the nativization phase. Indeed, after the stage of exonormative stabilization, during which the variety would have adhered to the BrE model – as it did in the case at hand –, came the nativization of AmE, characterized by the addition of new lexicon to the repertoire and the emergenge of distinct morphosyntactic patterns, among others (Schneider 2007: 278–9). As the data in this case study have suggested, this would also include the inception of new orthographic patterns, such as the *-or* spelling for words of the *colour* type.

These variants would progressively increase in usage and become indexical of the ever-growing feeling of Americanness of the eighteenth century. In this regard, Wolfram and Schilling-Estes (1998: 17) argue that "the very notion of American English itself was strongly tied to nationalism", and vice versa. Indeed, the sense of nationalism that permeated into the language and its spelling after the Declaration of Independence was crucial, thus leading – as per the discussion above – to the configuration of a new spelling. The codification of such a system came, as has been discussed before, by the hand of Webster in 1806. This action seems to have preceded the phase of endonormative stabilization. Nevertheless, Schneider (2007: 31) argues that while he describes "an ideal constellation, . . . in reality room must be provided for variation, fuzzy transitions, and overlapping". This comes to highlight that the model does accommodate the standardization of the *-or* spelling variant in the variety, from whence they were projected onto the rest of the world.

5. Conclusions

This chapter has explored the role(s) played by Webster in the orthographic configuration of *colour*-type words in historical AmE. While the lexicographer has typically been described as the main actor in the re-spelling of *-our* > *-or*, the present study has illustrated that his participation concerned the codification and maintenance of a variant that had been growing in usage for decades, but did not include its selection. Nevertheless, this finding should not downplay the significance of his historical figure. Webster was a visionary inasmuch as he identified a trifling change in orthography and transformed it into the keystone of a new orthographic system. In infusing the rising *-or* forms with the sense of Americanness and nationalism that were so ubiquitous in the brand new United States, Webster succeeded in marketing a variety that was clearly distinct from the British. In this regard, his role was neither innovative nor regulatory. Instead, it was patriotic. Little did John Adams know in the 1780s, when he claimed that AmE was "destined to be in the next and succeeding centuries more generally the language of the world than Latin was in the last" (Kahane 1983: 229), that an action as trivial as removing a *-u-* from a word like *colour* would certainly identify an American in writing.

Sources

Davies, Mark, *Corpus of Historical American English* (Brigham Young University, 2010). Available at https://www.english-corpora.org/coha/.

Evans Early American Imprints (Text Creation Partnership, 2011). Available at https://textcreationpartnership.org/tcp-texts/evans-tcp-evans-early-american-imprints/.

References

Algeo, John, 'The Effects of the Revolution on Language', in Jack P. Greene and Jack R. Pole, eds., *A Companion to the American Revolution* (Oxford: Blackwell, 2000), 594–9.

Anthony, Laurence, *AntConc*, version 3.5.9 (Tokyo: Waseda University, 2020).

Bartlett, John R., *Dictionary of Americanisms: A Glossary of Words and Phrases* (New York: Bartlett & Welford, 1848), https://archive.org/details/dictionaryofamer00bart/page/198/mode/2up, accessed 31 March 2023.

Burchfield, Robert, *Unlocking the English Language* (London: Faber, 1989).

Cooper, James F., *Notions of the Americans: Picked Up by a Travelling Bachelor* (Albany: State University of New York Press, 1991).

Franklin, Benjamin, *Political, Miscellaneous, and Philosophical Pieces* (London: J. Johnson, 1779).

Funk, Isaac K., *A Standard Dictionary of the English Language* (New York: Funk and Wagnalls Company, 1893), https://archive.org/details/standarddictiona01funkuoft/page/n3/mode/2up>, accessed 31 March 2023.

Goodrich, Chauncey, *Webster's American Dictionary of the English Language* (Springfield, Mass.: G. and C. Merriam, 1848), <https://archive.org/details/websteramericand00webs/page/n7/mode/2up>, accessed 31 March 2023.

Goodrich, Chauncey, and Noah Porter, *Webster's American Dictionary of the English Language* (Springfield, Mass.: G. and C. Merriam, 1865), <https://archive.org/details/americandictiona00websuoft/page/n9/mode/2up?view=theater>, accessed 31 March 2023.

Gramley, Stephan, Vivian Gramley, V and Kurt-Michael Pätzold, *A Survey of Modern English*, 3rd edition (London: Routledge, 2021).

Haveman, Heather A., *Magazines and the Making of America: Modernization, Community, and Print Culture, 1741–1860* (Princeton: Princeton University Press, 2015).

Horobin, Simon, *Does Spelling Matter?* (Oxford: Oxford University Press, 2013).

Kahane, Henry, 'American English: From a Colonial Substandard to a Prestige Language', in Braj B. Kachru, ed., *The Other Tongue: English Across Cultures* (New York: Pergamon Press, 1983), 229–36.

O'Sullivan, John L., 'Introduction', *The United States Democratic Review* (1838), 1–15, <https://babel.hathitrust.org/cgi/pt?id=coo.31924077700031&view=1up&seq=3>, accessed 31 March 2023.

Oxford English Dictionary (Oxford: Oxford University Press, n.d.), http://www.oed.com/, accessed 31 March 2023.

Pacheco-Franco, Marta and Javier Calle-Martín, 'Suffixes in Competition: On the Use of *–our* and *–or* in Early Modern English', *International Journal of English Studies* 20/2 (2020), 169–83.

Porter, Noah, *Webster's International Dictionary of the English Language* (Springfield, Mass.: G. and C. Merriam, 1898), <https://archive.org/details/webstersinternat00port/page/n1/mode/2up>, accessed 31 March 2023.

Schneider, Edgar. W., *Postcolonial English: Varieties around the World* (Cambridge: Cambridge University Press, 2007).

Simpson, David, *The Politics of American English, 1776–1850* (New York; Oxford: Oxford University Press, 1986).

Trudgill, Peter and Jean Hannah, *International English: A Guide to Varieties of Standard English*, 6th edition (London; New York: E. Arnold, 2017).

Upward, Christopher and George Davidson, *The History of English Spelling* (Chichester: Wiley-Blackwell, 2011).

Venezky, Richard L., 'Spelling', in John Algeo, ed., *The Cambridge History of the English Language*, Vol. 6 (Cambridge: Cambridge University Press, 2001), 340–57.

Webster, Noah, *Dissertations on the English Language* (Boston: I. Thomas & Company, 1789), <https://archive.org/details/dissertationsone00webs/page/n5/mode/2up?view=theater>, accessed 31 March 2023.

——, *The American Spelling Book*, 2nd edition (Boston: I. Thomas & E. T. Andrews, 1790), <https://www.loc.gov/item/11012477/>, accessed 31 March 2023.

——, *A Compendious Dictionary of the English Language* (New Haven: Sydney's Press, 1806), <https://archive.org/details/compendiousdictionaryoftheenglishlanguage1806>, accessed 31 March 2023.

——, *An American Dictionary of the English Language* (New York: S. Converse, 1828), <https://archive.org/details/americandictiona02websrich/page/n5/mode/2up>, accessed 31 March 2023.

Wolfram, Walt and Natalie Schilling-Estes, *American English* (Oxford: Blackwell, 1998).

Worcester, Joseph E., *A Comprehensive Pronouncing and Explanatory Dictionary of the English Language* (Boston: Hilliard, Gray, Little & Wilkins, 1830), <https://play.google.com/books/reader?id=D_qfMYuoXasC&pg=GBS.PP9&hl=es>, accessed 31 March 2023.

——, *A Universal and Critical Dictionary of the English Language* (Boston: Wilkins, Carter & Company, 1846), <https://ia801607.us.archive.org/3/items/cu31924027443336/cu31924027443336.pdf>, accessed 31 March 2023.

——, *Dictionary of the English Language* (Boston: Hickling, Swan & Brewer, 1860), <https://ia800205.us.archive.org/22/items/cu31924027443393/cu31924027443393.pdf>, accessed 31 March 2023.

Marta Pacheco-Franco and Javier Calle-Martín

Verbal Contractions in Late Modern English[1]

1. Introduction

The habit of contracting words originates in the intrinsic tendency of languages to assimilate the pronunciation of two neighbouring sounds. In Present-day English, this phenomenon is most plainly observed in the so-called "telescoped phrases", a term that refers to all those cases of elision affecting auxiliary verbs, as exemplified by *it's* and *doesn't* (Peters 2004: 126). Among these contractions, however, distinctions must be drawn. There are, on the one hand, the contractions featured in operators, i.e., "the larger class containing the NICE verbs in *all* their uses" (Huddleston and Pullum 2002: 104n, our emphasis).[2] In these cases, the element contracted is a verb, either in its functional or lexical uses, and the elision takes place at the beginning of the word, as in *it's* for *it is* or *they've* for *they have*. On the other hand, the negative adverb *not* may also be contracted to *n't* when it modifies an operator, thereby losing its mid-word vowel and its free-word status in the process. The examples *doesn't* for *does not* and *isn't* for *is not* illustrate this phenomenon, with the exception of the negative modal *can't*, which stands for the univocal full form *cannot*. In contrast to other examples of lexical contractions,

1 The present research has been funded by the Spanish Ministry of Science and Innovation (grant number PID2021-126496NB-I00), the Spanish Ministry of Universities (grant number FPU19/05104) and by the Andalusian Regional Government (grant numbers PY18-2782 and UMA18-FEDERJA-129). These grants are hereby gratefully acknowledged.

2 NICE, according to Huddleston and Pullum (2002: 93), stands for negation, inversion, code and emphasis, which are the syntactic properties of auxiliary verbs.

these shortened phrases present a uniform punctuation across varieties of English as signposted by the apostrophe (Peters 2004: 126).

This practice can be traced back to Old English, where we find that unstressed vowels in hiatus were already elided, as in the use of *bufan* for *be* + *ufan*, *þoþer* for *þe* + *oþer* (Dobson 1968: 836), or the so-called negative contraction, where the adverb *ne* was attached to the ensuing word, either verbs such as *nis* for *ne* + *is* or adverbs as in *næfre* for *ne* + *æfre* (Hogg 2006: 357). Even though medieval scribes contributed to the development of this practice with word-final elisions followed by a vowel or an aspirate without the break of an apostrophe (Petti 1977: 25) – *cham* for *ich am* or *tother* for *the other* –, Early Modern writers were responsible for the actual spread of the phenomenon after the introduction of the apostrophe in the English writing system (Schlüter 2012: 592). This symbol, introduced by the learned printers in the second half of the sixteenth century, first functioned as a marker of certain forms of elision, as in *th'onely* "the only" or *o'man* "woman" and later specialized in other orthographic environments, such as the expression of the genitive form of the noun (i.e. *the king's men*) or the past tense forms of regular verbs (i.e. *lov'd* and *lik'd*).

These contractions are found to be already on the rise in dramatic texts of the late sixteenth century, just two or three decades after the incorporation of the apostrophe into the English writing system.[3] Forms such as *wee'l* and *hee's* coexisted with their concomitant full forms *wee will* and *hee is*, even though the development of the former was neither straightforward nor free of controversy (Salmon 1999: 18). The issue was that contractions did not meet with the approval of some of

3 The origin of these contractions, however, was also a moot point in the previous century. Even though today it is almost a consensus that these contracted forms originated in the spoken language and were later imported into the written medium, it has also been interpreted that 'many contractions appeared first in writing and only later entered the spoken language to be pronounced as they are written' (Hendrickson 1971: 46). Hendrickson relies on the widespread use of the English Court-Hand until well into the eighteenth century, which favoured the rendering of contracted forms which had no correlation in speech. If speech habit had been responsible for contractions, in his opinion, the written forms would have been drastically different, such as *wu'not* or *d'not* instead of *wouldn't* or *don't*.

the seventeenth-century grammarians, who were on the whole sceptical about their use and preferred not to be contentious. Jonson, for instance, argued that "who can justly blame me" if nothing is more familiar in our common speech (1947 [1640]: 529). The eighteenth century, however, stands out for the advent of the proscriptive bias to the construction, which eventually derived in what Leonard later termed as "the war upon contractions" (1929: 170; Sundby, Bjørge and Haugland 1991: 159–160). This censure was pioneered by both Swift and Addison, the former in particular, who in his famous onslaughts complained about the use of "these new fashions in the way of writing English at the time" (Gailor 2011: 10–15), concluding satirically that "the usual Pretence is, That they spell as they speak: A noble Standard for Language!" (Bond 1987: 194). It is a fact, however, that both Swift and Addison were not familiar with the language of their predecessors, as this practice had been widespread among early Modern English writers of renown, Shakespeare and Dryden among them.

Notwithstanding the trend of discontent towards contractions at the time, they had found their own niche in the English writing system and the nineteenth century witnessed both the progressive standardization of their spelling (i.e. *it's* instead of *'tis*, *it'd* instead of *'twould* or *don't* instead of *d'not*, among some others) and their overall acceptance by the community.[4] These dual forms were not mere alternatives available for the writer, but they were in themselves subjected to some level of variation in many cases. Soon after their appearance in English, the contractions were taken to have a sociolinguistic bias associated with the language of uneducated lower-class speakers as an intrinsic characteristic of their "vulgar and sloppy" pronunciation (Görlach 1999: 530). The passing of time, in turn, coined other patterns of usage of these shortened forms. In her analysis of Robert Lowth's correspondence, Tieken-Boon van Ostade witnessed the proliferation of these forms in this register and, more particularly, in cases of increased familiarity between the writer and the addressee (2009: 125). This practice is

4 Standardization is well underway already in the eighteenth century. It was a systematic process according to which the auxiliary verb is now enclitically attached to the pronoun (*it's, it'll*), while 'until the end of the seventeenth century it was typically the pronoun that was clipped (*'tis, 'twas, 'twill*)' (Nevalainen 2006: 129).

surely the precursor of the present-day use of contractions, considered to be in many manuals and usage books a characteristic feature of informal writing – fiction and news in particular – and spoken English (see Britain 2010; Biber et al. 1999: 166). Even though distinctive of this type of writing, they are progressively finding more room in Present-day English since "the interactive quality that contractions lend to a style is these days often sought, in business and elsewhere. They facilitate reading by reducing the space taken up by predictable elements in the verb phrase and help to establish the underlying rhythms of prose" (Peters 2004: 127).[5]

The previous state of the art has shown that the inception and eventual rise of these contracted forms in English took place in the period 1550–1800, a timespan of more than three hundred years when both printers and grammarians necessarily had to take a stand on the propriety of the use of the shortened forms in English writing. It was certainly a moot point in the period. It goes without saying that printers endorsed the use of these contracted forms after their sudden irruption in the English writing system while grammarians, in turn, expressed their own disturbance in their attempt to put some order out of the chaos, with a plethora of spelling variants for the rendering of auxiliary verbs. As it stands, this is another case at hand showing the controversy between the two groups and, more importantly, which one became "more influential in determining the eventual form of a standard orthography" (Salmon 1999: 18). This dilemma between norm and usage is then sorted out in favour of the latter, which progressively facilitated the incorporation of these contracted forms to the system. Today, however, they cannot compete with the full forms and have been mostly relegated to more informal types of writing.

The present paper has been conceived as a register analysis of the phenomenon so as to obtain further insight into particular patterns of linguistic variation. The study is then concerned with the standardization of the contractions in the period 1600–1999 and pursues the following objectives: (a) to study the development of the phenomenon over time assessing its origin and spread in English; (b) to analyse its distribution

5 For a comprehensive description of the phenomenon in Present-day English, see Biber et al.'s specific appendix on the use of contractions (1999: 1128–32).

across registers and gender; and (c) to consider the factors which may have rendered the construction informal in Present-day English. The analysis explores the instances of contraction with the verb *be*, the verb *have*, the shortened forms of the negative particle *not* and the modal auxiliary verbs *will* and *would*.

2. Methodology

The source of information is *A Representative Corpus of Historical English Registers* or *ARCHER* 3.2., "a multi-genre historical corpus of [3.3] million words of British and American English covering the period 1600–1999" (Yáñez-Bouza 2011: 205). It represents a wide range of register diversity that encompasses material from 12 different text types, including personal styles of communication, fiction prose, popular and specialist exposition and scientific prose (Yáñez-Bouza 2011: 207). It should be noted, however, that some of these genres have been collated into seven in the present study and some others have been renamed. Ego-writing now comprises diaries and letters; literature does so with drama, early prose and fiction; periodicals, with journals and news; and science, with medicine and science. Whereas advertising remains the same, legal texts and sermons have been redefined as law and religion, respectively.

On methodological grounds, the process was not straightforward in view of the particularities of the corpus and the intrinsic nature of the phenomenon at hand. Even though *ARCHER* is offered both in plain text and tagged formats, the former was chosen as the ideal input since the modern version of the corpus presents some shortcomings with the tagging of the contractions, not always tagged as an auxiliary verb (with the tag VB) but as a singular letter of the alphabet (tagged as ZZ1).[6]

6 In this fashion, the sentence *that iewel's mine* is tagged as *that*_DD1 *iewel*_(NN1) '_NULL *s*_ZZ1 *mine*_NN1, where the contracted for of the verb be is taken as a letter of the alphabet rather than as a verb itself. In addition to this, note the erroneous tagging of the pronoun *mine*, given as a singular noun instead of as a possessive pronoun with the tag _PPGE.

This significantly complicated the task of data retrieval in view of the absence of an umbrella string for the generation of the complete set of instances with a contracted spelling. For accuracy, the study relies on the following four searches: (a) the contracted forms of the verb *be* (i.e. '*m* > am, '*re* > *are*, '*s* > *is*); (b) the contracted forms of the verb *have* (i.e. '*ve* > *have*, '*s* > *has* and '*d* > *had*); (c) the contracted forms of negative auxiliary verbs (i.e. *n't* > *can't*); and (d) the contracted forms of modal auxiliaries (i.e. '*ll* > *will*, '*d* > *would*).

This process, as expected, is not free of noise and some disambiguation was required to select the appropriate input in view of the context to discern, for example, whether the string '*s* corresponded to *is*, *has* or an instance of the Saxon genitive, or whether the string '*d* stood for *had*, *would* or the regular past tense morpheme, often shortened at the time. In addition to this, the present study has also retrieved the full forms of all the contractions in order to calculate the rate of occurrence of the contracted and uncontracted forms both over time and across registers and gender. All in all, the present study eventually relies on a total of 125,971 instances, of which 17,192 appear with the contracted form and 108,779 instances with the full form. Table 1 reproduces the instances according to the particularities of the construction, whether the verbs *be* or *have* or if in combination with a modal auxiliary or a negated verb. For the purposes of the study, however, the absolute frequencies have been normalized to a common base of 10,000 words, thus enabling the analysis of the data diachronically, as well as the register and gender variation studies.

Table 1: Corpus data

	Be		***Have***		**Negative**		**Modals**	
	Abs. freq.	*%*	***Abs. freq.***	*%*	***Abs. freq.***	*%*	***Abs. freq.***	*%*
Contracted forms	6,863	12.9	1,527	3.9	6,074	28.8	2,728	14.7
Uncontracted forms	46,201	87.1	37,007	96.1	15,006	71.2	15,869	85.3
TOTAL	53,064		38,534		21,080		18,597	

3. Data Analysis

This section addresses the development of contractions in the period 1600–1999 when the phenomenon is found to have its most widespread diffusion after its inception in the history of English. The paper has also been conceived as a variationist study exploring the distribution of contractions across genres and gender in order to determine the pioneering forces that may have contributed to the dissemination and eventual diffusion of contractions in the late Modern English period.

3.1. Contractions over Time

Figure 1 presents the distribution of the contracted and the full forms of the verbs *be* and *have*, of the negative particle *not* and of the modal auxiliaries *will* and *would* in the period under scrutiny, thereby shedding light on the development of contractions and on their relationship to the full forms over time. In the first place, the figure shows that the short forms were already in use by the beginning of the seventeenth century, which conforms with their introduction during the second half of the 16th. However, these variants were not very frequent yet with a score of n.f. 12.54 instances at the beginning of the 1600s. The contractions would develop steadily throughout the seventeeth century, while they would diffuse during the eighteenth and nineteenth centuries. Despite having almost doubled in frequency by the early 1800s, their growth was not always progressive, as the experienced a slight decrease in the period 1750–1799. Nevertheless, they continued spreading soon after. In the end, the dissemination of contractions in the late Modern period would ultimately trigger their dramatic expansion throughout the twentieth century, when the frequency of the shortened forms spiked.

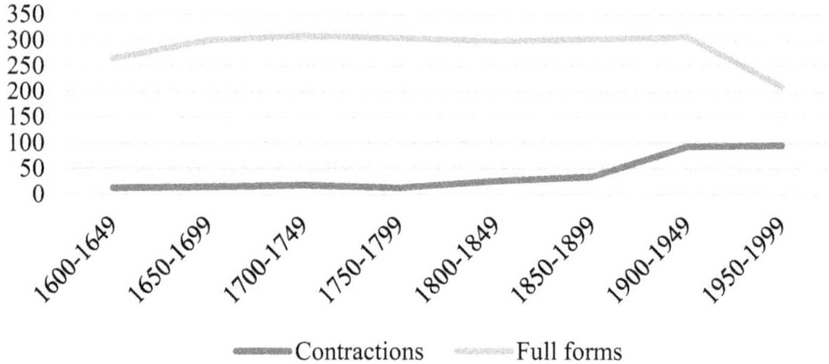

Figure 1: Contractions and their full forms over time (n.f.).

The figure also provides insight into the relationship between the short and full variants from a diachronic perspective. Although the co-occurrence of synonymous linguistic forms performing the same function would often result in linguistic competition (Aronoff 2019: 42–3; Marchand 1969: 241–2), this phenomenon never seemed to operate between contractions and their full analogues. Although the two sets of variants seem to be converging by the end of the period, the truth is that, from a diachronic perspective, the ups and downs experienced by the contracted forms never had an impact on their counterparts, thus suggesting that these developed independently from the full forms. In the end, since the latter presented such a high incidence in use, it stands to reason that their frequency would have no effect on the former. This restriction evokes the phenomenon of blocking, which Bauer (2006: 181) described as occurring between linguistic competitors and leading to preference for the earliest form by virtue of its hold among speakers. However, because there is no evidence to argue for competition, blocking was not possible. In any event, there is the possibility that such processes might have taken place for some of the variants, but not for all.

3.2. The Operators of Contractions

The data displayed so far have only engaged with the diachronic development of contractions from a broad perspective. Since the phenomenon merits in-depth attention, the present section breaks down the data to shed some light on the roles played by the operators and the co-text, if any, in the spread of these forms. For that purpose, Figure 2 presents the development of the contracted forms over time to better reproduce the rise of the contractions in the period, where each case is found to evolve at a different rate. The shortened forms of the verb *be* and negative auxiliary verbs diffused earlier than the other contracted forms, with a moderate rise in the period 1800–1849 followed by their definite dissemination one century later, becoming twice as frequent in the period 1900–1949. The other contracted forms, in turn, seem to lag behind with a negligible distribution throughout the nineteenth century. It was not until the beginning of the twentieth century when they timidly increased their frequency surely as a result of the growing influence of the previous types of contractions, which had already acquired a prominent role in the system. Interestingly enough, these two types of contractions never reached the frequency of the negative contraction, perhaps as a consequence of some kind of bias in the speakers' minds. Negative contractions and, in this same vein, *be*-contractions tend to be considered as a single unit in speech processing, therefore making it more productive (Biber et al. 1999: 164–5). Modal auxiliaries, in turn, could have been deemed as multiple units, which to a broad extent might explain their moderate success in the period. The shortened form of the verb *have* is negligible in our data, systematically outnumbered by its full form.

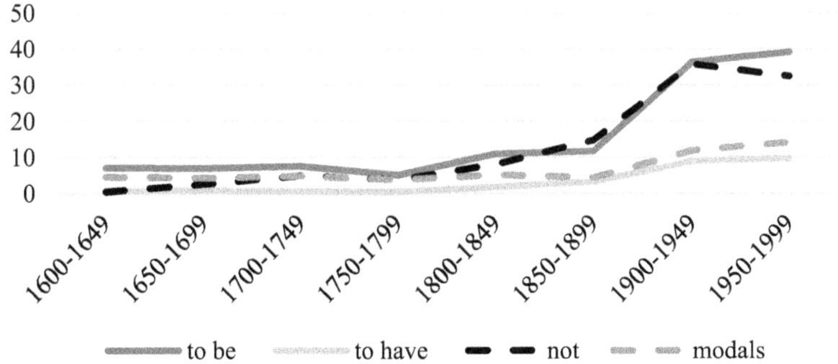

Figure 2: The operators of the contractions (n.f.).

Figure 3 itemizes these data of the contracted operators even further and shows the distribution of the linguistic material preceding the contracted form of auxiliary verbs. According to Peters (2004: 127), "auxiliary verbs can be telescoped with almost any kind of word or phrase which serves as the subject", though these are perhaps more common with pronouns. The figure illustrates, as expected, that personal pronouns have predominated over all the other grammatical categories since the seventeenth century and their frequency is also found to increase significantly in the early decades of the nineteenth century. The other types of subject, however, lag considerably behind personal pronouns, the list consisting of other pronouns (i.e. *somebody*, *nothing*, *there*, etc.), interrogative pronouns, common nouns and adverbs, respectively.

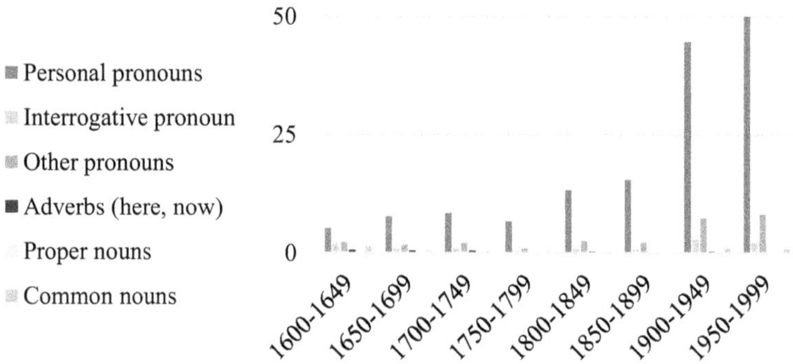

Figure 3: The subjects of the contractions (n.f.).

Finally, Figure 4 presents the classification of the operators participating in negative contractions. As shown, the phenomenon is systematically preffered in combination with the operator *do* soon after the spread of contractions in the seventeenth and the eighteenth centuries, the latter in particular. This tendency remained constant throughtout the following century to such an extent that this operator becomes three times more frequent than all the other operators in the course of the twentieth century. In addition to the general preference for *do* in these contexts, negative contractions are found to have the same pattern of distribution from the beginning of the nineteenth centuty, as they are more typically bound to appear with the operators *can/could* followed, in turn, by *will/would* and the verbs *be* and *have*, respectively.

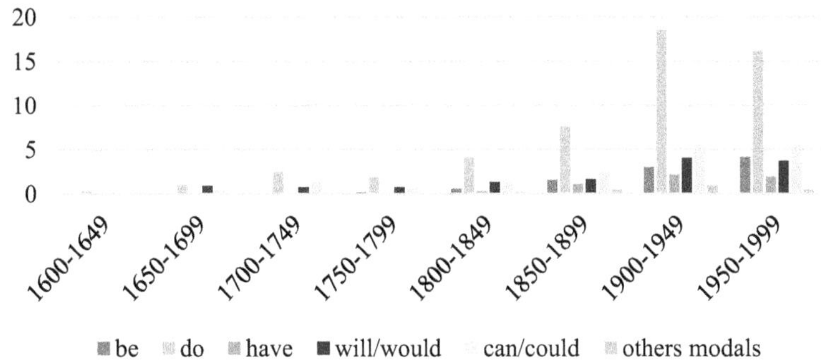

Figure 4: The operators of negative contractions over time (n.f.).

3.3. Contractions across Genre

Figures 5 and 6 illustrate the dissemination of the contractions and the full forms by genre, respectively, for the purpose of inquiring into their Present-day English distributional restrictions. In essence, the figures show that the full forms have always been more scattered across text types than the contractions. This pattern of usage holds true over time and is clearly observable in the very first subperiod, with contractions being negligible in legal texts despite these being one of the two genres sampled at that stage. The incorporation of more text types into the corpus in subsequent periods only highlights this state of affairs. Whereas contractions occur more commonly in literature and, from the eighteenth century onwards, also in ego-writing, their counterparts are found in genres such as law, periodicals and science, alongside the other two. That there exists a clear-cut distinction in the distribution of the variants, however, does not mean that the short forms are entirely exempt from appearing in more formal text types. Though with a minor incidence, advertising, law and periodicals also feature some contractions, especially throughout the twentieth century. Interestingly, these variants are virtually non-existent in scientific texts over time, a genre in which they peaked in the period 1650–1699 with just 8 tokens and n.f. 1.56. The figures ultimately corroborate the claims that contractions have always been characteristic of colloquial registers, even if they feature a greater dispersion across text types in the twentieth century.

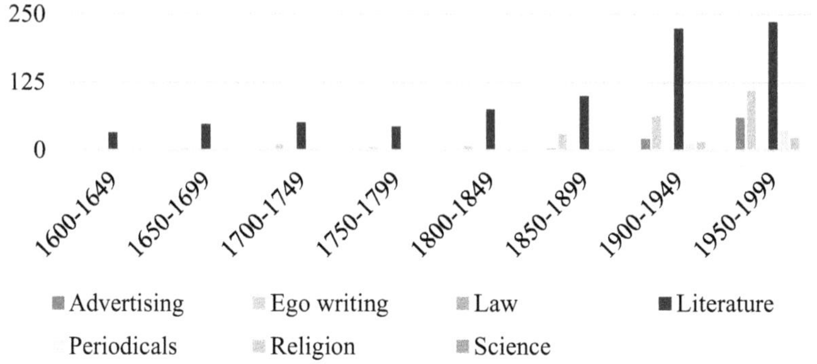

Figure 5: The contractions across genre (n.f.).

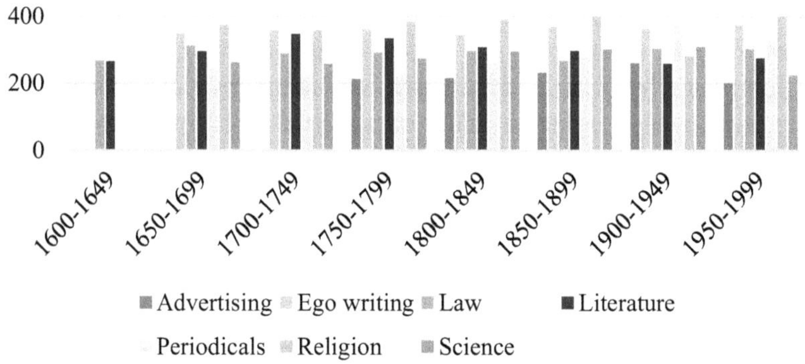

Figure 6: The full forms across genre (n.f.).

3.4. Contractions across Gender

The fossilization of contractions in colloquial English turns out to be yet more interesting when considered from the perspective of the speakers' gender. Figure 7 depicts the selection of these forms by male and female speakers in the corpus, as well as it includes data from authors whose gender is unknown.[7] On the whole, the figure shows that the

7 It should be noted that the occurrence of contractions in these texts is inconsequential. Nevertheless, the data have been included in the interest of transparency, especially since this variable exhibits their greater frequency when it comes to the full forms, as represented in Figure 4.

spread of the contractions was pioneered by female authors from the beginning of the period and all the way to the eighteenth century.[8] Indeed, the data indicate that, starting in the 1650s, women were more likely to employ these contractions than men, a trend that was on the rise throughout the next 100 years. As discussed before, the overall frequency of these forms decreases in the period 1750–1799, while they are still more often found in female-authored texts. All the while, the gap in usage between men and women seems to be growing smaller. Whereas the selection of the contractions had a ratio of 1:3 in the seventeenth century, the use of these forms seemed to have evened out by the mid-1700s, with men presenting a normalized score of 16.73 and women, of 20.6. During the nineteenth century, the selectional pattern drastically changed and men started heading the use of these forms. In the last years of the late Modern period, the distribution of contractions across gender would become more balanced and more consistent with the Present-day English distributional paradigm.

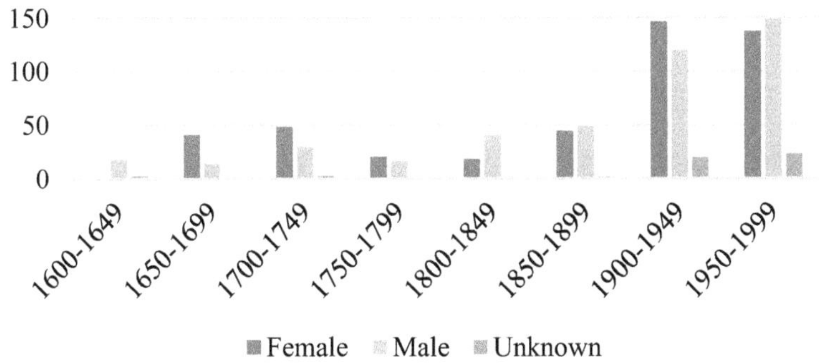

Figure 7: The contractions across gender (n.f.).

8 The figure shows no data from females in the period 1600–1649, in all likelihood due to corpus bias. There are only 3,450 words produced by women in this period, which stand in stark contrast to the 63,390 words written by men. This disparity in the corpus design thus accounts for the lack of tokens in this particular case, especially since the use of contractions was not so frequent a phenomenon at that stage.

For the sake of consistency, Figure 8 displays the distribution of the full forms across gender. The figure manifests, quite straightforwardly, that the full forms were equally distributed regardless of the gender variable all throughout the period. Although the data show that women were often more likely to use these items than men, there is still a sensible balance in the selection of the forms, also true for those texts whose authorship remains unknown. All in all, the point of this figure is to serve as contrast for the data discussed above: by establishing what a "normal" distributional pattern looks like, the role played by women in the spread of contractions, as suggested above, is more strongly emphasized. In any event, the pull exercized by female authors in the promotion of these forms has only been corroborated from a quantitative perspective. Consequently, the following section will focus on the matter adopting a qualitative stance.

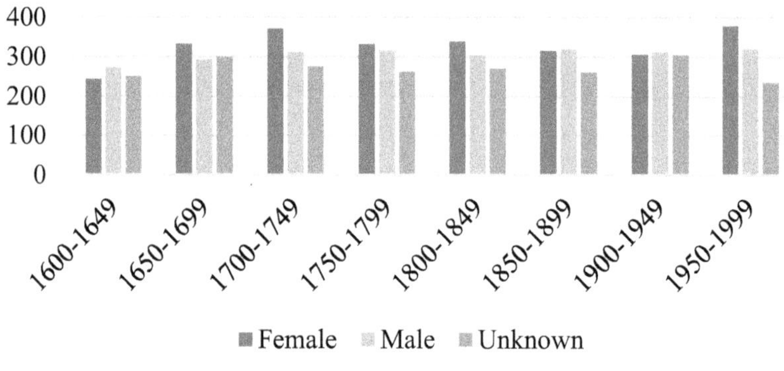

Figure 8: The full forms across gender (n.f.).

4. Discussion

Though the wide spread of the contractions took place in the twentieth century, the late Modern period was crucial to their diffusion among speakers and, ultimately, to their Present-day English configuration. The data analysis has corroborated that these shortened forms were, from the beginning of the period, more recurrent in colloquial registers than in formal ones respectively. These findings answer, on the one hand, to the greater correlation between informal text types and speech and, on the other, to the notions of involvement and intimacy within the communicative exchange. Indeed, the contractions considered in the present paper are characteristic of spoken English (Britain 2010: 44; Peters 2004: 127) and, as such, they permeate more conspicuously in genres that are written to be read aloud. Furthermore, it seems that in the case of letter-writing the relationship between the writer and the addressee is a decisive factor for the selection of such forms: the more intimacy there is between the participants, there more colloquial the language becomes (Tieken-Boon van Ostade 2009: 125). Biber and Finegan (1992: 692, 696) had arrived at similar conclusions in their diachronic study on genre variation, where they found letters and drama to present more personal involvement and, in turn, more informal structures than prose fiction and essay writing over time.

Our treatment of genre variation in Section 3.3 fell short at detecting the differences in distribution between drama and prose fiction given that they were contained within the same text type. To illustrate the selection of the contractions in these genres separately, Table 2 breaks down these data. As anticipated by Biber and Finegan (1992: 692), the shortened forms were far more frequent in drama than they were in prose all throughout the period. Nevertheless, contractions become more and more recurrent in fiction with the passing of time and, in fact, they record a higher incidence than ego-writing starting in the period 1750–1799 and continuing thereafter. The spread of contractions in fiction over time is not surprising at all. Whereas seventeenth- and eighteenth-century prose was characterized by its grandiloquent style, loaded with complex structures and elevated lexicon (see Jones 1953), literary figures such as Charles Dickens and Emily Brontë had, by the nineteenth century, grown interested in representing their characters' often "non-standard and/or regional" speech (Beal 2016: 17). This would directly reflect on the spread of colloquial forms in writing, including contractions. Their expansion would culminate, in fiction as well as in drama and other genres, during the twentieth century, at a time when linguistic colloquization was prevalent.

Table 2: The contractions in drama and fiction over time (n.f.)

	1600–1649	**1650–1699**	**1700–1749**	**1750–1799**	**1800–1849**	**1850–1899**	**1900–1949**	**1950–1999**
Drama	31.87	105.3	117.2	89.6	124.8	152.4	344.4	336.2
Fict.	-	2.1	5.8	10	33.91	57.18	118.7	164.2

On the question of the speakers' gender, the data indicated that women pioneered the use and spread of contractions in the early years of the late Modern period. Whereas the under-representation of female-authored texts in the period 1600–1649 rendered no tokens, the truth is that "women never actually initiated linguistic change, but [...] took the lead only after a change had been set in motion" (Tieken-Boon van Ostade 2009: 115). This path of development is not only consistent with the data presented in Section 3.4, but also with previous linguistic changes, such as the substitution of the subject pronoun *ye* by the objective form *you* (Nevalainen 2006: 136). Labov (2001: 292) formulates female participation in linguistic innovation as Principle 4, which reads as follows: "In linguistic change from below, women use higher frequencies of innovative forms than men do". Nonetheless, the nature of their role as innovators lies in their social standing throughout history.[9] In this regard, Tieken-Boon van Ostade (2009: 115) argues that

> due to limited educational and economic possibilities women were less strongly integrated into their social networks. Rather than being as much subject to the norm enforcement mechanism of their social networks as their male counterparts, they would adopt network external features

In this particular case, the external features, i.e., the contractions, might first be found in colloquial discourse, from whence they may have permeated onto written language. In the light of women's promotion of these forms and of their restricted involvement in the public domain, it is hardly surprising that the contractions should extend across the more informal registers.

9 Interestingly, some have ascribed women's linguistic behaviour to some biological endowment that makes them more perceptive of linguistic change than men (see Chambers 1995: 132–3).

The corpus itself attests to the limited social opportunities opened up for late Modern women. *ARCHER* contains 268 texts with females featuring as the first author, out of which 71.26 per cent fall into the category of ego-writing (191) and 21.27 per cent into literary texts (57), while the remaining 7.47 per cent are either periodical (14), scientific (4) or religious (2) publications. Moreover, the latter were published either in the nineteenth (8) or in the twentieth (12) centuries, thereby corroborating that the participation of women in society was limited to the private sphere for most of the period (Kiełkiewicz-Janowiak 2012: 317; Nevalainen 2006: 136). Considering that the use of contractions has been stigmatized at least since the early eighteenth century, there arise questions regarding their spread among women: did female authors employ these forms because they were writing informal texts or were they unaware of this stigmatization? Labov (2001: 293) provides insight with what he terms "the gender paradox" and explains that "women conform more closely than men to sociolinguistic norms that are overtly prescribed, but conform less than men when they are not". When considered in the case at hand, the arguments suggest that both female and male speakers were informed as to the register restrictions of contractions, thus the patterns of usage discussed above.[10] Ultimately, the explosion of the shortened forms during the twentieth century substantiates these claims, as the linguistic ideology of the late Modern period was actively obstructing their expansion onto other distributional domains.

Attitudes towards language in the late Modern period are best described in terms of linguistic insecurity. The rise of the new middle class in the eighteenth and nineteenth centuries disturbed the balance

---

10 In her discussion of gender-based patterns of use, Kiełkiewicz-Janowiak (2012: 314–7) provides further grounds supporting the claim that women were aware of linguistic norms. Whereas most grammarians' prescriptions towards language were universal, the insertion of women in public life set up certain expectations regarding their use of language: women ought to be sympathetic and to use refined linguistic forms with 'grace and elegance' (Kiełkiewicz-Janowiak 2012: 315, original emphasis). These ideas became widespread with publications aimed towards young women, such as Harvey Newcomb's *How to Be a Lady: A Book for Girls, Containing Useful Hints on the Formation of Character*, published in 1850.

of the class system, ultimately blurring the lines between old and new money and leaving language as the only remaining marker of social standing. Beal (2004: 94) thus describes a society where "gentlemen and ladies [wished] to avoid being confused with their social inferiors" and where the new rich 'aspired to attain such "purity and politeness of expression" in order to achieve the veneer of gentility'. This socio-historical context thus favoured the flourishing of linguistic prescription, founded by figures like Jonathan Swift and Joseph Addison. Their views on the use of contractions in particular were, as discussed elsewhere, proscriptive, just like on many other questions of uncertain nature (Leonard 1962: 10–11, 40). For Tieken-Boon van Ostade, however, "the Age of Prescriptivism is *now*", since these attitudes towards use are "very much alive in the general public's consciousness" (2010: 9, original emphasis). The author argues that the publication and expansion of the usage guide, fathered by Fowler's *A Dictionary of Modern English Usage* (1926), was only the beginning of a persisting tradition of linguistic commentary and correctness surrounding all of society. Nevertheless, this picture does not entirely correspond with the reality of contraction-usage nor of the attitudes towards it.

Despite his authoritative stance towards language, Fowler does not comment on the contractions in his work. Such disregard on his part does in no way sanction their usage. In fact, the author never seems to employ the shortened forms in his prose, although he does include them in the quotes illustrating other points, such as "You see it's like a portmanteau" for the entry on the noun (Fowler 1926: 445). A few years later, Rice (1935: 420–2) advises their inclusion in textbooks and grammars to avoid orthographic errors like 'writ[ing] the word "of" as a substitute for "have"'. The author also claims that the use of contractions should be encouraged in writing so as to "obliterate [the] needless distinction between the written and the spoken language" (Rice 1935: 421). In this last claim, Rice seems to have perceived the colloquialization of the written mode that was unfolding during his time, corroborated by the expansion of the contractions in usage, along with other features of spoken language (Biber and Finegan 1992). It is our contention that this colloquialization takes part of a greater trend towards the democratization of the language.

Leech et al. (2009: 259) define democratization as the tendency to "phase out markers of distance, respect, superiority [...] to aim at the expression of greater equality and familiarity". Although the authors illustrate this point with the decline of titular nouns such as *Mr.* and *Mrs.* over time, the process may also be observable in other linguistic forms that are less directly related to power structures. Baker, for instance, claims that the spread of the negative contraction from the 1930s onward in certain modal verbs answers to the democratization of the language in the twentieth century. The fact that, as discussed in Section 3.2, *n't* commonly occurs with *will*, *would* and *can*, but is rare with *may* and *might*, ultimately denotes that the latter "are more likely to occur in formal and thus old-fashioned contexts" (Baker 2017: 103). The wider dissemination of contractions across genres also substantiates the hypothesis that formal registers were approaching the colloquial. Nevertheless, the democratization of language is, ultimately, "a reflection [...] of changing norms in personal relations" (Leech et al. 2009: 259), thereby suggesting that social change must have preceded this phenomenon. The twentieth century, especially in contrast to the nineteenth, was a turning point in social policies for a number of minorities, as embodied by women's suffrage and the civil rights movement. Though a period of instability mostly due to the world wars, the 1900s eventually levelled the social field and put an end to the rigid system that had characterized the late Modern period. In the end, the dyke preventing the flood of contractions in eighteenth- and nineteenth-century English gave way to more democratic patterns of use.

5. Conclusions

Even though the habit of contracting words can be dated back to the second half of the sixteenth century as a result of the printers' adoption of the apostrophe as a marker of certain forms of elision, the actual dissemination of contractions is in itself a late Modern English phenomenon. The apostrophe fulfilled a plethora of functions immediately after its incorporation into the English writing system and, among them, contractions and the expression of the possessive case are perhaps the most notorious ones in view of their impact on present-day English. In our opinion, contractions deserve special attention since they have eventually managed to find their own room notwithstanding their proscriptive bias in many grammars and usage guides since the eighteenth century. The present paper has outlined the diachronic development of contractions in the history of English paying attention to its distribution over time and its variation across registers and gender. The operators in the contracted forms of the negative and auxiliary verbs have also been examined to discern whether the dissemination of the phenomenon is pioneered by the particularities of the linguistic context. The study has led us to gather the following conclusions.

Historically speaking, the phenomenon has been unevenly distributed. The shortened forms of the verb *be* and the negative auxiliary verbs pioneered the process in the first half of the nineteenth century while the other contracted forms lagged behind, spreading timidly one century later surely as a result of the growing influence of the previous contractions in the English writing system. The study has shed light on the intrinsic preference for the auxiliary *do* with negative contractions and for personal pronouns with the auxiliary verbs from the beginning of the 1700s.

Register analysis has corroborated the claims that contractions have always been characteristic of the more colloquial registers as they occur more commonly in literature and ego-writing, followed by other registers such as advertising, law and periodicals, where they hold just a minor incidence. Notwithstanding this, the study has also confirmed a greater dispersion of contractions across twentieth-century registers, thus pointing to their increasing role in present-day English. Gender analysis, in turn, has shown that women have historically employed contractions more frequently than men, especially from the second half of the seventeenth century and, since then, they have been on the rise until the second half of the following century.

All in all, the present study has contributed to our understanding of the origin and diffusion of contractions in the history of English along with the symptoms of its twentieth-century democratization. It is not possible, however, to elaborate on the complete set of linguistic and extra-linguistic factors which may have historically participated in the development of the phenomenon as they have been surely biased by the grammarians' proscriptive attitudes, on the one hand, or the so-called accusations of informality, on the other. The issue still awaits the labour of an insightful scholar to provide a more convincing explanation of the origin of contractions, whether in speech or writing, or their growing dissemination in twenty-first-century English. For now, we can safely conclude that contractions were in themselves a late Modern English phenomenon which diffused in particular genres and, more importantly, under the shelter of female writers.

Source

Denison, David and Nuria Yáñez-Bouza, eds., *A Representative Corpus of Historical English Registers 3.2* (expanded version, originally compiled by Douglas Biber and Edward Finegan) (University of Manchester, 2013). Available at https://www.llc.manchester.ac.uk/research/projects/archer/.

References

Aronoff, Mark, 'Competitors and Alternants in Linguistic Morphology', in Franz Rainer, Wolfgang U. Dressler, Francesco Gardani, and Hans Christian Luschützky, eds., *Competition in Inflection and Word-Formation* (Cham: Springer, 2019), 39–66.

Baker, Paul, *American and British English: Divided by a Common Language?* (Cambridge: Cambridge University Press, 2017).

Bauer, Laurie, 'Competition in English Word Formation', in Ans van Kemenade and Bettelou Los, eds., *The Handbook of the History of English* (Oxford: Blackwell, 2006), 177–98.

Beal, Joan C., *English in Modern Times* (New York: Arnold, 2004)

——, 'Nineteenth-Century Dialect Literature and the Enregisterment of Urban Vernaculars', in Jane Hodson, ed., *Dialect and Literature in the Long Nineteenth Century* (London: Routledge, 2016), 17–32.

Biber, Douglas and Edward Finegan, 'The Linguistic Evolution of Five Writtena dn Speech-Based English Genres from the 17th to the 20th Centuries', in Matti Rissanen, Ossi Ihalainen, Terttu Nevalainen and Irma Taavitsainen, eds., *History of Englishes: New Methods and Interpretations in Historical Linguistics* (Berlin, Boston: Mouton de Gruyter, 1992), 688–704.

——, Stig Johansson, Geoffrey Leech, Susan Conrad and Edward Finegan, eds., *Longman Grammar of Spoken and Written English* (London: Longman, 1999).

Bond, D. F, ed., *The Spectator, Volume II* (Oxford: Clarendon Press, 1965).

Britain, David, 'Grammatical Variation in the Contemporary Spoken English of England', in Andy Kirkpatrick, ed., *The Routledge Handbook of World Englishes* (London/New York: Routledge, 2010), 37–58.

Chambers, J. K, *Sociolinguistic Theory* (Oxford: Blackwell, 1995).

Dobson, Eric John, *English Pronunciation 1500–1700*, Vol. 2 (Oxford: Clarendon, 1968).

Fowler, Henry W., *A Dictionary of Modern English Usage* (Oxford: Clarendon, 1926).

Gailor, Denis, 'Early Modern English Contractions and Their Relevance to Present-Day English', *English Today* 27 (2011), 10–15.

Görlach, Manfred, 'Regional and Social Variation', in Roger Lass, ed., *The Cambridge History of the English Language*, Vol. 3 (Cambridge: Cambridge University Press, 1999), 459–538.

Hendrickson, John, 'A Question about Contractions: Are All of 'em colloquial?', *College Composition and Communication* 22/1 (1971), 46–8.

Hogg, Richard, 'English in Britain', in Richard Hogg and David Denison, eds., *A History of the English Language* (Cambridge: Cambridge University Press, 2006), 352–83.

Huddleston, Rodney and Geoffrey K. Pullum, *The Cambridge Grammar of the English Language* (Cambridge: Cambridge University Press, 2002).

Jones, Richard Foster, *The Triumph of the English Language: A Survey of Opinions Concerning the Vernacular from the Introduction of Printing to the Restoration* (Oxford: Oxford University Press, 1953).

Jonson, Ben, *The English Grammar*, in Charles Harold Herford, Percy Simpson and Evelyn Simpson, eds., *The Works* (Oxford: Clarendon, 1947 [1649]), 463–553.

Kiełkiewicz-Janowiak, Agnieszka, 'Class, Age, and Gender-Based Patterns', in Juan Manuel Hernández-Campoy and Juan Camilo-Conde Silvestre, eds., *The Handbook of Historical Sociolinguistics* (Oxford: Blackwell, 2012), 307–31.

Labov, William, *Principles of Linguistic Change*, Vol. 2 (Oxford: Blackwell, 2001).

Leech, Geoffrey, Marianne Hundt, Christian Mair and Nicholas Smith, *Change in Contemporary English: A Grammatical Study* (Cambridge: Cambridge University Press, 2009).

Leonard, Sterling Andrus, *The Doctrine of Correctness in English Usage 1700–1800* (New York: Russell and Russell, 1962 [1929]).

Marchand, Hans, *The Categories and Types of Present-Day English Word-Formation: A Synchronic-Diachronic Approach* (Munich: C. H. Beck'sche, 1969).

Nevalainen, Terttu, *Introduction to Early Modern English* (Edinburgh: Edinburgh University Press, 2006).

Peters, Pam, *The Cambridge Guide to English Usage* (Cambridge: Cambridge University Press, 2004).

Petti, Anthony G., *English Literary Hands from Chaucer to Dryden* (Cambridge, MA: Harvard University Press, 1977).

Rice, Wallace, 'Usage Counsel: Contractions', *The English Journal* 24/5 (1935), 420–22.

Salmon, Vivian, 'Orthography and Punctuation', in Roger Lass, ed., *The Cambridge History of the English Language*, Vol. 3 (Cambridge: Cambridge University Press, 1999), 13–55.

Schlüter, Julia, 'Early Modern English: Phonology', in Alexander Bergs and Laurel J. Brinton, eds., *English Historical Linguistics*, Vol. 1 (Berlin: Mouton de Gruyter, 2012), 589–604.

Sundby, Bertil, Anne Kari Bjørge and Kari E. Haugland, *A Dictionary of English Normative Grammar 1700–1800 (DENG)* (Amsterdam: John Benjamins, 1991).

Tieken-Boon van Ostade, Ingrid, *An Introduction to Late Modern English* (Edinburgh: Edinburgh University Press, 2009).

——, 'Usage Guides and the Age of Prescriptivism', in Claudia Claridge and Birte Bos, eds., *Norms and Conventions in the History of English* (Amsterdam/Philadelphia: John Benjamin's, 2019), 7–28.

Yáñez-Bouza, Nuria, '*ARCHER* Past and Present (1990–2010)', *ICAME Journal* 35 (2011), 205–36.

Alicia Rodríguez-Álvarez and Sara von der Fecht-Fernández

Amerindian Loanwords in Richard Hakluyt's *The Principall Navigations* (1589) and Their Inclusion in Early and Late Modern English Dictionaries: Applications and Limitations of Digital Corpora, Databases and Tools in Lexicographical Research[1]

1. Introduction

One of the key topics in lexicographic studies is the use of primary sources in the compilation of dictionaries (Atkins and Rundell 2008: 45–96; Hawke 2016; Stamper 2020: 11–3). An example of this is the numerous debates that have arisen regarding the use of the sources that serve as documentary support for the headwords of the nomenclature of the *Oxford English Dictionary* (henceforth *OED*). Among

1 This work was carried out within the framework of the research project with reference PID2019-104199GB-100, "Americanismos léxicos en las lenguas española e inglesa documentados en textos sobre América anteriores a 1700: AMERLEX-DATABASE (Lexical Americanisms in the Spanish and English languages documented in texts on the Americas prior to 1700: AMERLEX-DATABASE") funded by the Government of Spain's State Research Agency, under the Ministry of Science and Innovation, in the 2019 call for R&D&I projects. It was also co-financed by the Canary Islands' Agency for Research, Innovation and the Society of Information, under the Ministry of Economy, Knowledge and Employment; and by the European Social Fund (ESF), Integrated Operational Program of the Canary Islands 2014–2020, Axis 3, Priority Topic 74 (85 per cent).

other issues, some scholars point to the scant female presence among sources (Brewer 2009), the over-reliance on canonical literary authors (Brewer 2005; Brewer 2010), and even the limited number of citations of secondary sources, such as dictionaries (Osselton 1995: 137–47), while others point to the changes introduced in the *OED* thanks to the examination of new sources (Durkin 2002). In this work, we will focus on one of the top 1,000 sources used in the *OED* to illustrate the use of numerous headwords of Amerindian origin that entered the English language, mainly through Spanish: Richard Hakluyt[2] (c. 1552–1616); among whose works, the most cited by far is *The Principall Navigations* (1589, henceforth *TPN*), with excerpts in 722 entries. This work aims to examine the presence of a well-defined group of Amerindian loanwords used in *TPN* in the first dictionaries compiled at the end of the sixteenth century, tracing their presence over the course of the seventeenth century and into the dictionaries of the eighteenth. To carry out this work in the most efficient way, we turned to digitized corpora and lexical and lexicographical databases in order to automate as many tasks as possible, which allowed us to assess the possibilities and limitations of automated searches in historical lexicography.

When we speak of *Amerindian loanwords* in this work we are referring to those words of Amerindian origin that were used in the territories of the New World occupied by settlers from the Iberian Peninsula, and that, therefore, in most cases, were mainly transferred to English through Spanish; and, to a lesser extent, through Portuguese (Durkin 2014: 353; 365). In other words, we are referring to those terms that Cutler (1994) calls "West Indian words" or "Latin American words", as well as the first group of the classification established by Serjeantson (1935: 250), which covers the American languages spoken in "South and Central America, Mexico, and the West Indies".

These languages furnished English with over 1,500 words (Cutler 1994: 44) and, although many were incorporated as a result of the proximity of British colonies to Spanish-American territories, the transmission of Amerindian loanwords to English actually began before British colonization (Dohan 1974: 115), as Spanish initially functioned as an intermediary language between English and the West Indian languages

2 See "Top 1000 Sources in the *OED*", https://www.oed.com/sources.

(Schlaugh 1960: 97; Algeo 1996: 13; Belda Medina 2002: 26). Thus, as Watson (1938: 108) indicates, the first loanwords from Nahuatl, dating back to the sixteenth century, penetrated English through Spanish. Spain's knowledge of the New World and its political and economic hegemony during the sixteenth century favoured an increase in loanwords from Spanish to English, including terms that were, in turn, of Amerindian origin (Algeo 1996: 20–1). This trend continued until the middle of the seventeenth century (Durkin 2014: 365), after which, according to Algeo (1996: 22), by the eighteenth century a significant decline in the spread of loanwords in general can be detected.

When the Spaniards arrived in the Americas they not only discovered new territories and natural elements, but also unfamiliar peoples who spoke a multitude of languages. It is not surprising, then, that the first explorers adopted Amerindian loanwords from these languages to designate the new phenomena they found in their expeditions (Zamora 2002: 197–8). Christopher Columbus was a pioneer in the inclusion of Amerindian loanwords in his writings on the New World (Cutler 1994: 44; Belda Medina 2002: 26), although he would soon be followed by the testimonies of successive Spanish and Portuguese expeditions. These texts would be translated into English for the benefit of British navigators, respecting, in many cases, the presence of their Amerindian loanwords, as in the case of Eden's translation of *The Decades of the New World* (1555), which introduced at least 17 "Latin American words" (Cutler 1994: 45–6).

But not all were translations of words related to Spanish and Portuguese exploration and travel in the New World. In fact, the first record of an Amerindian loanword in the English language dates back to T. Pyrell's translation of a medical treatise in Latin in 1553, which included the Latinized form *guaiacum* (Serjeantson 1935: 251; Cutler 1994: 44; Carney 1997: 190). In addition, the English sailors themselves, who for various reasons ended up landing in Spanish America (López de Mariscal 2003), would soon describe their experiences, incorporating the Amerindian names of those exotic elements constituting potential commercial goods:

> When the naval power of England began to grow, and Englishmen came into contact, even though this was hostile contact, with Spaniards upon the high seas, in the West Indies and on the coasts of Mexico and South America, they adopted from

> them the names they used for the inhabitants, animals, plants, etc., some of them being really Spanish words [. . .], while others were taken over by the Spaniards themselves from the natives [. . .]. English sailors brought back such words to England, and many of them gained currency rapidly as stories and products of the New World spread in this country. Many of them appear from the first time in the tales of voyages collected and published by Hakluyt. (Serjeantson 1935: 195–6)

As Serjeantson points out, Hakluyt's work takes on special importance because, unlike Eden's translation, it was a compilation of texts originally written in English. With the intention of encouraging his country's expansion beyond its borders, and being able to compete with other colonizing powers of the time, Hakluyt undertook to compile all the records on the travels and discoveries of his countrymen over the course of history (Markham 1896: 7–8). Contemporary texts were added to the old ones, often commissioned by himself, thanks to the close relationships he maintained with sailors and merchant companies (Parks 1961). The fact that Hakluyt is recognized as a "non-interventionist editor" who republished the texts "with remarkable fidelity" to the original sources (MacCrossan 2009: 105) ensures a reliable study of the testimonies of the authors, as they are first-hand accounts.

The precedent set by Hakluyt's compilation was so important to later English travel literature that, even in the eighteenth century, when *TPN* no longer played such an important role in the nationalism of the day, publications continued to emerge that were indebted to Hakluyt's work. As Day wrote (2016: 85) "no eighteenth-century collection followed *The Principal Navigations* in every respect, but almost every anthology discloses some aspect of its nationalistic practice and discourse".

As indicated at the beginning of this section, this work will analyse the integration of the Amerindian loanwords introduced by the authors of *TPN* into the first English dictionaries, both monolingual and bilingual. The work will focus on the macrostructure of the dictionaries, such that the multiple spellings presented by the headwords in the corpus, as well as the definitions and other issues more related to the microstructure of these entries, fall outside the scope of this study.

The corpus of the study corresponds to the third volume of *TPN*, which is dedicated to England's "valiant attempts in searching almost all the corners of the vast and new world of *America*" (Hakluyt 1589: cover), and is composed of 33 travel narratives by different authors, and 44 texts of other kinds, such as letters, patents and itineraries, according to Quinn's classification (1974: 341–77).

The two research questions that this work seeks to answer are: (i) given the popularity that *TPN* achieved, can we assume that the Amerindian loanwords employed by the authors featured in it were included in the hard-word dictionaries that began to be compiled around the same time that *TPN* was published? and (ii) if so, did they continue to form part of the nomenclature of the more general dictionaries of the eighteenth century? To answer these questions, in this paper we intend firstly to identify the Amerindian loanwords present in the corpus and analyse the frequency of their usage, then to seek occurrences of these Amerindian loanwords in other contemporary travel narratives that might have led to their inclusion in dictionaries, and finally to study the incorporation of Amerindian loanwords in the bilingual and monolingual English dictionaries of the sixteenth, seventeenth and eighteenth centuries.

2. Amerindian Loanwords in *TPN*: Identification and Frequency of Use

In order to extract the list of Amerindian loanwords used in *TPN* forming the basis of our study, we proceeded to read the corpus and identify the terms potentially of indigenous origin. This phase of the work had to be carried out *manually* by examining the digitized text of *TPN*, obtained through *Early English Books Online* (henceforth *EEBO*), since the 1589 text is not yet part of the Text Creation Partnership, which "has produced thousands of accurate, searchable, full-text transcriptions of early print books" (https://textcreationpartnership.org/). Therefore, it was only possible to consult the digitized images of the 1589 volume, which do not allow for searches. Moreover, when dealing with terms featuring highly dynamic spellings, we do not have stable and reliable search terms.

The task of identifying Amerindian loanwords involved certain difficulties resulting from English narrators' exposure to completely unknown indigenous languages. With regards to this phenomenon, Belda Medina (2002: 66–7) argues that the settlers in the New World found the Amerindian loanwords unpronounceable, such that, in the process of adapting them to their phonological systems, their spellings constantly changed. Although this author argues that when the loanword was transmitted to English through another European language much of the adaptation process had already been carried out in the intermediate language, we have found cases in which this does not seem to have happened. This is because, at times, the English navigators who were authors of the corpus did not know these terms through Spanish, but rather through oral contact with the inhabitants. Hence, when they registered a word unknown to them, they did so through a personal interpretation of the sounds that made it up. As an example of this, we find the spellings *aluacatas* (1589: 547)[3] for *aguacate* "avocado"; *nege* (1589: 594) for *maguey* "agave, aloe"; *miskito* (1589: 547) for *mesquite* "a type of tree"; *nochole* (1589: 570) for *nocheztli* "*cochineal*", and *clashacally* (1589: 569) for *tlaxcal* "*corn bread*".

In these cases, the context was decisive to discern the meaning, as were consultations of the extensive register of spelling variations found in the *OED*. This dictionary also provided us with other data necessary to carry out this study, such as the source language of the headword, and the date and name of the first English-language sources that included it.

Reading and analysis of the corpus revealed the use of a total of 25 Amerindian terms by English chroniclers, of which 22 are recorded in the *OED* (those that are not are marked with * in Table 1 and presented with the spelling found in the *Diccionario de americanismos*). Most date from 1555, prior to the publication of *TPN* (the dates of entry into the English language are also indicated in Table 1). Once the Amerindian loanwords were identified, we counted the appearances of these terms, based on two factors: (a) the number of times a given Amerindian loanword appears in the corpus, and (b) the number of different texts containing a given Amerindian loanword. We believe that our analysis of the frequency of use of the Amerindian loanwords (that is, our study of the number of times that the same word is used in all

3 To avoid unnecessary repetition, all citations of *TPN* will indicate the publication date and the corresponding page number (s).

the texts, and evaluation of its greater or lesser distribution among the different authors) can shed light on what may have been an important factor determining the inclusion of these terms in the dictionaries of the time.

Regarding the frequency of use of these items in total terms, Table 1 presents the headwords identified in *TPN* together with the number of times they are found in the corpus, regardless of the number of different works in which they appear:

Table 1: Amerindian loanwords in *TPN*: Frequency of use and *OED* entry date

aguacate (*OED* 1633)	1	*canoe* (*OED* 1555 [1541])	84	*guava* (*OED* 1555)	3	*mammee* (*OED* 1555)	3	*tecuán* *	2
cacao (*OED* 1555)	10	*capulin* (*OED* n.d.)	1	*guaiacum* (*OED* 1533)	2	*mesquite* (*OED* 1589)	1	*tiburon*[4] (*OED* 1555)	1
cacique (*OED* 1555)	4	*Carib* (*OED* 1555)	5	*hurricane* (*OED* 1555)	4	*nocheztli* *	1	*tlaxcal* *	1
Campeachy wood (*OED* 1652)	1	*cassava* (*OED* 1555)	7	*maguey* (*OED* 1555)	4	*potato*[5] (*OED* 1565)	8	*tuna* (*OED* 1555)	2
cannibal (1553)	16	*guano* (*OED* 1697)	1	*maize* (*OED* 1555 [1544])	23	*pulque* (*OED* 1589)	1	*sapota* (*OED* 1589)	2

4 Although the *OED* lists this headword as *origin uncertain*, it also states the following: "probably taken into Spanish or Portuguese from some West Indian or East Indian language" (oed.com). Taking into account that this word first appeared in texts on American territories, we decided to include it on our list. Although some authors theorise that the English word "*shark*" could come from the Yucatecan word *xoc* (Jones: 1985), this is not an accepted fact, so *shark* will not be part of our inventory.

5 Although we opted to follow the trend in the various studies that deal with this word as an indigenous one, it is important to clarify that it is actually a Spanish creation, a combination of two Amerindian headwords: *papa* and *batata* (see the entry for *patata* in the *DLE*).

Based on these total numbers, the words appearing 10 or more times are, in descending order, *canoe* (84), *maize* (23), *cannibal* (16) and *cacao* (10).

It is not surprising that *canoe* appears far more frequently than the other Amerindian loanwords. First of all, it was a means of transport widely used by the natives, so it would not have gone unnoticed by English sailors; secondly, as many of the accounts indicate, in the New World the conveyance of goods using this type of boat was frequent. As for its incorporation into the English language, we find that it was one of the first Amerindian loanwords transferred to English, dating back to Eden's translation of *The Decades*, in 1555 (Carney 1997: 190), so it is possible that English navigators of the time may have already been familiar with it. Moreover, taking into account that Spanish was the mediating language when transferring *canoe* into English, it is important to consider the information provided by Zamora (1970: 98):

> Usually words from the languages learned first were preferred. *Canoa* is the Antillean Indian word for boat, but for the Spaniards it became the name for any Indian boat, even in places so far removed from the Caribbean as Peru.

In this way, like the Spanish settlers, the English travellers called any boat of the indigenous people a *canoe,* regardless of the area, thus increasing the number of times this word appears, with it even being used in some reports on other territories. For example, in North American territories far from the Spanish-speaking colonies, English explorers also used the word *canoe* to refer to the small boats of local peoples, as seen in the following fragments of stories compiled in *TPN*, the first of which belongs to *The voyage of Iohn Dauis, for the discouerie of the Northwest passage*, 1585; and the second *An accompt of the particularities of the imployment of the English men left in Virginia vnder the charge and gouerment of Ralfe Lane, written by himself*:

> At length there came 10 ***Canoas*** from the other Ilands, and two of them came so neere the shoare where we were, that they talked with vs, the other being in their boats a pretie way off. (1589: 778; our emphasis)

> Amongst other things he tolde me, that going three dayes iourney in a **canoa** by his Riuer of *Choanoke*, and descending to the land, you are within foure dayes iourney to passe ouer land Northeast to a certaine Kings countrey [. . .]. (1589: 738; our emphasis)

In addition, *maize*, *cannibal* and *cacao* correspond to the description of the new American reality. In the case of *maize* and *cacao*, we are not only talking about potentially lucrative goods for the English, but they also played an important role in the lives of Native Americans beyond food, for example functioning as tribute. As for *cannibals*, the fear inspired by those man-eating tribes was evident in accounts of the navigators' adventures, whether when comparing other groups of natives to them, in confrontations with them, or due to the need to avoid them. We must also bear in mind that the *OED* records the entry of these indigenous loanwords into the English language at an early date (*cacao* in 1555, *cannibal* in 1553, and *maize* in 1555, although it already appeared in a manuscript of 1544), indicating that they were probably familiar to English explorers.

The second factor that we took into account when evaluating the use of these Amerindian loanwords was their distribution in different texts. Certainly, the repetition of a headword in the compilation is not necessarily a faithful indicator of its spread, since it could have been used many times, but just by one author. Therefore, in order to expand on the information presented and reach a more accurate conclusion regarding its use, we carried out a second count, this time classifying the terms according to the number of different texts in which they appear, which is included in Table 2.

Table 2: Number of texts in *TPN* in which Amerindian loanwords are used

aguacate	1	*canoe*	20	*Guava*	2	*mammee*	3	*tecuán*	1
cacao	3	*capulin*	1	*Guaiacum*	2	*mesquite*	1	*Tiburon*	1
cacique	2	*Carib*	1	*Hurricane*	3	*Nocheztli*	1	*tlaxcal*	1
Campeachy	1	*cassava*	5	*maguey*	2	*potato*	6	*tuna*	2
cannibal	6	*guano*	1	*maize*	6	*pulque*	1	*sapota*	2

If we select those Amerindian loanwords that appear in five or more texts, we observe that *canoe* (20 texts) continues to be the most common, followed by *cannibal* (16), *maize* (6), *potato* (6) and *cassava* (5). These results show little variation with respect to Table 1, such that they reinforce the ideas extracted from the overall count. The only word with more than 10 appearances in Table 1 that does not appear in more than five texts in Table 2 is *cacao*, although two new words are included that also refer to food that were both a commercial good and a means of subsistence for natives and foreigners: *potato* and *cassava*.

Having extracted the data from Hakluyt's work, we proceeded to study the distribution of these Amerindian loanwords in other English travel books on the New World from the era, as we decided that this could be another factor favouring the inclusion of these indigenous loanwords in dictionaries. For this phase of the work we turned to *AMERLEX*, a database currently in the development phase, to which we had access in a test format. *AMERLEX* aims to compile lexical Americanisms[6] present in a selection of Spanish and English texts on the Americas published during the sixteenth and seventeenth centuries (https://iatext.ulpgc.es/es/aplicaciones)[7]. Access to this tool allowed us to verify in which other sixteenth-century travel narratives the Amerindian loanwords being studied were used, and to elucidate whether the Amerindian loanwords used by the authors of the corpus were common in the narratives about the new American territories in the sixteenth century or, on the contrary, they were lexical rarities. The following graph expresses the distribution of the headwords between these documents, differentiating between foreign texts translated into English and those that were originally written in English:

6 This term refers to both words from Amerindian languages and words from Spanish which acquired a new meaning in America.

7 At this time, the works that have been uploaded date from the sixteenth century.

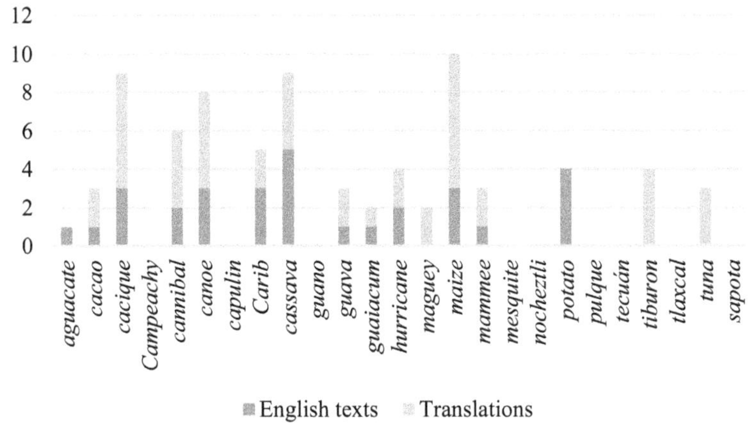

Figure 1: The distribution of the corpus Amerindian loanwords in sixteenth-century travel texts on the New World.

Of the 25 headwords on our list, 16 were found in other texts registered in *AMERLEX*. By establishing the cut-off at at least five texts, we found that the word with the greatest dispersal between the English texts was *cassava* (five texts). If we look at translations, *maize* was the leader (seven texts), followed by *cacique* (six texts) and *canoe* (five texts). With the exception of *cacique*, the rest of the Amerindian loanwords mostly? used by authors who were contemporaries of Hakluyt coincide with those most repeated in *TPN*, suggesting the general predominance of these Amerindian loanwords in the different works of English travel literature of the time. As with the earlier Amerindian loanwords, *cacique* and *cassava* are examples of early registration in the English language (both in 1555).

From another point of view, the Amerindian loanwords under study usually appear more frequently in translations than in English texts. This phenomenon is not strange, since most of the translations took works in Spanish as their source material, a language that, as already indicated, acted as a conduit of Amerindian words into English. The English text that contains the most Amerindian loanwords is *The Discouerie of the Large, Rich and Bewtiful Empire of Guiana* (1596), by Walter Raleigh (seven headwords); while the translation containing the most is *The Decades of the Newe Worlde or West India* (1555) by Pietro Martire d'Anghiera, which was translated by Richard Eden (12 headwords).

3. The Incorporation of Amerindian Loanwords in *TPN* into the English Lexicography of the Sixteenth, Seventeenth and Eighteenth Centuries: *LEME* as a Tool for AUTOMATED Searches

To study the incorporation of the Amerindian loanwords extracted from *TPN* into the English lexicography of the sixteenth to the eighteenth centuries, we compiled a list of the English monolingual and bilingual English-Spanish dictionaries released after the publication of Hakluyt's work and during the following two centuries (Table 3). In addition, in the case of bilingual dictionaries, John Florio's English-Italian dictionary *A Worlde of Wordes* (1598) was also included, due to the enormous influence it exerted on the compilation of subsequent bilingual and monolingual English dictionaries (Starnes 1937: 1012; Steiner 1970: 39; Hayashi 1978: 55; Domínguez-Rodríguez 2016: 154).

Table 3: List of dictionaries consulted for this study

	YEAR	AUTHOR	TITLE
Sixteenth century	1590	Del Corro/Thorius	*The Spanish Grammer [The Spanish Dictionarie]*
	1591	Perceval	*Bibliotheca Hispanica*
	1591	Stepney	*The Spanish Schoole-master*
	1598	Florio	*A Worlde of Words*
	1599	Perceval/Minsheu	*A Dictionarie in Spanish and English*
Seventeenth century	1604	Cawdrey	*A Table Alphabetical*
	1616	Bullokar	*An English Exhibitor*
	1623	Cockeram	*The English Dictionarie*
	1656	Blount	*Glossographia*
	1658	Phillips	*The New World of English Words*
	1676	Coles	*An English Dictionary*
	1689	Hogarth	*Gazophylacium Anglicanum*
Eighteenth century	1702	Kersey	*A New English Dictionary*
	1704	Cocker	*Cocker's English Dictionary*
	1706	Kersey/Phillips	*The New World of English Words*
	1706	Stevens	*A New Spanish and English Dictionary*
	1707	Anon	*Glossographia Anglicana Nova*
	1708	Kersey	*Dictionariun Anglo-Britannicum*
	1721	Bailey	*An Universal Etymological English Dictionary*

Table 3: *Continued*

YEAR	AUTHOR	TITLE
1727	Bailey	*The Universal Etymological English Dictionary, vol. II*
1730	Bailey	*Dictionarium Britannicum*
1735	Dyche and Pardon	*A New General English Dictionary*
1735	Defoe	*A New English Dictionary*
1740	Pineda	*Nuevo Dicionario, Español e Ingles e Ingles y Español*
1749	Martin	*Lingua Britannica Reformata*
1753	Anon	*A Pocket Dictionary or Complete English Expositor*
1753	[Wesley]	*The Complete English Dictionary*
1755	Scott / Bailey	*A New Universal Etymological English Dictionary*
1755	Johnson	*A Dictionary of the English Language*
1763	Giral del Pino	*A Dictionary Spanish and English, and English and Spanish*
1773	Kenrick	*A New Dictionary of the English Language*
1774	Barclay	*A Complete and Universal English Dictionary on a New Plan*
1775	Ash	*The New and Complete Dictionary of the English Language*
1778	Baretti	*A Dictionary, Spanish and English, and English and Spanish*
1797–1798	Connelly and Higgins	*Diccionario Nuevo de las Dos Lenguas Española ê Inglesa*

Term queries were run for the first editions of these 35 dictionaries, of which 10 are bilingual and 25 monolingual. Chronologically, the 35 dictionaries are distributed as follows: five of them, all bilingual, belong to the sixteenth century; seven monolingual ones correspond to the seventeenth century; and, finally, of the 23 dictionaries from the eighteenth century, five are bilingual and 18 are monolingual.

The digital tool that was clearly able to facilitate the time-consuming task of searching, one by one, the corpus of Amerindian loanwords in the different dictionaries was *Lexicons of Early Modern English (LEME)*, "a historical database of monolingual, bilingual, and polyglot dictionaries, lexical encyclopaedias, hard-word glossaries, spelling lists, and lexically-valuable treatises surviving in print or manuscript from about 1475 to 1755" (leme.library.utoronto.ca). *LEME* seemed to be the most suitable tool for this type of study, since it allows for the optimization of time and resources. However, there are many dictionaries whose bibliographic data have been recorded, but whose contents have not been uploaded; and other dictionaries that have not even been registered. In the first group are the dictionaries of Perceval (1591), Cockeram (1623), Cocker (1704), Stevens (1706), Anon. (1707), Kersey (1708), Bailey (1721), and (1730), Pineda (1740), Martin (1749) and Anon. (1753). Dictionaries that were not included in *LEME* as of the writing of this work include Coles (1676)[8], Kersey and Phillips (1706), Bayley (1727), Dyche and Pardon (1735), Wesley (1753), Giral del Pino (1763), Kenrick (1773), Barclay (1774), Ash (1775), Baretti (1778) and Connelly and Higgins (1797–1798). The fact that the nomenclatures of these dictionaries are not included in *LEME* meant that out of the 35 dictionaries that constitute the lexicographical corpus for this work's consultations, we could only use 13. What implications would this have for our study? It might be best to illustrate this with some examples that show the data obtained through searches in *LEME*.

This tool allows searches to be conducted in different ways. For example, a search can be run by placing the current headword in the Modern-English Headwords Search tab, which allows one to ascertain which dictionaries contain, for example, the word that today we identify as *guava* (following the spelling in the *OED*, which *LEME* uses), regardless of its form in the different dictionaries. This search carried out in *LEME* revealed that this term is only found in Bullokar's dictionary (1616), in which it appears with the spelling *guaiauas* (Figure 2):

8 The *LEME* records the 1677 edition, whose text is meta-searchable.

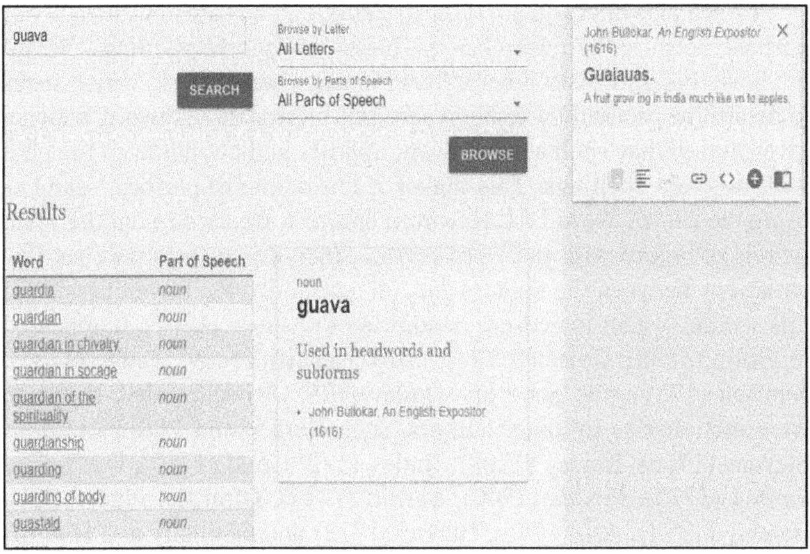

Figure 2: Caption of *LEME* "Modern-English Headwords Search": *guava.*

However, "manual" consultation of this same term in the reference dictionaries selected expands the number of dictionaries to 14: one from the sixteenth century (*guyávas*, in Perceval 1599), two from the seventeenth (*guaiauas*, in Bullokar 1616 and Coles 1676), and 11 from the eighteenth (*guajavas*, in Cocker 1704; *guábas*, in Stevens 1706 and Pineda 1740; *guaiavas*, in Kersey 1708 and Bailey 1721; *guai'avas*, in Bailey 1730; *gua'iava. gua'va*, in Johnson 1755; *gua'bas*, in Giral del Pino 1763 and Baretti 1778; *guaia'vas*, in Ash 1775; *guayába*, in Connelly and Higgins 1798).

The same problem is found with *cacao*. If we use *LEME's* Modern-English Headwords Search tab, only Kersey's dictionary (1702) is indicated, while a manual search reveals the inclusion of this word in 20 dictionaries, as shown in Table 4. In addition to these problems there is the fact that many words included in the *OED* are not found through the Modern-English Headwords Search; this is the case of *aguacate*, *cacique*, *Campeachy*, *Carib*, *guano*, *maguey*, *mammee*, *pulque*, *tiburon*, *tuna* and *sapota*.

LEME also offers other search systems, but they are not suited to our purpose because their searches are based on specific spellings. We do not have this information beforehand in this type of work, which seeks to determine precisely whether a certain Amerindian loanword, which a given author may spell a certain way, appears in dictionaries of the time with different spellings. This makes it unfeasible to perform searches using the *LEME* Word List. However, as a test, we carried out the same search as before with the word *cacao*, since it is a term that has few variations between the authors and, unexpectedly, the hits obtained via this search system increased; in addition to Kersey (1702), it appeared in Florio (1598), Coles (1677 = 1676), Hogarth (1689), Defoe (1735), Johnson (1755), and Scott and Bailey (1755). Not detected, however, were dictionaries by other authors, such Kersey and Phillips (1706), Stevens (1706), Kersey (1708), Bailey (1721), and (1730), Dyche and Pardon (1735), Pineda (1740), Martin (1749), Giral del Pino (1763), Barclay (1774), Ash (1775), Baretti (1778) and Connelly and Higgins (1798), which do register entries for this headword. A simple search for the word *cacao* in *LEME* yielded the same results.

Table 4: Number of dictionaries that include the Amerindian loanwords in *TPN*

WORD (OED entry)	**Sixteenth century (bilingual)**	**Seventeenth century (monolingual)**	**Eighteenth century**	**TOTAL**
aguacate	0	0	7 (5 bil. + 2 monol.)	7 (5 bil. + 2 monol.)
cacao	1	1	18 (5 bil. + 13 monol.)	20 (6 bil. + 14 monol.)
cacique	2	2	10 (5 bil. + 5 monol.)	14 (7 bil. + 7 monol.)
Campeachy wood	1	0	13 (4 bil. + 9 monol.)	14 (5 bil. + 9 monol.)
cannibal	1	4	14 (14 monol.)	19 (1 bil. + 18 monol.)
canoe	3	3	20 (5 bil. +15 monol.)	26 (8 bil. + 18 monol.)
capulí	0	0	1 (1 bil.)	1 (1 bil.)
Carib	1	0	10 (3 bil. + 7 monol.)	11 (4 bil. + 7 monol.)

Table 4: *Continued*

WORD (OED entry)	**Sixteenth century (bilingual)**	**Seventeenth century (monolingual)**	**Eighteenth century**	**TOTAL**
cassava	0	2	13 (3 bil. + 10 monol.)	15 (3 bil. + 12 monol.)
guano	0	0	5 (4 bil. + 1 monol.)	5 (4 bil. + 1 monol.)
guava	1	2	11 (5 bil. + 6 monol.)	14 (6 bil. + 8 monol.)
guaiacum	1	3	17 (5 bil. + 12 monol.)	21 (6 bil. + 15 monol.)
hurricane	0	4	21 (5 bil. + 16 monol.)	25 (5 bil. + 20 monol.)
maguey	1	0	4 (4 bil.)	5 (5 bil.)
maize	2	0	19 (5 bil. + 14 monol.)	21 (7 bil. + 14 monol.)
mammee	1	0	11 (4 bil. + 7 monol.)	12 (5 bil. + 7 monol.)
mesquite	0	0	1 (1 bil.)	1 (1 bil.)
nocheztli	0	0	0	0
potato	2	3	20 (5 bil. +15 monol.)	25 (7 bil. + 18 monol.)
pulque	0	0	3 (3 bil.)	3 (3 bil.)
tecuán	0	0	0	0
tiburon	2	0	5 (5 bil.)	7 (7 bil.)
tlaxcal	0	0	0	0
tuna	0	0	11 (5 bil. + 6 monol.)	11 (11 bil. + 6 monol.)
sapota	0	0	6 (5 bil. + 1 monol.)	6 (bil. + 1 monol.)

These problems are aggravated if it is a headword featuring several spellings in the different dictionaries, such as *canoe*. Using the Modern-English Headwords Search, we discovered its inclusion in Phillips (1658, *canow*), Hogarth (1689, *canow*), Kersey (1702, *canoo*) and Defoe (1735, *canoo*); besides, when we explored in the *LEME* Word List the same spellings recorded in *TPN* (*canoe*, *canowa*, *canoe* and *canow*) we discovered that, in addition to the previous dictionaries, it is also recorded in Coles (1677, *canow* = 1676) and Johnson (1755, *canoes*). Inexplicably, however, the tool did not report its inclusion in a set of dictionaries in which it appears, sometimes even with the same spellings: Perceval (1591, *canoa*), Florio (1598, *canóa*), Perceval and Minsheu (1599, *canóa*), Kersey and Phillips (1706, *canoo* or *canow*), Stevens (1706, *canóa*), Kersey (1708, *canoo* or *canow*), Bailey (1721, *canoo*, *canow*), Bailey (1730, *cano'e*), Dyche and Parcon (1735, *canoo*), Pineda (1740, *canóa*), Martin (1749, *cano'o, cano'w*), Anon. (1753, *cano'o*), Wesley (1753, *cano'o*), Scott and Bailey (1755, *cano'a, or cano'*e), Giral del Pino (1763, *cano'a*), Kenrick (1773, *cano'*e), Barclay (1774, *cano'a*, or *cano'e*), Ash (1775, *cano'a*, *cano'e),* Baretti (1778, *cano'a*) and Connelly and Higgins (1798, *canóa*), which seems to indicate that *LEME* does not detect words bearing punctuation marks, such as apostrophes or accents, something that poses a great problem when searching for many of the corpus headwords.

Thus, the powerful *LEME* database has not been useful for this particular work because it omits a great number of dictionaries in which the Amerindian loanwords in question do actually appear. Limiting ourselves, therefore, to the use of *LEME* would distort the results of the work, not only due to the omission of quantitative information, but also qualitative information, such as the definitions themselves, which we would not be able to consult. Faced with these drawbacks, we opted for manual searches of the headwords in the digitized works available through *EEBO*, *ECCO* (*Eighteenth-Century Collections Online*), and Google Books. The results obtained are presented in Table 4, which shows that, of our inventory of 25 Amerindian loanwords, 13 were listed in dictionaries from the sixteenth century, nine in dictionaries from the seventeenth century, and 22 in dictionaries from the eighteenth century. There were only three words that were not found in any of the dictionaries indicated: *nocheztli, tecuán* and *tlaxcal.*

There are several conclusions that can be drawn from the results presented in Table 4. First of all, the correlation between this lexicographic data and the data on these same terms' frequency of use and diffusion in the primary sources – in our case *TPN* and other texts on voyages to the Americas in the sixteenth century (Tables 1, and 2 and Figure 1) – indicates that the frequency of use of headwords and their dispersal do seem to have been a key factor determining the inclusion of the word in the first dictionaries. The most-listed word in the sixteenth-century dictionaries, *canoe* (three of the five consulted) is, precisely, one of the words most frequently found in *TPN* (84 appearances, Table 1), and the one that appears in the greatest number of *TPN* narratives (20 texts, Table 2). *Canoe* is one of the words most frequently found among the texts in English on expeditions to the Americas (Figure 1). Continuing with the sixteenth century, the dictionaries published on dates close to the publication of *TPN* also list entries coinciding with words often found in that text; especially, *maize*, with 23 appearances in *TPN*, and present in six texts of the compilation, and in seven other works on voyages in the Americas.

We must bear in mind, however, that the sixteenth-century dictionaries were bilingual, Spanish-English (except Florio 1589), such that a greater tendency to include in these works words more related to New World territories colonized by the Spaniards is to be expected. With this in mind, it is interesting to observe the evolution of these entries in monolingual hard-word dictionaries from the seventeenth century. Some of the most important Amerindian loanwords in the sixteenth-century texts, such as *canoe*, recur in seventeenth-century dictionaries. However, it is striking to see how the term *maize*, with a high frequency of use and considerable dispersal throughout the sixteenth century, was not included in seventeenth-century dictionaries. Meanwhile, words like *hurricane* and *cassava* make their entry, the latter with great diffusion in texts on the Americas of the sixteenth century, both in translations into English and texts originally written in this language (Figure 1).

The great explosion of Amerindian loanwords in English lexicography, both bilingual and monolingual, undoubtedly took place in the eighteenth century, which saw a huge increase in the number of dictionaries listing terms like *hurricane*, *potato* and *canoe*, for example. Several reasons may account for this dramatic increase. Firstly, in the eighteenth century commercial interests in goods from the Caribbean spawned the publication of numerous volumes providing information on trade routes and products. In fact, one of the first documents published in this regard at the beginning of said century was Captain Stevens' translation of Joseph Veitia Linage's text, which included the commercial legislation governing trade with the Americas, *The Spanish Rule of Trade to the West-Indies: Containing an Account of the Casa de Contratación, or India-House* (1702), which includes, at the end, a list of the goods that could be exported to the colonies and the names of the products that were imported from there, many of them Amerindian loanwords. A little later, we find texts such as Herman Moll's *A View of the Coasts, Countries and Islands within the Limits of the South-Sea-Company* (1711), which clearly states that it will deal with "the Product, People, Manufactures, Trade and Riches of the several Places". And the document that best embodies the institutional desire to boost trade with the New World is the text issued by the British Parliament entitled *Act for the Encouragement of the Trade to America* (Great Britain 1708), which specifically mentions those American products that are of special interest to British importers, along the same lines as the text *The Considerable Advantages of a South Sea Trade to Our English Nation* (1711), aimed at promoting trade relations with the New World.

In addition to this boom in the publications of volumes on the Americas, which led to the entry of numerous Amerindian loanwords into the English language, there was a surge in the publication of dictionaries throughout the eighteenth century. During this era, more dictionaries were published than during the previous centuries, which resulted in a greater number of volumes that, at least in theory, were able to include these terms. As a consequence of this increase, and taking into account the standard practice among lexicographers of taking previous dictionaries as starting points for the compilation of their own, it is logical to expect that the authors would repeat the entries found in previous dictionaries (not to mention the definitions, which will be the object of a future study). Thus, Captain Stevens, the translator of the text on commercial legislation that we have just mentioned, was also the author of the bilingual dictionary that inaugurated the eighteenth century with a great number of Amerindian loanwords (see the Appendix at the end of this paper), which made their way into the bilingual dictionaries that followed, with slight variations in number. Similarly, the monolingual dictionary by Kersey and Phillips, published in the same year as Stevens' (1706), listed a number of Amerindian loanwords that had never been published before and that were taken up by many subsequent lexicographers, only slightly surpassed by Ash (1775).

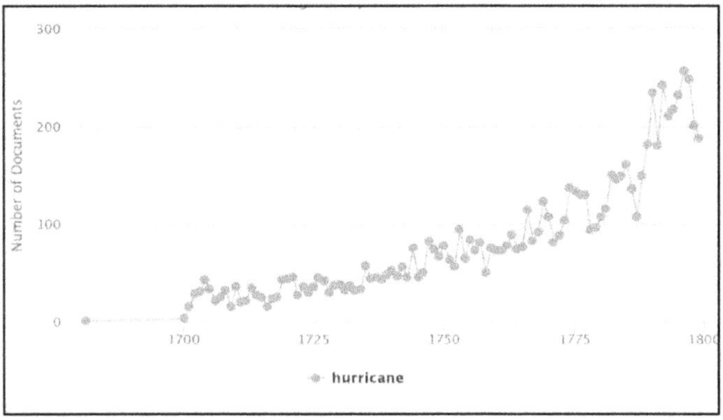
300
200
100
0
Number of Documents
1700
1725
1750
1775
1800
hurricane

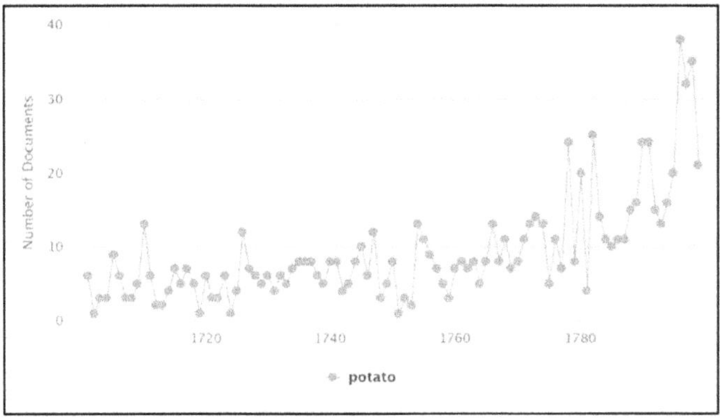
40
30
20
10
0
Number of Documents
1720
1740
1760
1780
potato

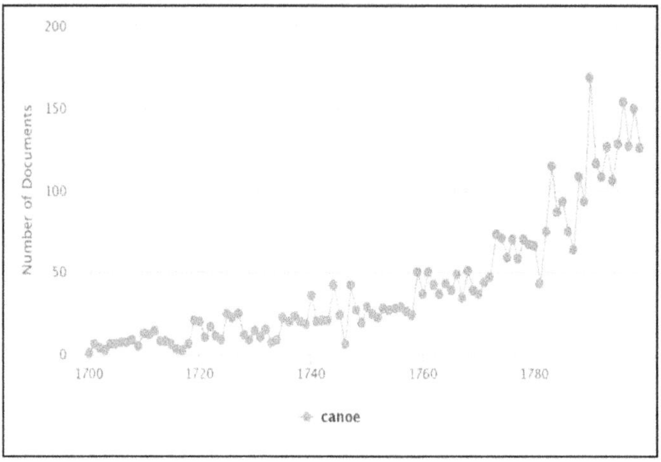

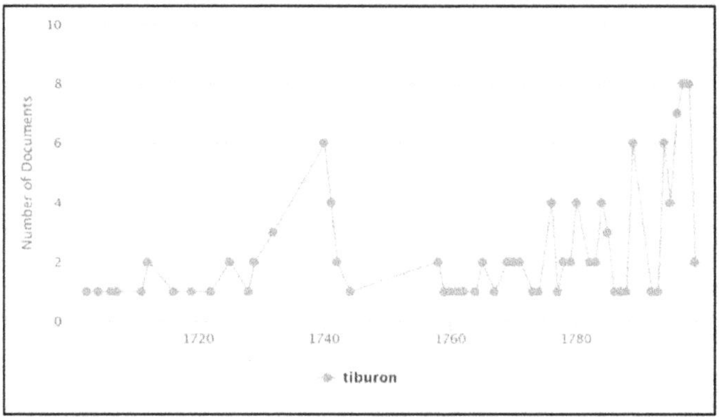

Figures 3, 4, 5, and 6: Number of texts per year (eighteenth century) including the words *hurricane*, *potato*, *canoe* and *tiburon* (source: *ECCO* search results for "Term frequency").

Did Hakluyt's compilation and its inclusion and preservation of the Amerindian loanwords appearing in its texts have an impact on the dictionaries compiled in the eighteenth century? We cannot answer this question with complete certainty, but automated searches of meta-searchable corpuses, such as the *ECCO*, reveal that Hakluyt and his work were regular references in up to 270 travel chronicles, naval histories, geographical descriptions, histories of the Americas, trade documents and other texts. Undoubtedly, these authors' exposure to the

Amerindian loanwords found in *TPN* favoured their usage and their consequent inclusion in English dictionaries. A search of the most listed words in the dictionaries of the eighteenth century in the digitized corpus of the *ECCO* reveals that *hurricane*, *potato* and *canoe* were widespread terms in eighteenth-century texts, with this explaining their inclusion in a large number of dictionaries of the time, while the scant use of the term *tiburón* "shark" in texts of the same era explains why it was included in few dictionaries.

4. Conclusions

This study on the reception of the Amerindian loanwords used in *TPN* in the dictionaries of the sixteenth, seventeenth and eighteenth centuries has shown that lexicological and lexicographic research can benefit from the use of digital tools that yield reliable and verified results. However, the excellent digital corpora, meta-searchable collections and databases available do not always allow for automated searches to streamline some very laborious tasks.

The problems we encountered were varied, and we had to find *ad hoc* solutions for each phase of the study. First of all, the Text Creation Partnership project has not yet undertaken a meta-searchable transcription of the text of *TPN* (1589), which forced us to read and run manual searches of the Amerindian loanwords. These searches revealed the use of 25 Amerindian loanwords, the most frequent being *canoe* (84 appearances), *maize* (23), *cannibal* (16) and *cacao* (10). Of these, *canoe*, *cannibal* and *maize* were also among those found in the largest number of texts: 20, 16 and 6, respectively. The task of searching for appearances of these words was carried out manually because, even if we had had meta-searchable texts, it would have been difficult to find all the Amerindian loanwords since they were recently incorporated terms featuring a range of different spellings.

As for the study of these terms in other texts of exploration, we discarded searches using the *EEBO* and *ECCO* because their advanced searches were not concrete enough. Thus, we opted to use a database currently under development that specifically contains Amerindian loanwords and Spanish words that took on new meanings in the New World colonies: the *AMERLEX*-database. At this time this database features Americanisms from sixteenth-century Spanish and English works on New World expeditions, geographical relationships, natural histories, administrative documents, etc. Its staff is currently working on the inclusion of seventeenth-century works, and is expected to go on to include eighteenth-century ones as well. Searches of *AMERLEX* confirmed that the words found most frequently and widely in *TPN* were also the most widespread in similar sixteenth-century works.

After identifying the Amerindian loanwords in *TPN* and establishing which ones were the most frequent and widespread in the primary sources, we proceeded to study the secondary ones. For this phase of the project, we had access to a very valuable tool that has facilitated many lexicographical studies: *LEME*. It features a search system that, *a priori*, we thought could greatly facilitate the work: the Modern-English Headwords Search, which allows a search for a certain headword to be conducted regardless of its spelling in the dictionaries. However, this search system, and others that we used, failed to detect many of the dictionaries that listed Amerindian loanwords found in *TPN*, such that, again, we had to carry out manual scanning of the dictionaries. In this phase of the work we reached valuable conclusions: (i) the sixteenth-century bilingual dictionaries list words often used in texts from that century on New World expeditions, their lexicographers echoing recent words whose use was increasingly widespread; (ii) the monolingual dictionaries of the seventeenth century did not undergo great changes with respect to the inclusion of Amerindian loanwords, adding very few words absent from sixteenth-century dictionaries; (iii) in contrast, eighteenth-century bilingual and monolingual dictionaries included much greater numbers of Amerindian loanwords. This increase was not by chance, but owing to clear historical reasons: commercial interest in South America and the Caribbean in eighteenth-century England gave rise to the publication of a great number of texts on these regions. The statistics on frequency of use that we were able to establish using *ECCO* clearly show that both the Amerindian loanwords most often found in eighteenth-century dictionaries and those that were less widespread have a similar diffusion in the primary sources.

References

Primary Sources

Anghiera, Pietro Martire d', *The Decades of the Newe Worlde or West India* (Londini: In ædibus Guilhelmi Powell, 1555).

Anon., *Glossographia Anglicana Nova* (London: Dan. Brown, 1707).

Anon., *The Considerable Advantages of a South Sea Trade to Our English Nation* (London: Printed for S. Popping, at the Black Raven in Pater-Noster-Row, 1711).

Anon., *A Pocket Dictionary of Complete English Expositor* (London: printed for J. Newbery, at th Bible and Sun, 1753).

Ash, John, *The New and Complete Dictionary of the English Language* (London: printed for Edward and Charles Dilly in the Poultry, 1755).

Bailey, Nathan, *An Universal Etymological English Dictionary* (London: printed for E. Bell, J. Darby, A. et al., 1721).

Bailey, Nathan, *The Universal Etymological English Dictionary* (London: printed for T. Cox, at the Lamb, 1727).

Bailey, Nathan, *Dictionarium Britannicum* (London: printed for T. Cox, at the Lamb, 1730).

Barclay, James, *A Complete and Universal English Dictionary on a New Plan* (London: printed for Richardson and Urquhart; W. Otridge et al., 1774).

Baretti, Giuseppe, *A Dictionary, Spanish and English, and English and Spanish* (London: printed for J. Nourse, Bookseller to His Majesty, 1778).

Blount, Thomas, *Glossographia* (London: Tho. Newcomb, 1656).

Bullokar, John, *An English Expositor* (London: Iohn Legatt, 1616).

Cawdrey, Robert, *A Table Alphabeticall* (London: I. R., 1604).

Cocker, Edward, *Cocker's English Dictionary* (London: John Overton, 1704).

Cockeram, Henry, *The English Dictioinarie: or, An Interpreter of Hard English Words* (London: Eliot's Court Press, 1623).

Coles, Elisha, *An English Dictionary* (London: Samuel Crouch, 1676).

Connelly, Thomas and Thomas Higgins, *Diccionario Nuevo de las Dos Lenguas Española ê Inglesa* (Madrid: en la imprenta real. Por Don Pedro Julian Pereyra, impresor de cámara de S.M., 1797–1798).

Defoe, Benjamin Norton, *A New English Dictionary* (Westminster: printed for John Brindley, at the King's-Arms, 1735).

Del Corro, Antonio and John Thorius, *The Spanish Grammer* (London: Iohn Wolfe, 1590).

Dyche, Thomas and William Pardon, *A New General English Dictionary* (London: printed for Richard Ware, 1735).

Florio, John, *A Worlde of Wordes* (London: T. Orwin, 1598).

Giral del Pino, Hipólito San Joseph, *A Dictionary Spanish and English, and English and Spanish* (London: printed for A. Millar, J. Nourse, and P. Vaillant, 1763).

Great Britain, *Act for the encouragement of the Trade to America* (London: printed by Charles Bill, and the executrix of Thomas Newcomb, deceas'd, 1708).

Hakluyt, Richard, *The Principall Navigations, Voiages and Discoueries of the English Nation* (Imprinted at London: by George Bishop and Ralph Newberie, 1589).

Hogarth, Richard, *Gazophylacium Anglicanum* (London: E. Holt, 1689).

Johnson, Samuel, *A Dictionary of the English Language* (London: printed by W. Strahan, 1755).

Kenrick, William, *A New Dictionary of the English Language* (London: printed for John and Francis Rivington, William Johnston et al., 1773).

Kersey, John, *A New English Dictionary* (London: Printed for Henry Bonwicke, at the Red Lion, 1702).

Kersey, John, *Dictionarium Anglo-Britannicum* (London: J. Wilde, 1708).

Kersey, John and Edward Phillips, *The New World of English Words* (London: printed for J. Phillips, at the King's Arms, 1706).

Martin, Benjamin, *Lingua Britannica Reformata* (London: printed for J. Hodges; S. Austen et al., 1749).

Moll, Herman, *A View of the Coasts, Countries and Islands within the Limits of the South-Sea-Company* (London: printed for J. Morphew near Stationers Hall, 1711).

Perceval, Richard, *Bibliotheca Hispanica* (London: London: Iohn Iackson, 1591).

Perceval, Richard and John Minsheu, *A Dictionarie in Spanish and English* (London: Edm. Bollifant. 1599).

Phillips, Edward, *The New World of English Words* (London: E. Tyler, 1658).

Pineda, Pedro, *Nuevo Diccionario, Español e Ingles e Ingles y Español. A New Dictionary, Spanish and English and English and Spanish* (London: printed for F. Gyles; T. Woodward et al., 1740).

Raleigh, Walter, *The Discouerie of the Large, Rich and Bewtiful Empire of Guiana* (London: Robert Robinson, 1596).

Scott, Joseph Nicol and Nathan Bailey, *A New Universal Etymological English Dictionary* (London: printed for T. Osborne and J. Shipton; J. Hodges et al., 1755).

Stepney, William, *The Spanish Schoole-Master* (London: R. Field, 1591).

Stevens, John, *A New Spanish and English Dictionary* (London: George Sawbridge, 1706).

Veitia Linage, Joseph, *The Spanish Rule of Trade to the West-Indies* (London: printed for Samuel Crouch, at the Corner of Pope's-Head-Alley in Cornhil, 1702).

Wesley, John, *The Complete English Dictionary* (London: printed by W. Strahan, 1753).

Secondary Sources

Algeo, John, 'Spanish Loanwords in English by 1900', in Félix Rodríguez González, Félix, ed., *Spanish Loanwords in the English Language* (Berlin / New York: Mouton de Gruyter, 1996), 13–40.

AMERLEX database. <https://tip.iatext.ulpgc.es/amerlex/>. (in preparation)

Atkins, B. T. Sue and Michael Rundell, *The Oxford Guide to Practical Lexicography* (Oxford: Oxford University Press, 2008).

Belda Medina, José Ramón, *Languages of Discovery: A Comparative Linguistic Study of English and Spanish after the Discovery of America* (Alicante: Editorial Club Universitario, 2002).

Brewer, Charlotte, 'Examining the OED. Period Coverage', https://oed.hertford.ox.ac.uk/quotations/period-coverage/, 2005–.

Brewer, Charlotte, 'The *Oxford English Dictionary*'s Treatment of Female-Authored Sources of the Eighteenth-Century', in Ingrid Tieken-Boon van Ostade and Wim van der Wurff, eds., *Current Issues in Late Modern English* (Bern: Peter Lang, 2009), 209–238.

Brewer, Charlotte, 'The Use of Literary Quotations in the Oxford English Dictionary', *The Review of English Studies* 61/248 (2010), 93–125.

Carney, Ginny, 'Native American Loanwords in American English', *Wicazo Sa Review* 12/1 (1997), 189–203.

Cutler, Charles L., *O Brave New Words! Native American Loanwords in Current English* (Norman: University of Oklahoma Press, 1994)

Day, Matthew, '"HONOUT TO OURNATION": Nationalism, *The Principal Navigations* and Travel Collections in the Long Eighteenth Century', in Daniel Carey and Claire Jowitt, eds., *Richard Hakluyt and Travel Writing in Early Modern Europe* (London / New York: Routledge, 2016), 77–86.

Diccionario de Americanismos. Asociación de Academias de la Lengua Española. < https://www.asale.org/damer/>

DLE = Diccionario de la Lengua Española. Real Academia Española. < https://dle.rae.es/>

Dohan, Mary Helen, *Our Own Words* (New York: Alfred A. Knopf, 1974).

Domínguez-Rodríguez, M.ª Victoria, 'Thomas Blount's *Glossographia* (1656): An Approach to Citation Styles in the Medical Entries', in Mª Victoria Domínguez-Rodríguez, Alicia Rodríguez-Álvarez, Gregorio Rodríguez Herrera and Verónica C. Trujillo-González, Verónica C., eds., *Words across History: Advances in Historical Lexicography and Lexicology* (Las Palmas de Gran Canaria: Servicio de Publicaciones y Difusión Científica de la ULPGC, 2016), 149–166.

Durkin, Philip, 'Changing Documentation in the Third Edition of the *Oxford English Dictionary*. Sixteenth-Century Vocabulary as a Test-Case', in Teresa Fanego, Belén Méndez-Naya and Elena

Seoane, eds., *Sounds, Words, Texts and Change*, Vol. 2 (Amsterdam / Philadelphia: John Benjamins, 2002), 65–81.

Durkin, Philip, *Borrowed Words. A History of Loanwords in English* (Oxford: Oxford University Press, 2014).

ECCO = *Eighteenth Century Collections Online*. <https://www.gale.com/intl/primary-sources/eighteenth-century-collections-online>.

EEBO = *Early english Books Online*. <https://www.proquest.com/eebo>.

Hawke, Andrew, 'Quotation Evidence and Definitions', in Philip Durkin, ed., *The Oxford Handbook of Lexicography* (Oxford: Oxford University Press, 2016), 176–202.

Hayashi, Tetsuro, *The Theory of English Lexicography, 1530–1791* (Amsterdam: John Benjamins, 1978).

Jones, Tom, 'The *Xoc*, the *Sharke*, and the Sea Dogs: An Historical Encountert', in Virginia M. Fields, ed., *Fifth Palenque Round Table, 1983* (San Francisco: The Pre-Columbian Art Research Institute, 1985), 211–222.

LEME = *Lexicons of Early Modern English*. <https://leme.library.utoronto.ca/>

López de Mariscal, Blanca, 'Otros Hombres con Libros Luteranos: Viajeros Ingleses en la Nueva España en el siglo XVI', *Revista de Humanidades: Tecnológico de Monterrey* 15 (2003), 187–208.

MacCrossan, Colm, 'New Journeys thorugh Old Voyages: Literary Approaches to Richard Hakluyt and Early Modern Travel Writing', *Literature Compass* 6/1 (2009), 97–112.

Markham, Clements R., *Richard Hakluyt: His Life and Work. With a Short Account of the Aims and Achievements of the Hakluyt Society* (London: Bedford Press, 1896).

OED = *Oxford English Dictionary Online*. <https://www.oed.com/>.

Osselton, N. E., *Chosen Words. Past and Present Problems for Dictionary Makers* (Exeter: University of Exeter Press, 1995).

Parks, G. Bruner, *Richard Hakluyt and the English Voyages,* 2nd edition (New York: Frederick Ungar Publishing Co., 1961).

Quinn, D. B., *The Hakluyt Handbook.* Volume II (London: The Hakluyt Society, 1974).

Schlauch, Margaret, *The Gift of Tongues* (1st edition 1943) (London: Allen and Unwin, 1960).

Serjeantson, Mary S., *A History of Foreign Words in English* (1st imp. 1935) (London: Routledge and Kegan Paul, 1961).

Stamper, Kory, 'How a Word Gets into an English Dictionary', in Sarah Ogilvie, ed., *The Cambridge Companion to English Dictionaries* (Cambridge: Cambridge University Press, 2020), 7–17.

Starnes, de Witt T., 'Bilingual Dictionaries of Shakespeare's Day', *Publications of the Modern Language Association of America* 52 (1937), 1005–1018.

Steiner, Roger J., *Two Centuries of Spanish and English Bilingual Lexicography (1590–1800)* (The Hague / Paris: Mouton, 1970).

Text Creation Partnership. < https://textcreationpartnership.org/>

Watson, George, 'Nahuatl Words in American English', *American Speech* 13/2 (1938), 108–121.

Zamora, Juan C., 'Indian Loanwords in Early American Spanish: A Preliminary Report', *NEMLA Newsletter* 2/4 (1970), 97–100.

Zamora, Juan C., 'Indigenismos en la Lengua de los Conquistadores', *Hesperia. Anuario de Filología Hispánica* V (2002), 195–209.

Appendix: Distribution of Amerindian Loanwords in Early and Late Modern English Dictionaries

YEAR	AUTHOR	TYPE	Nr.	aguacate	cacao	cacique	Campeachy	cannibal	canoe	copal	Carib	cassava	guano	guava	guaiacum	hurricane	maguey	maize	mammee	mesquite	nochetli	potato	pulque	tecuán	tiburon	tlaxcal	tuna	zapote
1590	Del Corro/Thorius	bilingual	0																									
1591	Percival	trilingual	2			X			X																			
1591	Stepney	bilingual	0																									
1598	Florio	bilingual	8		X			X	X						X		X	X				X			X			
1599	Percival/Minsheu	bilingual	8			X	X		X		X			X				X	X			X			X			
1604	Cawdrey	monolingual	0																									
1616	Bullokar	monolingual	4					X				X		X	X													
1623	Cockeram	monolingual	0																									
1656	Blount	monolingual	2					X								X												
1658	Phillips	monolingual	5			X			X						X	X						X						
1676	Coles	monolingual	9		X	X			X			X		X	X	X						X					X	
1689	Anon. (Hogarth)	monolingual	3						X							X						X						
1702	J.K.	monolingual	6		X			X	X							X		X				X						
1704	Cocker	monolingual	5					X				X		X	X							X						
1706	Kersey/Phillips	monolingual	13		X	X	X	X	X		X	X			X	X		X	X			X					X	
1706	Stevens	bilingual	15	X	X	X	X		X				X	X	X	X	X	X	X			X			X		X	X
1707	Anon.	monolingual	1													X												
1708	Kersey	monolingual	14		X	X	X	X	X		X	X		X	X	X		X	X			X					X	
1721	Bailey	monolingual	13		X	X	X	X	X		X	X		X	X	X		X				X					X	
1727	Bailey	monolingual	4													X		X	X			X						
1730	Bailey et al.	monolingual	14		X	X	X	X	X		X	X		X	X	X		X	X			X					X	
1735	Dyche & Pardon	monolingual	7		X		X		X		X				X	X		X										
1735	Defoe	monolingual	5		X			X	X							X						X						
1740	Pineda	bilingual	15	X	X	X	X		X				X	X	X	X	X	X	X			X			X		X	X
1749	Martin	monolingual	8		X		X		X			X				X		X				X					X	
1753	Anon.	monolingual	8		X		X	X	X						X	X		X				X						
1753	[John Wesley]	monolingual	3					X	X									X										
1755	Johnson	monolingual	11	X	X			X	X			X		X	X	X		X	X			X						
1755	Scott/Bailey	monolingual	11	X	X		X	X	X			X			X	X		X	X			X						
1763	Giral del Pino	bilingual	19	X	X	X	X		X		X	X	X	X	X	X	X	X	X			X	X		X		X	X
1773	Kenrick	monolingual	6					X	X						X	X		X				X						
1774	Barclay	monolingual	8		X			X	X		X	X			X	X						X						
1775	Ash	monolingual	16		X	X	X	X	X		X	X	X	X	X	X		X	X			X					X	X
1778	Baretti	bilingual	17	X	X	X	X		X		X	X	X	X	X	X		X				X	X		X		X	X
1797-	Connelly & Higgins	bilingual	19	X	X	X			X	X	X	X		X	X	X	X	X	X	X		X	X		X		X	X
1798																												

Nuria Yáñez-Bouza and Tino Oudesluijs

"My dearest friend . . . Ever Yours, Mary Hamilton": Exploring Forms of Address in the Late Georgian Period[1]

1. Introduction

In the late Georgian period, increasingly dynamic social mobility resulted in a greater awareness of an individual's identity in relation to those of other social positions. This in turn strengthened the notion of politeness as an "ideal that was aspired to in all aspects of daily life" (Jucker 2020: 117), in which language was a valuable commodity (see also Klein 1994, Fitzmaurice 2010). Previous studies on language use in this context have investigated the diversity of linguistic and pragmatic strategies through which individuals construct their own social identities in light of their relations with others, and one such strategy here involves the selection of forms of address in private correspondence. As Nevala (2004a: 85) notes, address "is widely used as a customary feature in personal correspondence even today" and, furthermore, it is "crucial" – from a sociopragmatic perspective – "not only because it indicates the recipient, but also because it is a means to show both the relationship between the writer and the recipient and to emphasize the social and relative status of both correspondents".

1 *Unlocking the Mary Hamilton Papers* is a three-year research project funded by the Arts & Humanities Research Council (AH/S007121/1), based at the University of Manchester in collaboration with University of Vigo and the University of York (www.maryhamiltonpapers.alc.manchester.ac.uk). Yáñez- Bouza would also like to acknowledge Grant ED431C 2021/52 (Xunta de Galicia).

For our research strand within the project *Unlocking the Mary Hamilton Papers*, we take Minna Nevala's (2004a) work as an inspiring point of departure for an exploration of expressions concerning both direct address (i.e. addressee-oriented formulae, e.g. *My dearest friend*) and self-reference (i.e. author-oriented formulae, e.g. *ever yours, M Hamilton*) in private correspondence from the Late Modern English (LModE) period.[2] In particular, we are interested "in how people address each other and how this reflects diachronic variation and change at both the societal and interactive level of communication", and we understand address as a means "to define and to refer" to the recipient of a written message and a means to bring the addressee closer to the writer, or indeed to create greater distance between the two (Nevala 2004a: 4).

Nevala's research, as well as related studies by Nevalainen and Raumolin-Brunberg (1995) and Raumolin-Brunberg (1996), has focussed largely on data from the Early Modern English (EModE) period (1500–1700), but, as she notes, the trends observed "may be challenged by further material, either literary or authentic" (Nevala 2004a: 147). Taking Nevala's sociopragmatic approach as our framework, and following up on this observation, we seek to examine the use of address in a subset of ego-documents in *The Mary Hamilton Papers (c.1740 –c.1850)*, a data source which covers the late eighteenth and early nineteenth centuries and which has not hitherto been explored in depth. More specifically, our focus is on intra-speaker variation in Mary Hamilton's private correspondence between 1776 and 1814 to various members of a rich social network, including family, friends, acquaintances and members of the Royal family. As Jucker and Taavitsainen (2003: 2) point out, the criteria for selecting address terms "are culture dependent and change in the course of time as old criteria become obsolete and come to be replaced by new criteria, and other criteria may be added to create a new system". It is therefore the aim of our research to build on previous findings from EModE letter-writing practices and social relations and offer a window onto forms of address in the eighteenth century.

---

2 Nevala's (2004a) monograph compiles various individual publications, namely Nevala (1998, 2002, 2003, 2004b, 2004c); the latter source includes data from the eighteenth century as well.

The outline of this paper is as follows: in Section 2 we contextualize the framework of our case study, followed in Section 3 by the description of the data and methodology. In Section 4 we present the analysis of expressions of direct address and self-reference, in terms of both letter structure (salutation, body, subscription) and the individual recipients to whom Mary Hamilton wrote (including their gender). The paper ends with some concluding remarks and suggestions for future research (Section 5).

2. Framework

Following Nevala, our approach to the study of address is "deeply embedded in, and makes use of, both historical sociolinguistics and historical pragmatics", in the belief that both theoretical frameworks are "inseparable and complementary parts of a whole" (2004a: 4). Nevala, like Nevalainen and Raumolin-Brunberg (1995), takes a socio-pragmatic approach in the general sense of the term provided by Leech (1983: 10), where variation and change are investigated at a more "local" level of language use by considering the social and societal dimensions involved (Nevalainen and Raumolin-Brunberg 1995: 542, Nevala 2009a: 239). More recently, the combination of frameworks and perspectives from historical sociolinguistics and historical pragmatics has led to the emergence of the field of historical sociopragmatics, as proposed by Culpeper (2009, 2011) and Włodarczyk and Taavitsainen (2017), the essence of which lies in the study of "language use in its situational context, and how those situational contexts engender norms which speakers engage or exploit for pragmatic purposes" (Culpeper 2011: 4). Our research also takes a historical sociopragmatic approach to the study of the linguistic strategies used to refer to recipients and writers in *The Mary Hamilton Papers*, a collection of manuscript material in which we can explore the ways in which correspondents "expressed their views on their mutual relationship through the use of address" (Nevala 2004a: 134–5).

Most attention in the literature has been paid to trends in address formulae to refer to the recipient of the correspondence, but, as Nevala points out, "the placing of the subscription formulae", a strategy of self-reference on the part of the writer, "follows them closely" here (Nevala 2004a: 137, n.9). Our study therefore maps both addressee-oriented and author-oriented reference expressions: formulae expressing direct address to the recipient reflect the writer's evaluation or interpretation of their societal relation, usually included in the opening salutation, and self-references carry a dual function in that they "describe the status or the emotional state of the writer at the same time as they address the recipient of the letter" (2004a: 95). Furthermore, in the context of subscription formulae, self-references "are used to close a letter, and they reflect more the image the writer has of him/herself in the relationship with the recipient" (2004a: 128), that is, more so than direct address oriented towards the recipient that typically figures in the opening of the letter.

Direct address may appear in the salutation, body and subscription of a letter, and self-reference expressions may occur in the main text and subscription. In our research, we take a broad approach which explores the entire structure of a letter, so that we can gain an overall view of the strategies employed by the letter-writer (Nevala 2004a: 119, 126). This wide scope has been adopted in previous studies exploring EModE correspondence among kin and non-kin letter-writers (e.g. Nevala 1998, 2003, 2004b) as well as LModE letter collections of individual authors such as John Wesley, John Gay, Robert Lowth and Jane Austen (Baker 1980; Tieken-Boon van Ostade 1999, 2011, 2014). At the same time, some studies have offered fruitful insights into practices of individual writers, focussing on either direct address forms to recipients, in the salutation formulae or the salutation and the main body of the letter (Nevalainen and Raumolin-Brunberg 1995; Raumolin-Brunberg 1996; Nevala 2004b, 2004c) or on the expressions of self-reference in subscription formulae (Bijkerk 2004; Navest 2004). In addition, the study of addressee-oriented and author-oriented strategies has also been explored along with third-person oriented expressions and in the context of social deixis (Nevala 2009a, 2009b, 2009c, 2010a; Nurmi and Nevala 2010).

With regard to the parameters which may govern the selection of forms of address, Nevala (2004a: 4) points out that the core factors include both "more sociolinguistically oriented notions, such as social rank, age, gender [. . .] as well as notions that are traditionally connected with pragmatic language use in human relationships, such as power, distance and politeness". Given that the current paper constitutes a first look at the use of direct address and self-reference in Mary Hamilton's correspondence, we will begin by exploring forms of address in light of both the general structure of her letters and notes, as well as the individual participants to whom she writes, also taking into account their gender. We will scrutinize sociopragmatic parameters in greater detail in further studies, as noted in Section 5.

3. *The Mary Hamilton Papers*

3.1. Mary Hamilton and Her Circles

Mary Hamilton (1756–1816) was the daughter of Charles Hamilton (1721–1771), soldier and son of Lord Archibald Hamilton and Lady Mary Catherine Hamilton (née Dufresne, d. 1778). Hamilton's father died when she was just fifteen, and following his death she lived in a variety of places, including Northampton, and in her early twenties she was recruited as a sub-governess at Court to assist Queen Charlotte with the young princesses. On retiring in late 1782, she became a member of the Bas Bleu (Bluestocking) circle and counted Hannah More, Frances Burney and Mary Delany among her literary friends. She enjoyed lifelong friendships with a number of female friends and a fond and mutually supportive relationship with her uncle Sir William Hamilton, ambassador to the Court of Naples. In 1785 she married John Dickenson (c.1757–1842), son of John Dickenson of Birch Hall, near Manchester. They had one child, Louisa Dickenson (later Anson), born in 1787, and lived in Taxal (Derbyshire), Leighton Buzzard (Bedfordshire) and London. Mary Hamilton fell ill and died in May 1816, aged sixty. She was not a public figure or a published writer, but her private writings shed light on her role as an educated and well-connected woman who stood as a nexus of several interlocking royal, aristocratic, literary and artistic circles in late eighteenth- and early nineteenth-century England (see also Crawley 2014).

The Mary Hamilton Papers is a digital edition of ego-documents, consisting of private correspondence and diaries, as well as other personal items such as account books, commonplace books and anthologies, currently consisting of over 3,200 items dating from the 1740s to the 1850s. Hamilton's autograph diaries and a large body of her correspondence have been transcribed (see Section 3.2) and can be investigated from a variety of different disciplinary perspectives, e.g. linguistic, literary, historical (cf. Coulombeau 2021; Ulph 2021; Denison and Oudesluijs 2022; Wallis to appear, Yáñez- Bouza to appear a, to appear b, ms; Oudesluijs and Yáñez- Bouza to appear). For the purposes of this paper, we will concentrate on the set of private correspondence, consisting of both letters and notes, written by Hamilton from 1776 to 1814 (c.53,000 words, see Table 1). The limited size of our dataset is due to the fact that the larger archive from which the majority of the material has been drawn is Mary Hamilton's own collection, hence containing items written *to* her rather than *by* her (see details in Denison et al. this volume).

Table 1: Data under study in Mary Hamilton's correspondence

Parameter	Details	
Contents	170 items	139 letters (82 %) 31 notes (18 %)
Time span	1776–1814	1779–1782: 129 items (76 %) 1782–1785: 27 items (16 %)
Correspondents	22 recipients (24 individuals)	81 items to Charlotte M. Gunning (48 %) 61 items to George, Prince of Wales (36 %)
Gender	female: 14 recipients	102 items, 81 to Charlotte M. Gunning
	male: 7 recipients	67 items, 61 to George, Prince of Wales
	male & female: 1 recipient	
Distance	family: 5 items	
	friends: 96 items	81 items to Charlotte M. Gunning
	acquaintances: 6 items	
	Royal family: 63 items	61 items to George, Prince of Wales
Power/Status	equal: 93 items	81 items to Charlotte M. Gunning
	inferior to superior: 77 items	61 items to George, Prince of Wales

The dataset comprises 139 letters and thirty-one notes. Forty-seven items are either copies or drafts, which, with regard to forms of address, we believe to be largely faithful to the originals (cf. Oudesluijs to appear). Thirty-six copies have been bound together as "Volume of Copy Letters" (HAM/1/15/2/31), and are catalogued as a single item in the archive. For this paper, however, we examine them individually. Furthermore, twenty-six items are incomplete; either the sheets have partially deteriorated, corners of pages have been cut off, or additional sheets are missing. We are aware of these issues and how they might affect our analysis, but, like other researchers in this field, we are "making the best use of 'bad' data" (Nevalainen 1999), and have erred on the side of inclusiveness on the grounds that what has been preserved may contain data relevant for our research.

The dataset covers four periods of Mary Hamilton's life: (i) the year 1776, before she joined Court as a sub-governess; (ii) 1779–November 1782, the period in which she worked at Court; (iii) November 1782 – June 1785, the years Hamilton spent after leaving Court but prior to her marriage to John Dickenson; and (iv) her married life as Mrs Dickenson. Most of the 170 items were written in period (ii), 142 of which belong to two sets of correspondence; the first between Hamilton and George, Prince of Wales, later George IV (1762–1830), from April–December 1779, and the second between Hamilton and her close friend Charlotte Margaret Gunning (1759–1794), dated between 1779 and 1790 (see Oudesluijs and Yáñez- Bouza to appear for more detail on these two correspondence sets).

Most of the twenty letters written by Hamilton in period (iii) are addressed to close friends who also worked as royal governesses at Court, such as Charlotte Finch (1725–1813) and Martha Goldsworthy (1740–1816). Another female correspondent in this period is Lady Mary Wake (c.1744–1823), a long-time friend from Hamilton's years in Northampton. Fewer letters have survived from period (iv), but they show a rich variety of correspondents, including family (e.g. Hamilton's sisters-in-law Sarah and Elizabeth Dickenson), acquaintances at Court (e.g. Louisa Clayton), as well as new friends from the Bluestocking circle like Horace Walpole (1717–1797) and Frances Burney (1752–1840).

While the number of correspondents in the subset of letters addressed to Hamilton in *The Mary Hamilton Papers* amounts to approximately 135 different writers, the number of addressees to whom Hamilton wrote is only twenty-two (see Table 2[3]), and, as mentioned above, the majority of letters involve two individuals (Charlotte Gunning and George, Prince of Wales) and are from the period when she worked at Court. For fifteen of these correspondents only one letter is preserved. The few recipients of whom we preserve between two and four of Hamilton's letters include her friends Charlotte Finch, Martha Goldsworthy, the Bluestocking Mary Delany (1700–1788) and two friends from before her time at Court: Ann Litchfield and Mary Wake. There are two items in the dataset each addressed to two recipients: one to Hamilton's sisters-in-law (Sarah and Elizabeth Dickenson) and one to Leonard and Jane Smelt, acquaintances at Court. In terms of gender, fourteen of the twenty-two correspondents are female (both family and friends), seven are men (also both family and friends), plus there is the joint letter to the Smelts.

Table 2: List of correspondents and number of items written to them

Correspondent	Items	Correspondent	Items
Robert Henry Blosset (née Peckwell)	1	Sir William Hamilton	1
Frances Burney (later D'Arblay)	1	Mary Johanna Jackson	1
Lady Louisa Clayton (née Fermor)	1	Anne King	1
Charles de Guiffardière	1	Ann Litchfield	3
Mary Delany (née Granville)	2	David Murray (Lord Stormont)	1
Sarah Dickenson and Elizabeth Dickenson (later Palombi)	1	unknown princess	1
Lady Charlotte Finch (née Fermor)	2	Queen Charlotte	1
George, Prince of Wales (later George IV)	61	Jean Baptiste Louis Georges Seroux d'Agincourt	1
Martha Carolina Goldsworthy	2	Leonard Smelt and Jane Smet (née Campbell)	1
Charlotte Margaret Gunning (later Digby)	81	Lady Mary Wake (née Fenton)	4
Johanna Louisa Hagedorn	1	Horace Walpole	1

3 The spelling of the names reflect contemporary practice when Mary Hamilton wrote to them.

3.2 Methodology

The Mary Hamilton Papers is a digital edition containing high-resolution images of all the materials we have been able to trace, written either to or by Mary Hamilton, as well as transcriptions of her diaries and a large selection of private correspondence (c.1 million words). The transcriptions are created in XML and conform to TEI (Text Encoding Initiative) guidelines (P5). During the transcription process we created specific tags which identify relevant strings of text with linguistic strategies relating to addressee-oriented and author-oriented forms of address. These concern nominal phrases with head nouns such as terms of friendship, kinship or endearment, as well as personal names and honorific terms. Pronominal forms of address go beyond the scope of the research strand within our project (cf. Nevala 2002, 2004a for a study of pronominal forms). This mark-up was added to the four structural parts of the letter: salutation, body and subscription on the "inside", and superscription on the "outside". This case study concerns the "inside" only, given the differences that exist between the two strategies in terms of audience (private on the inside, public on the outside) and of the social conventions established in letter-writing manuals (cf. Nevala 2004a: 229–56; Yáñez- Bouza ms). For the data analysis we have extracted the relevant strings directly from the XML mark-up in the individual files, and the metadata have been drawn from the project's personography database which stores biographical data on all writers and individuals mentioned in the materials compiled. An overview of the mark-up for direct address to the recipient is given in Table 3 and for self-reference expressions in Table 4.[4]

4 For our general editorial practices, see the project website. Illustrative examples in this paper have been normalized as far as spelling, capitalization and abbreviations are concerned; the edition of *The Mary Hamilton Papers* preserves these features as in the original.

Table 3: Mark-up for expressions of direct address

Part of the letter		**TEI/XML tag**	**Example**
Salutation		<salute n="opening">	*My dearest Mifs Goldsworthy*
Body	opening lines	<seg type="openSalute">	You will *my dearest* very easily comprehend . . .
	main body	<seg type="bodySalute">	But Oh *my friend* let that ardour be tempered
	final lines, introducing closure	<seg type="bodySalute" n= "closing">	Adieu *my dear friend.*
Subscription		<seg type="closeSalute">	I am *my dear Lord* ever most affectionately yours & I have the honor to remain *Your Ladyship*s affectionate friend & servant

Table 4: Mark-up for expressions of self-reference

Part of the letter		**TEI/XML tag**	**Example**
Body		<seg type="author">	I am *your friend* & as such must feel . . .
Subscription	subscription formula	<seg type="closeFormula">	I will be *your firm & faithful friend*
	signature	<signed>	*M. Hamilton*

Direct address to the recipient may appear in any part of the letter and has been marked up with five different tags:

(1) The tag <salute n="opening"> marks the opening formula in the salutation of the letter/note, as in *My friend* (GEO/ADD/3/83/9) or *My dear love* (HAM/1/15/2/15(3)).

(2) Sometimes there is no direct address in the structural salutation of a letter, but the recipient is addressed in the first lines of the body of the main text with the same pragmatic function, as in "Forgive me *Sir* disappointing you" (GEO/ADD/3/83/58) or "Highly grateful as I was *my dear Uncle* for the affectionate proof of your regard" (HAM/1/4/4/2). This is tagged with <seg type="openSalute">.

(3) The tag <seg type="bodySalute"> marks direct address in the main text, such as "But Oh *my friend* let that ardour be tempered with discretion" (GEO/ADD/3/83/11) or "from a sincere heartfelt regard & esteem I have for *Your Ladyship* which makes me feel interested" (HAM/1/9/83).
(4) When a direct form of address appears in the main body but close to the structural subscription of the letter, and as such functions as the lead-in to the closing section, it is tagged with <seg type="bodySalute" n= "closing">. Examples include "Adieu Adieu *my beloved*. send me the character of the Court female" (HAM/1/15/2/9) or "the many marks of gracious attention & condescending regard which You *Madam* – have so often shewn" (HAM/1/1/2/8).
(5) The subscription part of a letter may also include a direct form of address to the recipient, which is tagged with <seg type="closeSalute">. This usually appears before the subscription formula, e.g. "I remain, *my dear Lady Wake* your sincere & obliged friend" (HAM/1/8/8/31), but it may occasionally be integrated as a possessive determiner in the lexical phrase of the formula, e.g. "I have the honor to be remain *Your Ladyship*s affectionate friend & servant" (HAM/1/9/83).

Self-references to the author appear in the body and subscription parts of a letter/note and are marked with three different tags:

(1) Self-references in the main text are tagged with <seg type= "author">, such as "I am *your friend* & as such must feel" (GEO/ADD/3/83/34) or "I tell you this because I know every thing that gives *Miranda* satisfaction affords pleasure to Astrea" (HAM/1/15/2/4(2)).
(2) The subscription formula is tagged with <seg type="closeFormula">, such as *your sincere and affectionate friend* (HAM/1/12/52(2)) or *ever sincerely yours* (HAM/1/14/105).
(3) The third type of self-reference is the signature, marked with <signed>, e.g. *M: Hamilton* (HAM/1/8/8/21) or *Mary Dickenson* (HAM/1/1/1/13).

In addition to these three author-oriented tags, given the significance of the subscription part of the letter for the study of self-reference strategies, our editing practices have taken into account the complex structures in which subscription formulae and signatures are embedded so that other elements which function as an introductory phrase are also marked up with the tag <salute n="closing">. Examples include expressions such as *I am ever sincerely yours* (HAM/1/14/105), *I remain with respect & true affection your neice & friend* (HAM/1/4/4/2, sic) or *believe me your sincere friend* (GEO/ADD/3/83/6). The relevance of the introductory phrase has also been noted in other sets of eighteenth-century correspondence, for instance in Baker's (1980) study of John Wesley's writings.

4. Data Analysis

This section presents the analysis of our dataset of 170 letters and notes written by Mary Hamilton to twenty-two recipients. As mentioned in the introduction, for this paper we consider the structural parts of the items (Section 4.1) as well as the individual correspondents (Section 4.2) and their gender (Section 4.3).

4.1. Trends in Text Structure

Table 5 presents the overall distribution of Mary Hamilton's use of direct address to recipients and self-reference expressions according to the structure of the letter. It lists the number of items in which these occur, as well as the number of individual instances of address (out of a total of 264), including expressions crossed out by Hamilton; instances in apposition such as "As *your friend, your true friend* I look upon it..." are counted as two tokens (HAM/1/9/66).

Table 5: Distribution of expressions of direct address and self-reference in the text structure of the letter

Direct address		**Items (total 170)**		**Instances (total 264)**	
Salutation	Opening formula	29	17.1 %	29	11 %
Body	Opening lines	54	31.8 %	54	20.5 %
	Main text	66	38.8 %	119	45.1 %
	Final lines introducing closure	42	24.7 %	46	17.4 %
Subscription	Inside/around subscription formula	16	9.4 %	16	6.1 %
Self-reference		**Items (total 170)**		**Instances (total 161)**	
Body	Main text	28	16.5 %	39	24.2 %
Subscription	Introductory phrase	20	11.8 %	20	12.4 %
	Subscription formula	52	30.6 %	53	32.9 %
	Signature	49	28.8 %	49	30.4 %

At first glance, we see that Mary Hamilton tends to use more expressions of direct address than of self-reference (264 vs. 161). It should also be mentioned that not all the items in the dataset include a form of address, unlike other sets of EModE correspondence in which at least one expression has been attested in each item (Nevala 2004a: 86). Overall, in Hamilton's dataset there are thirty-five items without an explicit either direct address or self-reference, forty-six lack any kind of direct address to the recipient and ninety-eight items lack expressions of self-reference. In fact, very few items display what can be labelled a complete set, that is, including a form of direct address to open the letter (either a conventional salutation formula or within the opening lines of the body), direct address in the body followed by direct address in the subscription, and two self-reference expressions in the subscription (subscription formula and signature). Among the few instances of this kind, Hamilton writes *My dear Lord / your Lordship / I am, my dear Lord, ever most affectionately Yours / M: Dickenson* to her cousin-in-law Lord Stormont (HAM/1/18/180).

Hamilton uses expressions of direct address most often in the body of the letter. Not only does she frequently address the recipient in the main text (119 times), she also prefers to do this in the opening lines of the body, as opposed to using a more conventional formula in the salutation (fifty-four vs. twenty-nine items), and similarly in the final lines of the body as opposed to in the subscription (forty-two vs. sixteen items).

The absence of an explicit conventional salutation formula at the start of the letter relates to a strategy known as "no-naming", a term coined by Ervin-Tripp (1972), whereby the writer either chooses to refer to the addressee in the opening lines of the body (by title, relation or pronoun) or not at all (cited in Nevala 2004a: 98). This practice is said to have declined during the EModE period, being "practically non-existent in the latest collections" of the seventeenth century examined by Nevalainen and Raumolin-Brunberg (1995: 561). However, individual variation persists, and letters with no-naming are still found in the eighteenth century, particularly in correspondence with recipients of an equal status (Nevala 2004a: 99). This may relate to the fact that no-naming was originally a common convention in official correspondence, a more formal context, and then expanded to private correspondence with members of kin and friends in the EModE period, indicating that no-naming was "not necessarily a sign of lack of familiarity or even distance" (Nevalainen and Raumolin-Brunberg 1995: 582). As Table 5 reveals, Mary Hamilton makes use of direct address in both the salutation and the opening lines of the body, which is in line with eighteenth-century letter-writing manuals that "strongly emphasize the importance of using a proper form of address in the letter salutation and the body of the letter" (Nevala 2004a: 98–9). Hamilton's preference for no-naming corroborates the idea that, although the strategy was in decline, it was still an appropriate and suitable sociopragmatic choice in the late eighteenth century. Furthermore, her use is also in line with trends in sets of correspondence by other writers with regard to the social context, in that direct address in the opening lines of the body is more common in letters to friends and acquaintances than to correspondents of a superior rank.

With regard to forms of direct address in the subscription part of the letter, letter-writing manuals in the late seventeenth and eighteenth centuries advise correspondents to repeat the expression from the opening salutation, especially in correspondence to addressees of a superior rank. Eighteenth-century letter writers followed this to varying degrees. On the one hand, John Wesley seems to conform "usually" to this practice in the early decades of the century (Baker 1980: 59, cited in Tieken-Boon van Ostade 1999: 104–5), and Robert Lowth does so in the mid-late decades, albeit with more inter-speaker variation (Tieken-Boon van Ostade 2011: 154–5). On the other hand, John Gay in the early eighteenth century often omits direct address in the subscription and sometimes, rather than matching the expression from the one in the opening salutation, opts for a different expression, to either increase or decrease the level of formality according to the correspondent (Tieken-Boon van Ostade 1999: 105). Similarly, Jane Austen at the turn of the century seems to follow the normative advice "only rarely", and when she does so it is not necessarily in the context of formality or of an addressee with a superior social rank (Tieken-Boon van Ostade 2014: 69). As shown in Table 5, Mary Hamilton's use of direct address in the subscription part is relatively infrequent and more in line with the practice observed in Gay and Austen, and when Hamilton does use it, she generally follows the instructions in letter-writing manuals. She matches the closing expression with the one from the opening salutation in a number of letters, such as *Dear Sir* in the letter to Robert Blosset (HAM/1/8/2/32), *My dearest friend* in a letter to Mary Wake (HAM/1/8/8/1) and *My dear Lord* in a letter to Lord Stormont (HAM/1/18/180). Besides, in some other texts she mirrors the expressions by employing an honorific term in both structural parts, although the form itself varies: *My dearest Madam* and *My dearest Lady Charlotte* in a letter to Lady Charlotte Finch (HAM/1/12/52(2)) and *Madam* and *Your Majestie* in a letter to Queen Charlotte (HAM/1/1/2/8).

Turning to author-oriented expressions, the usual place for self-reference is the subscription of the letter, which encloses the subscription formula and the signature. It is thus not surprising that these two strategies are employed by Mary Hamilton more often than self-reference in the body of the letter (see Table 5). In EModE correspondence, subscription formulae were found to be "almost always followed by the writer's signature" (Nevala 2004a: 96). However, trends seem to have been different in LModE correspondence. For instance, the signature is often missing in John Gay's letters and is "usually lacking" in letters by Robert Lowth (Tieken-Boon van Ostade 1999: 104–7; 2011: 157). Mary Hamilton's preference is difficult to assess given the number of items in the dataset that are either incomplete, have sustained damage at the bottom part of the last page, or which are copies/drafts in which it would not have been necessary to include elements such as her signature (see Section 3.1). Despite these caveats, it is notable that not one of the sixty-one items written to George, Prince of Wales is signed, whereas most of the letters to her friend Charlotte Gunning do contain a signature, copies and drafts included (see also Oudesluijs and Yáñez- Bouza to appear). We can also observe that when Hamilton uses a subscription formula, she chooses to complete the self-reference with a signature more than half the time (thirty-two times in fifty-two items), e.g. *Your affectionate friend – Mary Hamilton* to Mrs Hagedorn (HAM/1/7/13/5(2)) or *ever most affectionately & faithfully yours – M: Dickenson* to Frances Burney (HAM/1/6/5/2). At the same time, Hamilton also sometimes opts for simpler structures with just a signature and no subscription formula; this is the case in seventeen items addressed to friends such as Charlotte Gunning (14), Anne King (1) and Mary Wake (1).

As noted in Section 3.2, our analysis takes into account the introductory phrase in the subscription. Research on other sets of eighteenth-century correspondence has reported diverging trends of use in terms of frequency over time and the lexical phrase selected. For instance, Austin (1998: 335) observes that expressions such as *I (must) conclude* occur "most frequently in letters of a more informal or humbler sort", as with the Clifton family, whereas "[t]he letters of literate writers in the seventeenth and early eighteenth century almost always finish with 'I am'", as observed in writings by Daniel Defoe and Samuel Johnson. The alternative phrase *So I remain* is said to have been "current from at least the seventeenth century, if not earlier, in certain spheres" (Austin 1998: 336), as in Samuel Pepys' correspondence. After a decrease in use by literary writers in the first half of the eighteenth century, this phrase seems to resurface in the second half – for example, "quite frequently" in the letters by Dorothy Wordsworth, and "occasionally" with Jane Austen, and for John Keats it carries "a more formal" connotation (Austin 1998: 336). Mary Hamilton's practice seems to be in line with the occasional use of an introductory phrase as she omits it more often than not (twenty of fifty-two items). When she does opt for including it, she seems to endorse the general preference of literary writers for the lexical phrases *I am* and *I remain*, variants of which are attested in all but two of the introductory phrases with structures containing a verb, such as *I afsure you I am... I am & Ever will be...*, *I will be...*, *I have the honor of being...* or *& I have the honor to remain....* These phrases are used in letters to superiors as well as to friends on an equal social footing. Other variants Hamilton uses include *believe me...*, to George, Prince of Wales and to an acquaintance, and *I embrace you*, to her friend Charlotte Gunning.

4.2 Trends with Individual Correspondents

As shown in Table 1 above, the dataset under study contains letters and notes addressed to twenty-two recipients (recall that two items were written to two individuals each – the letter to the Dickenson sisters and the letter to the Smelts). Tieken-Boon van Ostade (1999: 99) makes the point that letter-writers "must have had a certain amount of freedom to match the relative formality of their letters with their relationship with the correspondent or with the content of the letter by means of a creative use of the epistolary conventions", although, naturally, there will be repetition in the lexical choice of certain expressions. What is interesting in our dataset is not so much Mary Hamilton's lexical choices (cf. Yáñez- Bouza to appear a, b on personal names and honorific titles), but her preference for direct address or self-reference depending on the individual correspondent to whom she is writing. Tables 6 and 7 present the distribution of all types of address attested in the 170 items examined. In contrast to Table 5, here we group together direct address in the salutation and opening lines of the body in that they share the same pragmatic function, i.e. to address the recipient at the start of the letter.

Table 6: Distribution of expressions of direct address by correspondent

Correspondent (N=22)	**Direct address**		
	Opening	**Body**	**Subscrip.**
Blosset, Robert H.	salutation	--	✓
Burney, Frances	open. lines	--	--
Clayton, Louisa	salutation	main text	✓
de Guiffardière, Charles	--	--	--
Delany, Mary	open. lines	--	--
Dickenson, Sarah & Elizabeth	--	main text	--
Finch, Charlotte	salutation open. lines	main text closing lines	✓
George, Prince of Wales	salutation open. lines	main text closing lines	✓
Goldsworthy, Martha C.	salutation	--	--
Gunning, Charlotte M.	salutation open. lines	main text closing lines	✓
Hagedorn, Johanna L.	open. lines	--	--
Hamilton, William	open. lines	main text closing lines	--
Jackson, Mary J.	--	--	--
King, Anne	open. lines	--	--
Litchfield, Ann	salutation open. lines	main text closing lines	--
Murray, David	salutation	main text	✓
Princess (unknown)	--	--	--
Queen Charlotte	salutation	main text closing lines	✓
Seroux d'Agincourt, Jean Baptiste Louis Georges	open. lines	main text	--
Smelt, Leonard & Jane	open. lines	main text	✓
Wake, Mary	salutation open. lines	main text closing lines	✓
Walpole, Horace	open. lines	--	--
Total	salutations: 10 open. lines: 13	main text: 12 closing lines: 7	subscrip.: 9

Table 7: Distribution of expressions of self-reference by correspondent

Correspondent (N=22)	**Self-reference**		
	Body	**Subscrip.**	**Signature**
Blosset, Robert H.	--	intr. phrase formula	✓
Burney, Frances	--	intr. phrase formula	✓
Clayton, Louisa	--	intr. phrase formula	✓
de Guiffardière, Charles	--	--	--
Delany, Mary	✓	formula	✓
Dickenson, Sarah & Elizabeth	--	--	--
Finch, Charlotte	--	intr. phrase formula	✓
George, Prince of Wales	✓	intr. phrase formula	--
Goldsworthy, Martha C.	--	intr. phrase formula	✓
Gunning, Charlotte M.	✓	intr. phrase formula	✓
Hagedorn, Johanna L.	--	formula	✓
Hamilton, William	--	intr. phrase formula	✓
Jackson, Mary J.	--	--	--
King, Anne	--	--	✓
Litchfield, Ann	--	--	--
Murray, David	--	intr. phrase formula	✓
Princess (unknown)	✓	--	--
Queen Charlotte	--	formula	✓
Seroux d'Agincourt, Jean Baptiste Louis Georges	✓	intr. phrase formula	--
Smelt, Leonard & Jane	--	intr. phrase formula	✓
Wake, Mary	✓	intr. phrase formula	✓
Walpole, Horace	✓	--	--
Total	main text: 7	intr.phrase: 12 formula: 15	signature: 14

First, in the letters to two recipients, i.e. Charles de Guiffardière, an acquaintance from Court, and Mary Jackson, her goddaughter, Hamilton omits any type of direct address or self-reference expression. Furthermore, the letter to an unknown princess includes a self-reference expression in the body but no direct address to the princess. The reverse strategy, with references to the addressee but not to the author, occurs in the letter to the Dickenson sisters and in the three letters to Ann Litchfield. This scarcity of forms of address in Hamilton's correspondence here is, however, the exception rather than general practice in her letters.

With her close friends Charlotte Gunning and Mary Wake we find forms of direct address in all parts of the letter, as well as self-references in both the body and the subscription parts, including in the signatures. With five other recipients Hamilton includes the full range of types of address except for self-references in the body, and this occurs regardless of the relation with the correspondent in terms of gender, distance and relative power: in non-kin family members such as Hamilton's cousin-in-law Lord Stormont, friends like Charlotte Finch, acquaintances like the Smelts and Louisa Clayton, and also Queen Charlotte of the Royal family. The collection of notes and letters to George, Prince of Wales is remarkable in that it contains forms of direct address in all parts of the letter, and Hamilton also adds self-references in the body and subscription formulae, but none of the sixty-one items preserved are signed. This may well be the result of her attempts to keep their correspondence private and secret (see Coulombeau 2021, Oudesluijs and Yáñez- Bouza to appear).

The overview in Tables 6 and 7 also highlights Hamilton's common practice of including both direct address in the opening parts of the letter and self-reference in the subscription formulae, with at least one type of address used for fifteen of the twenty recipients. In most of these letters, Hamilton also adds a form of direct address in the body, but not always. For instance, it is absent in the letters to acquaintances such as Henry Blosset and Louisa Hagedorn, to the Bluestocking members Frances Burney and Mary Delany, and to her Court friend Martha Goldsworthy. At the same time, on a few occasions Hamilton addresses the recipient in both the opening and the body of the letter but omits direct address in the subscription, which is the case in the letters to correspondents who are friends of equal rank, like Ann Litchfield, but also when writing to superiors in rank like her uncle Sir William Hamilton and the Smelts.

In Hamilton's correspondence with recipients for whom more than one item is preserved, we see her alternate between direct address in the salutation structure and in the opening lines of the body of the letter. This concerns friends like Charlotte Gunning, Mary Wake and Charlotte Finch, as well as George, Prince of Wales. With other recipients of whom we preserve just one letter, Hamilton at times chooses the conventional salutation, as with acquaintances like Robert Blosset and Louisa Clayton, non-kin family like Lord Stormont, the Queen and friends like Martha Goldsworthy. All but the latter correspondent are superior in rank. The recipients whom Hamilton addresses in the opening lines of the body instead of in the salutation also span a wide social range in terms of distance and power status: acquaintances from Court (Johanna Hagedorn, the Smelts, Jean Baptiste Seroux d'Agincourt), friends (Frances Burney, Mary Delany, Horace Walpole) and family members (William Hamilton, Anne King). Linguistic practices in other sets of correspondence from contemporary writers such as Jane Austen, John Wesley and John Gay suggest that the absence of direct address in a letter, both in the salutation part and in the body, "may be the closest sign of intimacy with the addressee" (Tieken-Boon van Ostade 2014: 66). Gay tends to omit salutations even in letters to socially superior correspondents (Tieken-Boon van Ostade 1999: 101). However, Mary Hamilton does not follow this practice of omitting direct address in the opening parts of the letter, even with her closest friends. For instance, as pointed out above, some of the letters to her friends Charlotte Finch, Charlotte Gunning and Mary Wake show expressions of direct address of both types, and all of the letters to other friends include either one or the other type of address.

The subscription formula is a common feature in Mary Hamilton's private correspondence, only absent in letters to three of the eighteen correspondents with whom she uses self-reference expressions. An introductory phrase in the subscription occurs, however, with only twelve of the twenty-two correspondents, ranging from close friends to acquaintances and George, Prince of Wales. It is also missing in letters to friends like Mary Delany, acquaintances like Johanna Hagedorn and the Queen. When the introductory phrase is present, it is generally followed by the subscription formula, but the latter expression of self-reference is omitted in a letter to Charlotte Gunning where Hamilton ends with a signature: *Adieu I have only time to add that I embrace you with tenderneſs and sincerity – Mary Hamilton* (HAM/1/15/2/31–14).

Finally, the overview in Tables 6 and 7 shows that whenever Hamilton mentions the addressee in the body of the letter, this is preceded either by a conventional formula in the salutation part of the letter or by a form of direct address in the opening lines of the body; the only exception is the letter to the Dickenson sisters. Likewise, when the recipient is addressed directly in the subscription part of the letter, this is preceded by a direct address form in the body of the text, with again one exception in the letter to Robert Blosset.

4.3. Trends by Gender

The role of gender as a social factor in relation to language variation and change has been well accounted for in historical sociolinguistic studies on EModE and LModE correspondence (e.g. Nevalainen and Raumoling-Brunberg 2003: 110–32, Nevalainen *et al.* 2018). The trends in terms of intra-speaker variation in Mary Hamilton's correspondence according to the gender of her correspondents are presented in Tables 8 and 9; expressions of direct address in the salutation part and in the opening lines of the body are shown together, as was the case in Table 6. As described in Section 3.1, the dataset consists of fourteen female correspondents (102 items), including one letter written to Sarah and Elizabeth Dickenson, and seven male correspondents (sixty-seven items), plus a letter to Mr and Mrs Smelt (Table 2). The letters to Mary Jackson and Charles de Guiffardière do not contain any forms of address. As also pointed out in the description of the dataset, there is an unbalanced proportion of materials as the majority of items written to female correspondents are to Charlotte Gunning (eighty-one of 102 items) and the majority of those written to male correspondents are to George, Prince of Wales (sixty-one of sixty-seven items). As such, the tendencies and patterns reported here should be taken more as indicative of Hamilton's relationships with these two particular correspondents rather than with female or male recipients in general (see Oudesluijs and Yáñez- Bouza to appear).

The analysis reveals contexts in which differences emerge depending on whether Hamilton writes to a female or male correspondent, and also contexts in which the gender factor seems to play no role in her choice of address. Starting with the latter, there are three scenarios in which Hamilton's practices hold true for both female and male correspondents: first, her preference for addressing the recipient in the opening lines of the body rather than in a conventional salutation formula; second, her tendency to include self-reference expressions in the subscription rather than in the closing lines of the body, although in the items to George, Prince of Wales this difference is less marked; and third, her common practice of including a self-reference expression in the form of a subscription formula.

Regarding Hamilton's use of forms of address in which intra-speaker variation does occurs depending on gender we observe that Hamilton tends to add more expressions of direct address in letters to female correspondents, which is consistent across the three parts of the letter. In the main text of the body, the difference is still there but less marked. For self-reference expressions, the trends are more varied depending on the part of the letter and the type of address. First, Hamilton tends to use more self-reference expressions in the body when the recipient is male. Second, she also seems to be more inclined to add an introductory phrase in the subscription when writing to male correspondents. Third, the signature is absent not only from the letters to the Prince (see above), but also from the letters to three other male correspondents, Horace Walpole, Jean Baptiste Louis Georges Seroux d'Agincourt and Charles de Guiffardière. By contrast, among the fourteen female correspondents, unsigned letters appear with three of them: those to the Dickenson sisters and to the unknown princess, and the three letters to Ann Litchfield. In the collection of letters to Gunning, a signature is absent in fifty out of eighty-one items, but we should recall that many of these are copies or drafts (twenty of the fifty unsigned items).

Table 8: Distribution of expressions of direct address according to the gender of the correspondent

Gender (items)	Direct address		
	Opening	**Body**	**Subscrip.**
female (102)	salutation: 22 open. lines: 35	main text: 41 closing: 31	10
male (67)	salutation: 7 open. lines: 18	main text: 24 closing: 11	5
male & female (1)	open. lines: 1	main text: 1	1
Total (170)	salutation: 29 open. lines: 54	main text: 66 closing: 42	subscrip.:16

Table 9: Distribution of expressions of self-reference according to the gender of the correspondent

Gender (items)	Self-reference		
	Body	**Subscription**	**Signature**
female (102)	11	intr. phrase: 8 formula: 31	45
male (67)	17	intr. phrase: 11 formula: 20	3
male & female (1)	--	intr. phrase: 1 formula: 1	1
Total (170)	main text: 28	intr. phrase: 20 formula: 52	signature: 49

5. Concluding Remarks

The research presented in this paper has been conducted as part of the project *Unlocking the Mary Hamilton Papers* and focusses on the study of address by means of expressions of direct address and self-reference in the correspondence of Mary Hamilton (1776–1814). Taking Nevala's research on EModE correspondence as a point of departure, the aim was to present an initial exploration of Hamilton's practices and intra-speaker variation in terms of both the structure of her writing and the recipients involved. As such, our analysis has shed new light on Hamilton's overall distributional patterns in the salutation, body and subscription parts of the letter, and on her preferences as governed by the individual correspondent and, to some extent, their gender.

This case study is part of a larger research strand within the project, and thus there are many more research paths to explore. First, other sociolinguistic and sociopragmatic factors need to be investigated (cf. Nevala's words in Section 2), some of which have been mentioned above, such as the social groups into which the correspondents can be classified (family, friends, acquaintances), as well as their social status (superior or equal to Mary Hamilton). Another area of interest is Hamilton's lexical choice for addressee- and author-oriented expressions in her writings, for instance regarding variation between head nouns expressing terms of friendship, kinship or personal names, or the presence or absence of pre-modifying elements such as possessive determiners and/or terms of endearment (see Yáñez- Bouza to appear a, b). Ultimately, our aim in future work is to carry out data-driven social network analyses using Hamilton's letters as well as those written to her (Denison and Oudesluijs in preparation). At present, the number of transcribed items to Hamilton number c.1600 items written by c.100 individual authors (c.900,000 words), which will allow us to explore both intra- and inter-speaker variation in light of additional variables.

Given the dynamics of the sociocultural context in which the items in *The Mary Hamilton Papers* were written, and the salience of the ideal of politeness in the late Georgian period, we intend to examine the use of direct address and self-reference as an index of politeness whereby Mary Hamilton, and other correspondents, construct their social identity and subsequently negotiate their relationships with others (Oudesluijs and Yáñez- Bouza to appear). Building on Nevala's (2004a, 2009a) work, as well as earlier work by Nevalainen and Raumolin-Brunberg (1995) and Raumoling-Brunberg (1996), we are interested in mapping the so-called politeness continuum identified for EModE correspondence onto the LModE period. Nevalainen and Raumolin-Brunberg (1995: 557) emphasize that "the interpretation of the use of a given term depends on the context" and Nevala (2004a: 136–7) explains that, in her methodology, setting expressions of address on the politeness scale "has not been made by calculating any particular values to the different parts of the form, but by analysing the approximate weight of the address form on the whole". It is this approximate weight that we need to explore further in the context of eighteenth-century letter-writing practices and politeness. As Langford (2003: 311) observes, politeness is "a keyword with a meaning and implications that open doors into the mentality of a period" (cf. Fitzmaurice 2010), and thus, as Nevala notes, "carries along a range of context-dependent connotations" (Nevala 2010b: 439). The relevant socio-pragmatic factors, as Nevala (2004a: 4) aptly observes, will be "further described by the social history of Late Middle and Early and Late Modern England, which is needed in order to place the variation and change in the use of address in a wider perspective".

Source

Denison, David, Nuria Yáñez-Bouza, Tino Oudesluijs, Cassandra Ulph, Christina Wallis, Hannah Barker and Sophie Coulombeau, eds., *The Mary Hamilton Papers (c.1740–c.1850)* (University of Manchester, 2019–2023). Available at https://doi.org/10.48420/21687809.

References

Austin, Frances O., 'Epistolary Conventions in the Clift Family Correspondence', in Mats Rydén, Ingrid Tieken-Boon van Ostade and Merja Kytö, eds., *A Reader in Early Modern English* (Frankfurt am Main: Peter Lang, 1998), 319–47.

Baker, Frank, *The Works of John Wesley, Vol. 25: Letters, I: 1721–1739* (Oxford: Clarendon Press, 1980).

Bijkerk, Annemieke, '*Yours Sincerely* and *Yours Affectionately*: On the Origin and Development of Two Positive Politeness Markers', *Journal of Historical Pragmatics* 5/2 (2004), 297–311.

Coulombeau, Sophie, 'This Is Not a Love Story', *History Today* 71/10 (2021), 64–75.

Crawley, Lisa, 'A Life Recovered: Mary Hamilton 1756–1816. *Bulletin of the John Rylands University Library of Manchester* 90/2 (2014), 27–46.

Culpeper, Jonathan, 'Historical Sociopragmatics: An Introduction', *Journal of Historical Pragmatics* 10/2 (2009), 179–86.

——, ed., *Historical Sociopragmatics* (Amsterdam: Benjamins, 2011)

Denison, David and Tino Oudesluijs, 'Tracking Verb Changes in a Corpus of Non-Printed Manuscript Materials', *9th International Conference on Grammar and Corpora*, University of Ghent, 30 June–2 July 2022.

——, 'Reconstructing Mary Hamilton's Social Networks', in Sophie Coulombeau, David Denison and Nuria Yáñez-Bouza, eds., *Mary Hamilton and Her Circles: An Edited Collection* (Manchester: Manchester University Press, in preparation)

Denison, David, Nuria Yáñez-Bouza and Tino Oudesluijs. 'Editing *The Mary Hamilton Papers (c.1740 – c.1850)*, in Javier Calle-Martín and Jesús Romero-Barranco, eds., Corpora and Language Change in Late Modern English (Bern: Peter Lang, 2024).

Fitzmaurice, Susan M., 'Changes in the Meanings of Politeness in Eighteenth-Century England: Discourse Analysis and Historical Evidence', in Jonathan Culpeper and Dániel Z. Kádár, eds., *Historical (Im)politeness* (Bern: Peter Lang, 2010), 87–116.

Jucker, Andreas H., *Politeness in the History of English. From the Middle Ages to the Present Day* (Cambridge: Cambridge University Press, 2020).

Jucker, Andreas H. and Irma Taavitsainen, 'Diachronic Perspectives on Address Term Systems: Introduction', in Irma Taavitsainen and Andreas H. Jucker, eds., *Diachronic Perspectives on Address Term Systems* (Amsterdam: John Benjamins, 2003), 1–25.

Klein, Lawrence, '"Politeness" as Linguistic Ideology in Late Seventeenth- and Eighteenth-Century England', in Dieter Stein and Ingrid Tieken-Boon van Ostade, eds., *Towards a Standard English, 1600–1800* (Berlin: Mouton de Gruyter, 1994), 31–50.

Langford, Paul, 'The Uses of Eighteenth-Century Politeness', *Transactions of the Royal History Society* 12 (2002), 311–31.

Leech, Geoffrey, *Principles of Pragmatics* (London: Longman, 1983).

Navest, Karlijn, 'A Painter's Will to Please: Reynolds' Use of *Yours Affectionately / Yours Sincerely*', *Historical Sociolinguistics and Sociohistorical Linguistics* 4 (2004), <http://www.hum2.leidenuniv.nl/hsl_shl/reynolds%20letters.htm>.

Nevala, Minna, '*By Him that Loves You*: Address Forms in Letters Written to Sixteenth-Century Social Aspirers', in Antoinette Renouf, ed., *Explorations in Corpus Linguistics* (Amsterdam: Rodopi, 1998), 147–57.

——, '*Youre Moder Send a Letter to The*: Pronouns of Address in Private Correspondence from Late Middle to Late Modern English', in Helena Raumolin-Brunberg, Minna Nevala, Arja Nurmi and Matti Rissanen, eds., *Variation Past and Present: VAREING Studies on English for Terttu Nevalainen* (Helsinki: Société Néophilologique, 2002), 135–55.

——, 'Family First: Address and Subscription Formulae in English Family Correspondence from the Fifteenth to the Seventeenth Century', in Irma Taavitsainen and Andreas H. Jucker, eds., *Diachronic Perspectives on Address Term Systems* (Amsterdam: John Benjamins, 2003), 147–76.

——, *Address in Early English Correspondence: Its Forms and Socio-Pragmatic Functions* (Helsinki: Société Néophilologique, 2004a).

——, 'Accessing Politeness Axes: On Forms of Address and Terms of Reference in Early English Correspondence', *Journal of Pragmatics* 36 (2004b), 2125–60.

——, 'Inside and Out: Forms of Address in Seventeenth- and Eighteenth-Century Letters', *Journal of Historical Pragmatics* 5/2 (2004c), 273–98.

——, 'Altering Distance and Defining Authority: Person Reference in Late Modern English', *Journal of Historical Pragmatics* 10/2 (2009a), 238–59.

——, 'Referential Terms and Expressions in Eighteenth-Century Letters: A Case Study on the Lunar Men of Birmingham', in Arja Nurmi, Minna Nevala and Minna Palander-Collin, eds., *The Language of Daily Life in England (1400–1800)* (Amsterdam: Benjamins, 2009b), 75–103.

——, 'Friends Will Be Friends? The Sociopragmatics of Referential Terms in Early English Letters', in Andreas H. Jucker, Daniel Schreier and Marianne Hundt, eds., *Corpora: Pragmatics and Discourse. Papers from the 29th International Conference on*

English Language Research on Computerized Corpora (ICAME 29). Ascona, Switzerland, 14–18 May 2008 (Brill: Rodopi, 2009c), 83–103.

——, 'Keeping up Appearances: Facework in Self- and Addressee-Oriented Person Reference', in Jonathan Culpeper and Dániel Z. Kádár, eds., *Historical (Im)politeness* (Bern: Peter Lang, 2010a), 147–73.

——, 'Politeness', in Andreas H. Jucker and Irma Taavitsainen, eds., *Historical Pragmatics* (Berlin: Mouton de Gruyter, 2010b), 419–50.

Nevalainen, Terttu,'Making the Best Use of 'Bad' Data: Evidence for Sociolinguistic Variation in Early Modern English', *Neuphilologische Mitteilungen* 100/4 (1999), 499–533.

Nevalainen, Terttu and Helena Raumolin-Brunberg, 'Constraints on Politeness: The Pragmatics of Address Formulae in Early English Correspondence', in Andreas H. Jucker, ed., *Historical Pragmatics: Pragmatic Developments in the History of English* (Amsterdam: John Benjamins, 1995), 541–601.

Oudesluijs, Tino, ' "No criticism or remarks & pray burn it as fast as you read it" – Exploring Copying Practices in Mary Hamilton's Private Correspondence', in Luisella Caon, Thijs Porck and Mo Gordon, eds., *Proceedings of ICEHL-21, 7–11 June 2021, Leiden* (Amsterdam/Philadelphia: John Benjamins, to appear).

Oudesluijs, Tino and Nuria Yáñez-Bouza, 'Constructing Identities and Negotiating Relationships in Late Eighteenth-Century England: Mary Hamilton and her Correspondents at Court, *International Journal of English Studies* (to appear).

Raumolin-Brunberg, Helena, 'Forms of Address in Early English Correspondence', in Terttu Nevalainen and Helena Raumolin-Brunberg, eds., *Sociolinguistics and Language History: Studies based on the Corpus of Early English Correspondence* (Amsterdam: Rodopi, 1996), 167–81.

Tieken-Boon van Ostade, Ingrid, 'Of Formulas and Friends: Expressions of Politeness in John Gay's Letters', in Guy A. J. Tops, Betty Devriendt and Steven Geukens, eds., *Thinking English Grammar. To Honour Xavier Dekeyser, Professor Emeritus* (Louvain: Peeters, 1999), 99–112.

Tieken-Boon van Ostade, Ingrid, *The Bishop's grammar. Robert Lowth and the Rise of Prescriptivism in English* (Oxford: Oxford University Press, 2011).

Tieken-Boon van Ostade, Ingrid, *In Search of Jane Austen: The Language of the Letters* (Oxford: Oxford University Press, 2014).

Ulph, Cassandra, 'Intimacy, Creativity and Networks: Reading Practices in *The Mary Hamilton Papers'*, *GOTH 1st Annual Research Symposium'*, The Open University, 20–21 May 2021.

Wallis, Christine, 'Like Father, Like Son? Scottish English and Intra-Writer Variation in *The Mary Hamilton Papers'*, in Samantha M. Litty and Nils Langer, eds., *Historical Interplays between Language Ideology, Language Policy, and Language Practices* (Bern: Peter Lang, to appear).

Włodarczyk, Matylda and Irma Taavitsainen, eds., 'Historical (Socio) pragmatics at Present', Special Issue in *Journal of Historical Pragmatics* 18/2 (2017).

Yáñez Bouza, Nuria, ' "By Miranda, Mary Hamilton, Mrs Dickenson" – Self-Reference in Late Modern English Private Correspondence', *Neuphilologische Mitteilungen* 124.2 (2023), 220–254.

——, ' "My dearest Clara ... my dear friend" – Personal Names and Direct Address in Mary Hamilton's Private Correspondence', *Journal of Historical Sociolinguistics* (forthcoming).

——, ' "Directions for Addressing Persons of All Ranks" in *Late Eighteenth-Century Letter-Writing Manuals'*, ms.

Notes on Contributors

Carolina P. Amador-Moreno is Professor of English Linguistics. She is currently based at the University of Extremadura. At the time of writing the chapter for this volume she was Full Professor of English Linguistics at the University of Bergen, Norway (2020–2023). She has held different teaching positions at the Universities of Limerick (Ireland), University College Dublin (Ireland), Extremadura (Spain) and Bergen (Norway). Her research interests centre on the English spoken in Ireland with a more recent focus on historical sociolinguistics and corpus linguistics. Her work has also dealt with stylistics, discourse analysis and pragmatics. Her publications include articles and chapters dealing with these topics. She is the author, among others, of *Orality in Written Texts: Using Historical Corpora to Investigate Irish English (1700–1900)* (Routledge, 2019); *An Introduction to Irish English* (Equinox, 2010); the co-edited volumes *Digitally-Assisted Historical English Linguistics* (Routledge, 2024); *Expanding the Landscapes of Irish English Research* (Routledge, 2022); *Irish Identities: Sociolinguistic Perspectives* (Mouton de Gruyter, 2020); *Voice and Discourse in the Irish Context* (Palgrave-Macmillan, 2017); *Pragmatic Markers in Irish English* (John Benjamins, 2015); and *Fictionalising Orality*, a special issue of the journal *Sociolinguistic Studies* (2011). She is an associate member of CALS (Centre for Applied Language Studies), and IVACS (Inter-Variational Applied Corpus Linguistics network), both at the University of Limerick. She is also a member of the research groups DING (English Dialectology and the History of the English Language), University of Salamanca; Language Data and Language Change (University of Bergen) and LINGLAP (the Research Institute for Linguistics and Applied Language at the University of Extremadura), which she was Director of until August 2020.

Cristina Blanco-García holds a BA in English Philology at the University of Santiago de Compostela. She completed an MA in Advanced English studies at the same University, where she also wrote her Master's dissertation on "Ephemeral Adverbial Subordinators in the Early Modern English Period: Concession as a Case in Point" under the supervision of Prof. María José López-Couso. She was a full-time post-graduate researcher at the Department of English and German of the University of Santiago de Compostela, under funding from the Spanish Ministry of Economy and Competitiveness. Her PhD dissertation to be defended in April 2023 is on ephemerality in adverbial subordinators in Middle and Modern English. From Septernber 2020, she is an assistant lecturer at the Department of English of the University of Extremadura (Cáceres). Cristina's research interests include linguistic variation, change and grammaticalization processes and corpus linguistics.

Zeltia Blanco-Suárez is Senior Lecturer at the Department of English and German Philology of the University of Santiago de Compostela, where she teaches several English Linguistics courses at both graduate and undergraduate level. She is currently the coordinator of the *Inter-university Master in Advanced English Studies and its Applications* and a member of the research unit *Variation, Linguistic Change and Grammaticalization* (https://www.usc-vlcg.es/ZBS.htm) at the University of Santiago de Compostela. Her main research interests lie mostly within the field of (Historical) Linguistics and Corpus Linguistics, with a focus on English intensifiers, grammaticalization and subjectification. She has authored several articles and book chapters on these topics in international peer-reviewed journals and edited volumes and has participated in several national projects on language change and grammaticalization. She is also the director of the panel "Linguistic variation and change through corpora" of the Spanish Association for Corpus Linguistics (AELINCO).

Javier Calle-Martín is Professor of English Linguistics at the University of Málaga, (Spain), where he teaches History of English and Quantitative Linguistics. He is the editor of *The Middle English Version of De viribus herbarum* in MS Hunter 497 (2012), *A Late Middle English Remedybook* in MS Wellcome 542 (2013) and a synoptic edition of John Arderon's *De judiciis urinarum* in MS Hunter 328 and MS Rylands 1310 (2020). He is also lead researcher of the Early and Late Modern English components of *The Málaga Corpus of Early*

English Scientific Prose. His research interests are the History of the English Language and Manuscript Studies, Late Middle English and Early Modern English scientific manuscripts in particular. In the last few years, he has also developed some interest in the standardization of English and the connection between usage and prescription in Late Modern English. His most recent publications include contributions in collective works like the *The Cambridge Handbook of Historical Orthography* (Cambridge UP), *A History of Punctuation in English Literature* (Cambridge UP) and *Graphic Practice and Literacies in the History of English* (Brepols), and research articles in journals like *English Language and Linguistics*, *English Today* or *Australian Journal of Linguistics*.

Begoña Crespo-García is a Full Professor in English Linguistics at the University of A Coruña. She has taught several courses on the English Language, Etymology, Dialectology, English Grammar, History of the English Language, History and Culture of the English-Speaking Countries, Translation Studies, Linguistic Models, Variation and Change, Corpus Linguistics and Varieties of English. She has published on lexicon enlargement in the History of English, genre/text-type taxonomy and the diachrony of English scientific writing, corpus compilation and corpus exploitation for discursive purposes, especially female language uses in writing science. She has supervised several PhD dissertations on the language of science and on intercultural relations. She has published in high-quality and indexed journals such as *Studia Neophilologica*, *Nordic Journal of English Studies*, *Neuphilologische Mitteilungen*, *English Studies*, *Studia Anglica Posnaniensia*, *Literary and Linguistic Computing* and *Linguistica Praguensia*, among others, as well as book chapters in D.S Brewer, Rodopi, Peter Lang, Lincom Europa or John Benjamins, some of these publishing houses are included in the Scholarly Publishers Indicators (SPI) ranking occupying the top ten positions. She has also participated and/or coordinated several regional, national and European projects such as "Development of the interdisciplinary master program on Computational Linguistics at Central Asian UniverSitieS/CLASS"; "Flipped Impact", code: 2018-1-TR01-KA201-059386; "Création de Capacités institutionnelles d'intégration des Réfugiés dans l'Enseignement Supérieur", code: 610023-EPP-1-2019-1-DZEPPKA2-CBHE-SP, Universidade sem Fronteiras, 0685_UNISF_1_P; "Etiquetado electrónico de textos científico-técnicos en lengua inglesa entre los siglos XVII y XX (1–5): Coruña Corpus"; "La representación lingüística del 'otro: redefinición del concepto de 'extranjero' en el discurso institucional de Alemania, España, Reino Unido y la UE desde 1940 hasta nuestros días".

Miriam Criado-Peña is a Lecturer in English Language at the University of Granada (Spain). Her research interests lie within the fields of Historical Linguistics, Manuscript Studies, Corpus Linguistics and World Englishes. She is currently involved in the compilation of *The Malaga Corpus of Early English Scientific Prose*, and she has published in journals such as *Australian Journal of Linguistics*, *Studia Neophilologica* and *Nordic Journal of English Studies*, among others.

David Denison is Emeritus Professor of English Linguistics at the University of Manchester and a Fellow of the British Academy. He was a founding editor of the journal *English Language and Linguistics* and was President of the International Society for the Linguistics of English (ISLE) 2008–2011. He has published on syntax and semantics in all periods of the history of English, including current change. His other interests include gradience in linguistics and corpus linguistics. His work on the project *Unlocking the Mary Hamilton Papers* involves textual editing and commentary, technical work on TEI/XML, syntactic change in the eighteenth-century verbal system, and social network analysis.

Sara von der Fecht-Fernández is a research fellow at the Research Institute of Text Analysis and Applications (IATEXT) of the Universidad de Las Palmas de Gran Canaria (Spain), where she teaches English language courses in the Degree of Modern Languages. Currently, she is pursuing the PhD programme "Linguistic and Literary Studies in their Sociocultural Contexts" with a thesis on the Spanish and Amerindian words in Richard Hakluyt's *The Principal Navigations* (1589). Thus, her research interests include Early Modern English lexicology and lexicography and Renaissance travel texts. Her forthcoming publication is "The Role of Richard Hakluyt's *The Principall*

Nauigations (1589) in the Introduction and Dissemination of Spanish Loanwords in the English language", in Neophilologus, co-authored with Alicia Rodríguez-Álvarez.

Jesús Fernández-Domínguez, PhD (University of Jaén), is Associate Professor of English Language and Linguistics at the University of Granada, where he teaches courses on English grammar, text linguistics and corpus linguistics. His research interests are related to the formal and semantic aspects of English synchronic lexical morphology, such as productivity, the interaction between morphological processes or an onomasiological approach to word-formation. His most recent publications include contributions in collective works like the *Oxford Research Encyclopedia of Linguistics* and *The Wiley Blackwell Companion to Diachronic Linguistics*, and research articles in journals like *The Mental Lexicon*, *Anglia* or *Studia Neophilologica*. He has participated in several publicly funded research projects on English derivational morphology.

María F. García-Bermejo Giner is retired Senior Lecturer at the Department of English Philology of the University of Salamanca, Spain. Her main research interests are English Historical Dialectology in the Early and Late Modern English periods, and the literary representation of British English dialects as a source for the study of British English dialects. She has published extensively in these fields. Since 2004 she has been the Supervisor of the research project that brought about *The Salamanca Corpus* (www.thesalamancacorpus.com), an open access corpus of British English dialect texts held at the University of Salamanca digital repository (GREDOS). It comprises not only texts representative of the literary use of dialects and dialect literature but also glossaries and early and late Modern English papers on English dialects.

Turo Hiltunen is Senior University Lecturer in English at the University of Helsinki, Finland. His research interests include corpus linguistics and register analysis, and he has worked on grammatical and phraseological variation of scientific English past and present, compilation of specialized corpora, and democratization in the context of parliamentary discourse. His recent publications include co-edited volumes *Corpus Pragmatic Studies on the History of Medical Discourse* (John Benjamins 2022, with Irma Taavitsainen) and *Discourse-Pragmatic Variation and Change* (Cambridge University Press 2022, with Elizabeth Peterson and Joseph Kern).

Juan Lorente-Sánchez is a member of the Department of English French and German Philology at the University of Málaga (Spain), where he has taught English for International Tourism, and currently teaches English Language as well as English Phonetics and Phonology. He graduated in English Studies in 2016 and later obtained two Masters' degree at the same university: the first in Teaching English as a Foreign Language (2017), and the second in English Studies, Multilingual and Intercultural Communication (2018). He has recently completed his PhD dissertation (2022), which deals with the edition, corpus compilation and philological study of Glasgow University Library, MS Ferguson 7. He has also collaborated in the compilation and POS-tagging of the Late Modern English component of *The Málaga Corpus of Early English Scientific Prose* (1700–1900). His research interests include text editing, manuscript studies, historical linguistics and corpus linguistics.

Isabel Moskowich holds a chair in English Philology at the University of A Coruña where she leads the MuStE group. Her research covers different aspects of the History of English, mainly the Ikd Norse lexical elements and sociolinguistic implications during the Middle Ages. However, since 2003, she has directed the compilation of the *Coruña Corpus of English Scientific Writing* and the study of the origins of ESP from a socio-pragmatic approach. She has published extensively in international journals such as *Folia Linguistica Historica, SELIM, Neuphilologische Mitteilungen, Studia Anglica Posnaniensia, Studia Neophilologica, Literary and Linguistic Computing, Australian Journal of Linguistics, English Studies* or *Studies About Languages,* and has edited or co-edited different volumes. Prof Moskowich has also served in several journal editorial boards and scientific committees.She has been responsible for several research projects funded both by the Galician and the Spanish Governments.

Tino Oudesluijs is an Honorary Research Fellow in the School of Arts, Languages & Cultures at the University of Manchester. His research interests lie in historical sociolinguistics and diachronic aspects of language variation and change in English, with a focus on letter-writing and copying practices, as well as supralocalization and standardization processes. He has previously worked on the role of historical urban vernaculars in standardization processes in the *Emerging Standards* project (2014–2019), as well as on the compilation of the *Mary Hamilton Papers* digital edition in the *Unlocking the Mary Hamilton Papers* project (2019–2022).

Marta Pacheco-Franco is a researcher in the Department of English at the University of Málaga. After graduating in English Studies (2017), she interned at the University of Guelph, ON (2018), and later obtained her MAs on Teaching Spanish as a Foreign Language (2019) and on English Studies and Multilingual Communication (2020). She has most recently completed her PhD (2023) with a doctoral grant from the Spanish Ministry of Universities. Her research interests, like her dissertation, lie in the fields of historical linguistics and world Englishes, with a particular interest for orthographic variation.

Javier Ruano-García is Associate Professor of the History of the English Language at the University of Salamanca, where he teaches undergraduate courses on English historical linguistics, linguistic variation in Early Modern English, and MA courses on academic writing. His main research interests lie in the fields of historical language variation, with a focus on regional dialects of the Early and Late Modern English periods, historical sociolinguistics, corpus linguistics, historical dialect lexicography, and manuscript editing. He has been involved in the compilation of the Salamanca Corpus for the past ten years, taking care of specimens representative of the Lancashire dialect and other varieties of northern English. He is the author of *Early Modern Northern English Lexis: A Literary Corpus-Based Study* (Peter Lang, 2010) and has edited White Kennett's *Etymological Collections of English Words and Provincial Expressions* for Oxford University Press (2018).

Alicia Rodríguez-Álvarez is Professor of History of the English Language at the Universidad de Las Palmas de Gran Canaria, Instituto Universitario de Análisis y Aplicaciones Textuales (IATEXT). Her main research interests include the language of Early and Late Modern English medical texts, the history of the paratextual apparatus in non-literary English texts and English historical lexicography. Her recent publications include "An Approach to Persuasive Advertising Strategies in the Prefatory Matter of Seventeenth-century English Midwifery Treatises", in *The Dynamics of Text and Framing Phenomena. Historical Approaches to Paratext and Metadiscourse in English* (John Benjamins, 2020); "The Treatment of 'monstrous births' in 17th-century English Obstetrical Treatises: between the Prodigy Narrative and the Scientific Text", in *Ágora. Estudos Clássicos em Debate* (2021); "Robert Barret's Glossary of Military Terms in *The Theorike and Practike of Moderne Warres* (1558)" in *International Journal of Lexicography* (2023); and "The Role of Richard Hakluyt's *The Principall Nauigations* (1589) in the Introduction and Dissemination of Spanish Loanwords in the English Language", in *Neophilologus* (forthcoming). Currently, she is the co-Principal Investigator of the research project entitled "Lexical Americanisms in the Spanish and English Languages Documented in Texts about America (1650–1740): Development of the AMERLEX Database".

Carla Suhr is a University Lecturer in English Philology at the University of Helsinki. Her research interests lie primarily in the field of historical discourse analysis, pragmatics, corpus linguistics, and book history. She is a co-compiler of two corpora of historical medical texts, Early Modern English Texts (2010) and Late Modern English Medical Texts (2019), and has published several articles in international journals and edited volumes on topics such as genre development, advertising and marketing, paratextual elements, and fake news in historical medical and news discourse. She has also published a book on Early Modern English witchcraft pamphlets (2011). Currently she is a collaborator in the Early Modern Graphic Literacies project, an Academy of Finland-funded project based at the University of Turku.

Irma Taavitsainen is Professor Emerita of English Philology at the University of Helsinki. Her research focuses on historical pragmatics, corpus linguistics, genre and register variation and the evolution of scientific thought styles. She has published widely in these fields, and she is also a corpus compiler. She is a founding editor of the *Journal of Historical Pragmatics* (JHP, 2000–). Her most recent co-edited volumes are *Late Modern English Medical Texts: Writing Medicine in the Eighteenth Century,* (John Benjamins 2019, with Turo Hiltunen); *Manners, Norms and Transgressions: Literary and Linguistic Approaches* (John Benjamins 2020, with Andreas H. Jucker); *Corpus Pragmatic Studies on the History of Medical Discourse* (John Benjamins 2022, with Turo Hiltunen); and *Genre in Early Modern Medical English: Sociocultural Contexts of Production and Use, 1500–1800* (Cambridge University Press 2022, with Carla Suhr, Turo Hiltunen, and Jeremy Smith). Forthcoming is also *Genre Variation and Genre Change across Registers of Writing* (with Matylda Włodarczyk, accepted for *The Wiley Blackwell Companion to Diachronic Linguistics*).

Nuria Yáñez-Bouza is Senior Lecturer in the Department of English Philology at the University of Vigo (Spain) and Honorary Research Fellow in the Department of English Language and Linguistics at the University of Manchester (UK). Her research interests lie in historical sociolinguistics with a focus on the eighteenth-century grammar writing tradition (*Grammar, Rhetoric and Usage in English. Preposition Placement 1500–1900*, 2015; *The Eighteenth-Century English Grammars Database*), pronouncing dictionaries (*The Eighteenth-Century English Phonology Database*) and letter-writing practices (*Unlocking the Mary Hamilton Papers*). She has been actively involved in the field of Digital Humanities with the compilation of multi-register historical corpora and electronic historical databases. She is currently a member of the ICAME Board and of the Editorial Board of the journal *English Language and Linguistics*.

Linguistic Insights

Studies in Language and Communication

This series aims to promote specialist language studies in the fields of linguistic theory and applied linguistics, by publishing volumes that focus on specific aspects of language use in one or several languages and provide valuable insights into language and communication research. A cross-disciplinary approach is favoured and most European languages are accepted.

The series includes two types of books:

- Monographs – featuring in-depth studies on special aspects of language theory, language analysis or language teaching.
- Collected papers – assembling papers from workshops, conferences or symposia.

Each volume of the series is subjected to a double peer-reviewing process.

Vol. 1 Maurizio Gotti & Marina Dossena (eds)
Modality in Specialized Texts. Selected Papers of the 1st CERLIS Conference.
421 pages. 2001. ISBN 3-906767-10-8 · US-ISBN 0-8204-5340-4

Vol. 2 Giuseppina Cortese & Philip Riley (eds)
Domain-specific English. Textual Practices across Communities and Classrooms.
420 pages. 2002. ISBN 3-906768-98-8 · US-ISBN 0-8204-5884-8

Vol. 3 Maurizio Gotti, Dorothee Heller & Marina Dossena (eds)
Conflict and Negotiation in Specialized Texts. Selected Papers of the 2nd CERLIS Conference.
470 pages. 2002. ISBN 3-906769-12-7 · US-ISBN 0-8204-5887-2

Vol. 4 Maurizio Gotti, Marina Dossena, Richard Dury, Roberta Facchinetti & Maria Lima
Variation in Central Modals. A Repertoire of Forms and Types of Usage in Middle English and Early Modern English.
364 pages. 2002. ISBN 3-906769-84-4 · US-ISBN 0-8204-5898-8

Editorial address:

Prof. Maurizio Gotti
Università di Bergamo, Dipartimento di Lingue, Letterature e Culture Straniere Piazza Rosate 2, 24129 Bergamo, Italy
Fax: +39 035 2052789, E-Mail: m.gotti@unibg.it

Vol. 5 Stefania Nuccorini (ed.)
Phrases and Phraseology. Data and Descriptions.
187 pages. 2002. ISBN 3-906770-08-7 · US-ISBN 0-8204-5933-X

Vol. 6 Vijay Bhatia, Christopher N. Candlin & Maurizio Gotti (eds)
Legal Discourse in Multilingual and Multicultural Contexts.
Arbitration Texts in Europe.
385 pages. 2003. ISBN 3-906770-85-0 · US-ISBN 0-8204-6254-3

Vol. 7 Marina Dossena & Charles Jones (eds)
Insights into Late Modern English. 2nd edition.
378 pages. 2003, 2007. ISBN 978-3-03911-257-9 · US-ISBN 978-0-8204-8927-8

Vol. 8 Maurizio Gotti
Specialized Discourse. Linguistic Features and Changing Conventions.
351 pages. 2003, 2005. ISBN 3-03910-606-6 · US-ISBN 0-8204-7000-7

Vol. 9 Alan Partington, John Morley & Louann Haarman (eds)
Corpora and Discourse.
420 pages. 2004. ISBN 3-03910-026-2 · US-ISBN 0-8204-6262-4

Vol. 10 Martina Möllering
The Acquisition of German Modal Particles. A Corpus-Based Approach.
290 pages. 2004. ISBN 3-03910-043-2 · US-ISBN 0-8204-6273-X

Vol. 11 David Hart (ed.)
English Modality in Context. Diachronic Perspectives.
261 pages. 2003. ISBN 3-03910-046-7 · US-ISBN 0-8204-6852-5

Vol. 12 Wendy Swanson
Modes of Co-reference as an Indicator of Genre.
430 pages. 2003. ISBN 3-03910-052-1 · US-ISBN 0-8204-6855-X

Vol. 13 Gina Poncini
Discursive Strategies in Multicultural Business Meetings. 2nd edition.
338 pages. 2004, 2007. ISBN 978-3-03911-296-8 · US-ISBN 978-0-8204-8937-7

Vol. 14 Christopher N. Candlin & Maurizio Gotti (eds)
Intercultural Aspects of Specialized Communication. 2nd edition.
369 pages. 2004, 2007. ISBN 978-3-03911-258-6 · US-ISBN 978-0-8204-8926-1

Vol. 15 Gabriella Del Lungo Camiciotti & Elena Tognini Bonelli (eds)
Academic Discourse. New Insights into Evaluation.
234 pages. 2004. ISBN 3-03910-353-9 · US-ISBN 0-8204-7016-3

Vol. 16 Marina Dossena & Roger Lass (eds)
Methods and Data in English Historical Dialectology.
405 pages. 2004. ISBN 3-03910-362-8 · US-ISBN 0-8204-7018-X

Vol. 17 Judy Noguchi
The Science Review Article. An Opportune Genre in the Construction of Science.
274 pages. 2006. ISBN 3-03910-426-8 · US-ISBN 0-8204-7034-1

Vol. 18 Giuseppina Cortese & Anna Duszak (eds)
Identity, Community, Discourse. English in Intercultural Settings.
495 pages. 2005. ISBN 3-03910-632-5 · US-ISBN 0-8204-7163-1

Vol. 19 Anna Trosborg & Poul Erik Flyvholm Jørgensen (eds)
Business Discourse. Texts and Contexts.
250 pages. 2005. ISBN 3-03910-606-6 · US-ISBN 0-8204-7000-7

Vol. 20 Christopher Williams
Tradition and Change in Legal English. Verbal Constructions in Prescriptive Texts.
2nd revised edition.
216 pages. 2005, 2007. ISBN 978-3-03911-444-3.

Vol. 21 Katarzyna Dziubalska-Kolaczyk & Joanna Przedlacka (eds)
English Pronunciation Models: A Changing Scene.
2nd edition. 476 pages. 2005, 2008. ISBN 978-3-03911-682-9.

Vol. 22 Christián Abello-Contesse, Rubén Chacón-Beltrán,
M. Dolores López-Jiménez & M. Mar Torreblanca-López (eds)
Age in L2 Acquisition and Teaching.
214 pages. 2006. ISBN 3-03910-668-6 · US-ISBN 0-8204-7174-7

Vol. 23 Vijay K. Bhatia, Maurizio Gotti, Jan Engberg & Dorothee Heller (eds)
Vagueness in Normative Texts.
474 pages. 2005. ISBN 3-03910-653-8 · US-ISBN 0-8204-7169-0

Vol. 24 Paul Gillaerts & Maurizio Gotti (eds)
Genre Variation in Business Letters. 2nd printing.
407 pages. 2008. ISBN 978-3-03911-681-2.

Vol. 25 Ana María Hornero, María José Luzón & Silvia Murillo (eds)
Corpus Linguistics. Applications for the Study of English. 2nd printing.
526 pages. 2006, 2008. ISBN 978-3-03911-726-0

Vol. 26 J. Lachlan Mackenzie & María de los Ángeles Gómez-González (eds)
Studies in Functional Discourse Grammar.
259 pages. 2005. ISBN 3-03910-696-1 · US-ISBN 0-8204-7558-0

Vol. 27 Debbie G. E. Ho
Classroom Talk. Exploring the Sociocultural Structure of Formal ESL Learning. 2nd edition.
254 pages. 2006, 2007. ISBN 978-3-03911-434-4

Vol. 28 Javier Pérez-Guerra, Dolores González-Álvarez, Jorge L. Bueno-Alonso & Esperanza Rama-Martínez (eds)
'Of Varying Language and Opposing Creed'. New Insights into Late Modern English.
455 pages. 2007. ISBN 978-3-03910-788-9

Vol. 29 Francesca Bargiela-Chiappini & Maurizio Gotti (eds)
Asian Business Discourse(s).
350 pages. 2005. ISBN 3-03910-804-2 · US-ISBN 0-8204-7574-2

Vol. 30 Nicholas Brownlees (ed.)
News Discourse in Early Modern Britain. Selected Papers of CHINED 2004.
300 pages. 2006. ISBN 3-03910-805-0 · US-ISBN 0-8204-8025-8

Vol. 31 Roberta Facchinetti & Matti Rissanen (eds)
Corpus-based Studies of Diachronic English.
300 pages. 2006. ISBN 3-03910-851-4 · US-ISBN 0-8204-8040-1

Vol. 32 Marina Dossena & Susan M. Fitzmaurice (eds)
Business and Official Correspondence. Historical Investigations.
209 pages. 2006. ISBN 3-03910-880-8 · US-ISBN 0-8204-8352-4

Vol. 33 Giuliana Garzone & Srikant Sarangi (eds)
Discourse, Ideology and Specialized Communication.
494 pages. 2007. ISBN 978-3-03910-888-6

Vol. 34 Giuliana Garzone & Cornelia Ilie (eds)
The Use of English in Institutional and Business Settings. An Intercultural Perspective.
372 pages. 2007. ISBN 978-3-03910-889-3

Vol. 35 Vijay K. Bhatia & Maurizio Gotti (eds) Explorations in Specialized Genres.
316 pages. 2006. ISBN 3-03910-995-2 · US-ISBN 0-8204-8372-9

Vol. 36 Heribert Picht (ed.)
Modern Approaches to Terminological Theories and Applications.
432 pages. 2006. ISBN 3-03911-156-6 · US-ISBN 0-8204-8380-X

Vol. 37 Anne Wagner & Sophie Cacciaguidi-Fahy (eds)
Legal Language and the Search for Clarity / Le langage juridique et la quête de clarté.
Practice and Tools / Pratiques et instruments.
487 pages. 2006. ISBN 3-03911-169-8 · US-ISBN 0-8204-8388-5

Vol. 38 Juan Carlos Palmer-Silveira, Miguel F. Ruiz-Garrido & Inmaculada Fortanet-Gómez (eds)
Intercultural and International Business Communication. Theory, Research and Teaching.
2nd edition.
343 pages. 2006, 2008. ISBN 978-3-03911-680-5

Vol. 39 Christiane Dalton-Puffer, Dieter Kastovsky, Nikolaus Ritt & Herbert Schendl (eds)
Syntax, Style and Grammatical Norms. English from 1500–2000.
250 pages. 2006. ISBN 3-03911-181-7 · US-ISBN 0-8204-8394-X

Vol. 40 Marina Dossena & Irma Taavitsainen (eds)
Diachronic Perspectives on Domain-Specific English.
280 pages. 2006. ISBN 3-03910-176-0 · US-ISBN 0-8204-8391-5

Vol. 41 John Flowerdew & Maurizio Gotti (eds)
Studies in Specialized Discourse.
293 pages. 2006. ISBN 3-03911-178-7

Vol. 42 Ken Hyland & Marina Bondi (eds)
Academic Discourse Across Disciplines.
320 pages. 2006. ISBN 3-03911-183-3 · US-ISBN 0-8204-8396-6

Vol. 43 Paul Gillaerts & Philip Shaw (eds)
The Map and the Landscape. Norms and Practices in Genre.
256 pages. 2006. ISBN 3-03911-182-5 · US-ISBN 0-8204-8395-4

Vol. 44 Maurizio Gotti & Davide Giannoni (eds)
New Trends in Specialized Discourse Analysis.
301 pages. 2006. ISBN 3-03911-184-1 · US-ISBN 0-8204-8381-8

Vol. 45 Maurizio Gotti & Françoise Salager-Meyer (eds)
Advances in Medical Discourse Analysis. Oral and Written Contexts.
492 pages. 2006. ISBN 3-03911-185-X · US-ISBN 0-8204-8382-6

Vol. 46 Maurizio Gotti & Susan Šarcevic' (eds)
Insights into Specialized Translation.
396 pages. 2006. ISBN 3-03911-186-8 · US-ISBN 0-8204-8383-4

Vol. 47 Khurshid Ahmad & Margaret Rogers (eds)
Evidence-based LSP. Translation, Text and Terminology.
584 pages. 2007. ISBN 978-3-03911-187-9

Vol. 48 Hao Sun & Dániel Z. Kádár (eds)
It's the Dragon's Turn. Chinese Institutional Discourses.
262 pages. 2008. ISBN 978-3-03911-175-6

Vol. 49 Cristina Suárez-Gómez
Relativization in Early English (950-1250). the Position of Relative Clauses.
149 pages. 2006. ISBN 3-03911-203-1 · US-ISBN 0-8204-8904-2

Vol. 50 Maria Vittoria Calvi & Luisa Chierichetti (eds)
Nuevas tendencias en el discurso de especialidad.
319 pages. 2006. ISBN 978-3-03911-261-6

Vol. 51 Mari Carmen Campoy & María José Luzón (eds)
Spoken Corpora in Applied Linguistics.
274 pages. 2008. ISBN 978-3-03911-275-3

Vol. 52 Konrad Ehlich & Dorothee Heller (Hrsg.)
Die Wissenschaft und ihre Sprachen.
323 pages. 2006. ISBN 978-3-03911-272-2

Vol. 53 Jingyu Zhang
The Semantic Salience Hierarchy Model. The L2 Acquisition of Psych Predicates
273 pages. 2007. ISBN 978-3-03911-300-2

Vol. 54 Norman Fairclough, Giuseppina Cortese & Patrizia Ardizzone (eds)
Discourse and Contemporary Social Change.
555 pages. 2007. ISBN 978-3-03911-276-0

Vol. 55 Jan Engberg, Marianne Grove Ditlevsen, Peter Kastberg & Martin Stegu (eds)
New Directions in LSP Teaching.
331 pages. 2007. ISBN 978-3-03911-433-7

Vol. 56 Dorothee Heller & Konrad Ehlich (Hrsg.)
Studien zur Rechtskommunikation.
322 pages. 2007. ISBN 978-3-03911-436-8

Vol. 57 Teruhiro Ishiguro & Kang-kwong Luke (eds)
Grammar in Cross-Linguistic Perspective. The Syntax, Semantics, and Pragmatics of Japanese and Chinese.
304 pages. 2012. ISBN 978-3-03911-445-0

Vol. 58 Carmen Frehner Email – SMS – MMS
294 pages. 2008. ISBN 978-3-03911-451-1

Vol. 59 Isabel Balteiro
The Directionality of Conversion in English. A Dia-Synchronic Study.
276 pages. 2007. ISBN 978-3-03911-241-8

Vol. 60 Maria Milagros Del Saz Rubio
English Discourse Markers of Reformulation.
237 pages. 2007. ISBN 978-3-03911-196-1

Vol. 61 Sally Burgess & Pedro Martín-Martín (eds)
English as an Additional Language in Research Publication and Communication.
259 pages. 2008. ISBN 978-3-03911-462-7

Vol. 62 Sandrine Onillon
Pratiques et représentations de l'écrit.
458 pages. 2008. ISBN 978-3-03911-464-1

Vol. 63 Hugo Bowles & Paul Seedhouse (eds)
Conversation Analysis and Language for Specific Purposes. 2nd edition.
337 pages. 2007, 2009. ISBN 978-3-0343-0045-2

Vol. 64 Vijay K. Bhatia, Christopher N. Candlin & Paola Evangelisti Allori (eds)
Language, Culture and the Law. The Formulation of Legal Concepts across Systems and Cultures.
342 pages. 2008. ISBN 978-3-03911-470-2

Vol. 65 Jonathan Culpeper & Dániel Z. Kádár (eds)
Historical (Im)politeness.
300 pages. 2010. ISBN 978-3-03911-496-2

Vol. 66 Linda Lombardo (ed.)
Using Corpora to Learn about Language and Discourse.
237 pages. 2009. ISBN 978-3-03911-522-8

Vol. 67 Natsumi Wakamoto
Extroversion/Introversion in Foreign Language Learning. Interactions with Learner Strategy Use.
159 pages. 2009. ISBN 978-3-03911-596-9

Vol. 68 Eva Alcón-Soler (ed.)
Learning How to Request in an Instructed Language Learning Context.
260 pages. 2008. ISBN 978-3-03911-601-0

Vol. 69 Domenico Pezzini
The Translation of Religious Texts in the Middle Ages.
428 pages. 2008. ISBN 978-3-03911-600-3

Vol. 70 Tomoko Tode
Effects of Frequency in Classroom Second Language Learning. Quasi-experiment and stimulated-recall analysis.
195 pages. 2008. ISBN 978-3-03911-602-7

Vol. 71 Egor Tsedryk
Fusion symétrique et alternances ditransitives.
211 pages. 2009. ISBN 978-3-03911-609-6

Vol. 72 Cynthia J. Kellett Bidoli & Elana Ochse (eds)
English in International Deaf Communication.
444 pages. 2008. ISBN 978-3-03911-610-2

Vol. 73 Joan C. Beal, Carmela Nocera & Massimo Sturiale (eds)
Perspectives on Prescriptivism.
269 pages. 2008. ISBN 978-3-03911-632-4

Vol. 74 Carol Taylor Torsello, Katherine Ackerley & Erik Castello (eds)
Corpora for University Language Teachers.
308 pages. 2008. ISBN 978-3-03911-639-3

Vol. 75 María Luisa Pérez Cañado (ed.)
English Language Teaching in the European Credit Transfer System. Facing the Challenge.
251 pages. 2009. ISBN 978-3-03911-654-6

Vol. 76 Marina Dossena & Ingrid Tieken-Boon van Ostade (eds)
Studies in Late Modern English Correspondence. Methodology and Data.
291 pages. 2008. ISBN 978-3-03911-658-4

Vol. 77 Ingrid Tieken-Boon van Ostade & Wim van der Wurff (eds)
Current Issues in Late Modern English.
436 pages. 2009. ISBN 978-3-03911-660-7

Vol. 78 Marta Navarro Coy (ed.)
Practical Approaches to Foreign Language Teaching and Learning.
297 pages. 2009. ISBN 978-3-03911-661-4

Vol. 79 Qing Ma
Second Language Vocabulary Acquisition.
333 pages. 2009. ISBN 978-3-03911-666-9

Vol. 80 Martin Solly, Michelangelo Conoscenti & Sandra Campagna (eds)
Verbal/Visual Narrative Texts in Higher Education.
384 pages. 2008. ISBN 978-3-03911-672-0

Vol. 81 Meiko Matsumoto
From Simple Verbs to Periphrastic Expressions. The Historical Development of Composite Predicates, Phrasal Verbs, and Related Constructions in English.
235 pages. 2008. ISBN 978-3-03911-675-1

Vol. 82 Melinda Dooly
Doing Diversity. Teachers' Construction of Their Classroom Reality.
180 pages. 2009. ISBN 978-3-03911-687-4

Vol. 83 Victoria Guillén-Nieto, Carmen Marimón-Llorca & Chelo Vargas-Sierra (eds)
Intercultural Business Communication and Simulation and Gaming Methodology.
392 pages. 2009. ISBN 978-3-03911-688-1

Vol. 84 Maria Grazia Guido
English as a Lingua Franca in Cross-cultural Immigration Domains.
285 pages. 2008. ISBN 978-3-03911-689-8

Vol. 85 Erik Castello
Text Complexity and Reading Comprehension Tests.
352 pages. 2008. ISBN 978-3-03911-717-8

Vol. 86 Maria-Lluisa Gea-Valor, Isabel García-Izquierdo & Maria-José Esteve (eds)
Linguistic and Translation Studies in Scientific Communication.
317 pages. 2010. ISBN 978-3-0343-0069-8

Vol. 87 Carmen Navarro, Rosa Ma Rodríguez Abella, Francesca Dalle Pezze & Renzo Miotti (eds)
La comunicación especializada.
355 pages. 2008. ISBN 978-3-03911-733-8

Vol. 88 Kiriko Sato
The Development from Case-Forms to Prepositional Constructions in Old English Prose.
231 pages. 2009. ISBN 978-3-03911-763-5

Vol. 89 Dorothee Heller (Hrsg.)
Formulierungsmuster in deutscher und italienischer Fachkommunikation. Intra- und interlinguale Perspektiven.
315 pages. 2008. ISBN 978-3-03911-778-9

Vol. 90 Henning Bergenholtz, Sandro Nielsen & Sven Tarp (eds)
Lexicography at a Crossroads. Dictionaries and Encyclopedias Today, Lexicographical Tools Tomorrow.
372 pages. 2009. ISBN 978-3-03911-799-4

Vol. 91 Manouchehr Moshtagh Khorasani
The Development of Controversies. From the Early Modern Period to Online Discussion Forums.
317 pages. 2009. ISBN 978-3-3911-711-6

Vol. 92 María Luisa Carrió-Pastor (ed.)
Content and Language Integrated Learning. Cultural Diversity.
178 pages. 2009. ISBN 978-3-3911-818-2

Vol. 93 Roger Berry
Terminology in English Language Teaching. Nature and Use.
262 pages. 2010. ISBN 978-3-0343-0013-1

Vol. 94 Roberto Cagliero & Jennifer Jenkins (eds)
Discourses, Communities, and Global Englishes
240 pages. 2010. ISBN 978-3-0343-0012-4

Vol. 95 Facchinetti Roberta, Crystal David, Seidlhofer Barbara (eds)
From International to Local English – And Back Again.
268 pages. 2010. ISBN 978-3-0343-0011-7

Vol. 96 Cesare Gagliardi & Alan Maley (eds)
EIL, ELF, Global English. Teaching and Learning Issues
376 pages. 2010. ISBN 978-3-0343-0010-0

Vol. 97 Sylvie Hancil (ed.)
The Role of Prosody in Affective Speech.
403 pages. 2009. ISBN 978-3-03911-696-6

Vol. 98 Marina Dossena & Roger Lass (eds)
Studies in English and European Historical Dialectology.
257 pages. 2009. ISBN 978-3-0343-0024-7

Vol. 99 Christine Béal
Les interactions quotidiennes en français et en anglais.
De l'approche comparative à l'analyse des situations interculturelles.
424 pages. 2010. ISBN 978-3-0343-0027-8

Vol. 100 Maurizio Gotti (ed.)
Commonality and Individuality in Academic Discourse.
398 pages. 2009. ISBN 978-3-0343-0023-0

Vol. 101 Javier E. Díaz Vera & Rosario Caballero (eds)
Textual Healing. Studies in Medieval English Medical, Scientific and Technical Texts.
213 pages. 2009. ISBN 978-3-03911-822-9

Vol. 102 Nuria Edo Marzá
The Specialised Lexicographical Approach. A Step further in Dictionary-making.
316 pages. 2009. ISBN 978-3-0343-0043-8

Vol. 103 Carlos Prado-Alonso, Lidia Gómez-García, Iria Pastor-Gómez & David Tizón-Couto (eds)
New Trends and Methodologies in Applied English Language Research. Diachronic, Diatopic and Contrastive Studies.
348 pages. 2009. ISBN 978-3-0343-0046-9

Vol. 104 Françoise Salager-Meyer & Beverly A. Lewin Crossed Words. Criticism in Scholarly Writing?
371 pages. 2011. ISBN 978-3-0343-0049-0.

Vol. 105 Javier Ruano-García
Early Modern Northern English Lexis. A Literary Corpus-Based Study.
611 pages. 2010. ISBN 978-3-0343-0058-2

Vol. 106 Rafael Monroy-Casas
Systems for the Phonetic Transcription of English. Theory and Texts.
280 pages. 2011. ISBN 978-3-0343-0059-9

Vol. 107 Nicola T. Owtram
The Pragmatics of Academic Writing.
A Relevance Approach to the Analysis of Research Article Introductions.
311 pages. 2009. ISBN 978-3-0343-0060-5

Vol. 108 Yolanda Ruiz de Zarobe, Juan Manuel Sierra & Francisco Gallardo del Puerto (eds)
Content and Foreign Language Integrated Learning. Contributions to Multilingualism in European Contexts 343 pages. 2011. ISBN 978-3-0343-0074-2

Vol. 109 Ángeles Linde López & Rosalía Crespo Jiménez (eds)
Professional English in the European context. The EHEA challenge.
374 pages. 2010. ISBN 978-3-0343-0088-9

Vol. 110 Rosalía Rodríguez-Vázquez
The Rhythm of Speech, Verse and Vocal Music. A New Theory.
394 pages. 2010. ISBN 978-3-0343-0309-5

Vol. 111 Anastasios Tsangalidis & Roberta Facchinetti (eds)
Studies on English Modality. In Honour of Frank Palmer.
392 pages. 2009. ISBN 978-3-0343-0310-1

Vol. 112 Jing Huang
Autonomy, Agency and Identity in Foreign Language Learning and Teaching.
400 pages. 2013. ISBN 978-3-0343-0370-5

Vol. 113 Mihhail Lotman & Maria-Kristiina Lotman (eds)
Frontiers in Comparative Prosody. In memoriam: Mikhail Gasparov.
426 pages. 2011. ISBN 978-3-0343-0373-6

Vol. 114 Merja Kytö, John Scahill & Harumi Tanabe (eds)
Language Change and Variation from Old English to Late Modern English. A Festschrift for Minoji Akimoto
422 pages. 2010. ISBN 978-3-0343-0372-9

Vol. 115 Giuliana Garzone & Paola Catenaccio (eds)
Identities across Media and Modes. Discursive Perspectives.
379 pages. 2009. ISBN 978-3-0343-0386-6

Vol. 116 Elena Landone
Los marcadores del discurso y cortesía verbal en español.
390 pages. 2010. ISBN 978-3-0343-0413-9

Vol. 117 Maurizio Gotti & Christopher Williams (eds)
Legal Discourse across Languages and Cultures.
339 pages. 2010. ISBN 978-3-0343-0425-2

Vol. 118 David Hirsh
Academic Vocabulary in Context.
217 pages. 2010. ISBN 978-3-0343-0426-9

Vol. 119 Yvonne Dröschel
Lingua Franca English. The Role of Simplification and Transfer.
358 pages. 2011. ISBN 978-3-0343-0432-0

Vol. 120 Tengku Sepora Tengku Mahadi, Helia Vaezian & Mahmoud Akbari Corpora in Translation. A Practical Guide.
135 pages. 2010. ISBN 978-3-0343-0434-4

Vol. 121 Davide Simone Giannoni & Celina Frade (eds)
Researching Language and the Law. Textual Features and Translation Issues.
278 pages. 2010. ISBN 978-3-0343-0443-6

Vol. 122 Daniel Madrid & Stephen Hughes (eds)
Studies in Bilingual Education.
472 pages. 2011. ISBN 978-3-0343-0474-0

Vol. 123 Vijay K. Bhatia, Christopher N. Candlin & Maurizio Gotti (eds)
The Discourses of Dispute Resolution.
290 pages. 2010. ISBN 978-3-0343-0476-4

Vol. 124 Davide Simone Giannoni
Mapping Academic Values in the Disciplines. A Corpus-Based Approach.
288 pages. 2010. ISBN 978-3-0343-0488-7

Vol. 125 Giuliana Garzone & James Archibald (eds)
Discourse, Identities and Roles in Specialized Communication.
419 pages. 2010. ISBN 978-3-0343-0494-8

Vol. 126 Iria Pastor-Gómez
The Status and Development of N+N Sequences in Contemporary English Noun Phrases.
216 pages. 2011. ISBN 978-3-0343-0534-1

Vol. 127 Carlos Prado-Alonso
Full-verb Inversion in Written and Spoken English.
261 pages. 2011. ISBN 978-3-0343-0535-8

Vol. 128 Tony Harris & María Moreno Jaén (eds)
Corpus Linguistics in Language Teaching.
214 pages. 2010. ISBN 978-3-0343-0524-2

Vol. 129 Tetsuji Oda & Hiroyuki Eto (eds)
Multiple Perspectives on English Philology and History of Linguistics. A Festschrift for Shoichi Watanabe on his 80th Birthday.
378 pages. 2010. ISBN 978-3-0343-0480-1

Vol. 130 Luisa Chierichetti & Giovanni Garofalo (eds)
Lengua y Derecho. líneas de investigación interdisciplinaria.
283 pages. 2010. ISBN 978-3-0343-0463-4

Vol. 131 Paola Evangelisti Allori & Giuliana Garzone (eds)
Discourse, Identities and Genres in Corporate Communication. Sponsorship, Advertising and Organizational Communication.
324 pages. 2011. ISBN 978-3-0343-0591-4

Vol. 132 Leyre Ruiz de Zarobe & Yolanda Ruiz de Zarobe (eds)
Speech Acts and Politeness across Languages and Cultures.
402 pages. 2012. ISBN 978-3-0343-0611-9

Vol. 133 Thomas Christiansen
Cohesion. A Discourse Perspective.
387 pages. 2011. ISBN 978-3-0343-0619-5

Vol. 134 Giuliana Garzone & Maurizio Gotti
Discourse, Communication and the Enterprise. Genres and Trends.
451 pages. 2011. ISBN 978-3-0343-0620-1

Vol. 135 Zsuzsa Hoffmann
Ways of the World's Words. Language Contact in the Age of Globalization.
334 pages 2011. ISBN 978-3-0343-0673-7

Vol. 136 Cecilia Varcasia (ed.) Becoming Multilingual.
Language Learning and Language Policy between Attitudes and Identities.
213 pages. 2011. ISBN 978-3-0343-0687-5

Vol. 137 Susy Macqueen
The Emergence of Patterns in Second Language Writing. A Sociocognitive Exploration of Lexical Trails.
325 pages. 2012. ISBN 978-3-0343-1010-9

Vol. 138 Maria Vittoria Calvi & Giovanna Mapelli (eds)
La lengua del turismo. Géneros discursivos y terminología.
365 pages. 2011. ISBN 978-3-0343-1011-6

Vol. 139 Ken Lau
Learning to Become a Professional in a Textually-Mediated World. A Text-Oriented Study of Placement Practices.
261 pages. 2012. ISBN 978-3-0343-1016-1

Vol. 140 Sandra Campagna, Giuliana Garzone, Cornelia Ilie & Elizabeth Rowley-Jolivet (eds)
Evolving Genres in Web-mediated Communication.
337 pages. 2012. ISBN 978-3-0343-1013-0

Vol. 141 Edith Esch & Martin Solly (eds)
The Sociolinguistics of Language Education in International Contexts.
263 pages. 2012. ISBN 978-3-0343-1009-3

Vol. 142 Forthcoming.

Vol. 143 David Tizón-Couto
Left Dislocation in English. A Functional-Discoursal Approach.
416 pages. 2012. ISBN 978-3-0343-1037-6

Vol. 144 Margrethe Petersen & Jan Engberg (eds)
Current Trends in LSP Research. Aims and Methods.
323 pages. 2011. ISBN 978-3-0343-1054-3

Vol. 145 David Tizón-Couto, Beatriz Tizón-Couto, Iria Pastor-Gómez & Paula Rodríguez-Puente (eds)
New Trends and Methodologies in Applied English Language Research II.
Studies in Language Variation, Meaning and Learning.
283 pages. 2012. ISBN 978-3-0343-1061-1

Vol. 146 Rita Salvi & Hiromasa Tanaka (eds)
Intercultural Interactions in Business and Management.
306 pages. 2011. ISBN 978-3-0343-1039-0

Vol. 147 Francesco Straniero Sergio & Caterina Falbo (eds)
Breaking Ground in Corpus-based Interpreting Studies.
254 pages. 2012. ISBN 978-3-0343-1071-0

Vol. 148 Forthcoming.

Vol. 149 Vijay K. Bhatia & Paola Evangelisti Allori (eds)
Discourse and Identity in the Professions. Legal, Corporate and Institutional Citizenship.
352 pages. 2011. ISBN 978-3-0343-1079-6

Vol. 150 Maurizio Gotti (ed.)
Academic Identity Traits. A Corpus-Based Investigation.
363 pages. 2012. ISBN 978-3-0343-1141-0

Vol. 151 Priscilla Heynderickx, Sylvain Dieltjens, Geert Jacobs, Paul Gillaerts & Elizabeth de Groot (eds)
The Language Factor in International Business. New Perspectives on Research, Teaching and Practice.
320 pages. 2012. ISBN 978-3-0343-1090-1

Vol. 152 Paul Gillaerts, Elizabeth de Groot, Sylvain Dieltjens, Priscilla Heynderickx & Geert Jacobs (eds)
Researching Discourse in Business Genres. Cases and Corpora.
215 pages. 2012. ISBN 978-3-0343-1092-5

Vol. 153 Yongyan Zheng
Dynamic Vocabulary Development in a Foreign Language.
262 pages. 2012. ISBN 978-3-0343-1106-9

Vol. 154 Carmen Argondizzo (ed.)
Creativity and Innovation in Language Education.
357 pages. 2012. ISBN 978-3-0343-1080-2

Vol. 155 David Hirsh (ed.)
Current Perspectives in Second Language Vocabulary Research.
180 pages. 2012. ISBN 978-3-0343-1108-3

Vol. 156 Seiji Shinkawa
Unhistorical Gender Assignment in Lahamon's *Brut*. A Case Study of a Late Stage in the Development of Grammatical Gender toward its Ultimate Loss.
186 pages. 2012. ISBN 978-3-0343-1124-3

Vol. 157 Yeonkwon Jung
Basics of Organizational Writing: A Critical Reading Approach.
151 pages. 2014. ISBN 978-3-0343-1137-3.

Vol. 158 Bárbara Eizaga Rebollar (ed.) Studies in Linguistics and Cognition.
301 pages. 2012. ISBN 978-3-0343-1138-0

Vol. 159 Giuliana Garzone, Paola Catenaccio, Chiara Degano (eds)
Genre Change in the Contemporary World. Short-term Diachronic Perspectives.
329 pages. 2012. ISBN 978-3-0343-1214-1

Vol. 160 Carol Berkenkotter, Vijay K. Bhatia & Maurizio Gotti (eds)
Insights into Academic Genres.
468 pages. 2012. ISBN 978-3-0343-1211-0

Vol. 161 Beatriz Tizón-Couto
Clausal Complements in Native and Learner Spoken English. A corpus-based study with Lindsei and Vicolse.
357 pages. 2013. ISBN 978-3-0343-1184-7

Vol. 162 Patrizia Anesa
Jury Trials and the Popularization of Legal Language. A Discourse Analytical Approach.
247 pages. 2012. ISBN 978-3-0343-1231-8

Vol. 163 David Hirsh
Endangered Languages, Knowledge Systems and Belief Systems.
153 pages. 2013. ISBN 978-3-0343-1232-5

Vol. 164 Eugenia Sainz (ed.)
De la estructura de la frase al tejido del discurso. Estudios contrastivos español/italiano.
305 pages. 2014. ISBN 978-3-0343-1253-0

Vol. 165 Julia Bamford, Franca Poppi & Davide Mazzi (eds)
Space, Place and the Discursive Construction of Identity.
367 pages. 2014. ISBN 978-3-0343-1249-3

Vol. 166 Rita Salvi & Janet Bowker (eds)
Space, Time and the Construction of Identity. Discursive Indexicality in Cultural, Institutional and Professional Fields.
324 pages. 2013. ISBN 978-3-0343-1254-7

Vol. 167 Shunji Yamazaki & Robert Sigley (eds)
Approaching Language Variation through Corpora. A Festschrift in Honour of Toshio Saito.
421 pages. 2013. ISBN 978-3-0343-1264-6

Vol. 168 Franca Poppi
Global Interactions in English as a Lingua Franca. How written communication is changing under the influence of electronic media and new contexts of use.
249 pages. 2012. ISBN 978-3-0343-1276-9

Vol. 169 Miguel A. Aijón Oliva & María José Serrano
Style in syntax. Investigating variation in Spanish pronoun subjects.
239 pages. 2013. ISBN 978-3-0343-1244-8

Vol. 170 Inés Olza, Óscar Loureda & Manuel Casado-Velarde (eds)
Language Use in the Public Sphere. Methodological Perspectives and Empirical Applications
564 pages. 2014. ISBN 978-3-0343-1286-8

Vol. 171 Aleksandra Matulewska
Legilinguistic Translatology. A Parametric Approach to Legal Translation.
279 pages. 2013. ISBN 978-3-0343-1287-5

Vol. 172 Maurizio Gotti & Carmen Sancho Guinda (eds)
Narratives in Academic and Professional Genres.
513 pages. 2013. ISBN 978-3-0343-1371-1

Vol. 173 Madalina Chitez
Learner corpus profiles. The case of Romanian Learner English.
244 pages. 2014. ISBN 978-3-0343-1410-7

Vol. 174 Chihiro Inoue
Task Equivalence in Speaking Tests.
251 pages. 2013. ISBN 978-3-0343-1417-6

Vol. 175 Gabriel Quiroz & Pedro Patiño (eds.)
LSP in Colombia: advances and challenges.
339 pages. 2014. ISBN 978-3-0343-1434-3

Vol. 176 Catherine Resche
Economic Terms and Beyond: Capitalising on the Wealth of Notions.
How Researchers in Specialised Varieties of English Can Benefit from Focusing on Terms.
332 pages. 2013. ISBN 978-3-0343-1435-0

Vol. 177 Wei Wang
Media representation of migrant workers in China. Identities and stances
198 pages. 2018. ISBN 978-3-0343-1436-7

Vol. 178 Cécile Desoutter & Caroline Mellet (dir.)
Le discours rapporté: approches linguistiques et perspectives didactiques.
270 pages. 2013. ISBN 978-3-0343-1292-9

Vol. 179 Ana Díaz-Negrillo & Francisco Javier Díaz-Pérez (eds)
Specialisation and Variation in Language Corpora.
341 pages. 2014. ISBN 978-3-0343-1316-2

Vol. 180 Pilar Alonso
A Multi-dimensional Approach to Discourse Coherence. From Standardness to Creativity.
247 pages. 2014. ISBN 978-3-0343-1325-4

Vol. 181 Alejandro Alcaraz-Sintes & Salvador Valera-Hernández (eds)
Diachrony and Synchrony in English Corpus Linguistics.
393 pages. 2014. ISBN 978-3-0343-1326-1

Vol. 182 Runhan Zhang
Investigating Linguistic Knowledge of a Second Language.
207 pages. 2015. ISBN 978-3-0343-1330-8

Vol. 183 Hajar Abdul Rahim & Shakila Abdul Manan (eds.)
English in Malaysia. Postcolonial and Beyond.
267 pages. 2014. ISBN 978-3-0343-1341-4

Vol. 184 Virginie Fasel Lauzon
Comprendre et apprendre dans l'interaction. Les séquences d'explication en classe de français langue seconde.
292 pages. 2014. ISBN 978-3-0343-1451-0

Vol. 185 Forthcoming.

Vol. 186 Wei Ren
L2 Pragmatic Development in Study Abroad Contexts
256 pages. 2015. ISBN 978-3-0343-1358-2

Vol. 187 Marina Bondi & Rosa Lorés Sanz (eds)
Abstracts in Academic Discourse. Variation and Change.
361 pages. 2014. ISBN 978-3-0343-1483-1

Vol. 188 Giuditta Caliendo
Rethinking Community. Discourse, Identity and Citizenship in the European Union.
240 pages. 2017. ISBN 978-3-0343-1561-6

Vol. 189 Paola Evangelisti Allori (ed.) Identities in and across Cultures.
315 pages. 2014. ISBN 978-3-0343-1458-9

Vol. 190 Erik Castello, Katherine Ackerley & Francesca Coccetta (eds).
Studies in Learner Corpus Linguistics. Research and Applications for Foreign Language Teaching and Assessment.
358 pages. 2015. ISBN 978-3-0343-1506-7

Vol. 191 Ruth Breeze, Maurizio Gotti & Carmen Sancho Guinda (eds)
Interpersonality in Legal Genres.
389 pages. 2014. ISBN 978-3-0343-1524-1

Vol. 192 Paola Evangelisti Allori, John Bateman & Vijay K. Bhatia (eds)
Evolution in Genre. Emergence, Variation, Multimodality.
364 pages. 2014. ISBN 978-3-0343-1533-3

Vol. 193 Jiyeon Kook
Agency in Arzt-Patient-Gesprächen. Zur interaktionistischen Konzeptualisierung von Agency
271 pages. 2015. ISBN 978-3-0343-1666-8

Vol. 194 Susana Nicolás Román & Juan José Torres Núñez (eds)
Drama and CLIL. A new challenge for the teaching approaches in bilingual education.
170 pages. 2015. ISBN 978-3-0343-1629-3

Vol. 195 Alessandra Molino & Serenella Zanotti (eds)
Observing Norm, Observing Usage. Lexis in Dictionaries and in the Media.
430 pages. 2015. ISBN 978-3-0343-1584-5

Vol. 196 Begoña Soneira
A Lexical Description of English for Architecture. A Corpus-based Approach.
267 pages. 2015. ISBN 978-3-0343-1602-6

Vol. 197 M Luisa Roca-Varela
False Friends in Learner Corpora. A corpus-based study of English false friends in the written and spoken production of Spanish learners.
348 pages. 2015. ISBN 978-3-0343-1620-0

Vol. 198 Rahma Al-Mahrooqi & Christopher Denman
Bridging the Gap between Education and Employment. English Language Instruction in EFL Contexts.
416 pages. 2015. ISBN 978-3-0343-1681-1

Vol. 199 Rita Salvi & Janet Bowker (eds)
The Dissemination of Contemporary Knowledge in English. Genres, discourse strategies and professional practices.
171 pages. 2015. ISBN 978-3-0343-1679-8

Vol. 200 Maurizio Gotti & Davide S. Giannoni (eds)
Corpus Analysis for Descriptive and Pedagogical Purposes. ESP Perspectives.
432 pages. 2014. ISBN 978-3-0343-1516-6

Vol. 201 Ida Ruffolo
The Perception of Nature in Travel Promotion Texts. A Corpus-based Discourse Analysis.
148 pages. 2015. ISBN 978-3-0343-1521-0

Vol. 202 Ives Trevian
English suffixes. Stress-assignment properties, productivity, selection and combinatorial processes.
471 pages. 2015. ISBN 978-3-0343-1576-0

Vol. 203 Maurizio Gotti, Stefania Maci & Michele Sala (eds) Insights into Medical Communication.
422 pages. 2015. ISBN 978-3-0343-1694-1

Vol. 204 Carmen Argondizzo (ed.)
European Projects in University Language Centres. Creativity, Dynamics, Best Practice.
371 pages. 2015. ISBN 978-3-0343-1696-5

Vol. 205 Aura Luz Duffé Montalván (ed.)
Estudios sobre el léxico. Puntos y contrapuntos.
502 pages. 2016. ISBN 978-3-0343-2011-5

Vol. 206 Maria Pavesi, Maicol Formentelli & Elisa Ghia (eds)
The Languages of Dubbing. Mainstream Audiovisual Translation in Italy.
275 pages. 2014. ISBN 978-3-0343-1646-0

Vol. 207 Ruth Breeze & Inés Olza (eds)
Evaluation in media discourse. European perspectives.
268 pages. 2017. ISBN 978-3-0343-2014-6

Vol. 208 Vijay K. Bhatia & Maurizio Gotti (eds)
Arbitration Discourse in Asia.
331 pages. 2015. ISBN 978-3-0343-2032-0

Vol. 209 Sofía Bemposta-Rivas, Carla Bouzada-Jabois, Yolanda Fernández-Pena, Tamara Bouso, Yolanda J. Calvo-Benzies, Iván Tamaredo (eds)
New trends and methodologies in applied English language research III. Synchronic and diachronic studies on discourse, lexis and grammar processing.
280 pages. 2017. ISBN 978-3-0343-2039-9

Vol. 210 Francisco Alonso Almeida, Laura Cruz García & Víctor González Ruiz (eds)
Corpus-based studies on language varieties.
285 pages. 2016. ISBN 978-3-0343-2044-3

Vol. 211 Juan Pedro Rica Peromingo
Aspectos lingüísticos y técnicos de la traducción audiovisual (TAV).
177 pages. 2016. ISBN 978-3-0343-2055-9

Vol. 212 Maria Vender
Disentangling Dyslexia. VenderPhonological and Processing Deficit in Developmental Dyslexia.
338 pages. 2017. ISBN 978-3-0343-2064-1

Vol. 213 Zhilong Xie
Bilingual Advantages. Contributions of Different Bilingual Experiences to Cognitive Control Differences Among Young-adult Bilinguals.
221 pages. 2016. ISBN 978-3-0343-2081-8

Vol. 214 Larissa D'Angelo
Academic posters. A textual and visual metadiscourse analysis.
367 pages. 2016. ISBN 978-3-0343-2083-2

Vol. 215 Evelyne Berger
Prendre la parole en L2. Regard sur la compétence d'interaction en classe de langue.
246 pages. 2016. ISBN 978-3-0343-2084-9

Vol. 216 David Lasagabaster and Aintzane Doiz (eds)
CLIL experiences in secondary and tertiary education: In search of good practices.
262 pages. 2016. ISBN 978-3-0343-2104-4

Vol. 217 Elena Kkese
Identifying Plosives in L2 English: The Case of L1 Cypriot Greek Speakers.
317 pages. 2016. ISBN 978-3-0343-2060-3

Vol. 218 Sandra Campagna, Elana Ochse, Virginia Pulcini & Martin Solly (eds)
Languaging in and across Communities: New Voices, New Identities. Studies in Honour of Giuseppina Cortese.
507 pages. 2016. ISBN 978-3-0343-2073-3

Vol. 219 Adriana Orlandi & Laura Giacomini (ed.)
Defining collocation for lexicographic purposes. From linguistic theory to lexicographic practice.
328 pages. 2016. ISBN 978-3-0343-2054-2

Vol. 220 Pietro Luigi Iaia
Analysing English as a Lingua Franca in Video Games. Linguistic Features, Experiential and Functional Dimensions of Online and Scripted Interactions.
139 pages. 2016. ISBN 978-3-0343-2138-9

Vol. 221 Dimitrinka G. Níkleva (ed.)
La formación de los docentes de español para inmigrantes en distintos contextos educativos.
390 pages. 2017. ISBN 978-3-0343-2135-8

Vol. 222 Katherine Ackerley, Marta Guarda & Francesca Helm (eds)
Sharing Perspectives on English-Medium Instruction.
308 pages. 2017. ISBN 978-3-0343-2537-0

Vol. 223 Juana I. Marín-Arrese, Julia Lavid-López, Marta Carretero, Elena Domínguez Romero, Ma Victoria Martín de la Rosa & María Pérez Blanco (eds)
Evidentiality and Modality in European Languages. Discourse-pragmatic perspectives.
427 pages. 2017. ISBN 978-3-0343-2437-3

Vol. 224 Gilles Col
Construction du sens : un modèle instructionnel pour la sémantique.
292 pages. 2017. ISBN 978-3-0343-2572-1

Vol. 225 Ana Chiquito & Gabriel Quiroz (eds)
Pobreza, Lenguaje y Medios en América Latina.
362 pages. 2017. ISBN 978-3-0343-2142-6

Vol. 226 Xu Zhang
English Quasi-Numeral Classifiers. A Corpus-Based Cognitive-Typological Study.
360 pages. 2017. ISBN 978-3-0343-2818-0

Vol. 227 María Ángeles Orts, Ruth Breeze & Maurizio Gotti (eds)
Power, Persuasion and Manipulation in Specialised Genres. Providing Keys to the Rhetoric of Professional Communities.
368 pages. 2017. ISBN 978-3-0343-3010-7

Vol. 228 Maurizio Gotti, Stefania Maci & Michele Sala (eds)
Ways of Seeing, Ways of Being: Representing the Voices of Tourism.
453 pages. 2017. ISBN 978-3-0343-3031-2

Vol. 229 Dino Selvaggi
Plurilingual Code-Switching between Standard and Local Varieties. A Socio-Psycholinguistic Approach
371 pages. 2018. ISBN 978-3-0343-2663-6

Vol. 230 Anca-Cristina Sterie
Interprofessional interactions at the hospital. Nurses' requests and reports of problems in calls with physicians.
371 pages. 2017. ISBN 978-3-0343-2734-3

Vol. 231 Xiaodong Zhang
Understanding Chinese EFL Teachers' Beliefs and Practices in the Textbook-Based Classroom.
189 pages. 2017. ISBN 978-3-0343-3053-4

Vol. 232 Manuela Caterina Moroni & Federica Ricci Garotti (Hrsg.)
Brücken schlagen zwischen Sprachwissenschaft und DaF-Didaktik.
345 pages. 2017. ISBN 978-3-0343-2667-4

Vol. 233 Dimitrinka Georgieva Níkleva
Necesidades y tendencias en la formación del profesorado de español como lengua extranjera
401 pages. 2017. ISBN 978-3-0343-2946-0

Vol. 234 Juan Santana-Lario & Salvador Valera (Hrsg.)
Competing patterns in English affixation.
272 pages. 2017. ISBN 978-3-0343-2701-5

Vol. 235 Francisco Salgado-Robles
Desarrollo de la competencia sociolingüística por aprendices de español en un contexto de inmersión en el extranjero
241 pages. 2018. ISBN 978-3-0343-2323-9

Vol. 236 Maria Chiara Janner
Sguardi linguistici sulla marca. Analisi morfosintattica dei nomi commerciali in italiano
345 pages. 2017. ISBN 978-3-0343-2667-4

Vol. 237 Bárbara Herrero Muñoz-Cobo & Otman
El Azami Zalachi La primavera del árabe marroquí.
192 pages. 2017. ISBN 978-3-0343-3104-3

Vol. 238 Consuelo Pascual Escagedo
El papel del oyente en la construcción de la conversación espontánea de estudiantes italianos en su interlengua y en su lengua materna
295 pages. 2017. ISBN 978-3-0343-3186-9

Vol. 239 Stefania M. Maci
The MS Digby 133 *Mary Magdalene*. Beyond scribal practices: language, discourse, values and attitudes.
336 pages. 2017. ISBN 978-3-0343-3256-9

Vol. 240 Eliecer Crespo-Fernández
Taboo in Discourse. Studies on Attenuation and Offence in Communication.
326 pages. 2018. ISBN 978-3-0343-3018-3

Vol. 241 Jana Altmanova, Maria Centrella, Katherine E. Russo (eds)
Terminology & Discourse / Terminologie et discours.
424 pages. 2018. ISBN 978-3-0343-2417-5

Vol. 242 Xavier Blanco et Inès Sfar (dir.)
Lexicologie(s) : approches croisées en sémantique lexicale.
442 pages. 2018. ISBN 978-3-0343-3056-5

Vol. 243 Yunfeng Ge
Resolution of Conflict of Interest in Chinese Civil Court Hearings. A Perspective of Discourse Information Theory.
302 pages. 2018. ISBN 978-3-0343-3313-9

Vol. 244 Carla Vergaro
Illocutionary Shell Nouns in English
322 pages. 2018. ISBN 978-3-0343-3069-5

Vol. 245 Paolo Frassi
L'adjectif en français et sa définition lexicographique.
270 pages. 2018. ISBN 978-3-0343-3394-8

Vol. 246 Suwilai Premsrirat and David Hirsh (eds)
Language Revitalization. Insights from Thailand
328 pages. 2018. ISBN 978-3-0343-3497-6

Vol. 247 Wei Wang
Researching Learning and Learners in Genre-based Academic Writing Instruction
282 pages. 2018. ISBN 978-3-0343-3297-2

Vol. 248 Isusi Alabarte, Alberto & Lahuerta Martínez, Ana Cristina (eds)
La comprensión lectora de lengua extranjera
Estudio de los factores de familiaridad, interés, género y métodos de evaluación
336 pages. 2018. ISBN 978-3-0343-3493-8

Vol. 249 Mercedes Eurrutia Cavero
Approche didactique du langage techno-scientifique Terminologie et discours
374 pages. 2018. ISBN 978-3-0343-3512-6

Vol. 250 Aurora Ruiz Mezcua (ed.)
Approaches to Telephone Interpretation Research, Innovation, Teaching and Transference
268 pages. 2018. ISBN 978-3-0343-3330-6

Vol. 251 Morini Massimiliano
A Day in the News A Stylistic Analysis of Newsspeak
188 pages. 2018. ISBN 978-3-0343-3507-2

Vol. 252 Ignacio Guillén-Galve & Ignacio Vázquez-Orta (eds.)
English as a Lingua Franca and Intercultural Communication Implications and Applications in the Field of English Language Teaching
414 pages. 2018. ISBN 978-3-0343-2763-3

Vol. 253 Bianca Del Villano
Using the Devil with Courtesy
Shakespeare and the Language of (Im)Politeness
216 pages. 2018. ISBN 978-3-0343-2315-4

Vol. 254 David Hirsh (ed.)
Explorations in Second Language Vocabulary Research
252 pages. 2018. ISBN 978-3-0343-2940-8

Vol. 255 Tania Baumann (ed.)
Reiseführer - Sprach- und Kulturmittlung im Tourismus / Le guide turistiche - mediazione linguistica e culturale in ambito turistico
270 pages. 2018. ISBN 978-3-0343-3402-0

Vol. 256 Ariadna Sánchez-Hernández & Ana Herraiz-Martínez (eds)
Learning second language pragmatics beyond traditional contexts
376 pages. 2018. ISBN 978-3-0343-3437-2

Vol. 257 Albert Bastardas-Boada, Emili Boix-Fuster, Rosa Maria Torrens (eds)
Family Multilingualism in Medium-Sized Linguistic Communities
336 pages. 2019. ISBN 978-3-0343-2536-3

Vol. 258 Yuyang Cai
Examining the Interaction among Components of English for Specific Purposes Ability in Reading. The Triple-Decker Model
296 pages. 2020. 978-3-0343-2913-2

Vol. 259 Catia Nannoni
Participe présent et gérondif dans la presse française contemporaine
176 pages. 2019. ISBN 978-3-0343-3631-4

Vol. 260 Nieves Rodríguez Pérez & Bárbara Heinsch (eds.)
Contextos multilingües. Mediadores interculturales, formación del profesorado de lenguas extranjeras
289 pages. 2019. ISBN 978-3-0343-3768-7

Vol. 261 Giuliana Elena Garzone, Mara Logaldo, Francesca Santulli (eds.)
Investigating Conflict Discourses in the Periodical Press
244 pages. 2020. ISBN 978-3-0343-3668-0

Vol. 262 Laura Nadal
Lingüística experimental y contraargumentación
233 pages. 2019. ISBN 978-3-0343-3791-5

Vol. 263 Claudia Claridge & Merja Kytö (eds.)
Punctuation in Context – Past and Present Perspectives
288 pages. 2019. ISBN 978-3-0343-3790-8

Vol. 264 Maurizio Gotti, Stefania Maci, Michele Sala (eds.)
Scholarly Pathways
530 pages. 2020. ISBN 978-3-0343-3860-8

Vol. 265 Ruth Breeze, Ana M. Fernández Vallejo (eds.)
Politics and populism across modes and media
350 pages. 2020. ISBN 978-3-0343-3707-6

Vol. 266 Jean Marguerite Jimenez
Understanding the Effects of Immediate Electronic Corrective Feedback on Second Language Development
252 pages. 2020. ISBN 978-3-0343-3815-8

Vol. 267 Sergio Rodríguez-Tapia, Adela González-Fernández (eds)
Lenguas y turismo: estudios en torno al discurso, la didáctica y la divulgación
380 pages. 2020. ISBN 978-3-0343-3881-3

Vol. 268 Ana Bocanegra-Valle (ed.)
Applied Linguistics and Knowledge Transfer. Employability, Internationalisation and Social Challenges
344 pages. 2020. ISBN 978-3-0343-3714-4

Vol. 269 Beatrice Garzelli
La traducción audiovisual español-italiano.Películas y cortos entre humor y habla soez
202 pages. 2020. ISBN 978-3-0343-4013-7

Vol. 270 Iván Tamaredo
Complexity, Efficiency, and Language Contact. Pronoun Omission in World Englishes
292 pages. 2020. ISBN 978-3-0343-3902-5

Vol. 271 Silvia Domenica Zollo
Origine et histoire du vocabulaire des arts de la table. Analyse lexicale et exploitation de corpus textuels
239 pages. 2020. ISBN 978-3-0343-3890-5

Vol. 272 Paola Paissa, Michelangelo Conoscenti, Ruggero Druetta, Martin Solly (eds.)
Metaphor and Conflict / Métaphore et conflit
385 pages. 2021. ISBN 978-3-0343-4068-7

Vol. 273 María Martínez-Atienza de Dios
Entre el léxico y la sintaxis: las fases de los eventos
178 pages. 2021. ISBN 978-3-0343-4173-8

Vol. 274 Noelia Castro-Chao
Argument Structure in Flux. The Development of Impersonal Constructions in Middle and Early Modern English, with Special Reference to Verbs of Desire.
300 pages. 2021. ISBN 978-3-0343-4189-9

Vol. 275 Gabriella Carobbio, Cécile Desoutter, Aurora Fragonara (eds.)
Macht, Ratio und Emotion: Diskurse im digitalen Zeitalter / Pouvoir, raison et émotion: les discours à l'ère du numérique
246 pages. 2020. ISBN 978-3-0343-4184-4

Vol. 276 Miguel Fuster-Márquez, José Santaemilia, Carmen Gregori-Signes, Paula Rodríguez-Abru-ñeiras (eds.)
Exploring discourse and ideology through corpora
293 pages. 2021. ISBN 978-3-0343-3969-8

Vol. 277 Tamara Bouso
Changes in Argument Structure
The Transitivizing Reaction Object Construction
392. 2021. ISBN 978-3-0343-4095-3

Vol. 278 Maria Luisa Maggioni, Amanda Murphy (eds.)
Back to the Future. English from Past to Present
250 pages. 2021. ISBN 978-3-0343-4273-5

Vol. 279 Luisa Chierichetti
Diálogos de serie. Una aproximación a la construcción discursiva de personajes basada en corpus
246 pages. 2021. ISBN 978-3-0343-4274-2

Vol. 280 Cristina Lastres-López
From subordination to insubordination. A functional-pragmatic approach to if/si-constructions in English, French and Spanish spoken discourse
258 pages. 2021. ISBN 978-3-0343-4220-9

Vol. 281 Eleonora Federici, Stefania Maci (eds.)
Gender issues. Translating and mediating languages, cultures and societies
500 pages. 2021. ISBN 978-3-0343-4022-9

Vol. 282 José Mateo, Francisco Yus (eds.)
Metaphor in Economics and specialised Discourse
354 pages. 2021. ISBN 978-3-0343-4048-9

Vol. 283 Nicholas Brownlees (ed.)
The Role of Context in the Production and Reception of Historical News Discourse
376 pages. 2021. ISBN 978-3-0343-4181-3

Vol. 284 Catalina Fuentes Rodriguez, María Ester Brenes Peña, Víctor Pérez Béjar (eds.)
Sintaxis discursiva: construcciones y operadores en español
396 pages. 2021. ISBN 978-3-0343-4306-0

Vol. 285 Dominic Stewart
Frequency in the dictionary. A corpus-assisted contrastive analysis of English and Italian
176 pages. 2021. ISBN 978-3-0343-4368-8

Vol. 286 Carla Bouzada-Jabois
Nonfinite supplements in the recent history of English
320 pages. 2021. ISBN 978-3-0343-4226-1

Vol. 287 Sofía Bemposta Rivas
Verb-governed infinitival complementation in the recent history of English
320 pages. 2021. ISBN 978-3-0343-4227-8

Vol. 288 Mirella Agorni
Translating Italy for the Nineteenth Century. Translators and an Imagined Nation in the Early Romantic Period 1816–1830s
180 pages. 2021. ISBN 978-3-0343-3612-3

Vol. 289 David Hirsh (ed.)
Research Perspectives in Language and Education
276 pages. 2021. ISBN 978-3-0343-4219-3

Vol. 290 Federica Vezzani
Terminologie numérique : conception, représentation et gestion
238 pages. 2022. ISBN 978-3-0343-4394-7

Vol. 291 Stefania M. Maci
Evidential verbs in the genre of medical posters. A corpus-based analysis
498 pages. 2022. ISBN 978-3-0343-4521-7

Vol. 292 Francisco J. Álvarez-Gil
Stance devices in tourism-related research articles: A corpus-based study
170 pages. 2022. ISBN 978-3-0343-4555-2

Vol. 293 Annalisa Baicchi / Stefania Biscetti (eds.)
The Language of Fashion. Linguistic, Cognitive, and Cultural Insights
190 pages. 2022. ISBN 978-3-0343-4428-9

Vol. 294 Ana Maria Piquer-Píriz
E-learning in EMI. Academic language for university students
200 pages. 2022. ISBN 978-3-0343-4589-7

Vol. 295 Geneviève Henrot Sostero (ed.)
Alle radici della fraseologia europea
400 pages. 2023. ISBN 978-3-0343-4645-0

Vol. 296 Klara Dankova
Les fibres textiles entre synchronie et diachronie: études terminologiques
300 pages. 2023. ISBN 978-3-0343-4587-3

Vol. 297 Marta Carretero, Juana I. Marín-Arrese, Elena Domínguez Romero, Mª Victoria Martín de la Rosa (eds.)
Evidentiality and Epistemic Modality. Conceptual and Descriptive issues
350 pages. 2023. ISBN 978-3-0343-3993-3

Vol. 298 Kim Grego, Alessandra Vicentini, Virpi Ylänne (eds.)
Age-Specific Issues. Language, Spaces, Technologies
300 pages. 2023. ISBN 978-3-0343-4411-1

Vol. 299 Giovanni Garofalo (ed.)
Estudios de género asistidos por corpus. Enfoques multidisciplinarios
292 pages. 2022. ISBN 978-3-0343-4548-4

Vol. 300 Giuseppe Palumbo, Katia Peruzzo, Gianluca Pontrandolfo (eds.)
What's Special About Specialised Translation? Essays in Honour of Federica Scarpa
296 pages. 2023. ISBN 978-3-0343-4411-1

Vol. 301 Raquel P. Romasanta
Probabilistic variability in clausal verb complementation in World Englishes
390 pages. 2023. ISBN 978-3-0343-4703-7

Vol. 302 Giulia Adriana Pennisi
A linguistic Insight into Legislative Drafting. Tradition and Change in the UK Legislation
330 pages. 2023. ISBN 978-3-0343-4700-6

Vol. 303 Javier Fernández-Cruz, Antonio Moreno-Ortiz
Economic terms in the news during the Great Recession. A diachronic sentiment and collocational analysis
193 pages. 2024. ISBN 978-3-0343-4778-5

Vol. 304 Stefania Maci, Mark McGlashan (eds.)
(Critical) Discourse Studies and the (new?) normal. Analysing discourse in times of crisis
400 pages. 2024. ISBN 978-3-0343-4767-9

Vol. 305 Ana Elvira Ojanguren López
Predications in competition and the rise of serial verb constructions in English. The verbal and nominal complementation of Old English aspectual and manipulative verbs
330 pages. 2024. ISBN 978-3-0343-4644-3

Vol. 306 Stefania Maci, Giovanni Garofalo (eds.)
Investigating Discourse and Text. Corpus-Assisted Analytical Perspectives
370 pages. 2023. ISBN 978-3-0343-4753-2

Vol. 307 Víctor Pérez Béjar
Las construcciones suspendidas en español. Un paradigma en gramática del discurso
494 pages. 2024. ISBN 978-3-0343-4799-0

Vol. 308 Javier Calle-Martín / Jesús Romero-Barranco (eds.)
Corpora and Language Change in Late Modern English
408 pages. 2024. ISBN 978-3-0343-4642-9

www.ingramcontent.com/pod-product-compliance
Ingram Content Group UK Ltd.
Pitfield, Milton Keynes, MK11 3LW, UK
UKHW020838290926
15470UKWH00004B/1420

9 783034 346429